REIMAGINING RESTORATIVE JUSTICE

In recent years, restorative-based interventions have expanded rapidly and are increasingly viewed as a legitimate, and even superior means of delivering justice. The result of this swift but piecemeal development has been that restorative justice practice has outpaced the development of restorative justice theory. This book takes up this challenge by 'reimagining' a new framework for the operation of restorative justice within criminal justice. In essence, it is contended that the core empowering values of 'agency' and 'accountability' provide a lens for reimagining how restorative justice works and the normative goals it ought to encompass.

Reimagining Restorative Justice

David O'Mahony and Jonathan Doak

HART
PUBLISHING
OXFORD AND PORTLAND, OREGON
2017

Hart Publishing
An imprint of Bloomsbury Publishing Plc

Hart Publishing Ltd	Bloomsbury Publishing Plc
Kemp House	50 Bedford Square
Chawley Park	London
Cumnor Hill	WC1B 3DP
Oxford OX2 9PH	UK
UK	

www.hartpub.co.uk
www.bloomsbury.com

Published in North America (US and Canada) by
Hart Publishing
c/o International Specialized Book Services
920 NE 58th Avenue, Suite 300
Portland, OR 97213-3786
USA

www.isbs.com

HART PUBLISHING, the Hart/Stag logo, BLOOMSBURY and the
Diana logo are trademarks of Bloomsbury Publishing Plc

First published 2017

© David O'Mahony and Jonathan Doak 2017

David O'Mahony and Jonathan Doak have asserted their right under the Copyright,
Designs and Patents Act 1988 to be identified as Authors of this work.

All rights reserved. No part of this publication may be reproduced or transmitted in any form or by any
means, electronic or mechanical, including photocopying, recording, or any information
storage or retrieval system, without prior permission in writing from the publishers.

While every care has been taken to ensure the accuracy of this work, no responsibility for loss or damage
occasioned to any person acting or refraining from action as a result of any statement
in it can be accepted by the authors, editors or publishers.

All UK Government legislation and other public sector information used in the work is Crown Copyright ©.
All House of Lords and House of Commons information used in the work is Parliamentary Copyright ©.
This information is reused under the terms of the Open Government Licence v3.0 (http://www.
nationalarchives.gov.uk/doc/open-government-licence/version/3) except where otherwise stated.

All Eur-lex material used in the work is © European Union, http://eur-lex.europa.eu/, 1998–2017.

British Library Cataloguing-in-Publication Data
A catalogue record for this book is available from the British Library.

ISBN: PB: 978-1-84946-056-9
       ePDF: 978-1-50990-106-7
       ePub: 978-1-78225-197-2

Library of Congress Cataloging-in-Publication Data

Names: O'Mahony, David. | Doak, Jonathan.
Title: Reimagining restorative justice / David O'Mahony and Jonathan Doak.
Description: Oxford ; Portland, Oregon : Hart Publishing, an imprint of Bloomsbury Publishing Plc, 2017. |
Includes bibliographical references and index.
Identifiers: LCCN 2017021992 (print) | LCCN 2017025881 (ebook) |
ISBN 9781782251972 (Epub) | ISBN 9781849460569 (pbk. : alk. paper)
Subjects: LCSH: Restorative justice. | Criminal justice, Administration of.
Classification: LCC HV8688 (ebook) | LCC HV8688 .O425 2017 (print) | DDC 364.6/8—dc23
LC record available at https://lccn.loc.gov/2017021992

Typeset by Compuscript Ltd, Shannon
Printed and bound in Great Britain by CPI Group (UK) Ltd, Croydon CR0 4YY

To find out more about our authors and books visit www.hartpublishing.co.uk. Here you will find extracts,
author information, details of forthcoming events and the option to sign up for our newsletters.

PREFACE

This book proposes a new theoretical lens through which the theory and practice of restorative justice can be analysed. Given the sheer pace of recent developments in the field, there has been a clear need to re-evaluate the utility of some of the prevailing benchmark theories and to reimagine the shape and role of theory in guiding restorative justice provision within criminal justice. Drawing on empowerment theory, we argue that the joint concepts 'agency' and 'accountability' (which we label the agency-accountability framework) provide a useful lens for reimagining how restorative justice works and the normative goals it ought to encompass. From our perspective, programmes which aspire to be regarded as 'fully restorative' should be designed, implemented and evaluated in such a way that agency and accountability are maximised.

The genesis of this book began some years ago, when we led a major evaluation of the newly mainstreamed restorative conferencing system in Northern Ireland following the ceasefires and peace agreement. Shortly after, we were commissioned to undertake an international review of restorative justice for the National Commission of Restorative Justice in Ireland. These projects—while valuable in their own right—prompted a myriad of questions concerning the lack of coherence in restorative justice theory, and how this could be married to the highly divergent range of practices that have emerged in recent years on a transnational basis. Whilst we cannot claim that the book offers definitive answers to the many conundrums regarding the role of restorative justice within criminal justice, it is hoped that the book will provide a useful contribution to ongoing debates about the values and practices which underpin contemporary criminal processes.

We would like to extend our sincere gratitude to a number of individuals who have (perhaps unwittingly) assisted us in developing and refining our ideas. Valuable insights were offered by participants at various conference sessions—most notably at meetings of the European Society of Criminology and the *Restorative Justice and Mediation in Penal Matters* project at the University of Greifswald. Three previous conferences around the theme of bridging theory and practice in restorative justice, hosted by Durham Law School and Nottingham Law School also generated many fruitful discussions. Particularly constructive questions and comments were offered *inter alia* by Tim Chapman, Frieder Dünkel, Simon Green, Kerry Clamp and Joanna Shapland. The excellent work of our former doctoral students at Durham University, Adeniyi Olayode, Kelly Stockdale and Elizabeth Tiarks, also provided us with valuable food for thought as they progressed through their own academic journeys. Colleagues at the Universities of Durham, Essex and Nottingham Trent have also provided helpful insights and encouragement. Particular thanks are owed to Lorna Fox O'Mahony who read and provided useful feedback on previous drafts of our work, and to Emily Braggins and the rest of the team at Hart. Our copyeditor, Ceri Warner, also provided excellent support in pulling the final draft together. Any errors or omissions remain our own.

Finally, we are indebted to our families—Lorna, Conor, Aidan and Benji (David) and Lauran, Miriam, Reuben and Benji (Jonathan)—for their love and support throughout this project. We dedicate this book to them.

David O'Mahony and Jonathan Doak
February 2017

CONTENTS

Preface v
Abbreviations xi

1. An Alternative Paradigm of Justice 1
   I. Introduction..1
      A. Victim-offender mediation 4
      B. Restorative Policing 5
      C. Community Reparation Panels..6
      D. Family Group Conferencing 7
      E. Other Forms of Restorative Justice 8
   II. Trailblazing and Standard-Setting 10
   III. Bridging Theory and Practice 13
   IV. Structure and Argument of this Book 19

2. Restorative Justice Theory: Concepts, Processes and Outcomes....................23
   I. Introduction..23
   II. Criminal Justice: A Paradigm in Crisis?...24
   III. Refining Restorative Justice Theory 27
      A. Restorative Justice Concepts: What is Being Restored?
         To Whom and by Whom? 30
         i. A Role for the State? 39
      B. Restorative Justice Processes: 'How?' and 'Why?' 41
      C. Restorative Justice Outcomes: The Nature and
         Form of Restoration 47
   IV. Mainstreaming Restorative Justice within
       Criminal Justice: The Challenge Ahead...53
   V. Conclusions..57

3. Theorising Restorative Justice in Criminal Justice 59
   I. Introduction..59
   II. Empowerment Theory 60
      A. Disempowerment Through Crime and the Criminal
         Justice System..61
         i. Empowerment and Restorative Justice 63
         ii. Empowerment and Restorative Themes........................65

viii Contents

        B. Restorative Agency and Accountability 69
           i. Agency 70
           ii. Accountability 71
           iii. Agency, Accountability and Criminal Justice 73
    III. Conclusions 74

4. Victims and Offenders: Agency and Accountability in Practice 75
    I. Victims and Restorative Justice 76
        A. Victim Participation 77
        B. Overcoming Non-participation 79
        C. The Experiences of Victims 83
           i. Restoration and Apology 86
        D. Safety as a Prerequisite for Delivering Agency
           and Accountability 90
    II. Offenders and Restorative Justice 92
        A. The Experiences of Offenders 93
        B. The Rights of the Offender 94
    III. Conclusions 98

5. Restorative Practices at the Periphery of Criminal Justice 100
    I. Introduction 100
    II. Community-based Programmes 101
    III. Restorative Policing 104
        A. Restorative Cautioning 109
    IV. Youth Offender Panels 116
    V. Schemes for Adult Offenders 118
        A. New Zealand 119
        B. England and Wales 121
    VI. Prison-based Restorative Programmes 123
    VII. Conclusions 128

6. Mediation and Restorative Justice in Continental Europe 132
    I. Introduction 132
    II. Background and Context 133
    III. Administration and Referral 135
    IV. Process and Agreement 138
    V. Evaluation 142
    VI. Developing Restorative Justice in Continental Europe 146
    VII. Conclusions 149

7. Mainstreamed Restorative Justice: Youth Conferencing 151
    I. Introduction 151
    II. The Process of Youth Conferencing 153
    III. Participation in Youth Conferencing 157
        A. Consent and Engagement 159
        B. A 'Soft Option'? 161

	IV.	Satisfaction and Procedural Justice..165
	V.	Agreement: Restoration and Apology..168
	VI.	Conclusions..172
8.	Restorative Justice and Recidivism...175
	I.	Introduction..175
		A. Restorative Cautioning and Recidivism 176
		B. Restorative Justice Programmes and Recidivism..........................180
		i. Meta-analyses..182
		ii. More Detailed Analyses of Recidivism 184
		iii. Factors Which Influence Recidivism 187
	II.	Conclusions..192
9.	Reimagining Restorative Justice: Towards Empowerment 196
	I.	Introduction..196
	II.	Agency and Accountability as Keys to Empowerment........................197
	III.	From Theory to Practice 199
	IV.	Extending the Reach of Restorative Justice 202
	V.	Challenges Ahead..203
		A. Quantity over Quality?...204
		B. Legalism and Institutionalisation 208
		C. Cultural Resistance 212
	VI.	Effecting Change..214

References..217
Index 247

ABBREVIATIONS

CPS	Crown Prosecution Service
CVORJ	Citizens, Victims, and Offenders Restoring Justice
FGC	Family Group Conferencing
JGG	Juvenile Criminal Code (Germany)
NGO	Non-governmental organisation
NICE	National Institute of Clinical Excellence
RISE	Re-integrative Shaming Experiments
StPO	Criminal Procedure Code (Germany)
VOM	Victim-offender mediation
VORP	Victim-offender reconciliation programmes

1
An Alternative Paradigm of Justice

I. Introduction

In this book we contend there is a pressing need to reimagine the role of restorative justice within modern criminal justice. The practice of restorative justice has rapidly expanded in recent years and has seen considerable transformation in terms of how it is delivered. These range from diversionary applications at the policing level and integrated approaches at the sentencing point, through to complementary approaches used during or following imprisonment. However, the underlying theory of restorative justice has not kept pace with the divergent range of practice developments. This has led to a lack of clarity in the underlying purpose and function of restorative justice. In this book we seek to address this challenge by proposing a new theoretical lens through which the role of restorative justice within criminal justice can be reimagined.

We begin the challenge by providing a contextual platform for our work. This chapter first considers the potential of restorative justice as an alternative paradigm. The chapter examines differing forms of restorative interventions, from victim-offender mediation to conferencing models, and how these have been influenced and shaped at national and international levels. It shows how developments in practice have indeed outstripped the theoretical debates underpinning restorative justice and highlights the pressing need for us to rethink fundamental questions about what it should seek to achieve and the premise of how and why it works.

As its nomenclature suggests, restorative justice is essentially a theory of justice which gravitates around the core notion of restoration. In this sense it represents a significant point of departure for criminal justice theory. It is perhaps surprising that the very concept of 'making amends' has not, until recently, featured prominently in criminal justice discourse. The penal systems in most western countries have been traditionally retributive in nature, an orientation that has been justified by reference to classic penal philosophies such as retribution, incapacitation, deterrence and just deserts. Yet, in recent years, restorative justice has been catapulted to the forefront of the political, academic and practitioner discourses currently dominating criminal justice policy debates on both national and international platforms. At the heart of this concept lies an analysis of criminal behaviour as something that is first and foremost a violation of people's rights and relationships. From that starting position the restorative process aims to develop strategies and processes whereby offenders can make amends for the harm that has been caused to victims and others impacted by crime. Restorative justice strategies downplay orthodox justifications for punishment such as retribution and 'just deserts'.[1] Ownership of the offence and the harm that is caused is thus divested away from the state, and re-invested in the hands of those most acutely affected by the harm.[2] Ordinarily, the process entails some form of face-to-face encounter between the victim and the offender in the presence of a trained mediator or facilitator. Family, friends, community members and various professionals such as police officers, social workers or probation officers may also participate or be in attendance, depending on circumstances and the form of intervention that is used. The aim of the restorative intervention is the formulation of an agreement on how to move forward from the offence, which will usually involve some measure of reparation to the victim as well as measures to reintegrate the offender back into the community. Although this may result in some form of punishment in the sense that a degree pain or burden may be still be inflicted on the offender, this is generally viewed as incidental to the more important task of restoring and reintegrating those most affected by the offence.[3]

As Daly remarks, 'no other justice practice has commanded so much scholarly attention in such a short period of time';[4] restorative justice is now widely considered to be a 'global social movement' which aims 'to transform the way contemporary societies view and respond to crime and related forms of troublesome behaviour'.[5] While its contemporary renaissance is often traced to practices promoted by the Christian Mennonite movement in North America during the mid-1970s,[6] its origins have also been traced back to practices of many ancient and acephalous societies. Such claims have sometimes been questioned on grounds that they tend to generate a 'nirvana story' which paints a false picture of a bygone 'golden age' of restoration.[7] Yet, although punitive and oppressive practices may also have been commonplace within such societies, Braithwaite's bold claim that restorative justice has been 'the dominant model of criminal justice through most of human history'[8] seems to contain more than a seed of truth. Criminal law as

---

[1] Zehr (1990).
[2] Braithwaite (2002a); Pavlich (2005).
[3] Braithwaite and Mugford (1994); Johnstone (2011).
[4] Daly (2004), 500.
[5] Johnstone and Van Ness (2007), 5.
[6] The modern use of restorative justice is often traced to an incident in Kitchener, Ontario in 1974, where two intoxicated youths committed criminal damage to over 20 vehicles in the local vicinity. Given the fact that the youths were well known in the town, and had no previous criminal record, the court accepted a recommendation from their probation officer that the young men meet the victims of their offences and provide some monetary reparations. See further Peachey (1989).
[7] Daly (2002), 61–64. See also Bottoms (2003); Sylvester (2003).
[8] Braithwaite (1998), 323.

we know it—in England at least—only began to develop following the Norman Invasion.[9] While retribution has become the predominant ideology in controlling undesirable behaviour in in most western legal systems, in many ancient societies it was a measure of last resort in circumstances where restitution was not possible.[10]

In more contemporary times, the remarkable global ascent of restorative justice can be attributed to a mélange of factors. Cosemans and Parmentier point to 'the rise of the international victim movement at national and international levels, criminal policy trends towards diversion, and the limits of prosecution in (post-conflict societies … abolitionism, the re-discovery of traditional concepts of conflict resolution), and informalisation and de-professionalisation'.[11] As we discuss in chapter two, the 1970s and 1980s witnessed a proliferation of academic literature critiquing the existing paradigm of criminal justice and calling for more innovative and informal processes of dispute resolution. Restorative justice came to emerge as a persuasive alternative, offering scope to view crime through a different 'lens'[12]—with victims, offenders and communities usurping the roles of lawyers, the state and the courts. This was matched on the ground by the development of restorative justice practices. Schemes in the 1970s and 1980s were generally 'bottom up' in nature, in that they emerged not from national policy initiatives, but from local criminal justice professionals and social workers seeking out innovative forms of practice in pursuit of a better solution than that offered by conventional criminal justice in order to meet the needs of those affected by crime.[13] The youth justice system, in particular, seemed to provide fertile soil for early prototypes of restorative practice. As *ad hoc* schemes began to gain a footing in England and Wales,[14] Australia[15] and North America,[16] New Zealand became the first jurisdiction to legislate for its widespread use through the family group conferencing model, whilst the use of mediation expanded and was moved onto a statutory footing in a number of European jurisdictions.[17]

During the 1990s there was a tendency for any and all alternative or informal approaches to justice to be swept under the collective banner of 'restorative justice'.[18] However, it is apparent that what is branded as 'restorative' in one quarter is not always perceived as such in another. Indeed Zehr and Mika pointed to a possibility that certain 'retributive and punitive programmes are simply being

---

[9] Liebmann (2007).
[10] Sylvester (2003), 512–14.
[11] Cosemans and Parmentier (2014), 233. See also Cunneen (2010); Richards (2009).
[12] Zehr (1990).
[13] Marshall (1996).
[14] See eg. Hinks and Smith (1985); Marshall (1996); Marshall and Merry (1990).
[15] Daly and Immarigeon (1998); Hayes and Daly (2003).
[16] See McCold (2006).
[17] Miers (2001); Pelikan and Trenczek (2006).
[18] Roche (2003), 6.

repacked as RJ initiatives'.[19] Certainly, there is no single 'prototype' format for practices that adopt the 'restorative' label, and programmes are capable of being classified in numerous different ways. For one thing, there is considerable divergence on the extent to which schemes may be integrated into existing criminal justice structures. In many jurisdictions, programmes tend to be community-led, localised initiatives with or without support from local government of criminal justice agencies. Such informal schemes typically lie on the fringes of the criminal justice system and, as such, may struggle to access operational resources and logistic support.[20] Programmes can be led by different agencies, such as the police, an independent conferencing service, or even local community mediation organisations. Schemes also differ according to the level of victim involvement, with some using face-to-face meetings, others using indirect mediation and some rarely involving victims at all. Even the nature of the offence and type of offender differ; some programmes may deal with only one type of offending (such as retail theft or anti-social behaviour), whilst others may cover a wide range of offences including serious violence, sexual offences and even domestic abuse. Traditionally, many programmes—particularly those enshrined in law—have been orientated towards young offenders, although in recent years there has been an increased willingness to use restorative justice strategies in cases involving adult offenders.

Across the wide range of programmes that have sought to operationalise the underlying values of restorative justice, one of the most common means of 'classifying' restorative responses is according to the specific mode of intervention. Broadly, there are four main forms of restorative interventions: victim-offender mediation; community sentencing panels; police-led restorative cautioning; and family group conferencing.

A. Victim-offender mediation

Victim-offender mediation (VOM) and victim-offender reconciliation programmes (VORP) have their roots in programmes that were developed in North America in the mid-1970s and still remain the most common form of restorative justice.[21] In Canada they have been largely promoted by the Christian Mennonite movement, with an emphasis on the values of forgiveness and reconciliation. These programmes, which still flourish today, bring together victims and offenders along with a facilitator or mediator, who is usually professionally trained.[22] The aim of mediation is to give victims and offenders a safe environment in which they are able to discuss the crime, its impact and the harm it may have caused, and to allow

---

[19] Zehr and Mika (1998), 49.
[20] Mika and McEvoy (2001).
[21] Bazemore and Schiff (2005).
[22] See Johnstone (2011); Dignan (2005).

an opportunity to 'put right' the harm. Some forms of VOM limit the role of the offender and victim by using 'shuttle' type interactions or go-betweens, thereby limiting victim-offender contact. More commonly, however, the mediation takes place on a face-to face basis between victim and offender, with the mediator acting as a neutral facilitator.

VOM has proved very popular and is currently the most common form of restorative practice in both North America and continental Europe. It has also seeded a more general practice of dispute resolution which is widely used to mediate in neighbourhood disputes, especially where there has been a history of conflict between the parties that has not been resolved by other forms of intervention. This model has also gained in popularity across many parts of Europe where, as we discuss in chapter six, it is currently the most dominant form of restorative justice practice. However, it should be noted that VOM is primarily directed at repairing the relationship between the victim and offender, and thus it is settlement-driven, rather than dialogue-driven.[23] This differs from the other forms of restorative justice noted below, in that the process remains focused on that relationship rather than the offence itself. While the circumstances surrounding the offending behaviour may be addressed as part of the mediation, the process is not primarily geared to developing an outcome that provides reparation for a specific offence.

B. Restorative Policing

Police-led restorative justice has its roots in Australia, where restorative approaches to cautioning were developed in the early 1990s as an alternative approach to traditional formal police cautioning.[24] The practice became widespread throughout Australia, New Zealand and North America (notably in Minnesota and Pennsylvania) in the mid to late 1990s.[25] In the United Kingdom, restorative cautioning was trialled in a number of police forces, including the Thames Valley police and the (then) Royal Ulster Constabulary in Northern Ireland. These methods became standard practice for delivering cautions across police forces in the United Kingdom,[26] with legislation now in place in England and Wales to embed the use of conditional cautions in many cases involving both adults[27] and juveniles.[28]

The concept of integrating restorative elements within the cautioning process draws heavily from Braithwaite's theory of 'reintegrative shaming',[29] whereby

---

[23] Umbreit (2001).
[24] Wemmers and Canuto (2002); Dignan (2005).
[25] McCold (2000).
[26] Paterson and Clamp (2012).
[27] Criminal Justice Act 2003, Pt III.
[28] Criminal Justice and Immigration Act 2008, s 48.
[29] Braithwaite (1989).

shaming is used as a positive tool to encourage offenders to reflect on their actions, make amends for their wrongdoing and thereby be reintegrated back into the moral community.[30] The approach is largely based around a structured dialogue between the offender and a trained police officer. The victim (or the victim's representative) may also be present. Some form of script or agenda is usually used to encourage the offender to understand why his or her actions were harmful to others and to help the offender to empathise with how victims might feel.[31] It may draw on methods associated with either VOM, conferencing or may entail a looser, more informal arrangement. In contrast to traditional cautioning, offenders will be actively encouraged to take concrete steps to repair the harm, such as offering pecuniary reparation or an apology to the victim.[32]

In addition to restorative cautioning, there has been a trend in recent years towards using restorative approaches in frontline or 'on the beat' policing. For example, in 2008 England and Wales introduced the 'Youth Restorative Disposal' system which enables officers to deal with low-level offending by way of a discretionary summary disposal based loosely on restorative principles. In line with general principles of restorative justice, it should only be used in those cases where the offender and victim agree to participate and may only be offered in circumstances where a young person has not previously been subject to a to a reprimand, final warning or caution.[33]

C. Community Reparation Panels

A third restorative justice format which has recently found favour in a number of jurisdictions is the community sentencing or reparation panel (also commonly referred to as a community sentencing panel or a community reparation/restorative board). The main goal of these panels is to promote community involvement and empowerment in relation to offending and to promote offender responsibility and victim reparation.[34] Such panels are typically composed of a small number of trained community representatives who hold face-to-face meetings with offenders following a referral by an agency—often the courts. The panel meet with the offender, decide on the sanction that should be imposed for the offence, monitor compliance and report back to the referring court or agency on its completion. While the origin of these panels in the United States can be traced as far back as the 1920s, modern examples began to emerge during the 1990s,[35] with the

---

[30] Crawford and Clear (2001).
[31] However, as Dignan (2005) notes, restorative cautioning schemes have (at least initially) placed a greater emphasis on the offender and issues of crime control, than on their ability to meet the needs of victims.
[32] O'Mahony and Doak (2004).
[33] O'Mahony (2012), 91–92. See further ch 4, III.
[34] Bazemore and Umbreit (2004).
[35] Bazemore and Umbreit (2001).

Vermont Community Reparative Board frequently cited as a trailblazer in respect of best practice.[36] The model has also been adopted in other jurisdictions, including England and Wales. As we outline in chapter five, 'referral orders' are made available to the youth courts as a primary court disposal method for first-time offenders between the ages of 10–17 years. The Young Offender Panel is required to devise a plan which provides some form of reparation to the victim or community, as well as tailoring specific interventions (such as victim awareness sessions or drug/alcohol/family counselling) to address the young person's offending behaviour and help to prevent future reoffending. If a young person refuses to agree to the plan or does not follow it through, he or she will be referred back to the court for sentencing.

D. Family Group Conferencing

Family Group Conferencing (FGC) involves a much wider circle of participants than the other models outlined above. First developed in New Zealand, the model was devised as part of a more general initiative which sought to address difficulties in the way young people were being treated in the criminal justice and welfare systems in New Zealand, perceived as particularly problematic within minority groups such as the Maori and Pacific Island Polynesians.[37] The model sought to reflect a more culturally sensitive approach to offending that emphasises inclusive participation and collective decision making, bringing together young people, their families and community to determine appropriate means of reintegrating young offenders and providing redress for victims. Discussions are structured around a script and are convened by a trained facilitator. Typically, the victim and the offender will be invited to give accounts of the incident with prompts (as necessary) from the facilitator. Family members, supporters or community representatives who are present may also provide input to the discussion. At the end of the session, a conference plan is agreed which will usually contain elements of reparation for the victim and/or community, as well as measures to support the young offender to help him or her desist from future offending.

Family group conferencing was introduced in New Zealand under a reform agenda that emphasised diverting young people away from criminal justice interventions. The legislation made conferencing the main avenue of disposal for all but the few most serious offences including murder and manslaughter. In effect, family group conferencing became the main statutory method of disposal for young offenders being prosecuted. Young people can only be prosecuted if they have been arrested and referred by the police through a family group conference. The courts are required to send offenders for family group conferences

---

[36] Bazemore and Umbreit (2001); Dooley (1995).
[37] Maxwell and Morris (1993).

and they have to consider the recommendations of the conference and generally do not deal with cases until they have had a conference recommendation.[38] The New Zealand model has been adopted by a range of other criminal justice systems across North America, Australia, Belgium and the United Kingdom, and was placed on a statutory footing in Northern Ireland in 2002. As will be argued in chapter 7, conferencing is perhaps the most effective means of delivering 'full' restorative justice.

E. Other Forms of Restorative Justice

As with any attempt to schematise justice systems, there are certain models that do not appear to fit neatly within the standard categories above. An ever-expanding range of practices seem capable of attracting the label; for those who subscribe to a 'maximalist' view of restorative justice, these may encompass victim support, peer mediation, specialist courts and compensation/reparations programmes. Some models of classification include 'sentencing circles' as a main model of restorative justice.[39] Their use has been documented across the world, although most of the literature explores their use by the Native American and First Nations peoples of what today constitute the United States and Canada. Although similar in many respects to a restorative conference, they tend to draw heavily on traditional indigenous techniques of conflict resolution. Among First Nations tribes, prayers may be used to open proceedings, and sometimes two circles are created (an 'inner' and 'outer' circle), the former comprising the victim, offender and their supporters, and the latter including professionals who may be asked to provide specific inputs at any point in the process. Power is vested in a 'keeper' to co-ordinate the discussions and provide guidance towards a suitable outcome.[40] Group discussions with a similar spiritual dimension are also commonplace among the Navajo people, where an egalitarian approach is used in conjunction with a *naat 'aaii*, or spiritual teacher, who advises as to appropriate outcomes.[41] These practices, in particular, have provided the backdrop to much of the theoretical literature to have emerged on restorative justice in North America at the turn of the century.[42] Informal tribal responses to conflict have also been documented in many parts of Africa, Asia and the Pacific region.[43] Whilst variation in the individual approaches should not be underestimated, many draw heavily on the core individual values of respect, equality, participation, repair and reintegration.

---

[38] Morris and Maxwell (1998).
[39] See eg Gavrielides (2008); King et al (2014), Menkel-Meadow (2007).
[40] See further Cayley (1998); Griffiths and Hamilton (1996); McCold (2001).
[41] Yazzie and Zion (1996); Yazzie (1998).
[42] See eg Karp and Drakulich (2004); McCold (2001); Sullivan and Tifft (2001), Winfree (2002).
[43] See generally Maxwell and Hayes (2007).

In essence, therefore, restorative justice programmes worldwide are highly diffuse in terms of what they do and how they achieve their outcomes. However, relatively few processes can be accurately classified as 'pure' forms of restorative justice, since many lack elements such as being fully participatory or truly consensual, or they do not conform to all of the values that the concept seeks to promote.[44] As such, it is no longer useful to simply assert whether or not a practice is restorative, but instead it is more useful to view the question of the degree of 'restorativeness' in terms of a spectrum.[45] In order to determine how restorative a particular programme may be, McCold and Wachtel suggest that its processes and outcomes should be evaluated in order to determine whether programme can be said to be 'fully restorative', 'mostly restorative' or 'partially restorative'.[46] By this measure, in order for a scheme to be legitimately deemed to be 'fully' restorative it is necessary that victims fully participate in the process, agree outcomes and are offered some form of reparation and, secondly, offenders must voluntarily assume responsibility for their actions, be willing to show remorse and be offered opportunities to reintegrate back into society.[47]

In contrast, some schemes offer some form of mediation, which provides victims with the opportunity to meet the offender, in a safe environment with a trained mediator, but do not seek to address the root causes of the offending behaviour, or may offer little by way of redress to the victim. Such programmes might be described as 'mostly restorative'. Other schemes only provide compensation or reparation for damage caused, which may be direct or indirect, with little input from the victim. Some simply offer victim awareness programmes to offenders, whereby they seek to confront offenders with the consequences of their actions. Such schemes can only be described as 'partly restorative'.[48]

On this basis, a distinction should also be made between 'restorative justice' and 'restorative practices'. For the purposes of this book, we argue that restorative justice requires the incorporation of all the core elements of what is defined as restorative justice. Thus they need to provide 'a process whereby all the parties with a stake in a particular offence come together to resolve collectively how to deal with the aftermath of the offence and its implications for the future'.[49] Practices which fall short of this, being either 'partly restorative' or 'mostly restorative' should only be described as being 'restorative practices' as they fall short of the restorative ideal.[50]

---

[44] Daly (2002), 6. The 'purist' position set out by McCold (2000) is often contrasted with the 'maximalist' view set out by Bazemore and Walgrave (1999). See further ch 2, III.

[45] Bolitho (2012); Braithwaite (2002a); Campbell et al (2006); Hoyle (2010); McCold and Wachtel (2002); Roche (2001); O'Mahony (2012).

[46] McCold and Wachtel (2002).

[47] McCold and Wachtel (2002).

[48] Wilcox and Hoyle (2004).

[49] See Marshall (1999).

[50] See further Daly (2002); Hoyle (2010), 14–15; O'Mahony (2012). This is not to suggest that restorative practices cannot deliver some of the aims of restorative justice, such as raising awareness of the impact of the crime, or seeking forgiveness and restitution.

II. Trailblazing and Standard-Setting

The divergence in practices highlighted above need not be viewed in an overly negative light; after all the legitimacy of restorative programmes hangs largely on the capability of governments as well as civil societies to formulate innovative programmes that are responsive to the needs of any given community. By the same token, however, it ought to be accepted that if restorative justice is used as a form of criminal sanction, it ought to be subject to international benchmarks of best practice. Increasingly, international institutions have become willing to engage in standard-setting, with a range of instruments laying down standards in respect of the key concepts of stakeholder participation, redress for victims, and due process protections for offenders. One of the first international instruments to reflect these values was the United Nations Vienna Declaration on Crime and Justice[51] which committed signature states:

> to introduce, where appropriate, national, regional and international action plans in support of victims of crime, such as mechanisms for mediation and restorative justice, and we establish 2002 as a target date for States to review their relevant practices, to develop further victim support services and awareness campaigns on the rights of victims and to consider the establishment of funds for victims, in addition to developing and implementing witness protection policies.[52]

Paragraph 28 of the Declaration further commits the Member States to implementing restorative justice policies that are 'respectful of the rights, needs and interests of victims, offenders, communities and all other parties'. At a subsequent meeting, the UN Congress on Crime Prevention formulated a draft proposal for Basic Principles on the Use of Restorative Justice Programmes in Criminal Matters. This instrument was formally adopted by the United Nations in August 2002.[53] The Basic Principles stipulate that restorative justice programmes should be generally accessible at all stages of the penal procedure; they should be used on a voluntary basis; participants should receive all relevant information and explanation; and power imbalances and differences in age and mental capacity need to be taken into account in devising processes. Core due process requirements should also be observed. Moreover, if restorative justice processes or outcomes are not possible or agreement cannot be reached, steps should be taken to support offenders to take responsibility for their actions to provide reparation to the victim and the community. Subsequently, the Eleventh UN Congress on the Prevention of Crime and the Treatment of Offenders (2005) encouraged Member States to acknowledge the importance of implementing restorative justice

---

[51] Vienna Declaration on Crime and Justice: Meeting the Challenges of the 21st Century (UN Doc A/CONF.187/4).
[52] Ibid, at [27].
[53] ECOSOC Res 2002/12 (24 July 2002).

policies, procedures and programmes that include alternatives to prosecution. The following year the United Nations published the *Handbook of Restorative Justice Programmes*,[54] which surveyed and benchmarked a range of international best practice in the implementation of restorative schemes.

Standard-setting has also become a key feature of restorative justice in Europe. The Council of Europe has called for the promotion of 'mediation, diversion ... and alternative dispute resolutions',[55] whilst the 2001 EU Framework Decision on the Standing of Victims in Criminal Proceedings calls on Member States to promote mediation in criminal cases for offences which it considers appropriate for this sort of measure.[56] Article 10(2) calls on Member States to ensure that 'any agreement between the victim and the offender reached in the course of such mediation in criminal cases can be taken into account'. 'Mediation' itself is defined broadly in Article 1(e) as 'the search prior to or during criminal proceedings, for a negotiated solution between the victim and the author of the offence, mediated by a competent person'. The Framework Decision was superseded by Directive 2012/29/EU, otherwise known the 'Victims' Directive'. The Directive establishes minimum standards on the rights, support and protection of victims of crime. Although it does not oblige Member States to make restorative justice programmes available and lacks the promotional obligation contained in the 2001 Framework Decision, Article 12(2) does provide that 'Member States shall facilitate the referral of cases, as appropriate to restorative justice services'. This is clearly a discretionary matter for individual states; no guidance is offered as to when it may or may not be appropriate to provide for such a referral. The focus of the Directive is on protecting the interests of victims where restorative justice is made available rather than stipulating a normative basis as to when this ought to be the case. Thus, for example, competent authorities must make victims aware of any restorative justice services that are in place. Further safeguards are contained in Article 12, which stipulates that restorative justice services should be used 'only if they are in the interest of the victim, subject to any safety considerations, and are based on a victim's free and informed consent which may be withdrawn at any time'.[57] Article 25(4) provides that Member States:

> shall encourage initiatives enabling those providing victim support and restorative justice services to receive adequate training to a level appropriate to their contact with victims and observe professional standards to ensure such services are provided in an impartial, respectful and professional manner.

The Council of Europe has also recognised the recent trend for Member States to integrate restorative measures within their criminal justice systems. In 1999, the Council issued a detailed set of principles in the form of Recommendation

---

[54] United Nations (2006).
[55] Council of Europe (2010), para 24, cited by Cunneen and Goldson (2015), 140.
[56] European Communities, Council Framework Decision (2001/220/JHA).
[57] Directive 2012/29/EU, Art 12(1).

(99)19 'Concerning Mediation in Penal Matters'.[58] The Recommendation, which consists of 34 articles, recognises the need for both victims and offenders to be actively involved in resolving cases themselves, with the assistance of an impartial third party. These provisions reflect internationally recognised principles of best practice, including (inter alia), the importance of specific training, the principle of voluntariness, the need for judicial supervision, and the need to ensure that procedural human rights guarantees are safeguarded. In addition, Member States are called on to promote research and evaluation of mediation processes. It should be noted, however, Council of Europe Recommendations are a form of 'soft law' that are non-binding on Member States, with national governments asked, in developing mediation schemes, to bear in mind the principles laid down in the Recommendation and to circulate the text as widely as possible.

The trend towards standard-setting is generally viewed as a positive development in the sense that it helps to develop benchmarks of best practice, and should also thereby help to ensure consistency and a shared understanding of what restorative justice ought to entail. Crucially, it may also safeguard against the risks of power imbalances or the abuse of process by the state in settings where legal representation is generally eschewed. On the other hand, there is nevertheless a risk that a move towards standardisation may ultimately erode some of the innovative, flexible and culturally sensitive practices that have developed from grassroots initiatives outside the terrain of the criminal justice system and well beyond the formal reaches of international forums.[59]

Notwithstanding its rapid expansion on the international academic and policy platforms, Hoyle has cautioned that 'restorative justice … is fast becoming the most over-evaluated and under-practised area of criminal justice'.[60] While policymakers have been keen to pay lip-service to the concept for the best part of two decades, many programmes have failed to penetrate the formal justice system and remain situated at the 'shallow end' of the criminal justice system, through their diversionary focus. They are often organised on an ad hoc basis by criminal justice agencies, local government, civil society or a mix of the above and—in common law jurisdictions at least—their role is rarely embedded in law. Practice is thus diverse and fragmented and varies considerably not only between jurisdictions, but also within jurisdictions. However, there is evidence that this scene is beginning to change. Recent years have seen a drive towards mainstreaming restorative justice, with an increasing number of schemes now anchored in legislation as an integral part of the state structures which attempt to deal with crime. A number of jurisdictions including the United Kingdom, Australia and within

---

[58] Council of Europe, Committee of Ministers (1999), Recommendation No R (99) 19.
[59] See further Braithwaite (2002b), who recognises the need for certain types of international standards which enshrine basic due process protections and place checks on the power of the state, but cautions against attempts to superimpose uniform models of practice.
[60] Hoyle (2010), 26.

continental Europe have moved to enshrine forms of restorative justice within legislation. In some jurisdictions, such as Northern Ireland, New Zealand and several Australian states, restorative justice now forms the predominant method for dealing with young offenders even at the so-called 'deep end' of criminal justice (covering serious offences, including sexual offences).[61] In such incidences, outcomes may incorporate various forms of retributive sanctions, including imprisonment.[62] Legislative provision has also been put in place in relation to adult offenders in the Australian Capital Territory,[63] New South Wales[64] and South Australia.[65] Statutory provisions exist in Western Australia[66] and England and Wales[67] for courts to adjourn sentence pending a report into a restorative intervention. Yet in order to 'do' restorative justice well, considerable resources need to be invested across a range of statutory agencies, and widespread training and a change in the (typically adversarial) working cultures of the police, prosecutors, lawyers, judges and other criminal justice professionals is required.[68] However, there is data that suggest that moves towards a mainstreamed restorative approach can prove cost-effective in the longer term.[69] As we will argue in this book, restorative justice offers considerable potential to modernise criminal justice, especially through a better understanding of its role and function, whereby its capacity to deliver a more intelligent form of justice represents is a valuable goal for the future.

III. Bridging Theory and Practice

As restorative justice praxis has expanded both its reach and its scope, so too there has been capacious academic inquiry into its core principles and values from a

---

[61] In relation to New Zealand, see generally Maxwell and Morris (2002), see Doak and O'Mahony (2011) re. Northern Ireland. See generally Larsen (2014), re Australia.

[62] Theory has also evolved; a number of scholars now accept that restorative justice should encompass some element of punishment: see eg Brooks (2012); Daly (2002); Duff (2003); Duff and Walgrave (2002); Garvey (2003).

[63] Crime (Restorative Justice) Act 2004 (ACT). King et al (2014) note that, at the time of writing, only those provisions concerning juvenile offenders were operational.

[64] Criminal Procedure Legislation 2010 (NSW), Pt 7.

[65] Criminal Law (Sentencing) Act 1988 (SA), s 9C.

[66] Sentencing Act 1995 (WA), ss 16, 27.

[67] Powers of Criminal Courts (Sentencing) Act 2000, s 1ZA as inserted by the Crime and Courts Act 2013, sch 16.

[68] It is undeniable that upfront costs are required to meet the training needs and operational restructuring that would be required across the criminal justice system. Also, in an era where many western countries are undergoing a period of economic austerity, it is unfortunate (if not unexpected) that many statutory schemes remain inadequately funded, or that promises to engage in radical overhaul of criminal justice systems remain unfulfilled, see Greene (2013); Padfield (2012).
King et al (2014), 51.

[69] See Bonta et al (2006); Maruna (2011a); Shapland et al (2008); Sherman and Strang (2012); Sherman et al (2015).

wide range of disciplinary perspectives.[70] While many would agree that the notion of restorative justice emanates positive overtones which may well address some of the long-standing criticisms that have been levelled at the retributive and adversarial status quo, there remains a deeply entrenched *conceptual* barrier that has hindered the mainstreaming of restorative justice and which existing theoretical debates have not yet satisfactorily addressed. Indeed, restorative praxis has developed so rapidly and often in a piecemeal manner, that the theoretical inquiry has struggled to keep pace with practice. This is evidenced by a diverse, sometimes disjointed, and occasionally conflicting body of literature which can give the impression that the concept lies in a state of 'a confused, seemingly incoherent assembly'.[71] In addition, longstanding theoretical assumptions about the proper role of restorative justice and its outcomes have not been readily subjected to much critical inquiry,[72] with evidence and argument often undermined by overzealous rhetoric.[73]

By the same token, however, it is possible to identify a broad alignment or overlap in terms of intuitive values and principles that are recurrent in the literature including respect, equality, fairness, inclusivity, truth telling, honesty, voluntariness, empathy, repair and reintegration.[74] There is also increasing consensus around the transformative potential of restorative justice in effecting outcomes such as genuine apologies, forgiveness and moral transformation, which have largely remained on the periphery of the conventional criminal process. However, there continues to be a need for greater conceptual clarity regarding which aims or values restorative justice should prioritise, how they interact with each other and how they ought to be realised in practice. Moreover, clarity is also needed as to how such aims and values should be applied within the specific context of utilising restorative justice as a *criminal justice* mechanism.[75]

For instance, one of the more common claims is that restorative justice seeks to 'make amends' or 'repair the harm'.[76] While it is relatively straightforward to envisage how, for example, a compensation payment might make amends for stolen goods or a broken window, it is considerably more difficult to outline how a process can make amends for a sexual offence, or indeed any offence that carries significant and lasting emotional harm or trauma for the victim. This conundrum is exacerbated further given the varied responses and needs of individual victims in the aftermath of crime.[77] Similar difficulties arise in respect of themes such as 'reconciliation', 'rehabilitation' and 'reintegration': how can reconciliation take

---

[70] King et al (2014), 51.
[71] Walgrave (2011), 94.
[72] Shapland et al (2006b).
[73] Ward and Langlands (2009).
[74] Dyck (2004); Pranis (2007). See further ch 3.
[75] Daly (2016), 11.
[76] See eg Bazemore et al (1997); Davis (1992); Morris (2002); Zehr and Mika (1998).
[77] See generally Shapland and Hall (2007).

place if the parties were not 'conciled' in the first place? What precisely does reintegration entail, and what happens if the victim's or offender's understanding of a rehabilitation act differs from what might normatively be acceptable to the community? Should reconciliation be afforded priority over traditional rationales for sentencing including incapacitation, denunciation and just deserts? These questions, and many more besides, continue to generate debate within the evolving literature.

In this book we contend that there is a pressing normative case for formulating criminal justice responses which consider the needs, rights and interests of the victim, the offender, the broader community, as well as the criminal justice system itself. In the case of the latter, careful thought needs to be afforded to the question of *what* police, prosecutors, and courts are tasked with doing, as well as the rationales for what they do, including the broader goals and traditional justifications of criminal justice. Whatever one feels about the state of punishment and the criminal justice system in general, the reality is that—for the foreseeable future at least—policymakers and the public generally hold steadfast to the view that the state ought to censure wrongdoing. This means that there is a need for a clearer understanding of how restorative justice works within criminal justice, including the extent to which it is capable of encapsulating core criminal justice values (such as accountability, proportionality and due process).

The confusion surrounding restorative justice's definitional clarity is unsurprising not only due to the various philosophical standpoints from which commentators tend to analyse the subject, but also given the wide variation in practice that exists globally. Yet it is vitally important that the complexity of theoretical conundrums does not obstruct attempts to seek conceptual clarity. Such clarity is an essential component in understanding how restorative justice works within the criminal justice system. Similarly, if policy and practice are to be evidence-based, they need to be driven by a coherent underlying theory. Without a coherent theory, all we have is raw data and mindless speculation about what it might mean, coloured by researchers' own personal, social and political views.[78] For example, evaluative data is often reported using 'satisfaction' as benchmark against which its success might be measured, with satisfaction typically flowing from participants' opportunities to achieve agreements or having the chance to express emotions and make an impact on the offender.[79] Satisfaction is also linked to opportunities that the process provides to meet the offender, to participate in decision making and obtain information on what happened.[80] Conversely, *dissatisfaction* has been linked to cases where processes or outcomes are poorly managed or delivered. For example, where restorative processes are not delivered effectively participants often report lower levels of satisfaction, usually related to insufficient planning,

---

[78] Duffee et al (2015), 426.
[79] Shapland et al 2007; Dignan (2005).
[80] Umbreit et al (2004).

unrealistic expectations, or bias that may be shown towards individual parties.[81] Likewise, bringing participants into a restorative process when they are not fully prepared can result in lower levels of satisfaction, as individuals may be unable to fully engage, participate and take responsibility for their actions, or they may even become uncooperative and dispute the 'facts'.[82]

Research relating processes and outcomes to the satisfaction of participants with restorative justice has been used as a key strategy to measure its effect,[83] but caution is needed in extrapolating effects across different studies. As noted above, programmes operate across a wide variety of legal and cultural settings. Although there is no shortage of robust evaluations, these often diverge in terms of the different styles and forms of restorative justice, different offence types, the range of participants and the point at which referral is made within the process. Confounding these are the disparity of methods adopted, ranging from small-scale observational studies to highly complex quantitative meta-analyses.[84] Generally speaking, research is largely positive in terms of satisfaction levels of victims and offenders, particularly when contrasted with conventional criminal processes.[85] Yet, these measures of 'satisfaction' are by no means clearly related to the more fundamental goals of restorative justice, such as reconciliation, restoration and reintegration.[86] Moreover, there is a lack of clear evidence that 'satisfaction' translates into what restorative justice is actually trying to achieve as a theory or as a set of goals.[87] Likewise, the 'success' of restorative justice is sometimes measured in terms of its capacity to reduce recidivism. Again, however, an overly mechanical focus on reoffending data overlooks other positive forms of impacts on a wide range of stakeholders, including victims and the wider community. In a similar vein to much of the research focusing on 'satisfaction', recidivism studies often tell us little about how and why the theoretical underpinnings of restorative justice may (or may not) impact on reoffending.

There is an expansive and diffuse literature concerning both the *normative* elements of restorative justice theory (ie why it may or may not be morally desirable, or which values it ought to espouse) as well as *explanatory* aspects of theory which seek to locate and explain how restorative justice operates within the criminal justice system.[88] There is also a growing body of evaluative research which tends to benchmark the success of restorative justice against vague concepts such as 'satisfaction' or blunt measures like 'recidivism'. Meanwhile, restorative justice discourses have unfolded at a remarkable pace across various (sub) disciplines, leading to a 'widespread conception of restorative justice as a work

---

[81] See eg Campbell et al (2006); Morris et al (1993); Shapland et al (2007); Strang (2002).
[82] Umbreit (1994); Shapland et al (2007); Morris et al (1993).
[83] Dignan (2005).
[84] Saulnier and Sivasubramaniam (2015a).
[85] Dignan (2005); Poulson (2003).
[86] See Braithwaite (1989); Zehr (1990); Pranis (2007).
[87] Dignan (2005); Bolívar (2010); Braithwaite (2002a).
[88] Braithwaite (2003).

in progress constantly being improved and sophisticated'.[89] Concepts, ideas and values have been readily proposed, dissected and applied, but there has been such a proliferation of literature on these matters that it lacks a sense of coherence. As Walgrave contends, there is no 'real story' of restorative justice; there are, in fact, many stories.[90] This is acutely evident in relation to the types of offences to which restorative justice might be applied, as well as its role within a broader (and often unrestorative) criminal justice system.[91]

By the same token, theory has arguably failed to keep pace with what is actually happening on the ground. This is not to suggest that the efforts of those who have designed and implemented individual programmes on the ground have not been theoretically informed. Many programmes—particularly those that are rolled out on a large scale at a national level—have drawn heavily on research into what works.[92] Yet, in her oft-cited paper, *Mind the Gap*,[93] Daly draws on empirical findings from the South Australian Juvenile Justice Project to show that the gap between theory and practice is often acute.[94] In short, there have been relatively few attempts to explain the *how* and *why* mechanisms of restorative justice operate in order to better engineer successful outcomes.[95]

In light of the sheer breadth of the theoretical literature and the heterogeneous nature of practice in the field, we have confined our discussion to examples of restorative justice practice within western criminal justice systems. While we acknowledge that there is an argument to be made that restorative justice should usurp, rather than complement, existing criminal justice structures,[96] this position appears to have fallen from favour in recent years[97] and, in any case, is not reflective of the reality of how restorative justice operates in practice. We also recognise that restorative justice principles have been applied in respect of conflicts beyond the parameters of the formal criminal justice system, including community-led programmes in neighbourhoods, schools, care facilities, prisons and the workplace, as well as in relation to peacebuilding and the reconciliation of political conflicts. While useful lessons may be drawn from the literature relating to restorative justice in such settings,[98] our primary concern is with how restorative justice operates within the formal justice setting.

Finally, our exploration of the discrepancy between theory and practice is centred on developments in western criminal justice systems. We have not

---

[89] Von Holderstein Holtermann (2009), 190.
[90] Walgrave (2012), 33 responding to Daly (2002).
[91] Von Holderstein Holtermann (2009), 191.
[92] King et al (2014).
[93] Daly (2002).
[94] See also Cunneen (2010); Cunneen and Goldson (2015).
[95] Saulnier and Sivasubramaniam (2015a).
[96] See eg Barnett (1977); Cantor (1976); Christie (1977); Zehr (1990).
[97] Gavrielides (2007).
[98] See eg Doak (2015), arguing that criminal justice could be 'enriched' through drawing on lessons from post-conflict arenas.

included in our scope the innovative and creative restorative practices that have been documented across Africa[99] and Asia[100] as well as applications within Islamic legal systems[101] and within the indigenous communities of North America[102] and Australia.[103] We acknowledge that this limits our analysis insofar as it draws primarily on western practices and we make no claim on the so-called 'origin myth' concerning its resonance (or lack thereof) to indigenous forms of justice.[104] While some may argue this risks painting an overly neo-liberal and/or state-centric view of what might be properly regarded as restorative justice in a global sense, our approach has been shaped by the practical difficulties in accurately charting the diffuse nature of an extremely wide variation of practices outside these settings.

Our focus on western countries (despite some cultural and demographic differences) has also been informed by the fact that they share political, socio-economic and cultural features.[105] There is also an enhanced capacity of strong states with strong markets and civil society networks to absorb and develop restorative justice as part of their regulatory frameworks.[106] More specifically, within the criminal justice context, many have undergone a 'punitive turn' in which the state response to crime has shifted along neo-liberal and 'law and order' rhetoric and policies,[107] including governance through risk[108] and a focus on managerialism.[109] This is not necessarily reflective of a genuine commitment by policymakers to overhaul the underlying paradigm of justice; but may instead be attributable to the 'bureaucratic convenience' of grafting new processes on to the existing structures of the criminal justice system.[110] Most western systems share similar paradigms of criminal justice, and it was these same paradigms that became the subject of widespread disillusionment in the latter part of the last century, and which in turn helped to catalyse the rapid expansion of restorative justice throughout the West.[111] We seek to move past a focus on the problems of delivering restorative justice in criminal justice. Through a new theoretical model, based on empowerment theory and the core goals of agency and accountability, we seek to offer a fresh conceptual platform from which to better understand the role of restorative justice and the potential it offers as a forward looking, constructive approach to criminal justice into the future.

---

[99] Elechi (1999); Jenkins (2006); Skelton (2007).
[100] Lo (2011); Ping Wang et al (2007); Ua-amnoey and Kittayarak (2004).
[101] Braithwaite and Gohar (2014); Irani and Funk (1998); Rahami (2007).
[102] Cayley (1998); Griffiths (1996); McCold (2001); Yazzie (1998); Yazzie and Zion (1996).
[103] Blagg (1997), (2002); Council and Durie-Hall (1999); Cunneen (2007).
[104] Blagg (2001); Bottoms (2003); Daly (2016).
[105] Huntington (1996); Thompson and Hickey (2005).
[106] Braithwaite (2006).
[107] Bell (2011); Garland (2001); Pratt et al (2013); Simon (2001); Rose (2000).
[108] Beck (1992); Gray (2009); McAlinden (2016).
[109] James and Raine (1998); McAlinden (2011); McLaughlin et al (2001). See further Bottoms (1995), who identifies four key 'movements of thought' on western criminal justice policy viz. popular punitivism; just deserts/human rights; managerialism and community.
[110] Pratt (2007), 140.
[111] Tonry (2005), 1268.

IV. Structure and Argument of this Book

This introductory chapter has sought to provide a contextual platform for our work. In the remainder of the book we explore the evolution of the underlying values and principles within restorative justice theory and seek to map it against the range of applications in practice. Given the rapid expansion of restorative justice over the past two decades and the highly divergent state of practice, there is a clear need to re-evaluate the utility of some of the prevailing benchmark theories and to reimagine the shape and role of theory in guiding restorative justice provision within criminal justice into the future. The underlying aim of this project is to clarify how restorative justice works and the normative goals it ought to encompass. We propose a new conceptual platform which advances both normative and explanatory debates. It enables us to understand more precisely the circumstances in which restorative justice works and the guiding principles upon which theory and praxis rest. Our vision for the criminal justice system is that re-empowerment is identified as fundamental normative goal. The book contends that agency and accountability are recognised as twin values which provide the justification for this goal, as well as the key drivers which explain why restorative justice works. Thus, (tweaking a pre-eminent aphorism from the realm of economic finance theory),[112] agency and accountability are both components of the engine that drives restorative justice praxis, as well as lens of the camera through which restorative justice can be observed.

The study begins with an appraisal of the current state of theory in the field. Thus, in chapter two we demonstrate that while multiple values and principles have been deployed to explain the normative and operational aspects of restorative justice, existing theory has gravitated around the abstract notions of conflict and harm. Yet, while there is broad normative support for the use of a restorative paradigm, considerably less is known about how, specifically, the mechanics of restorative justice are capable of resolving conflicts, or how that which is deemed to be 'broken' can somehow be 'fixed'. In this sense, existing theory which seeks to account for the role that restorative justice plays within criminal justice has been deficient in a number of respects. It fails to provide a succinct account of the core objectives that ought to underpin praxis, and also flounders in explaining how such objectives might be engineered in restorative encounters. In essence, while the growing body of restorative justice theory has connected to questions of restoration, particularly in relation to what is being restored, how it might be restored and the nature and form of the restorative measures, it is clear there is the need for an overarching theoretical paradigm through with we can begin to reimagine and reconceptualise restorative justice for the future.

---

[112] MacKenzie (2008).

In chapter three we take up the challenge of reimagining restorative justice within criminal justice. We set out our theoretical frame of reference, developed to help better understand how restorative justice can and should operate in within the confines of criminal justice. Drawing on empowerment theory, as developed in social psychology, we offer an alternative and pragmatic paradigm through which to build a broader understanding of the inter-relationship between restorative justice and criminal justice and thus a better theoretical framework for restorative practices in such contexts. By allowing us to reconceptualise restorative 'processes' and 'outcomes' as core empowering values of 'agency' and 'accountability', our theory which we label the 'agency–accountability framework' offers a distinct advantage for conceptualising restorative justice within criminal justice. It should be noted that our understanding of these terms differs from the frequently invoked negative or neo-liberal connotations of social control via the 'responsiblisation' of the individual.[113] As we explain in chapter three, by 'agency', we are referring to the empowerment of individual actors, through increasing their autonomous capacity to make effective choices and maximising their involvement throughout the process. This vision of agency contrasts directly with the processes and systems which underpin the conventional criminal justice system, and tend to disempower individuals and limit their capability to make autonomous choices. In a similar sense, we view 'accountability' as essentially conferring the power of accepting accountability *for* some action and *towards* others. It focuses on the freedom of the individual to create and accept obligations and commitments, as opposed to having them imposed from above through a retributive state-led sentencing process.[114] We demonstrate how our concept of 'agency' maps broadly onto the 'processes' of delivering restorative justice within criminal justice, whilst 'accountability' generally maps onto the 'outcomes' of restorative justice (eg the final agreement or sentence that follows).[115] In our model, the joined-up view of these concepts provides a clearer and more accurate explanation of the role of restoration in restorative justice. From this theoretical platform, we argue that in practical terms, programmes which aspire to be regarded as 'fully restorative' should be designed and implemented in such a way so that 'agency' and 'accountability' are maximised as goals throughout their delivery. Similarly, 'partially restorative' programmes can be guided and more effectively delivered if they realise elements of agency and accountability as underpinning objectives for their practice.

In chapter four the roles and experiences of victims and offenders are contrasted between restorative justice and the traditional adversarial criminal justice approach. It will be shown that direct deliberation between the parties is the key factor that distinguishes restorative justice experiences with the criminal justice process. Many of the goals and values that underpin restorative justice apply to

---

[113] See Garland (2001).
[114] Johnstone (2013); Johnstone and Van Ness (2007).
[115] Johnstone (2013); Johnstone and Van Ness (2007).

victims and offenders alike. These include the need to provide a process that is characterised by the respectful treatment of all parties; the need for all parties to be able to participate in the process and be empowered by that process; the ability to provide a flexible and responsive process that meets the needs of all of the participants, yet which provides safety for all; and the need for consensus amongst the participants, so agreements are genuine, likely to be achieved, and are productive and useful. Evaluations of restorative interventions indicate that offenders are generally satisfied with their experience of the restorative process. However, it should be borne in mind that the process of participation for offenders goes beyond simply having to speak—it needs to be an active process that involves them in dialogue, both holding them to account and engaging them so there is clear ownership of the dispute by all the parties. The discussion in chapter four enables us to better understand how the agency–accountability framework maps on to the experiences of victims and offenders and sheds light on their normative roles as well as providing key insights for effective practice.

In chapters five, six and seven we turn our attention to the nature and form of restorative interventions at various stages of the criminal process. Our aim here is to illustrate the key ways in which restorative practices play out within criminal justice, which will allow us to gain a better understanding of the gaps that exists between the normative principles of restorative justice and its practical implementation. Chapter five begins this analysis by outlining a number of formal, pre-trial programmes. Most of these are diversionary in nature and are primarily orientated towards juvenile offenders, and many are based around the family group conferencing model. Similarly, police-based conferences, which are practised widely across Australia, New Zealand, the United States and the United Kingdom, are primarily designed as a diversionary mechanism to avoid prosecution.

Our attention shifts to continental Europe in chapter six where restorative justice has also expanded considerably in recent years, although for the most part interventions centre around the victim-offender mediation model. The majority of the mediation projects available are used as forms of diversion away from criminal sanctioning and are usually restricted to either juvenile or adult offenders. The decision on whether to use mediation is often made by the prosecutor, before cases make it to court. It is argued, however, that most mediation programmes available are not explicitly restorative and only recently has there been an emphasis on providing programmes that have a strong restorative focus. Belgium, in particular, provides a useful insight into the expansion of restorative conferencing within a European setting and its considerable potential for the future.

Once a decision has been taken to prosecute the offender through the courts, or following sentencing, restorative justice in common law jurisdictions is often operationalised through conferencing. In chapter seven we draw heavily on research in Northern Ireland and New Zealand, where criminal justice institutions are under a statutory obligation to use restorative interventions as a mainstreamed approach to dealing with young offenders. Where relevant, we also explore various schemes that operate for adult offenders in New South Wales, South Australia, Belgium and England and Wales.

The issue of recidivism, which is often identified as one of the key measures of 'success' in restorative justice practice, is the focus of chapter eight. Here we seek to bring together the findings of a diverse range of research studies. It is difficult to elicit a single message here; as noted above, such difficulties are compounded by the fact that such research draws on a wide range of restorative interventions, at different stages in the criminal justice system, with different types of offenders and offences. Indeed, many had different ways of defining recidivism, from re-arrests, to convictions for offences committed after interventions. Nevertheless, the weight of evidence on recidivism from recent research studies demonstrates that restorative justice interventions usually have a modest but statistically significant impact in reducing recidivism. In particular, it is noted that restorative interventions appear to have a more powerful impact for violent and more serious offences, and appear to be better at reducing reoffending for higher-risk individuals and especially those who are not first-time offenders. In addition, the evidence suggests that restorative interventions that involve direct interactions between the offender and victim are generally more successful than those that have indirect or no victim involvement. However, we argue that it is important not to oversell the power of restorative justice in terms of its ability to reduce recidivism, or to frame it simply as a crime prevention scheme. After all, a single restorative intervention such as a conference lasting 60 to 90 minutes is unlikely to lead to radical changes in offending, particularly if it is not backed up with any other programmes that address offending.

The aim of chapters four to eight is to build an intricate picture of the diverse ways in which restorative justice operates in practice; not all schemes embrace all restorative principles in equal measure, and there is also considerable divergence on the extent to which schemes may be integrated into existing criminal justice structures. In turn, this analysis will enable us, in chapter nine, to map the ways which contemporary theories of restorative justice fail to account satisfactorily for the variety of ways in which restorative justice is used within criminal justice settings. Notwithstanding the intensity of ongoing debates about its precise meaning and scope, the key underlying principle that 'ownership' of criminal justice ought to be devolved downwards from the state towards offenders, victims and communities has been broadly accepted within both the academic and policy platforms.[116] Thus, we contend that the twin empowering goals of 'agency' and 'accountability' should be better ingrained throughout the process in order to deliver a more responsive, legitimate and emotionally intelligent criminal justice system.

---

[116] It is not our intention here to engage in a protracted debate with the critics of restorative justice; that task has been admirably accomplished elsewhere, see eg Johnstone (2007); Morris (2002); Van Ness (1993).

2
Restorative Justice Theory: Concepts, Processes and Outcomes

I. Introduction

This chapter begins by tracing how the existing paradigm of criminal justice came to be challenged in the years following the Second World War. As the visibility of crime victims increased, so it became apparent that the criminal justice system was failing to meet their needs. The latter years of the twentieth century subsequently witnessed a growing critique of the underlying structures and assumptions of the criminal justice system, which in turn triggered a rapid growth in both the theory and praxis of restorative justice as an alternative paradigm. As previously noted, the rapid global expansion of restorative justice programmes has arguably led to a 'gap' between how restorative justice operates in practice, and how theory has sought to explain its operation. Theory has particularly struggled in providing clarity as to how restorative justice should be delivered within a criminal justice context, but more fundamentally, in providing guidance and answers to why it works. While the nature and extent of this gap will be crystallised in subsequent chapters, this chapter aims to provide an analysis of the evolution of restorative justice theory. In doing so, it highlights some of the key areas which remain a source of contention, as well as exploring some of the theoretical conundrums which continue to rankle.

As restorative justice continues its growth and spread, a number of key conceptual challenges have arisen. This chapter locates these challenges under three broad heads. First, such challenges arise in relation to the fundamental concept of restorative justice itself. If restoration is to be accepted as a guiding principle of restorative justice within criminal justice, then clarity is needed on the question of *what* is being restored, by whom and to whom. While material harms are (relatively) straightforward to calculate, it is considerably more difficult to quantify the value of emotional and relational forms of harm which have not featured prominently, especially in relation to the conventional criminal process. For many restorative justice theorists to date, harm assumes the form of a moral debt that is owed by the offender to the victim, the community and, indeed, potentially the state. It is axiomatic that the identification of the nature and extent of the harm caused ought to map directly on to the outcomes of restorative justice, but the task of 'making amends' remains in need of conceptual clarification given the range of stakeholders—and their differing (and potentially competing) needs. Second, we explore the process of restoration, asking *how* the operation of a restorative process is capable of delivering outcomes capable of meeting the needs of victims and offenders. We note the deficiencies of the existing criminal process, before exploring some of the fruitful sociological insights which have advanced our understanding of how restorative justice can achieve such outcomes.[1] While Braithwaite's theory of reintegrative shaming has served to bolster understanding of this process for over two decades, more recent empirical research suggests that it is not shame per se, but rather the emotional intensity of the process that belies its potential for successful outcomes. Finally, our attention turns to the nature and form of those outcomes themselves. At this juncture we consider how the distinction between 'material' and 'symbolic' forms of restoration, along with the emphasis placed on tailor-made restoration packages, carry the potential to address the needs and demands of the stakeholders in a way that conventional criminal justice fails to do. In conclusion, we reflect on the state of theory in the field, and highlight the difficulties of translating diffuse sets of restorative goals and values into praxis within criminal justice, particularly without the benefit of a clear and overarching theoretical framework.

II. Criminal Justice: A Paradigm in Crisis?

Although criminal justice policy was not a widely contested political issue in the years following the Second World War, it was against the backdrop of emerging social rights in this period that a loose association of groups and individuals began to voice the view that the criminal justice system was failing victims. Campaigns by Margery Fry for victim compensation during the 1950s were followed by wider campaigns by the feminist movement during the 1960s and 1970s, which highlighted hidden aspects of victimisation, including those experienced by survivors of domestic violence, rape and child sex abuse. Likewise, research revealed the extent of such victimisation was a lot more prevalent than had been thought.[2] Throughout the 1980s and 1990s, a growing number of specific interest groups emerged, including organisations campaigning for the registration of sex offenders, incest survivor groups, relatives of murdered and missing children, relatives of victims of drunk driving, and those concerned with combating racism, homophobia and discrimination. While such groups were generally unconnected and pursued their independent agendas, the net effect of their efforts was to raise

---

[1] Rossner (2013). See further ch 3.
[2] Nash and West (1985); Glaser and Frosh (1988).

fundamental questions relating to how effectively the criminal justice system was serving the needs of victims.[3]

The rising visibility of the victim was undoubtedly a key contributory factor to the growth of victimology as an academic discipline, though it also acted as a catalyst to generate radical ideas which would question the underlying values and assumptions of the existing criminal justice paradigm. The psychologist Albert Eglash is often identified as having coined the term 'restorative justice'. In a series of articles during the latter part of the 1950s, Eglash described some of his work with adults and young offenders as a form of 'creative restitution'.[4] Unlike 'conventional restitution' as ordered by courts, 'creative restitution' went beyond the notion of restoring property or its pecuniary value to its rightful owner, to focus on restoring 'goodwill and harmony' through a constructive and self-determined act on the part of the offender.[5] The aim of this 'lifelong ... psychological exercise' was to achieve an outcome that was better and more constructive for all involved.[6] In addition to conferring benefits on victims and society as a whole, the process was expected to impact on the offender's self-esteem and thereby assist in future efforts to desist from offending. Although Eglash is rightly credited with coining the term 'restorative justice', he did not actually use it until some two decades later, when describing a model that entailed 'a deliberate opportunity for offender and victim to restore their relationship, along with a chance for the offender to come up with a means to repair the harm done to the victim'.[7]

Two seminal articles, published in 1977, engaged in a deeper critique of the existing criminal justice paradigm. The first of these was by Barnett, who identified the 'crisis of an old paradigm', which was based around an artificial construction of interpersonal harms as criminal offences against the state. Barnett called for a 'new paradigm', which he labelled 'pure restitution', whereby 'sentencing' would basically entail the payment of reparations directly to the victim. Under this model the state interest in denunciation, incapacitation or rehabilitation would be incidental to the reparatory interests of the victim. Drawing on Epstein's theory of tort liability,[8] Barnett called for an end to the distinction between public and private harms, and proposed 'a single system of corrective justice that looks to the conduct, broadly defined, of the parties to the case with a view toward the protection of individual liberty and private property',[9] an approach he described as a 'common sense view of crime'.[10]

---

[3] Mawby and Walklate (1994).
[4] Eglash (1958).
[5] Eglash (1958), 620.
[6] Eglash (1958), 622.
[7] Eglash (1977), 2.
[8] Epstein (1975).
[9] Barnett (1977), 290, citing Epstein (1975), 441.
[10] Barnett (1977), 288.

The second important contribution at this period was Christie's *Conflicts as Property*.[11] The paper opens by recalling a practice in a rural village in Tanzania, whereby a dispute was settled through a deliberative process involving the victim, the offender, family members and community elders. In his critique of western criminal justice, Christie notes how over the course of centuries, conflicts between individuals have been appropriated by the state and legal professionals. Christie describes lawyers as having 'stolen' the disputes of the protagonists, a state of affairs which is reflected in the organisation of the criminal process, the legalistic manner in which the criminal law is framed, and the ways in which offenders and victims are routinely sidelined by lawyers in court. He proceeds to outline an alternative vision for a justice system that revolves around the victim and the community, with outcomes designed to provide redress for the victim as well as reintegrating the offender into society. Unlike Barnett, Christie maintains that there is a role for a court to impose some form of additional punishment on the offender, which might exceed the reparation which might be required to rectify the harm caused to the victim.

Although they differ in the level of detail and the value they attach to the role of punishment within the criminal process, these early accounts have much in common.[12] They provide substantial critique of the conventional criminal justice system on the grounds that it tends to prioritise punishment over redress and to exclude the victim and the community from the conflict resolution process. Although the tenor of this early body of work provided a strong normative framework for criminal justice reform, it significantly preceded the rapid growth of restorative justice that was to take place towards the turn of the century. The calls for a paradigm shift and many of the proposals for reform were both imaginative and ambitious, although these authors were constrained by the prevailing paradigm which was so entrenched that the reforms they proposed were unlikely succeed in the short to medium term. While Barnett and Christie both made some effort to imagine how precisely criminal procedure might be reformed to accommodate restorative goals, their accounts failed to engage with the structural and cultural obstacles necessary to engineer such radical reform in practice. Challenges pertaining to how governments, judges, lawyers and others with vested interested in the status quo might react to such proposals were not unpacked in any depth; neither were questions pertaining to some of the risks of restorative justice (such as the protection of due process and other human rights, the need for proportionality, and the dangers of power imbalances) dealt with in any detail. It is only more recently, following the widespread development of restorative justice programmes, that such concerns have been addressed from both conceptual and practical perspectives. Nevertheless, the value of this theoretical groundwork cannot be underestimated; it provided a conceptual fabric for many of the more

---

[11] Christie (1977).

[12] Other less well-known accounts making similar arguments emerged around the same time: see eg Abel and Marsh (1984); Cantor (1976); Goldstein (1982); Harland (1978); and Klein (1978).

detailed and nuanced debates around the role of restorative justice that have burgeoned since the early 1990s.

III. Refining Restorative Justice Theory

Over the past quarter of a century, scholars have devoted considerable energy to developing a theoretical framework for restorative justice. There have also been numerous attempts to coin a universally acceptable definition of restorative justice. Yet, in spite of its growing popularity, restorative justice still remains a contested concept, which has proved difficult to define in concise terms and even more difficult to grasp theoretically. One key area of disagreement is whether restorative justice ought to be characterised in terms of a process, an outcome, a collection of values or principles, or a mixture of all of the above.

Process-based definitions have been proffered by Zehr and Mika: 'a process of justice which maximises opportunities for exchange of information, participation, dialogue and mutual consent between the victim and offender'.[13] Similarly, Marshall has defined it as 'a process whereby all the parties with a stake in a particular offence come together to resolve collectively how to deal with the aftermath of the offence and its implications for the future'.[14] Marshall's definition, in particular, is widely cited in the literature, though it has not been without its critics. Dignan, for example, has criticised it on the grounds that it is process-centric, and makes no reference to the nature of the outcomes that might be carried forward.[15] This critique might also be applied to perspectives advanced by Braithwaite, who contends that 'stakeholder deliberation determines what restoration means in a specific context',[16] or Morris' observation that 'any outcome—including a prison sentence—can be a restorative outcome if it is agreed to and considered appropriate by the key parties'.[17] The concern here is that such views do not take adequate account of the nature of the outcomes and thereby eschew fundamental principles of fairness and proportionality.[18] There are also inherent vagaries surrounding the nature, extent and form of stakeholder participation envisaged, or what restorative justice seeks to achieve.[19]

For Dignan, restorative justice comprises three core features: first, putting right the harm caused by an offence;[20] second, a balanced focus on the offender's

---

[13] Zehr and Mika (1998), 2.
[14] Marshall (1999), 5.
[15] Dignan (2005), 3–5.
[16] Braithwaite (1999), 6.
[17] Morris (2002), 599.
[18] Dignan (2005).
[19] Clamp and Doak (2012); McEvoy and Mika (2002).
[20] Dignan (2005).

personal accountability to those who have been harmed—including the victim and broader community—and on the victim's right to some form of reparative redress; and, third, a process that is inclusive and non-coercive, that 'encourages participation by the key participants in determining how an offence should be dealt with'.[21] Dignan's use of the term 'encouragement' is apt, since many process-related definitions have been described as 'purist', where they rely on the restorative ideal of such an encounter,[22] despite the fact that this may not be possible or even desirable[23] and that in such cases it may still be possible to utilise a process which draws on restorative principles.[24]

Pranis also conceives restorative justice in terms of fundamental values and principles which she details as being either 'process values' or 'individual values'.[25] Process values relate to the qualities of the restorative process itself and include practices that reflect concerns for respect, equality, inclusion and truth telling.[26] They may also encompass the maintenance and restoration of dignity through empathy, understanding and restitution[27] and should be based around fairness, honesty and respect, which seek to enhance the common good.[28] Similarly, equality, non-domination and community are considered core restorative values that shape effective practice.[29] On the other hand, individual values are those that a restorative process tries to draw out of the participants themselves. These include compassion, patience and open-mindedness.[30] Both the individual and process values provide a common ground for restorative justice to operate successfully, and as such should be regarded as the 'foundation of restorative justice' and a yardstick for assessing how it operates.[31]

Others take a more prescriptive approach: for example, Van Ness and Heetderks Strong contend that there are four critical values for restorative justice.[32] First, it must be inclusionary, so all affected parties are able to participate and engage in the process. Second, it must be encounter-based, with all of the parties given the opportunity to meet in a safe environment. Third, those responsible for the harm caused must take responsibility for making amends and repairing the harm. Fourth, reintegration must be facilitated, with means and opportunities provided for individuals to move beyond stigmatisation and rejoin their community. While others have presented competing accounts of what they consider 'essential'

---

[21] Dignan (2005), 8.
[22] McCold (2000).
[23] Clamp and Doak (2012).
[24] Doolin (2007). Such a process might include, for example, the use of surrogate victims: see ch 4, I (B).
[25] Pranis (2007).
[26] Dyck (2004).
[27] Herman (2004).
[28] Consedine (1995).
[29] Braithwaite and Parker (1999).
[30] Pranis (2007).
[31] Pranis (2007), 72.
[32] Van Ness and Heetderks Strong (2014).

restorative values, Pranis makes the useful observation that while there is no single accepted list of values, they are consistent in their importance in the delivery of effective restorative practices.[33]

Some commentators have been reluctant to lay down any specific process-based conditions as to what qualifies as restorative justice. The 'maximalist' position, as expounded by Bazemore and Walgrave, adopts a very broad view as to what constitutes restorative justice. For them, the label may be applied to 'every action that is primarily oriented towards doing justice by restoring the harm that has been caused by a crime'.[34] However, in failing to take into account any aspect of the process, this position fails to make any reference to the form of process adopted at all, and would thus potentially encapsulate broader victim support initiatives alongside restitutionary and compensatory remedies, which have been available through the conventional civil and criminal justice systems for many years. More recently, most commentators have accepted the need to marry process-based and outcome-based perspectives. Johnstone and Van Ness advance their definition, encompassing both process-based and outcome-based perspectives in defining restorative justice as 'the process in which the hurts and the needs of both the victim and the offender are addressed in such a way that both parties, as well as the community which they are part of, are healed'.[35] For Doolin, the tension might be resolved by developing 'an approach that emphasises the principles of the process (the involvement of the key stakeholders, the dialogue, the collective resolution, consensus decision-making, forward-looking approach) but, importantly, recognises that the outcome of restoration is the determining value that should govern both the process and the resolution'.[36]

Although it is claimed, in some contemporary commentaries, the values and principles of restorative justice 'form a consistent and coherent picture',[37] we contend that there is considerable divergence and disagreement and it is not at all clear what actually constitutes restorative justice. This lack of clarity has also adversely impacted attempts to progress our basic theoretical understanding of restorative justice. Indeed, Wood and Suzuki have rightly warned that the idea of restorative justice has been 'stretched to its conceptual limits'.[38] It seem, at least for some, the passage of time has proven that McCold's cautionary note that restorative justice 'has come to mean all things to all people'.[39] This lack of clarity, or even confusion in some cases, has even led to frustration amongst some commentators, with Daly contending that 'an inability to define RJ … is not fatal'.[40] Moreover, Daly has

---

[33] Pranis (2007).
[34] Bazemore and Walgrave (1999), 48.
[35] Johnstone and Van Ness (2005), 23.
[36] Doolin (2007), 431.
[37] Pranis (2007), 62.
[38] Wood and Suzuki (2016), 163.
[39] McCold (2000), 358.
[40] Daly (2006), 135.

recently changed her mind on the issue, contending that 'the research and development phase of RJ has now passed'.[41] However, we do not think it is advisable to attempt to progress the project of restorative justice without further serious consideration of what it actually is, together with a more fundamental understanding of its theoretical underpinnings. In particular, we identify the need for a deeper analysis of the purpose of restorative justice, shedding much needed light on what it should seek to achieve and why this is important, especially from the perspectives of those who participate within it.

While our understanding of restorative justice theory must be sufficiently broad to avoid legalism and allow for diversity of practice, we contend that a sharper degree of certainty is necessary to unravel the more complex questions about the role and limits of restorative justice within the criminal justice system, as well as ensuring basic levels of consistency in practice. Such conceptual clarity is vital in the criminal justice sphere since, ultimately, we are dealing with the fate of individuals who have committed acts proscribed by the criminal law. To aid this quest, we propose that an enhanced conceptual clarity is required on at least three questions that underpin any attempt to define the concept. To address this we first explore the question of what, precisely is being restored, from whom and to whom. Second, we consider the mechanics of the restorative process; how, precisely, does it engineer the transformation in relationships which so many of its advocates identify as a core characteristic? Finally, we turn to the question of restoration itself by asking the question how, if at all, can a process 'undo' the effects of harmful behaviour.

A. Restorative Justice Concepts: What is Being Restored? To Whom and by Whom?

In contrast to conventional criminal justice where crime is conceived first and foremost as an offence against the state, restorative justice theorises crime as a 'wound in human relationships' that 'creates an obligation to restore and repair'.[42] This obligation has been built around three core pillars: (1) harms and needs; (2) obligations; and (3) engagement. Thus, we should aim to acquire a far-reaching and inclusive understanding of the nature of the harm caused by the offender's actions. Such harm is caused not only to the victim, but also to the wider community and the offender. Once this understanding has been achieved, we can then proceed to understand the range of unmet needs that exist as a result of the harm. These needs create both obligations and liabilities: offenders are obliged to make amends for the harm that they have caused. This act of restoration serves to vindicate the victims and re-establish the normative order that has been flouted.

---

[41] Daly (2016), 13.
[42] Zehr (1990), 181.

For their part, the broader community also has obligations to help victims and offenders restore themselves and thus maintain the general welfare of all its members. Achieving these objectives can only be effected through some form of deliberative engagement by the stakeholders which should entail an exchange of information, dialogue and consent which should then provide a platform for recognising how forgiveness and reconciliation might best be accomplished.

This relational approach to justice is not new; Wielsch traces it back to Aristole's interpretation of corrective justice, and argues that '[it] is inherent in the early definitions of justice that link the term to the virtue of individuals'.[43] Thus even before the explosion of restorative justice literature in the latter part of the 1990s, the importance of relationships to the legal system was receiving increasing attention due to the perceived decline in community cohesion and increasing scepticism towards formalism and statism.[44] In an edited collection entitled *Relational Justice*, published in 1994, Schluter argues for a 'political philosophy which has as its starting point the centrality of human relationships, for it is in relationships that we define our identity and recognise our well-being'.[45]

How, then, might this relational approach to justice provide a better basis on which harm might be quantified? At first glance, it may appear to complicate rather than simplify matters. While the civil courts are closely tied to a rigid system of scales, formulae and precedents, relational justice demands that we construct a more nuanced picture of the nature of the fractured relationship, rather than embark on an attempt to measure accurately or objectively the nature of harm caused to the injured party. As Deklerck contends, 'friendships and familial relationships are not for sale, and cannot be expressed in a financial unit. Human warmth of human suffering in a personal relationship has no financial value. A home cannot be replaced by a more beautiful "house"'.[46] In this respect, human emotions assume a much more central place in attempting to ascertain the nature and extent of harm. In a widely cited 2002 presidential address to the American Society of Criminology, Lawrence Sherman called for an 'emotionally intelligent' approach to criminal justice,[47] 'in which the central tools will be inventions for helping offenders, victims, communities, and officials manage each other's emotions to minimise harm'.[48]

There is a significant variation in the manner in which crime impacts upon victims. While emotions such as powerlessness, fear, shame, loss of autonomy, self-blame, anger and a heightened sense of vulnerability are widely documented in the literature,[49] others may experience few symptoms or none of all.[50] On a more

---

[43] Wielsch (2013), 191.
[44] Daems (2008); Deklerck (2008); Schluter (1994).
[45] Schluter (1994), 19.
[46] Deklerck (2008), 165. See also Fox (2007).
[47] Sherman (2003).
[48] Sherman (2003), 6.
[49] See eg Achilles and Zehr (2001); Shapland and Hall (2007); Zehr (1990).
[50] Daly (2006).

abstract level, wrongs can damage 'morally adequate relationships' including 'victims' ability to cope and their confidence and trust in moral standards and the receptivity of those standards'.[51] Harms also cause damage through 'insulting' the victim since they infer that the victim's rights are inherently less important than those of the wrongdoer.[52] From the restorative justice perspective then, in *addition* to the more tangible losses which can be readily transposed into some pecuniary value, there is a need to make amends for the emotional after-effects of crime. As Braithwaite contends, ultimately the question of 'what is to be restored?' is 'whatever dimensions of restoration matter to the victims, offenders and communities affected by the crime'.[53] This theme will be revisited below as we consider how restorative justice attempts to address this challenge through engineering both symbolic and material forms of redress.

Thus restorative theory implies that the object of the reparation is some form of moral debt owed by the harm-doers to the persons who have suffered harm. In many cases, there will be a personal and identifiable victim to whom this debt is owed and the restorative paradigm provides a basic apparatus through which the duty might be discharged. Victims are provided with a channel through which they can offload their feelings about the impact of the offence, which in turn may allow them to make sense of their experiences.[54] The provision of a forum which does not seek to control or restrict what the victims say, and allows them to tell their stories using their own words, acknowledges the status of the victim as a genuine stakeholder who has suffered directly as the result of the offence. Through this process, Zehr argues, they may have 'this sense of personal power returned to them', so restoring some of the loss suffered from the impact of the offence.[55]

Of course, not all victims may want to meet with the offender. As will be noted in chapter seven, it is naturally the case that some victims wish to put the offence behind them as quickly as possible, and some have little inclination to engage in any way with the offender, especially where the offence was particularly violent in nature. At the other end of the spectrum, victims may even regard the process as a waste of time, particularly if the offence was relatively minor in nature.[56] In other cases, victims may opt not to come forward or cannot be traced.[57]

---

[51] Walker (2006).

[52] Radzik (2009).

[53] Braithwaite (2002a), 11.

[54] For victims, the importance of being allowed to participate significantly impacts their experience of justice and the understanding their victimisation. See Harber and Pennebaker (1992); Orbuch et al (1994); Harber and Wenberg (2005).

[55] Zehr (1990), 27.

[56] O'Mahony and Doak (2004).

[57] See ch 4, I(B). Here we note how organisers have developed innovative ways of sidestepping some of these barriers so that some degree of restorativeness can be preserved in the procedure. For instance, the mediator or facilitator may offer the victim an opportunity to communicate indirectly either through a letter, written statement or audio recording, or through some form of 'shuttle' mediation. The mediator or facilitator may attempt to 'feed in' a victim's perspective by informing the offender of the typical reaction and impact of the type of offence upon a victim of that particular type of offence.

In these circumstances, we must reconsider the question: to whom is the moral debt owed? If a personal victim exists, but either has not been identified or has refused to become involved in the process, the moral debt remains in place. In these instances, it might be said that the offender remains under an obligation to restore the debt. Even if the victim is opposed to receiving any form of material or symbolic reparation, arguably the offender should still be afforded the opportunity to atone for his wrongdoing in a restorative setting. According to Hegel, the offender has a right *to be* punished since, through this process, 'the criminal is honoured as a rational being'.[58] Irrespective of whether the outcome of a restorative event may properly be deemed 'punishment' or not, the offender is given the opportunity to participate in a mechanism through which the offender may atone for the moral debt that might be considered to be appropriate to the nature of the offence and the harm caused.

What then of those criminal offences which do not involve any direct harm or loss to an individual at all? Such 'victimless' offences may range from criminal damage to public property (eg public parks, schools or sites of historical or cultural importance) to many motoring offences. Other such offences will include some instances of fraud and deception, regulatory offences such as the infringement of intellectual property rights, insider trading, or supplying alcohol or pharmaceuticals without holding an appropriate licence, and unlawful possession of narcotics. Although it is difficult to point to an individual who has suffered direct harm in these types of cases, they ought not to be truly regarded as 'victimless', since in all cases either the state, the taxpayer, a corporate entity or a particular community will ultimately suffer some degree of harm and will bear the cost of putting it right. The moral debt on the part of the offender and the obligation to restore therefore remains.

As in the case of absent or untraceable victims, we face the challenge of attempting to conceive of how best to operationalise participation by non-personal victims. As we describe in chapter seven, programmes have utilised a variety of tools in order to do this. Thus, representatives from corporate bodies may participate in restorative programmes to stress the consequences of a particular offence to the wider community. A representative from an insurance company could, for instance, attend a conference to explain that insurance fraud results in higher premiums for all customers. A representative from a local school could attend to explain how the cost of repairing a damaged roof has meant that the school has been unable to afford to purchase new computers for the children to use. Those who have suffered harm or addiction as a result of drug abuse could explain the impact of supplying a particular drug; alternatively, a therapist or clinician could

---

Alternatively, it may be possible to substitute the actual victim with a 'surrogate' or 'indirect' victim who may have worked in a victim support role or who may have personally experienced a similar type of offence in the past.

[58] Hegel (1821), 100.

attend to explain the physical and psychological effects of drug addiction as well as the impact of addiction on an individual's family. Even the impact of motoring-related offences where there has been no road traffic incident can be linked to the harm they can potentially cause, which can be explained to the offender, particularly by a victim of a similar offence, a paramedic or a police officer.

The question nevertheless arises as to whether 'surrogate' victims, either in their capacities as corporate representatives or acting as a proxy for another in similar circumstances, ought to be regarded as having the capacity to forgive, or even ascent to a form of repair, where 'the crime or other acts of wrongdoing are a collective hurt or tear in the social fabric'.[59] Indeed, the same objection potentially applies where offenders seek to make amends on behalf of others in the event of collective wrongdoing. At one level, these questions must be answered in the negative, since one individual's decision to offer or accept a particular form of restoration will depend not only on the nature of the broken relationship between the (impersonal) victim and the offender, but will ultimately hinge on the emotional dynamics of the restorative event.[60] However, what is arguable is whether it succeeds in offering the best opportunity for healing the harm 'as much as possible'[61] through recognising and nurturing those relationships that do exist, even if they do not fully reflect the entirety of the harmful act.

Another way of conceiving of this is that even beyond personal, corporate and surrogate victims, the offender owes a moral debt to the community. But a significant challenge for restorative justice is how the concept of 'community' can be used in a practical sense. The notion of community is often portrayed as a third stakeholder in restorative justice literature, with proponents arguing for the need to divest authority from the state and reinvest this in the community, as a rightful owner.[62] The concept carries with it a certain innate appeal insofar as it evokes a social imperative to restore a sense of connectedness 'against a tide of individualism and a perceived decline of community life'.[63] Indeed, such participation carries three potential benefits. First, it may assist with localised problem-solving efforts in terms of contributing towards public safety and crime prevention.[64] To this end, community members are seen as being more effective than 'outside' professionals in encouraging offenders to take personal responsibility for their crimes and in reintegrating them back into the community, since they are in a better position to 'connect with the victim and offender and support them as they try to repair the harm from the crime'.[65] This comes from the expectation that community members are more like 'real people' to the offenders, who will identify more closely with

---

[59] Menkel-Meadow (2007), [10.2].
[60] See below, III(B).
[61] McCold and Wachtel (2003), 1.
[62] Christie (1977); Dzur and Olson (2004); Walgrave (2002).
[63] McCold and Wachtel (2003), 296.
[64] Braithwaite (2002a); McCold and Wachtel (1998); Zehr (1990).
[65] Dzur and Olson (2004).

these community members and care more what they think. In turn, communities that are proactive and mobilised may reduce reliance upon the resources and representatives of the state.[66]

Second, community input provides a framework for the restoration of harm and reintegration of the offender. Through offering a forum for the symbolic acknowledgement that harm has occurred,[67] community involvement may be said to have a denunciatory function. However, it simultaneously avoids stigmatising or ostracising the offender, and instead offers a forum where public disproval can be aired, but rituals of forgiveness can be invoked and a 'continuum of respect' may be left intact.[68] This is often described as 'reintegrative shaming'.[69]

A third benefit of community participation is that it may add a sense of legitimacy to the outcomes and agreements that result from restorative processes.[70] This is particularly pertinent in settings where there have been longstanding tensions between specific communities and criminal justice agencies.[71] In setting down norms of acceptable and unacceptable conduct, community participation can help foster a sense of civic ownership of disputes.[72] It follows that community involvement may be capable of adding a sense of moral authority to decision-making processes, which in turn may assist in developing a collective sense of understanding of the need to address offending behaviour.

Yet there are also certain inherent dangers in the nature of the power that might be exercised by community actors. Where non-state parties play a central role in the process, there is a risk that such processes may be seen as deficient in terms of accountability, transparency and human rights. Dignan highlights a dangerous presumption that communities are 'reasonably benign, tolerant, likely to espouse broadly progressive values', but proceeds to note that not all communities could be characterised in this manner.[73] Likewise, Pavlich warns of the 'totalitarian dangers that lurk beneath attempts to posit the community as an ontologically fixed entity' since images of community 'have featured prominently among social calculations behind the most horrific catastrophes of the twentieth century' including National Socialism and Stalinism.[74] Such views underline the need for some form of overarching check against vigilantism, authoritarianism or domination.[75] Even if communities themselves can be said to espouse collective liberal values, not all communities share the same resources or are equally well-placed to restore victims or reintegrate offenders.[76] The validity of such criticisms in relation to

---

[66] Weisberg (2003).
[67] Sullivan and Tifft (2001).
[68] Braithwaite (2002a), 78.
[69] Braithwaite (1989); Braithwaite (2002a).
[70] Shapland (2003); Weisberg (2003).
[71] O'Mahony and Doak (2006).
[72] Dzur and Olson (2004); Weisberg (2003).
[73] Dignan (2005), 101.
[74] Pavlich (2001), 58–59.
[75] Shapland (2003); Weisberg (2003).
[76] Crawford and Clear (2001).

specific restorative programmes will depend on a number of factors, including the nature of, or values held by, the community in question;[77] their underlying social, economic or political construction; the degree to which the views expressed by representatives are actually reflective of the community as a whole; and the role that the community actually plays in arriving at the conference agreement.[78]

Many epistemological ambiguities also remain concerning the very concept of 'community'.[79] While attempts have been undertaken to unpick the meaning of the term, the task is often more complex and difficult to define adequately.[80] Commonly defined in everyday usage in geographical terms (ie a locality, district, or neighbourhood), there is a broad consensus that this view tends to be simplistic and over-romanticised.[81] As such, the term is essentially a dynamic yet enigmatic sociological construct used to describe an 'ephemeral quality of identification through connection with others',[82] through a form of social network where individual lives converge through diverse media including work, neighbourhood, family, friends, leisure, religion or politics.[83] Membership is subjective and largely dependent on a sense of connectedness and interdependency.[84] Still, there is little agreement as to what level of 'connectedness' is sufficient to give rise to a community. While some commentators conceptualise 'community' as an all-encompassing term that includes anything or anyone that is distinct from the state,[85] others have suggested a more refined set of criteria that would need to be met before a 'community' can be truly said to exist.[86]

Despite the more recent focus on community in political rhetoric,[87] the utility of the concept within western societies has been questioned in an era where western urban communities are typically characterised by weak social ties, with low levels of social capital and interdependency.[88] While cyber communities continue their remarkable expansion, it is generally acknowledged that more traditional forms of social networks and interpersonal connections have largely declined due to a variety of social and economic factors—which have triggered mass social change over the past half century.[89] One consequence of this shift is that many

---

[77] McEvoy and Mika (2002).
[78] O'Mahony and Doak (2006).
[79] O'Mahony, MeEvoy, Geary and Morison (2000).
[80] Sullivan and Tifft (2001); Zehr (2002).
[81] Crawford and Clear (2001); Duff (2003); McCold and Wachtel (1997).
[82] Pavlich (2005), 85.
[83] Braithwaite (1989), 85; Walgrave (2003); Crawford and Clear (2001).
[84] McCold and Wachtel (1997).
[85] Van Ness (1997); Weisberg (2003).
[86] Frazer (1999).
[87] Garland (1996) traces the growing emphasis placed on community in criminal justice policy to the growth of responsibilisation, moving away from reliance upon conventional state agencies towards non-state organisations. See also Bottoms (1995); Day (2006); Frazer (1999).
[88] Crow (2002); Putnam (2000); Green (2014); Rossner and Bruce (2016).
[89] Putnam (2000); Crow (2002).

more individuals tend to lead isolated and inward-looking lives,[90] which may, in turn, increase their propensity towards social disorder.[91]

One of the key challenges for restorative justice thus concerns how to operationalise the vexed notion of 'community' within a practical setting.[92] Most obviously, perhaps, this entails inviting community volunteers to attend restorative events.[93] However, praxis suggests this is far from a straightforward exercise; as Shapland et al found, the notion of 'reintegration' into a community was very often flawed, since such communities simply did not exist.[94] Likewise, Cunneen and Goldson have warned of the omnipresent danger that restorative justice risks becoming a practice 'that excludes individuals because they are without community or without the *right* community'.[95] In order to counter such difficulties, many proponents emphasise the need to construct a 'micro-community' or 'community of care' comprising those who have been touched in some way by the offence. This may include family and extended family members; neighbours; friends; religious communities; social workers; community representatives and others) who have been directly affected in some way by the offence.[96] On the one hand, this seems to present itself as an innovative solution to sidestep the predicaments outlined above since it can 'allow for the creation of informal support systems or safety nets for victims and offenders than can be provided for by people who are not acquainted with the victim or the offender'.[97] On the other hand, empirical research has questioned the extent this can happen in practice with some evaluations showing low levels of wider community engagement in restorative programmes.[98] For example, discussed further in chapter five, the Thames Valley research on restorative policing revealed relatively little community engagement in the process, other than by family members or supporters of victims and offenders, who were said to constitute 'community representatives'.[99] Other similar programmes have been heavily reliant on small groups of 'repeat players' and 'quasi-professionals'.[100] As Rossner and Bruce contend, this need not necessarily be a bad thing; those with local knowledge and experience can help offender reintegration through developing bonds and identifying services and facilities that might enable social solidarity.[101]

---

[90] Bauman (2001).
[91] Braithwaite (1989); Putnam (2000).
[92] Hoyle (2010), 17.
[93] Rossner and Bruce (2016).
[94] Shapland et al (2006b).
[95] Cunneen and Goldson (2015), 145 (emphasis in original).
[96] See eg McCold (1996); Braithwaite (2002a).
[97] Hoyle and Rosenblatt (2016), 44.
[98] Newburn and Crawford (2002); Shapland et al (2006a); Rosenblatt (2015a); Rossner and Bruce (2016).
[99] Hoyle and Rosenblatt (2016), 40.
[100] Rossner and Bruce (2016).
[101] Rossner and Bruce (2016).

Careful thought also needs to be given to the organisation and facilitation of restorative justice to ensure that 'quasi-professional' voices do not override those of victims and offenders. The 'proper' role that such representatives might play is likely to differ significantly depending on the particular setting. For example, while some of these communities such as parents, friends or social workers, may have a role in supporting either the victim or the offender, others may have been indirectly harmed by the offence. In this sense, the 'moral debt' described above is not only owed to the victim, but also potentially to some or all of these communities. Messmer and Otto have suggested that:

> The community's injury is to shalom—right relationships—among members of the community. The injury is against peace, and requires a local effort to restore harmony in the community. There is a desperate need within our communities for 'socially integrative' interventions.[102]

Such an injury might therefore arise, for example, through criminal damage to public property, whereby neighbours of the offender are unable to make use of a local facility, such as a park or youth club. Even where a direct victim is identifiable—for example, through damage to a parked car or a corner shop—the local community may also suffer by experiencing heightened levels of anxiety and insecurity about crime or anti-social behaviour. On a more abstract level, the values and norms of such a community may appear to be threatened.[103] Members of a religious community, for example, may feel that they have been harmed where one of their members commits an act which violates certain religious norms.

This raises the normative question for restorative justice as to whether the process of discharging the debt to the victim is also capable of discharging the debt to the community. It may be that members of the community feel that a simple act of apology or token payment of compensation would be insufficient. Thus, some form of additional burden may need to be imposed on the offender—perhaps in the form of work—which could then provide a means to make good the wider harm imposed on those indirectly affected by the offence. Similarly, a parent may feel that a child who has been caught taking part in anti-social behaviour ought to undertake domestic chores to make amends for the personal sense of disappointment or anger that was triggered by the harm in question. However, the same conundrum we identified above in relation to non-personal victims emerges: who is entitled to act as a voice for the community, and in what capacity are they authorised to act when, for example, proposing or accepting a particular reparation offer? It appears that there are no straightforward answers here, but for restorative justice to be able to deliver a sense of community involvement to the process it is important that facilitators have the necessary skills to ensure that the community interests impacted by offending behaviour are represented in some

---

[102] Messmer and Otto (1992), 1.
[103] Hoyle (2012), 23.

form and preferably that suitable representatives of the community are able to participate within the restorative encounter.

i. A Role for the State?

While the restorative justice paradigm gravitates around the roles of the victim, the offender and the community as the three archetypal stakeholders, the question arises as to what—if any—role ought to be afforded to the state. Notwithstanding the spurt of innovative, bottom-up community-led programmes in recent years, the majority of schemes which have developed in western criminal justice systems have been devised, funded, overseen and managed by state agencies. As noted above, one of the main drivers behind the growth of the restorative justice movement has been the desire to reverse the historical 'appropriation' of conflicts by the state;[104] and reinforce a sense of communal ownership.[105] There is thus scepticism in some quarters that the restorative capacity of state-led programmes is inherently limited by the overarching role that continues to be exercised by the state. Cunneen and Goldson fear that embedding restorative justice within the confines of the pre-existing structures of the youth justice system constitutes an 'invitation for net-widening, system expansion and the co-existence of diversified (but interdependent) technologies of criminalisation, control and, ultimately, punishment'.[106] Similar fears lead Pavlich to warn of an *imitor paradox* developing, whereby the restorative nature of schemes may be endangered if they are subsumed within a state-led system that has been historically affixed to adversarial and retributive norms, as well as narrowly defined notions of 'crime', 'offender' and 'victim'.[107] The underlying irony at the heart of the paradox is that whilst restorative justice conceptualises crime as a 'harm' between victims, offenders and communities, its operationalisation within the criminal justice system depends on the parameters of the criminal law, as defined by the state. Formal co-option of restorative justice thus poses a threat to its traditional 'oppositional focus and specificity', leading it to become 'colonised' by repressive and punitive practices that are deeply ingrained within the existing apparatus.[108] This, in turn, leads to a risk that the goals and values of restorative practices will be supplanted by 'system' goals and outcomes, such as case-processing targets, efficiency and growth.[109] Indeed, there is empirical evidence to suggest that deeply ingrained cultural attitudes and working practices of the police, magistracy and other criminal justice professionals may stifle the potential of restorative justice within the formal criminal justice system.[110]

---

[104] Christie (1977).
[105] Achilles and Zehr (2001); McCold (1998); Mika and McEvoy (2002).
[106] Cunneen and Goldson (2015), 149.
[107] Pavlich (2005), 14.
[108] Pratt (2007), 142.
[109] Wood and Suzuki (2016), 155.
[110] Campbell et al (2006); Shapland et al (2011).

These are genuine dangers which cannot be ignored, particularly given the underlying fabric of the criminal justice system. Given the prevailing climate of popular punitivism, the reach of the formal system seems likely to extend still further in the years ahead.[111] As such, proponents of restorative justice cannot simply ignore or attempt to opt out of criminal justice; rather, they must consider questions as to how such risks might be minimised and how the restorative 'quality' of a state-led processes can be enshrined and protected.[112]

It is also important to shed conceptual clarity on the realistic role that the state ought to play. If we accept the Kantian view that crime distorts the moral equilibrium by creating a debt owed by the offender to wider society,[113] then it is difficult to see how such a debt can be restored within the tripartite stakeholder model. While the harm caused to direct victims and 'communities of care' may often be more tangible than the esoteric nature of harm caused to society at large, this wider debt to the state at large may remain unaddressed.[114] Moreover, wider societal interests also demand that the law has an instrumental function in protecting individuals from the actions of others and upholding community norms.[115] In this sense, an overarching legal framework operates to ensure not only that the rights of the stakeholders themselves are protected, but that the security of society is also safeguarded through processes and outcomes which are fair and broadly proportionate. Ultimately, the devolution of criminal justice away from the state should not usurp the underlying *public* function of the criminal justice system.[116]

Criticisms of state-led schemes have often drawn on their failure to take account of grassroots customs, expertise and practical knowledge as well as forging links with 'bottom up' initiatives.[117] In order to work effectively and engender legitimacy, some form of partnership with the local community is undoubtedly required. As Clamp has argued, effective partnerships between state and the community sector are often difficult to engineer given that state-based agencies are usually hierarchical, are not naturally calibrated to working with those outside its formal parameters, and there is relatively little evidence to demonstrate how such a partnership might operate on a practical level with any level of success for a sustained period.[118]

What is apparent for restorative justice is that an appropriate balance needs to be struck which gives individual programmes the necessary social and political space to evolve and adapt in order to maximise their effectiveness within the

---

[111] Garland (2001), (2013).
[112] See further ch 9, V(A).
[113] See generally Bradley (2003).
[114] McDermott (2002).
[115] Meares (2000).
[116] Luban (1995).
[117] Boyes-Watson (1999); McEvoy and Eriksson (2006); McEvoy and Mika (2002).
[118] Clamp (2014).

communities that they serve.[119] By the same token, in order to mainstream restorative justice as a cornerstone of the formal justice system, structures need to be put in place which are capable of maximising community participation within this system and which ensure the observation of protocols which are capable of maintaining a stable, yet dynamic, relationship between schemes operating at grassroots level and those operated by the state.[120]

B. Restorative Justice Processes: 'How?' and 'Why?'

On the basis of the above, it is therefore worth pausing to consider the questions of *how* and *why* restorative justice processes are better placed than the common law adversarial approach to restore the moral debt owed by the offender to the victim. It is already widely acknowledged that the adversarial courtroom is an alien and potentially harmful environment which undermines the victim's sense of power and autonomy:

> The main function of the victim within the adversarial trial is that of a witness … Their testimony must be shaped to bring out its maximum adversarial effect, and victims are thereby confined to answering questions within the parameters set down by the questioner. They have no opportunity to relay their account before the court using their own words, which seems something of an irony given that logic dictates that such an account should have a key role to play in arriving at the truth. In practice, counsel in adversarial trials seek to take control of the witness, and use questioning to elicit only those facts which he or she feels should be included. Questions are carefully framed to avoid the witness speaking about anything that counsel feels should be omitted from the testimony.[121]

As the adversarial process is lawyer-led, it is rare for either victims or offenders to make oral representations to the court (particularly regarding the nature and form of any reparation),[122] let alone to engage in any form of didactic communication with each other.[123]

It might be argued that the recent development of victim impact statements has gone some way to offsetting such deficiencies. There are two main types of victim impact statements: those which explain the physical, emotional or financial

---

[119] Woolford and Ratner (2008).
[120] Northern Ireland provides an interesting example of how a working relationship was built over time between community-led programmes and the state-led youth conferencing system: see further Doak and O'Mahony (2011).
[121] Doak (2008), 138.
[122] In England and Wales, expressions of remorse (or other emotions) on the part of the offender tend to be communicated to the court through pre-sentencing reports or the plea in mitigation. Victims are entitled to submit a written personal statement, which is appended to the judge's papers, but there is no right to read the statement orally. Many US and Australian states do, however, allow the victim to address the court. See further Doak (2008); Booth (2014).
[123] Doak and Taylor (2013).

impact of the offence on the victim alone (as is commonplace in Canada, New Zealand, Australia and the United Kingdom); and those which, in addition, lay down specific penal demands (as in some jurisdictions within the United States). Although the advent of victim impact evidence may be welcomed insofar as it opens a channel through which victims can communicate their emotions to the court, the emotional power of their stories is significantly diminished by the fact that they are unable to address either the defendant or the court in person. Victims may prepare their statement many months, or perhaps longer, before sentencing occurs. Often, the statement is ghost written or subject to revision by a police officer or prosecutor, rendering them somewhat formulaic and, on occasion, lacking any direct input from victims themselves.[124] Moreover, the emotions contained in that document may no longer reflect how the victim feels at the point of sentence. The passage of time, counselling, and other forms of support and assistance may have changed the impact of the offence on the victims, and their feelings towards the offender may have changed.[125] Perhaps the most pressing criticism is that such statements are addressed to the court, rather than to the offender in person. In some jurisdictions, such as England and Wales, it is also usual practice for the prosecutor to deliver the statement, thus raising the question whether victims can really be said to be exercising 'voice' whenever their agency to do so is undercut by a lawyer acting on their behalf. As McEvoy and McConnachie have noted in the context of transitional justice mechanisms, legal institutions tend to prefer lawyers or professional civil society actors to speak on behalf of victims rather than hearing from the victims themselves.[126] The same might well be said in respect of domestic criminal proceedings, where decisions are made by judges, with victims often not even being present at court.[127]

By contrast, restorative justice places a much higher emphasis on direct involvement by the parties,[128] the importance of which is underpinned by research that confirms that the process of a restorative encounter is frequently ranked as being more important to victims of crime than any material or financial compensation that may result.[129] Its strength lies in the fact that victims are able to establish an element of control over the process and offenders are encouraged to assume responsibility for their actions, whilst active community participation can strengthen the sense of community values which underpin the whole process.[130] In contrast to the formal setting of the courtroom which inherently suppresses the emotions of participants, restorative justice settings create a space for human emotions to be communicated and understood between those who have been

---

[124] Arrigo and Williams (2003); Doak and Taylor (2013).
[125] Doak and Taylor (2013).
[126] McEvoy and McConnachie (2013).
[127] Braithwaite (2002a); Shapland et al (2006b).
[128] Van Ness (1996); Menkel-Meadow (2007).
[129] Bradshaw and Umbreit (1998).
[130] Claassen (1995); Doak and O'Mahony (2011).

most intimately affected by the offence.[131] In terms of outcomes, whilst conventional sentencing proceedings in England and Wales are supposed to be guided by reference to the 'purposes' of sentencing as stipulated in the Criminal Justice Act 2003,[132] the restorative approach emphasises the four 'Rs': repair, restoration, reconciliation and reintegration.[133]

Framing proceedings in this manner may both promote psychological healing as well as procedural fairness. In recent years, the emergence of 'therapeutic jurisprudence' has proposed that legal processes ought to act in a way which enhances psychological well-being.[134] Despite its relatively nascent status and some concerns surrounding its normative clarity,[135] the concept has served as a useful framework for contrasting the psychologically detrimental effects of the adversarial process with the potential beneficial effects of restorative approaches which emphasise the centrality of security, self-respect and control.[136] Indeed, the therapeutic potential of restorative encounters tends to resonate closely with the considerable body of psychological evidence which links oral or written accounts to a reduction in feelings of anger, anxiety and depression,[137] to higher levels of self-confidence,[138] and even to improved physical health.[139] While there is no suggestion that restorative justice can or should replicate the work of professional therapy and counselling, it is difficult to imagine how it could be any less therapeutic than the conventional adversarial system, which has been so widely criticised for its exclusionary and demeaning treatment of victims.[140]

The potential of restorative justice to deliver therapeutic benefits hinges not only on the manner in which the victim is able to interact with offender, but it also depends on how fairly victims feel that they have been treated by the criminal justice system. Supported by a substantial body of evidence, procedural justice theory posits that even where victims are dissatisfied with specific *outcomes*, a sense of legitimacy can still prevail if *processes* are perceived as fair.[141] To a large extent, perceptions of procedural fairness often hinge upon the extent to which individuals feel able to exercise 'voice' in the decision-making process.[142] As Shapland et al suggest, this may be one reason why so many victims have associated the

---

[131] Braithwaite and Strang (2001), 10.
[132] Under s 142 of the Act, the purposes of sentencing are designated as punishment; deterrence; rehabilitation; protection of the public; and reparation. However, no particular priority is afforded to these purposes, and nor is there any guidance as to which method sentencers ought to adopt in deciding which of these aims to prioritise where the purposes may conflict.
[133] Menkel-Meadow (2007).
[134] Wexler (1998).
[135] See eg Arrigo (2004); Brakel (2007); Hoffman (2002); Slobogin (1995).
[136] Beven et al (2005).
[137] Orbuch et al (1994).
[138] Kellas and Manusov (2003).
[139] Enright and Fitzgibbons (2000).
[140] Doak (2008).
[141] Lind and Tyler (1988).
[142] Lind et al (1997).

traditional court process as unfair: their lack of *input* into proceedings means that they do not believe the courts and criminal justice professionals have received sufficient information from them on which to base their decisions.[143]

Many victims who feel that the restorative process is fair also report that these same procedures help them come to terms with the offence.[144] Three main reasons are suggested for this. First, victims who feel that they have lost an element of control through victimisation may feel that that power has been returned to them by having a say in how the offence is dealt with.[145] Second, it may help restore victims' lost faith in society, by offering them an official acknowledgement that they have suffered a wrong. Third, as Wemmers has highlighted, fair procedures can provide a 'cushion of support', so that decisions that would often seem unjust or burdensome would be made more palatable by the fact that the views of the victim were nevertheless taken seriously.[146]

Although these elements of restorative justice are widely vaunted by its proponents, it has been more difficult to determine *why* the process works in this way. The fact that the offender and victim are given freedom to express themselves in an open and safe environment, far removed from the austerity of a lawyer-dominated courtroom is undoubtedly facilitative. However, research to date has been less clear in establishing how the aims and values of the restorative process map on to the sociological and psychological dynamics necessary for agreement to be reached and reparation to occur.

In certain respects, the 'reintegrative shaming' theory developed by Braithwaite presents reasoning as to why restorative interventions appear to be more productive for offenders. The theory operates from the premise that when stigmatised as a criminal or a 'bad person', offenders find it difficult to reintegrate back into the community and thus are more likely to reoffend in the future. While the orthodox conception of shame degrades, humiliates and stifles opportunities for social reintegration,[147] 'reintegrative shaming', by contrast, involves expressing a form of social disapproval that is respectful of offenders and does not label them as inherently bad. The theory centres the idea that it is the wrongfulness of the offence, rather than of the offender, which needs to be the focus of disapproval.[148] Braithwaite argues that through shaming the *action*, rather than the *person*, the offender learns certain behaviours are morally wrong and they will begin to feel a greater sense of accountability to victims and the wider community.[149] It is argued that deeming offenders collectively as a group worthy of redemption,[150] offenders

---

[143] Shapland et al (2006b).
[144] Beven et al (2005); Lind and Tyler (1988); Sherman et al (2005); Wemmers and Cyr (2005).
[145] See further the discussion on empowerment theory at ch 3, II(A).
[146] Wemmers (1996).
[147] Braithwaite and Mugford (1994).
[148] Braithwaite (1989).
[149] Braithwaite (1989); Braithwaite (2002a).
[150] Saulnier and Sivasubramaniam (2015a).

are more likely to express remorse and apologise, and more likely to desist from future offending. Reintegrative shaming has also been evaluated by participants as fairer and more respectful than the shame that is experienced during the orthodox criminal process.

One of the most valuable aspects of Braithwaite's work and the research that has built on it, is his emphasis on the centrality of emotions to successful restorative encounters. Similarly, drawing on the work of Collins and his theory of interaction rituals,[151] Sherman et al contend that emotions in restorative encounters can act to create a new sense of shared experience and solidarity,[152] whereby the broken bond is transformed by the emotional energy into a new social bond, which will in turn boost the prospects of a successful restorative encounter. This 'interaction ritual' symbolises the efforts invested by both parties to repair the harm, and is consistent with the available data on victims' experiences of restorative justice.[153] It has been argued that such emotions are inextricably linked with both shared and individual notions of identity, which may subsequently be transformed in light of a new understanding of shared norms and values emerging from interpersonal interaction.[154]

Despite the richness of these conceptual insights,[155] our understanding of how self-conscious emotions—including shame, remorse, anger, fear and empathy—operate as the underpinning transformative mechanism of restorative justice remains underdeveloped and in need of further empirical analysis. For instance, studies have often reported that offenders dealt with through restorative encounters experience positive emotions resulting from a sense of participation, being able to move on from the offence, or being able to contribute to the process in a positive way.[156] Although these positive emotional results suggest that participants experience a change in their self-perceptions and their understanding of the broader impact of the offence, further analysis is needed to unpick the precise role of emotions within restorative events, as well as how they connect to the underlying theory of restorative justice.[157] Similarly, a sincere apology has been shown time and again to be a vital ingredient to successful restorative justice encounters.[158] Yet much of the existing research fails to uncover why the apology has such an important part in the process, or the deeper complexity of the interactions that take place in both the giving and receiving of a sincere apology. Indeed, as Daly has shown, there is considerable complexity in the role of verbal and non-verbal communications as they play out in these kinds of interactions—particularly when participants are vastly different in terms of their ages and social

---

[151] Collins (2004).
[152] Sherman et al (2005).
[153] See ch 4, I(C).
[154] Theidon (2006); Tyler et al (2007).
[155] See also Aertsen et al (2013); Bolívar (2010).
[156] See Shapland et al (2011); Strang (2002); Umbreit (1994).
[157] Bolívar (2010).
[158] Shapland et al (2011).

experiences.[159] It is axiomatic that some offenders are simply better equipped to verbalise what seems to be a genuine apology and some victims are more open to accepting the sincerity of an apology, irrespective of how it is communicated or received.[160]

Although there has been relatively little theoretical insight shedding light on the questions above, a significant exception can be found in the recent work of Rossner, who—again using Collin's theoretical framework on interaction rituals—undertook a detailed study into the 'microdynamics' of the role of emotions and rituals in restorative encounters.[161] Drawing on both her own observations of conferences and in-depth interviews with participants, as well as data from the RISE study,[162] her research explored how the micro-structures of conferences can result in a form of ritual that is transformative for the participants and results in successful outcomes. Analysing one particular conference, Rossner concluded that 'rhythmic dialogue, emotional entrainment, a balance of power and status, and identifiable emotional "turning points"' were key to ensuring the successful outcome.[163] Adopting a mixed methods approach to test this hypothesis, she concluded that these features together function to enable the offender to overcome stigmatisation and defiance, so producing a new sense of social solidarity. Such solidarity, in turn, provides an impetus for the offender to seek out similar positive experiences beyond the confines of the conference room, which can assist with both desistance and reintegration efforts. This is corroborated by Rossner's data analysis of the RISE study, in which she finds a correlation between measures of 'solidarity' and 'emotional energy' and longer-term re-arrest rates. This research challenges Braithwaite's theory, to suggest that it is not shame that serves to construct new bonds and promote reintegration, but the emotional intensity experienced within the conference itself.

Rossner's research undoubtedly provides valuable and much needed insight into the connections between the underpinning values of restorative justice and their translation into praxis; however, the research also raises further questions that are yet to be addressed. As Rossner notes, the role of the facilitator is crucial in maximising the emotional energy of the conferences. Yet achieving successful facilitation is not necessarily a straightforward task given the types of emotions that are commonly involved, including anger, shame and disgust. As van Stokkom has noted, Rossner does not address the question as to whether emotions such as compassion and remorse should be objectives of the planning process at all.[164] There are also unanswered questions relating to her argument that the emotional energy created in the conference is capable of contributing towards desistance and

---

[159] Daly (2008).
[160] Cunneen (2010), Daly (2008).
[161] Rossner (2013).
[162] Sherman and Strang (2007).
[163] Rossner (2013), 71.
[164] Van Stokkom (2015), 305.

reintegration in the longer term. Inevitably, many other factors such as employment prospects, family circumstances, peer pressure, rehabilitation programmes and community bonds are also likely to play an important part.[165]

C. Restorative Justice Outcomes: The Nature and Form of Restoration

Following from the above, while restorative approaches may appear to offer a quintessentially better process in many respects, the questions of how and why these processes work cannot be neatly extracted from the broader issues concerning what they are attempting to achieve. From the perspective of conventional criminal justice, the emphasis has been firmly placed on the classic penal objectives of retribution, incapacitation, deterrence and just deserts. The notion of an individual moral 'debt' between victim and offender (as opposed to the offender and society) is thus far removed from the normative basis of most western criminal justice systems. Nevertheless, the idea that reparation ought to be afforded some recognition within the criminal courts has gained traction in recent decades, and serves underline the fundamental normative tension concerning the place of reparation in a system that is structurally geared towards punishment of the offender. Limited forms of reparation, in the guise of compensation orders, have been available through the conventional sentencing process across most common law jurisdictions for some time. Since 1973, courts in England and Wales have been empowered to order the offender to pay compensation as part of a sentence for 'any personal injury, loss or damage resulting from the offence'.[166] Originally introduced as an ancillary penalty, from 1982 English courts were given the power to award compensation orders as penalties in their own right.[167] While it is still the norm for these to be awarded in conjunction with other penalties, the court may make a compensation order either instead of, or addition to, any other penal sanction.[168] Courts are under a duty to consider making orders in all cases and must now state reasons if not doing so.[169]

---

[165] See further Ward et al (2014).
[166] Originally contained in the Criminal Justice Act 1972, the power is now contained in the Powers of Criminal Courts (Sentencing) Act 2000, s 130.
[167] Criminal Justice Act 1982, s 67.
[168] Section 130(4) of the Criminal Courts (Sentencing) Act 2000 states that compensation 'shall be of such amount as the court considers appropriate, having regard to any evidence and to any representations that are made by or on behalf of the accused or the prosecutor, the Court'. The legislation further provides that compensation should be afforded priority over fines. Thus where an offender has insufficient means to pay both, the court should impose a compensation order rather than a fine: Powers of Criminal Courts (Sentencing) Act 2000, s 130(12).
[169] Powers of Criminal Courts (Sentencing) Act 2000, s 130(3). This provision was originally contained in s 104 of the Criminal Justice Act 1988. cf the Sentencing Act 1997 (Tasmania), which made compensation orders compulsory for property damage or loss resulting from certain crimes.

However, compensation orders appear to be made on an inconsistent basis, and the amount awarded is usually small given the limited means of most offenders.[170] Only rarely will victims receive compensation that is both full and immediate. It is much more likely that they will receive small, irregular amounts over a period of time, which means that they will continue to feel the effects of the offence for some time; they will not, for example, be able to replace stolen or damaged property immediately.[171] Even where the offender is able and willing to comply with a compensation order, a further weakness of the regime stems from the fact that, it only serves to cover very specific material losses to victims and, as such, fails to cover the emotional impact of victimisation.[172] Moreover, from the offender's perspective, it is arguable that a compensation order does not amount to any genuine form of accountability since there is a real risk that they will be unable to distinguish between a compensation order and a fine.[173] From a restorative justice perspective, it is doubtful whether such orders ought to be regarded as 'restorative' at all; not only is the underlying process fundamentally exclusionary, but ultimately the decision as to whether and how much compensation should be ordered is imposed by the court rather than being agreed between the parties.

Indeed, the organising principles of private law tend to place a high value on corrective justice, seeking to restore the *status quo ante* by placing the injured party on a similar footing to that which occurred prior to the harm in question.[174] In this sense, restorative justice shares a common objective with private law systems of many western societies. The law of obligations revolves around the ideas of *duties*, which may be either contractual or non-contractual in nature. Where a duty of care is breached, or a contractual obligation is breached, a corresponding right to a remedy exists whereby the court may order a wrongdoer to take steps to put the injured party back in the place he or she would have been in either (a) had the breach not occurred; or (b) had the wrongdoer fulfilled his or her duties to the full extent required by the law. For the most part, harm is envisaged within private law in predominantly pecuniary terms; as O'Malley remarks, '[m]oney is probably the most frequently used means of punishing, deterring, compensating and regulating throughout the legal system'.[175] Thus, damages within the civil courts are usually calculated on the basis of the financial loss

---

[170] Miers (2014).
[171] Van Ness and Nolan (1998, 95–86) propose a means of sidestepping the problem of an offender's inability to pay. They argue that the systems of state compensation and offender compensation ought to be combined. Restitution should first be ordered, and should be based on a formula that takes into account the daily income of the offender. If the amount of harm to the victim is greater than the restitution ordered, the victim would then be able to apply for state compensation to 'top up' the amount they would receive. If the amount of harm to the victim were, however, to be less than the restitution ordered, the surplus would be placed into the state compensation fund.
[172] Hanson et al (2010); Shapland et al (1985); Shapland and Hall (2007).
[173] Groenhuijsen (2004), 74.
[174] Weinrib (2012).
[175] O'Malley (2009), 1.

sustained by the injured parties. In some cases, this is a relatively straightforward calculation involving the calculation of tangible pecuniary or proprietary loss or damage caused by the defendant's actions, coupled with any specific losses (such as medical bills or repair bills) that have arisen as a result. The exercise, however, becomes more complicated where the harm has resulted in future losses and may involve, for example, calculating the loss of earnings, profits or opportunities or the event of proprietary loss or damage. More difficult still is the question of what monetary value can be placed on physical or emotional injuries, including loss of amenity. This type of loss is not capable of mathematical calculation, and assessments will inevitably be subject to some form of arbitrary scale, metric or tariff which can—at best—'guesstimate' the value of the harm caused.[176]

A similar exercise is regularly conducted in the criminal courts where attempts are made to measure harm for the purposes of calculating the seriousness of the offence. Most contemporary theories of punishment accept, to a greater or lesser extent, the Kantian view that the nature and extent of punishment must be based on the principle of equality, essentially meaning that the punishment and level of pain it entails should be balanced with the conduct of the offender.[177] Despite the recent development of sentencing guidelines to regulate this process, it remains fraught with difficulty, given that the level of pain will inevitably differ between offenders convicted of inflicting similar levels of harm, and that the impact of the offence will vary significantly according to the experiences of individual victims. The task is further complicated insofar as there is no universally accepted mechanism or consensus for arriving at the appropriate measures.[178]

Notwithstanding these conceptual challenges, a number of commentators have sought to formulate a means of determining proportionate punishments. Von Hirsch and Jareborg, for example, have devised a scale whereby the seriousness of harm is gauged through measuring the extent to which an offence interferes with an individual's 'living standard',[179] whilst other attempts have focused on the extent to which harm limits freedom of choice or capabilities.[180]

While the rules of evidence and procedure may be slightly less stringent in civil courts than in their criminal counterparts,[181] the process remains fundamentally adversarial and lawyer-led. The failure of both the civil and criminal justice systems to capture the full extent of the impact of a wrongful act on an individual victim means that restorative justice requires sharper tools than the orthodox legal process if it is to meet the needs of its stakeholders. The structure and form of reparation is likely to impact on a victim's sense of justice, and research appears to suggest that victims place as high a priority on symbolic reparation as they

---

[176] See generally Croley and Hanson (1995); Radin (1993).
[177] Easton and Piper (2012).
[178] Easton and Piper (2012).
[179] Von Hirsch and Jareborg (1991).
[180] See eg Feinberg (1984); Schiff (1997).
[181] Doak and McGourlay (2015), 2.

do upon material recompense.[182] Although the distinction between material and symbolic forms of redress is often cited as a key feature of restorative programmes, it can be noted that the appeal of this distinction is also reflected in recent international human rights instruments, such as the 2005 UN Basic Principles and Guidelines on the right to a remedy and reparation for victims of violations of international human rights and humanitarian law. The instrument categorises reparations according to whether they are material or symbolic in nature. Examples of the former include proprietary and pecuniary measures, most notably restitution of rights and property and compensation for physical and mental harm or damage to property, whereas symbolic restitution is potentially much broader, including concepts such as 'rehabilitation', 'satisfaction' (including verification of facts, official apologies, acts of commemoration and judicial sanctions against violations) and 'guarantees of non-repetition' (which may include entrenching international human rights standards and putting in place mechanisms to monitor conflict resolution). Of course, not all reparation programmes will be capable of realising all of these objectives, but the instrument reflects the fact that victims have a complex range of needs which ought to be addressed using a diverse range of methods.

Herein lies a distinctive advantage of restorative justice; it is widely accepted that material and symbolic forms of redress will form part of a restoration package, with the nature and form of this package varying according to the needs of the parties and the nature of the harm. For the most part, it seems that material forms of reparation payable directly to the victim are relatively uncommon; perhaps because many offenders lack the means to make financial restitution.[183] Although simple gestures—such as a handshake, an apology, an explanation for the behaviour, an acceptance of responsibility or an undertaking not to repeat the offence or commit any further act that would cause further distress to the victim—are arguably just as unable to 'undo' the harm caused by the offence as material forms of redress, they may still carry a beneficial role in helping victims move beyond anger and a sense of powerlessness by communicating that the offender has a personal desire to make amends.[184] Symbolic forms of reparation may also be undertaken indirectly through community service, such as picking up litter or cleaning graffiti in a public area, or some other form of voluntary work.

The variety of forms of reparation reflects the potential of restorative justice to respond to the emotional dimensions of crime. Apologies, in particular, appear to feature prominently within restorative justice literature. There are two reasons for this. First, on a theoretical level, it might be said that the victim is owed an apology arising from the moral debt owed by the offender.[185] Second, research

---

[182] Braithwaite (2002a); Campbell et al (2006); Retzinger and Scheff (1996); Strang (2002); Shapland et al (2011). Strang et al (2013).
[183] Campbell et al (2006); Hoyle et al (2002); Shapland et al (2006b).
[184] Sharpe (2007).
[185] Bennett (2008).

has consistently shown that victims place a particularly high value on receiving an apology and it is often one of the key motivating factors when agreeing to participate in a restorative encounter.[186] The issue of apologies in practical settings is discussed in more detail in chapter seven; the discussion here focuses on the potential of the apology to restore the moral debt.

In his seminal sociological study, Tavuchis argues that a genuine apology on the part of a wrongdoer constitutes a tacit acknowledgement of the legitimacy of the violated rule or social norm; an admission of full fault and responsibility; and an expression of regret for having caused the harm in question.[187] If lacking in any of these components, the apology must be regarded as incomplete. Indeed, the acceptance of responsibility, in particular, would appear to be a fundamental prerequisite.[188] Anything short of this, such as an excuse, explanation or qualification for the offender's behaviour, constitutes an *account* rather than a proper apology, and is less likely to constitute a basis for reconciliation. A genuine apology should include a visible expression of remorse, which signals to the victim that the offender genuinely regrets his or her behaviour and wishes to make amends. The victim is then empowered to choose whether to accept the apology (thereby restoring a state of equality) or reject it, allowing that moral imbalance to stay in place).[189] For some, this is not so much a choice, but a responsibility.[190]

Of course, the prospect of an apology being accepted will often depend on how the victim evaluates its sincerity. Tavuchis asserts that a genuine apology is only completed when two steps are complete: that the harm-doer must feel sorry and must say so. Drawing on Tavuchis' analysis, Moore argues that the perception of sincerity can be maximised when the offender drops all defences, including the defence of being 'childlike' or otherwise lacking moral responsibility.[191] Thus it is then that the victim is empowered to make the decision whether to accept or refuse the apology (discussed further in the next chapter).

It can be deduced from this that, in the longer term, apologies, like other symbolic forms of reparation, assist in providing victims with a sense of healing and closure.[192] They also help the community appreciate the atoning efforts made by the offender in the attempt to reintegrate himself/herself back into society.[193] However, the need for a tailor-made reparatory package to meet the individual needs of victims (as well as to match the capacities of offenders to deliver them) is also vital. While symbolic forms of reparation are clearly of importance, sometimes saying 'sorry' is not enough.[194] As a justice process, restorative justice risks

---

[186] Campbell et al (2006); Fercello and Umbreit (1998); Shapland et al (2006a); Strang (2002).
[187] Tavuchis (1991).
[188] Lazare (2004); Smith (2008).
[189] Petrucci (2002).
[190] Hudson and Galaway (1996).
[191] Moore (1993).
[192] Doak (2011); Schopp (1998); Wemmers and Cyr (2005).
[193] Minow (1998), 92.
[194] Shapland et al (2006b).

being undermined if not backed up by action which appears to impose some form of burden or 'restorative pain' on the offender,[195] although this may be tangible in nature (such as the restitution of property or financial compensation) or intangible (such as undertaking work in the community).[196] Although custodial penalties are often considered anathema to restorative justice, it is not unknown for them to form part of, or run parallel to a restorative process, particularly in relation to very serious offences.[197] The best form of reparation is likely to comprise a mixture of symbolic and material awards, what Zedner has labelled the 'elusive recipe for reparation'.[198]

However, locating the specific ingredients for such a recipe is unlikely to be a straightforward task for facilitators, with formulaic of tokenistic reparatory measures cited as problematic, particularly in some earlier restorative initiatives.[199] It is well established that the effects of victimisation vary considerably, with victims having divergent needs. Some victims will be traumatised by what may appear to be a relatively trivial offence; others may be able to find closure and healing soon after falling victim to a serious offence.[200] Financial assistance may help some victims; for others it may be a low priority, and may even be regarded as an insulting attempt to buy them off. Whatever the consequences of an offence may be for an individual victim, it seems only logical that the type of reparation provided by the state or the offender corresponds to the needs and preferences of the individual(s) concerned, and, as Zedner indicates, it should also take into account the social relationship which has been damaged by the act in question.

> Reparation is not synonymous with restitution, still less does it suggest a straightforward importation of civil into criminal law. Reparation should properly connote a wider set of aims. It involves more than 'making good' the damage done to property, body or psyche. It must entail recognition of the harm done to the social relationship between offender and victim, and the damage done to the victim's social rights in his or her property or person.[201]

Restoration, then, is not limited to meeting the needs of the victim, but it also touches on the notion of reconciliation—of healing the underlying relationship between the victim and the offender. As noted above, the notion of a violation of a broken bond features strongly in restorative justice theory.[202] Strictly speaking, it is questionable whether it is always appropriate to invoke the term 'restoration' since it imputes the existence of a prior connectivity or relationship that needs to

---

[195] See eg Gavrieledes (2013).
[196] Braithwaite (1989).
[197] Bonta et al (1998); Campbell et al (2006); Morris (2002).
[198] Zedner (1994), 238.
[199] See eg Marshall and Merry (1990); Davis (1992).
[200] Shapland et al (1985); Shapland and Hall (2007).
[201] Zedner (1994), 234.
[202] See p 45.

be repaired.[203] In such circumstances, the restorative justice event comprises just one element of a longer interactional chain between the parties in which it may be appropriate to think of ways in which the *status quo ante*.[204] However, in other cases, no prior relationship between the victim and offender will have existed at all; the relationship itself only arises through the occurrence of a harmful act.[205] In such a scenario, 'reconciliation' blurs into a rather nebulous concept of restoring whatever (non)-relationship existed in the first place, or else appears to presume that the victim and offender want to develop an ongoing relationship in the aftermath of the offence.[206] In addition to restoring the relationship with the victim and the community, offenders on an individual level are also in need of restoration, since their lives have been negatively affected by the offence.[207] Reintegration and rehabilitation are achieved through ensuring offenders are held accountable by accepting responsibility on an individual level and through 'earning their redemption' by completing their obligations to 'make good' the damage they have caused.[208] In this way, the offender's 'human capital' can be maximised, resulting in overall higher levels of social capital which may subsequently help offenders to desist from future offending.[209]

IV. Mainstreaming Restorative Justice within Criminal Justice: The Challenge Ahead

The spread of private reparatory interests into the public domain of criminal justice has been described by one writer as a 'conceptual cuckoo in the criminal law nest'.[210] Adherents of a 'purist' conception of criminal justice warn of the dangers of integrating reparatory elements into a justice system that revolves around the principle of 'just deserts',[211] while others, such as Barnett, Christie and Zehr, call for a complete paradigmatic overhaul of the system which either relegates (or removes) any notion of punishment in favour of reparation. In more recent times, the debate has matured as some scholars have attempted to bridge these seemingly incompatible paradigms of justice.

Indeed, it has been argued that the distinction between criminal and non-criminal harms is artificial *ab initio*: The criminal law evolved long after the law

---

[203] Clamp and Doak (2012); Kohen (2009).
[204] Shapland et al (2006b).
[205] Zehr (2005), 27.
[206] Kohen (2009), 407.
[207] Zehr and Mika (1998).
[208] Bazemore and Schiff (2005), 51.
[209] Bazemore and Schiff (2005); Shapland et al (2011).
[210] Campbell (1984), 343.
[211] See eg Ashworth (1993), (2002); Ashworth and Von Hirsch (1993); Morris (1968).

of tort as a means for the state to exert control over those wrongs that were deemed to be sufficiently injurious to the interests of the monarch.[212] Thus this is largely a subjective distinction, as there is no qualitative distinction that can be drawn between different forms of conflicts. Progressing Christie's arguments, Zedner has neatly summarised the position in the following terms:

> But one might go further and argue that not only has the State 'stolen' the conflict, by the artifice of legal language it has transformed the drama and emotion of social interaction and strife into technical categories which can be subjected to the ordering practices of the criminal process. That small proportion of conflicts which enter the criminal justice system undergo an elaborate process of inquiry, classification and judgment by police, lawyers and judges by means of which they are translated to fit the legal categories of crime. The criminal justice process may thus be seen as a means of repackaging conflicts in order to render them amenable to legal regulation.[213]

On the one hand, a fundamental problem with the 'public' character of the criminal justice system is that it fails to recognise the moral imperative to make amends for the private harm experienced by individual victims, which—in most cases—will be more acute, direct and tangible than harm any to the state, the community or the 'public interest'. In other words, a system of justice which revolves around the notion of retributivism or just desserts is only ever capable of capturing part of the harm caused by the offender's actions. Yet, on the other hand, a justice system which gravitates around reparation is arguably incapable of addressing the public dimension of harm, which might legitimately encompass other objectives such as denunciation, deterrence and 'just deserts'. It is not only that societal norms have been violated, but there may be a very real threat that the right to personal security of other individuals might be threatened if the public interest dimension were to be excluded from the purview of the courts. Moreover, it is incumbent that any system must have mechanisms in place to protect the offender from arbitrary or disproportionate reparatory burdens that might be imposed by such a process.[214]

For the most part, restorative theorists have placed less emphasis on linking the outcome to specific measures of harm of culpability, but have rather focused on the multi-faceted question of how the harm has impacted upon human relationships between victims, offenders and the community.[215] Some analysts have explored whether it is possible to conceive of some form of 'hybrid' or 'mixed' procedure which would be capable of pursuing redress alongside the public and social objectives of the penal law, thinking creatively about how a criminal justice system might enable 'denunciation to be expressed in a currency other than that of retributive-style punishments'.[216] A number of authors have expounded

---

[212] Doak (2008); Fattah (1998).
[213] Zedner (1994), 231.
[214] Ashworth (1993); von Holderstein Holtermann (2009).
[215] See Llewellyn and Howse (1998); McCold and Wachtel (2003).
[216] Wright (1991), 113.

normative models as to how this might be done,[217] although this work tends to speak in terms of values and principles rather than concrete detail as to how such a model might interact with (or replace) the existing criminal justice system.[218]

One of the most comprehensive proposals has been advanced by Cavadino and Dignan,[219] who reject the idea of strict proportionality on the grounds that, if enforced, it could potentially limit the scope for the victim and offender to be actively involved in shaping reparation, since the tariff would be pre-determined. As an alternative, they advocate an 'integrated restorative justice model', whereby reparation is carried out according to proportionality principles. This model is based around the idea of a 'public tariff', which would effectively seek to transpose traditional penal sanctions to forms of reparations for individual victims. In simple terms, this might include rendering the amount payable by way of a fine payable instead to the victim through a compensation order, or community service into a period of time instead geared towards helping specific victims. Ultimately, the nature and extent of reparation would be a decision for the court which, through clear guidance, would attempt to pass a sentence which reflected both the private interests of the victim and the public interests set out above. Private, informal agreements could be taken into account by the sentence, which would also ensure that 'retributive maximum' and 'retributive minimum' standards were applied in order to strike a balance between the private interests and those of the wider community, including potential victims. In cases where such informal agreements proved impossible, the principle of proportionality would provide a 'default setting' for determination of the final outcome. This proposal is not without its problems. In critiquing a similar proposal by Braithwaite,[220] von Holderstein Holdtermann warns that trying to convert orthodox disposals into a reparative format enters 'the dubious business of comparing oranges and apples— or … of finding out how many oranges it takes to exceed, say, ten apples'.[221] Yet, this objection tends to overlook the fact that the business of determining orthodox penal sanctions is also a rather dubious business. The sentencer's exercise, which usually consists of determining levels of culpability and harm, also involves an imprecise conversion exercise to calculate the form and quantum of the punishment to be imposed by the court. It is therefore arguable that if harm and culpability can be used as concepts to determine the degree of punishment, so too can they be used to determine the degree of reparation.

Whether or not such reparative measures would constitute a form of 'punishment' per se has been widely debated in the literature,[222] but for present purposes

---

[217] See eg Barton (2000); Braithwaite (2002a); Brooks (2012); Garvey (2003).
[218] Von Holderstein Holtermann (2009), 192.
[219] Cavadino and Dignan (1997).
[220] Braithwaite (2002a).
[221] Von Holderstein Holtermann (2009), 200.
[222] cf Barnett (1977), Barton (2000), Brooks (2012), Christie (1977), Garvey (2003); Daly (2002), Daly and Immarigeon (1998); Pavlich (2005); Walgrave (2008), Walgrave and Bazemore (1999); Woolford and Ratner (2008); Wright (1996); Zehr (2002).

we proceed on the basis that integrating reparation within the sentencing framework is not inherently incompatible with public interest justifications (which, in any case, often conflict with each other).[223] However, this position then posits a further question: if we accept the premise that reparation ought to be a legitimate objective for criminal justice, are the existing structures within the system capable of delivering it? As suggested above, the answer is almost certainly 'no'. The institutions and processes of the criminal justice system have evolved to reflect the purely public dimension of criminal harms. In order for an effective form of reparation to be ordered, that meets the needs of the victim, any process must be calibrated to uncovering the nature and extent of the harm caused. This will necessarily involve some mechanism of input or 'voice' for the victim, above and beyond what they are currently able to exercise in the courtroom.

This underscores the point above that restorative processes are inherently linked to restorative outcomes. Restoration—be it material or symbolic in nature—demands more than merely 'hearing' the victim, and more than a judicial assessment of the extent of damage to a person's body or property.[224] Since harm is also emotional and moral in nature, the quantum of reparation cannot be determined through the application of a quasi-mathematical formula. In order to construct a complete picture of the offence, from its precipitation, to the execution, through to its aftermath, the courts need to embark on a much more nuanced fact-finding exercise than that which is provided for under the existing paradigm. The best means of achieving this is thus to open some form of communication channel between the victim and offender, in order to allow for the circumstances of the offence to be fully probed and to allow for the possibility of expressions of remorse or forgiveness, which are highly unusual within the adversarial trial structure.[225] It is at this juncture of the trial process—after a finding or admission of guilt—that restorative justice presents itself as an alternative model which empowers the key stakeholders to engage with each other and advance their own views as to the most effective means of addressing the harm. Cavadino and Dignan contend that such conferences could be organised either by a criminal justice agency or a third party agency, whereby (as noted above) agreements could then be returned to the court for approval to ensure that they conform to 'retributive maximum' and 'retributive minimum' standards, and to ensure that other public interests are adequately taken into account in passing the final sentence.[226] As we illustrate in chapter four, referrals to mediation and restorative justice by sentencing courts are becoming increasingly commonplace. We contend that, with appropriate safeguards, such court-ordered mediation and conferencing could serve to substantially improve the legitimacy and coherence of existing sentence practice.

---

[223] Ashworth and Player (2005); Kaufman (2008); Padfield (2013).
[224] Davis et al (1988).
[225] Bibas and Bierschbach (2004), 288.
[226] Cavadino and Dignan (1997).

V. Conclusions

This chapter has sought to provide conceptual clarity surrounding key theoretical tensions within restorative justice, particularly in relation to what is being restored and how it might be restored, as well as the nature and form of restorative measures themselves. Restorative justice discourse has undoubtedly provided highly useful insights into these questions, though it is equally clear that they remain contested and that there is no one overarching theory. However, a number of common themes can be clearly elicited.

First, there is broad agreement on the deficiencies of the existing criminal justice system. If one accepts the normative premise that restoration ought to feature as an aim of criminal justice, then the system as it stands is poorly equipped to deliver it. While the literature gives us a laudable critique of the ways in which restorative justice provides a better alternative to conventional criminal justice for victims, offenders and the community, there remains an unresolved tension regarding the question as how (if at all) it can be realised against the embedded structures and values of a criminal justice system that have evolved to resolve a notional dichotomous conflict between the state and the accused. Criminal justice and restorative justice have almost contradictory functions and objectives, and restoration as a value sits uncomfortably as a novel interloper amongst the established *raisons d'être* of the existing paradigm.

Second, and in consequence of the above, not all restorative justice concepts map clearly on to the existing criminal justice system. The literature tends to rely heavily upon on abstract notions of 'conflict', 'harm' and 'responsibility'. This reflects the broad global reach of the subject, and is arguably a more accurate descriptor of what is at stake since the definition and scope of the criminal law arbitrarily depends upon the type of behaviour which the state has opted to criminalise. However, if we are serious about mainstreaming restorative justice within the parameters of the existing criminal justice system, important questions need to be addressed concerning the applicability of non-legal concepts for addressing legal questions pertaining to whether the elements of a particular offence are in place, whether burdens of proof have been discharged, whether due process has been maintained and whether a particular sentence can be deemed to be proportionate to the offence in question. Restorative justice has not evolved to act as a legal or fact-finding mechanism to resolve these issues and confronting them will reveal significant legal and policy challenges ahead.

The third challenge posed by the literature concerns the lack of a detailed account concerning how the values of restorative justice are channelled into praxis. As noted above, most commentators accept that restorative justice ought to be informed by certain values which include (inter alia) respect, equality, fairness, inclusivity, restoration, truth telling, honesty, voluntariness, empathy, repair and reintegration. Some of these values may be mapped on to the processes of restorative justice (such as what happens during conferencing and whether it instils values like fairness and participation), while others tend to refer to its outcomes (such as satisfaction with agreed plans or the achievement of agreements amongst participants). Some may apply to both. There remain, however, many unanswered questions concerning how and why such values are operationalised in practice. Indeed, many of the values of restorative justice appear to be implicitly related to more general theories of behavioural change across the social science and criminological fields, rather than on any direct connection to restorative justice theory.[227] Thus, concepts like reintegration, restoration and collective healing are often associated with labelling, control theory and social disorganisation perspectives.[228] Moreover, many values have often been identified post facto from the outcomes that practitioners observe through practice, rather than from the theoretical literature on restorative justice. While recent research, most notably Rossner's study, has shed some light on these issues, there is still a significant gap in our understanding as to how and why restorative justice works as a theory—or, as one writer surmises, what is actually in the 'black box' of restorative justice.[229] It is this third challenge that we explore in chapter three.

---

[227] Bazemore and Schiff (2005), 47.
[228] See eg Bazemore (1998); Bazemore and Schiff (2005); Hudson (2002); Braithwaite (1999); Wheeldon (2009).
[229] Choi (2008).

3
Theorising Restorative Justice in Criminal Justice

I. Introduction

Although the key theoretical insights discussed in the previous chapter have helped to chart and explain the operation of restorative justice, in this chapter we seek to build on this discussion by proposing a fresh framework to better understand both how restorative justice operates within the context of criminal justice, as well as the normative values which it ought to encapsulate in order to realise its full potential. For these purposes, we draw on empowerment theory, as developed in social psychology, to propose a paradigm through which a more nuanced understanding of how restorative justice operates within the criminal justice sphere with regard to its impacts on victims, offender and the broader community. Our theoretical framework seeks to clarify the underpinning processes and outcomes of restorative justice practice. More specifically, we show how two key empowering values, agency and accountability, can be used to reconfigure our understanding of restorative processes and outcomes, thus providing a theoretically informed framework for recalibrating praxis to deliver a better experience of justice for all stakeholders.

We begin by exploring the concept of empowerment theory and how it can act as a lens through which the operation of restorative justice can be better understood. We then proceed to show how both crime and the criminal justice process have considerable disempowering impacts on victim, offenders and communities, whilst highlighting how, conversely, restorative justice can be used to re-empower those who are adversely impacted by crime. As such, we argue that empowerment theory offers a way to better understand the apparently contradictory impacts of criminal justice against the goals of restorative justice. It helps us to comprehend how the impacts of crime and criminal justice disempower individuals while restorative justice seeks to re-empower; thus aiding our understanding of what restorative justice should seek to achieve, and why.

II. Empowerment Theory

As illustrated in the previous chapter, much of the underlying theory for restorative justice appears to be implicitly related to more general theories of behavioural change across the social science and criminological fields, rather than on any direct connection to restorative justice theory per se.[1] Thus concepts like restoration and collective healing are often associated with labelling, control theory and social disorganisation perspectives.[2] Moreover, such established theories have been largely identified post facto from the outcomes practitioners observe through practice, rather than from the theoretical literature on restorative justice. As such, general theories relating to individual behaviour and social interactions are usually used to validate positive results from restorative practice, rather than to develop restorative justice theory in its own right. Empowerment theory can assist in developing a more fundamental theoretical base for restorative justice within criminal justice by helping us to articulate more clearly how and why restorative justice 'works' at both individual and collective levels.

Both restorative processes and outcomes are key to our theoretical framework. As a process, empowerment enables people to gain control over their lives, achieve democratic participation within their 'community' and, for those lacking resources, gain greater access and control over their lives.[3] Empowerment theory is particularly relevant to understanding how those who lack control in their lives are able to gain control and participate in decisions that impact them. Zimmerman describes it as a process involving mutual respect, critical reflection and group participation, through which those lacking control are given greater access, participation and the ability to control their lives.[4] By the same token, empowering outcomes are often associated with a shift in a person's statement of mind, such as gaining a sense of worthiness or competency, coupled with personal power and control.[5]

Empowerment theory can therefore provide a useful theoretical platform through which restorative justice within criminal justice can be framed and better understood, through its focus on actions, events and processes which result in individuals losing control or becoming disempowered. This clearly resonates with the impacts of crime and criminal justice, which have often been described as ultimately disempowering for both victims and offenders.[6] Indeed, crime has been characterised as being a 'desecration of who we are, of what we believe, of our

---

[1] Bazemore and Schiff (2005), 47.
[2] See eg Bazemore (1998); Bazemore and Schiff (2005); Hudson (2002); Braithwaite (1999); Wheeldon (2009).
[3] Rappaport (1987).
[4] Zimmerman (1995).
[5] Choi et al (2010).
[6] Finkelhor and Brown (1985); Spalek (2005); Wright (2002).

private space'.[7] It thereby undermines two of the basic assumptions on which we base our lives: our belief that the world is orderly and meaningful, such that we can usually predict what will happen to us; and our belief in personal autonomy, such that we have power over what happens on our own lives.[8] In the aftermath of a criminal offence, victims are thus left with many unresolved questions concerning why they were victimised and what they could have done to prevent it. This may, in turn, result in a sense of powerlessness, undermining their sense of autonomy and control over their own lives by the very fact that someone else has taken control over their property, space and experiences.[9]

A. Disempowerment Through Crime and the Criminal Justice System

As noted in the previous chapter, research has shown that victims suffer a range of impacts as a result of crime, ranging from physical injuries and financial loss, to psychological trauma and helplessness, as well as powerlessness, loss of autonomy and vulnerability. The effects of crime on victims are qualitatively different from being the victim of an accident or disease, because crime generally involves someone (the offender) deliberately or recklessly harming another person. The impacts of crime vary according to the nature of the criminal incident; violent crimes are more likely to result in physical injuries, but equally they are also more likely to be psychologically traumatic for victims, often leaving them with feelings of shock, fear and anger.[10] Such emotions are particularly prevalent among victims of violent crimes, including sexual assaults and domestic abuse, which may cause significant psychological and psychiatric harm lasting for years after the event.[11] Profound feelings associated with a loss of control and dignity, including fear, guilt and shame, are often reported in the research literature.[12]

Even crimes that do not involve physical violence, such as property-related offences, can take a significant toll on victims. In addition to financial hardship, property crimes can create feelings of shock, violation and insecurity, again associated with a loss of control.[13] Burglary victims are also particularly vulnerable to negative psychological impacts associated with the violation of their private living space and home environment, which often connotes feelings of security, control and privacy.[14] Other types of property-related crime can have negative impacts

---

[7] Zehr (1990), 24.
[8] Zehr (1990).
[9] Zehr (1990).
[10] Janoff-Bulman (1985); Kilpatrick and Acierno (2003).
[11] Jones et al (2001); Ruback and Thompson (2001); Stanko and Hobdell (1993).
[12] Skogan (1987).
[13] Janoff-Bulman (1985); Maguire (1982).
[14] Maguire (1982); Mawby (2013).

on victims beyond the financial costs, particularly where victims feel helpless and insecure through being unable to control what happened.[15] More generally, the physical, mental, psychological, social and financial effects of crime extend beyond individual victims; when this affects families, friends and colleagues of the victim, they also become indirect victims of crime.[16] Indeed, successive sweeps of the British Crime Survey have shown that the effects of crime can have powerful negative consequences, including heightened fear of repeat victimisation. Even where victims of property and violent crime suffer relatively little physical or financial harm, they may still report significant emotional reactions including shock and anger, as well as raised fears of re-victimisation.[17] Taken together, the literature evidences a pressing need for many victims to regain a sense of power and control over their lives in order to recover some of the personal autonomy that has been lost.[18]

Beyond the negative impacts of crime itself, the disempowering effects of secondary victimisation within the criminal justice system have been widely documented. Victims have long been reported as feeling 'excluded' from the criminal justice process and the decisions that are made about 'their' cases, which can include not being told if a suspect has been arrested, whether they have been charged, whether the matter will be dealt with in court or what kind of sentence they received.[19] Despite a series of reforms aimed at improving the way that victims are kept informed by the police, prosecution and court service, there is still significant cultural resistance to further involving victims in the procedural aspects of their cases or in the wider decision-making process.[20] International surveys have repeatedly revealed that about half of victims feel the police did not do enough about the crime that impacted them.[21] Those called as witnesses report how intimidating and difficult this process can be, and that they feel at the mercy of questioning by defence and prosecution counsel alike.[22] Intense and degrading questioning can be especially damaging to vulnerable witnesses, despite the widespread availability of measures designed to protect such witnesses and ease the impact of testifying.[23] In particular, there is a considerable body of literature charting the experiences of child witnesses,[24] witnesses suffering from physical

---

[15] Button et al (2014); Deem (2000); Fox (2007).
[16] Shapland and Hall (2007).
[17] Deem (2000); Janoff-Bulman (1985); Shapland and Hall (2007).
[18] Zehr and Mika (1998).
[19] Doak (2008); Shapland and Hall (2007); Spalek (2005); Wemmers (2009).
[20] Hall (2012).
[21] Van Kesteren et al (2001).
[22] Jacobson et al (2015).
[23] See Hamlyn et al (2004). Almost half of vulnerable witnesses surveyed (48%) were upset 'a lot'. Almost three-quarters (71%) of those questioned found cross-examination to be 'upsetting'.
[24] Brennan and Brennan (1989); Cordon et al (2003); Goodman and Bottoms (1993); Spencer and Lamb (2012).

or learning disabilities,[25] complainants in sexual cases[26] and witnesses at risk of intimidation or repeat victimisation. However, these difficulties are not confined to vulnerable witnesses; a recent survey of almost 8,000 victims and witnesses in England and Wales found that one in five victims were 'dissatisfied', and one in ten were 'very dissatisfied' with the Crown Prosecution Service.[27] Half of those victims surveyed and over a third of the witnesses said they would not consent to being a witness in a criminal trial if they were asked to do so in the future. A subsequent report, by a coalition of 90 criminal justice organisations, *Structured Mayhem*, issued an even more damning indictment of the treatment of victims, witnesses and defendants.[28] Among its key findings were that 'those who might be presumed to be key players—the witnesses, victims and defendants—are in fact side-lined and tend to play only minor roles', and that '[t]he consequent delays, adjournments and scheduling problems often cause frustration, anxiety and inconvenience to victims, witnesses and defendants'.[29] The absence of any meaningful sense of 'voice' or legal representation was found to be a particular source of frustration for many victims and witnesses, who shared a 'marginalised outsider position'.[30]

In adversarial systems, the nature of criminal proceedings often demeans victims of crime, as the structure of proceedings reflects its normative conceptualisation of the case as a conflict between the State and the accused. In contrast to many continental legal systems, victims have no right to be heard or to give a narrative account.[31] Such problems are not unique to victims; as noted in the previous chapter, offenders are also structurally excluded from proceedings, and are disempowered through the lack of capacity to account for their actions or exercise their own voice. In this sense, both victims and offenders are 'conscripted' into operational roles within the criminal justice system and are treated as its servants or agents.[32]

i. Empowerment and Restorative Justice

Restorative justice is frequently presented as having the potential to re-empower victims of crime.[33] Similarly, much of the recent research evaluating restorative interventions and their impacts on victims of crime has emphasised their positive results in terms of producing outcomes, such as increasing victim satisfaction, as well as producing positive emotional and psychological benefits.[34]

---

[25] Clare and Murphy (2001); Kilcommins and Donnelly (2014); Voice UK et al (2001).
[26] Campbell (2006); Lees (1996); Vetten et al (2014).
[27] Wood et al (2015).
[28] Jacobson et al (2015).
[29] Jacobson et al (2015), 2.
[30] Jacobson et al (2015), 3.
[31] See ch 2, III.B. See further Doak (2008).
[32] Faulkner (2001), 226.
[33] See generally Sawin and Zehr (2007); Zehr and Mika (1998).
[34] Aertsen et al (2006). See further ch 7,III.

The concept of empowerment has even been described as a fundamental principle and value of restorative justice.[35] This has been highlighted in research findings which show how restorative programmes can provide opportunities for victims of crime to have their voices heard, receive answers to their questions, feel less fearful and gain a better sense of fairness and, ultimately, possibly achieve empathy with the offender and experience personal empowerment.[36] Likewise, offenders are afforded an opportunity to explain their actions directly to the victim, and reflect on the circumstances which to the offending behaviour and the nature of the harm it caused. Empowerment theory also adds to our understanding as to how the 'micro-dynamics' of restorative process, discussed in the previous chapter, might be able to engineer these outcomes. Research has highlighted how empowerment includes interpersonal, interactional and behavioural components, which all contribute towards gaining a sense of control at individual, organisational and community levels.[37] First, at an individual level, the *interpersonal* element of empowerment connects with the manner in which people think about themselves. It refers to the notion that individuals can gain influence and control over events in their lives and generally refers to beliefs about one's ability to exert influence in different life spheres, as well as a basic element that provides people with the initiative to engage in behaviours that influence desired outcomes.[38] Second, the *interactional* element of empowerment theory refers to the understanding people have about their community and the choices available to them. In this way, it may help people gain an understanding of the ways and resources necessary to allow them to achieve their goals. The interactional element includes decision making, problem solving and leadership skills, which may be developed in situations where participants have opportunities to become involved in decision making. In this sense, individuals become independent and better able to exert control over events, thereby becoming their own advocates. Third, the *behavioural* element of empowerment refers to the actions necessary to achieve desired objectives, namely active participation and being part of the deliberative process that shapes outcomes. For example, this might include involvement with community organisations and self-help groups which enable participants to regain a sense of control over events.[39]

Equally, empowerment theory has been used to critique restorative practices, particularly where specific practices adversely impact already socially marginalised populations, increasing their social exclusion.[40] Thus, empowerment has been used as a concept in assessing practices that fail to meet the needs of participants

---

[35] Choi et al (2010).
[36] For a good general discussion see the work of see Bazemore and Schiff (2005); Daly (2006); Strang et al (2006).
[37] Zimmerman (1995).
[38] Rappaport (1987).
[39] Zimmerman (1995).
[40] Richards (2011).

in certain circumstances. In an examination of the narratives of victims of crime, Choi et al argue that some restorative practices fall short in term of achieving positive outcomes, particularly if they fail to deliver a sense of empowerment for participants.[41] The authors contend that when victims do not feel that they are able to fully participate in the restorative process, when they are placed in passive roles and when they do not receive sincere apologies and genuine interactions they are more likely to feel the process was disappointing or even disempowering.[42] Conversely, when victims are able to share their experiences of victimisation, ask questions and receive answers, and thus get information through a restorative process, their narratives regarding their experiences are more likely to be empowering and restorative.[43] This serves as a useful reminder of the need to address the 'gap' between the goals of restorative justice and what is actually delivered in practice—particularly if this leaves participants feeling unable to meaningfully participate and engage in the process.[44]

ii. Empowerment and Restorative Themes

In the previous chapter, we observed how much of the debate about what restorative justice actually seeks to achieve is focused on the 'process' of delivering restorative justice—what happens during conferencing and whether it instils values like fairness and participation. Such debates also focus on the 'outcomes', such as satisfaction with agreed plans or the achievement of agreement amongst participants. However, this has led to a lack of clarity on the more fundamental questions related to how and why restorative justice works.[45] Similarly, as will become evident in subsequent chapters, the bulk of evaluative research has examined specific aspects of restorative 'processes' or 'outcomes', such as their delivery and their impacts, from interpersonal and individual perspectives.[46]

We argue that empowerment theory can provide a useful lens into how restorative justice works in practice, mapping restorative justice values against the broad concepts of 'empowering values', 'empowering processes' and 'empowering outcomes'.[47] Empowering values are the basic principles that underpin the concept of empowerment. From a social psychological perspective, social problems are often framed as the consequence of unequal distribution and access to resources. Thus empowerment values seek to allow people, organisations and communities to gain mastery over issues of concern to them.[48] Empowerment processes, such as personal control, community support, influencing change, working

---

[41] Choi et al (2010).
[42] Choi et al (2010).
[43] Choi et al (2010).
[44] Daly (2006).
[45] Choi et al (2012); Bolívar (2010); Daly (2006).
[46] See Zehr (2005); Van Ness (2004).
[47] Zimmerman (1995).
[48] Rappaport (1987).

cooperatively, collective decision making, capacity building and influencing change, create opportunities for individuals to control and influence decisions that affect their lives.[49] These experiences enable individuals, organisations and communities to gain greater access and control, such as through shared leadership, participation in community organisations and collective decision-making processes. Empowering outcomes, on the other hand, are the effects of interventions designed to empower participants and are the consequences of empowering processes. They are the results of the empowering process and include gaining control over events and decisions, which can include feeling a sense of control and competence, and a belief about one's ability to influence issues that impact our lives. These outcomes may have interactional components, whereby they bestow personal and interpersonal power to understand how events are controlled. In other words, this is the extent to which people understand and are able to manage the environment in which they find themselves. In addition, such outcomes may also comprise a behavioural component, which is the action that the individual takes to influence and exert control, such as through participation in organisations and groups.[50]

As illustrated in Figure 3.1, there is a considerable paradigmatic overlap between many of the guiding values and principles underpinning both empowerment theory and restorative justice. Restorative justice seeks to provide individuals with the opportunity for account-making (ie, to tell their story and be heard);[51] to be recognised as stakeholders rather than merely witnesses or defendants; to be able to receive answers to their questions; to be able to re-connect to their community; and to have meaningful interactions, on their own terms.[52] As an empowering mechanism, restorative justice also seeks to transform negative impacts of crime from isolation, silence and powerlessness into community support, shared healing, interaction, reengagement and empowerment.[53] As noted in chapter one, there is a burgeoning body of literature which explores the normative values which ought to guide restorative justice. Figure 3.1 encapsulates the normative range of values which tend to feature prominently in both empowerment theory and restorative justice.

---

[49] Zimmerman (1995).
[50] Zimmerman (1995).
[51] See further Dignan (2007); Orbuch et al (1994).
[52] See eg Doak (2008); Sherman (2003); Strang (2002); Zehr (2005).
[53] Van Ness and Heetderks Strong (2014); Bazemore and Schiff (2005).

Empowerment Theory 67

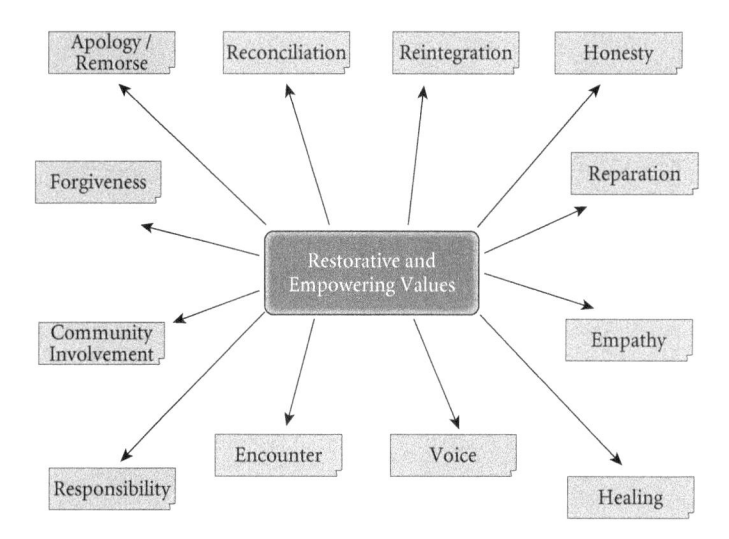

Figure 3.1: Overlapping Values and Principles

Values surrounding "Restorative and Empowering Values": Apology/Remorse, Reconciliation, Reintegration, Honesty, Forgiveness, Reparation, Community Involvement, Empathy, Responsibility, Encounter, Voice, Healing.

There has also been a considerable expansion on international benchmarks of best practice of restorative justice. These key facets of a restorative encounter tend to be associated with in positive outcomes and strongly resonate with practices widely identified as 'empowering' within social psychology literature as illustrated in Figure 3.2.

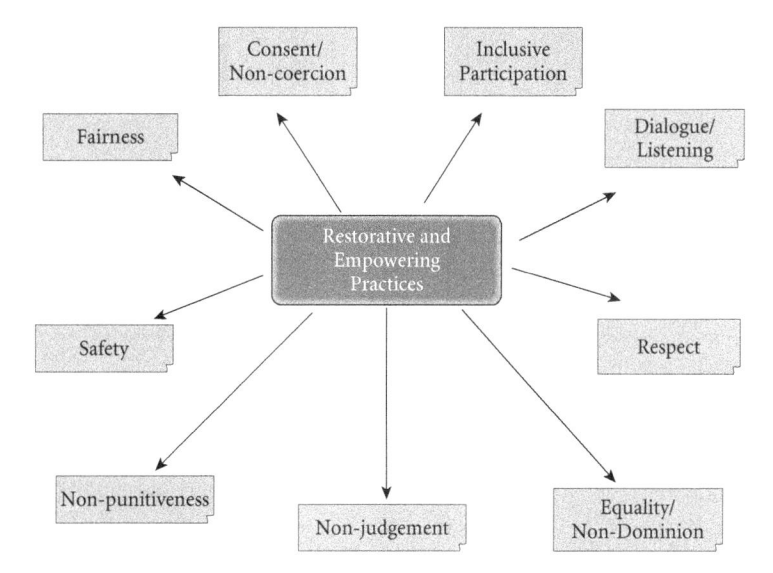

Figure 3.2: Restorative and Empowering Practices

Practices surrounding "Restorative and Empowering Practices": Consent/Non-coercion, Inclusive Participation, Fairness, Dialogue/Listening, Safety, Respect, Non-punitiveness, Non-judgement, Equality/Non-Dominion.

Empowerment theory allows us to re-examine how these values interact with each other in a restorative context, to give individuals both the power and the ability to understand the context in which they find themselves, as well as the ability to act and have real influence over events which directly impact them. However, Figures 3.1 and 3.2 represent just one (non-exhaustive) attempt to elicit the myriad of values, principles and practices which are widely cited in the literature. Broadly speaking, such concepts might individually be charted as drivers of Van Ness and Strong's four 'common goals' of restorative justice: 'encounter', 'participation', 'reparation' and 'reintegration' (see Figure 3.3).[54] In turn, these goals map on to the processes and outcome factors which have also been the subject of much of the evaluative and empirical research (see Figure 3.3).

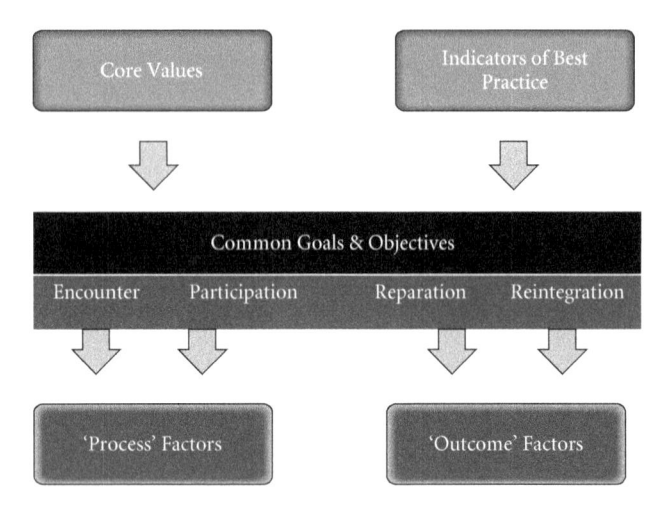

Figure 3.3: Common Goals and Objectives of Restorative Justice

Empowerment theory offers a distinct advantage for theorising restorative justice by allowing us to reconceptualise these restorative 'processes' and 'outcomes' as core empowering values, rather than merely as the products of restorative justice encounters. Indeed, we propose that two such values, those of 'agency' and 'accountability', can be mapped onto the process and outcome factors of restorative justice (see Figure 3.4). Thus, much of what is sought within the 'process' of restorative justice, where the focus is the impact of the restorative process on participants (its sense of legitimacy, fairness and justice) broadly maps onto the empowering value of 'agency' (referring to the capacity to provide empowering choices and decision-making abilities on participants; see further details below).[55] Similarly, the 'outcomes' of restorative justice (where the focus is on the agreement,

---

[54] Van Ness and Heetderks Strong (2014).
[55] See also Shapland et al (2006b); Woolford and Ratner (2008).

Empowerment Theory 69

making amends, rehabilitation and other products of the restorative encounter) broadly map onto the empowering value of accountability. Accountability, as viewed through the lens of empowerment theory, refers to the ways in which individuals make themselves accountable, take responsibility for the consequences of their actions and positively hold others to account. Within a restorative justice setting, this allows for concrete actions to rectify harms and address some of the factors which caused the offender to engage in wrongful behaviour.[56]

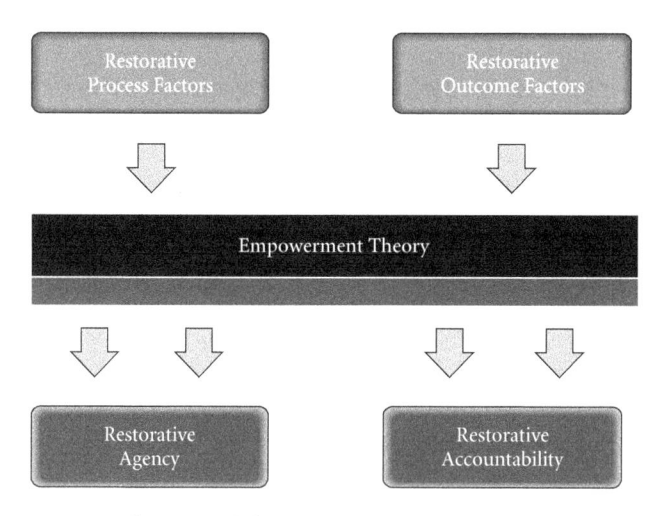

Figure 3.4: Agency and Accountability in Empowerment Theory

These interlinked goals of agency and accountability allow us to better frame and understand restorative justice within criminal justice. Throughout this book, we refer to this paradigm as the 'agency–accountability framework'. By analysing restorative encounters through this lens, we can move beyond the well-trodden analysis of the products of restorative justice, breaking down analyses focused on 'processes' and 'outcomes' and integrate these with the dynamics of interactions. As we argue below, the agency–accountability framework provides an alternative way of conceptualising and understanding restorative justice, providing a more fundamental understanding of how it works, why it works and how it can be successfully delivered in criminal justice practice.

B. Restorative Agency and Accountability

In order to clarify how the concepts of agency and accountability can be used in a theoretical framework for restorative justice, conceptual clarity is required as to

---

[56] Foley (2014); Johnstone and Van Ness (2005); Roche (2003).

what meaning is attached to these terms. As both labels are widely used within the social sciences, the following section unpacks our understanding of these terms and their connections to restorative processes and restorative outcomes. The discussion then turns to consider how the concepts of agency and accountability might be used as conceptual goals in order to improve both the coherency of restorative justice theory and render praxis more effective.

i. Agency

As a concept within empowerment theory, agency should be simply understood in its positive sense of allowing individuals the capacity to make choices. As Durkheim describes, it refers to individual and collective autonomy to make choices, giving actors the power to make their own decisions and the capacity to make their own choices amongst available alternatives.[57] However, this notion of agency is constrained by *structure*, which Giddens described as the societal constraints that are placed on us within society through organisations and social rules.[58] Notwithstanding these limits, Giddens argued that structures were also maintained and adapted by the exercise of individual agency, a process he refers to as *structuration*.

In specific relation to restorative justice, agency entails empowering and enabling those impacted by crime the capacity to make choices and play an active part in the process and decision-making that takes place throughout the criminal process. This phenomenon is widely reflected in research observations that highlight the importance of giving participants voice, responsibility and the capacity to change;[59] the importance of allowing a genuine apology and expressing feelings freely, while holding offenders to account;[60] and affording victims an input into decision-making processes.[61] Like all criminal processes, it is not claimed that restorative justice is capable of realising absolute agency for all stakeholders all of the time. As with any legal process, constraints such as the need to uphold due process and fair trial norms, and the need for proportionality (alongside other penal aims) mean that it would be nonsensical to adopt an absolutist agency-at-all-costs approach. Moreover, even if agency were to be afforded priority as an overriding value, underlying structures would inevitably impede its full potential. Nevertheless, if the empowerment of individual stakeholders is to be regarded a desirable objective of the criminal process, the facilitation of agency should be maximised wherever possible.

Nevertheless, the priority afforded to agency within restorative justice stands in sharp contrast to the disempowering impacts that traditional criminal

---

[57] Durkheim (1966); Hays (1994).
[58] Giddens (1982); Giddens (1984).
[59] Shapland et al (2011).
[60] Choi et al (2010).
[61] Zehr (2001).

justice practice has on victims and offenders.[62] As we noted in the previous chapter, Christie famously argued that modern criminal justice proceedings 'steal' the process of resolving conflicts from those who are directly involved, that is, the victim, offender and broader community. So, for example, in the modern criminal trial parties are represented by professional lawyers, who speak for them and decide what elements of the conflict are relevant to their legal and evidential needs.[63] The interests of victims themselves are notionally relegated to the civil courts, thereby effectively excluding them from criminal proceedings, unless required by the prosecutor to function as a witness to their own victimisation.[64] Similarly, the broader community interests are taken over by the state, by way of the prosecution service which assumes ownership of the communal interests. In practical terms, this means that the agency of individuals within modern criminal justice is effectively denied. The impact of the conflict on both victims and offenders, including their emotional trauma; their practical needs; the need to be heard and to explain what has happened to them, the need to understand why they were victimised and the need for an apology or some form of recompense—are structurally excluded by the criminal justice process. Rarely is any space created whereby offenders are able to apologise meaningfully to victims (and/or their communities) or make an offer of amends.[65] Thus, as a concept within empowerment theory, agency can be used as an underpinning goal for restorative justice within criminal justice, as it provides the individual and the collective the power to make choices and decisions amongst available alternatives.

ii. Accountability

The concept of accountability, like agency, is subject to frequent usage in the parlance of criminal justice policy, where it is often used to denote criminal prosecution, sanction and the imposition of punitive outcomes.[66] While criminal justice is frequently characterised as a sphere in which offenders are held to account for their actions, restorative justice aims to create a space where individuals render *themselves* accountable, by taking active responsibility for the consequences of their actions.[67] Accountability, within the context of our framework, thus needs to be understood in its positive and empowering sense, and is achieved when offenders admit their involvement in the offence, accept the harms they have caused, express remorse and accept collectively agreed resolutions that help contribute towards their reintegration and rehabilitation.

In much of the restorative justice literature, accountability can also be viewed as part of an empowering practice in which participants are empowered to express

---

[62] Christie (1977).
[63] Christie (1977).
[64] Doak (2008).
[65] Sawin and Zehr (2007), 45.
[66] Braithwaite and Roche (2001).
[67] Braithwaite and Roche (2001).

themselves and are held accountable both for the wrongfulness of the criminal act and for the negative consequences caused by crime. Thus, there is a moral accountability that emerges through restorative justice, whereby offenders accept accountability for their actions and give account, or explain and answer questions about their behaviour to the collective group. This account giving also encourages gestures of remorse by the offender and can lead to reintegration, whereby remorse can be met with gestures of reconciliation, breaking down the barriers between the victim, offender and community.[68] In many respects this involves confronting the reality of the pain they have caused others, thereby offering a chance for redemption.[69]

This concept of accountability contrasts vividly with what Matza described as 'techniques of neutralisation', whereby offenders can justify their behaviour by denying that it caused any real harm, or when they are allowed to mitigate their individual responsibility by 'hiding out' in the criminal justice process, where they are represented and spoken for by legal counsel.[70]

Thus, the facilitation of accountability in a restorative context is about creating and accepting obligations and commitments across the parties and within the parties.[71] Accountability is not just confined to the offender accepting what they have done as wrong and being willing to address the harms caused. The victim plays an important part in accountability by holding the offender to account for their actions, by participating in the conference, by hearing the offender's account of their actions and being willing to question the offender and reveal the consequences of the criminal incident and how it has impacted them. Accountability is therefore more broadly about facilitating a process in which individuals are able to be accountable for their actions, and giving individuals the space to hold others accountable for their behaviour, with a view to leading to genuine remorse and reconciliation.[72]

Accountability operates another key function through its potential to personify all of those who have been impacted by crime. Thus when offenders give account of their actions and accept the consequences of their behaviour, and when victims are willing to hold offenders to account by listening to their account and explaining the impact of the crime on them as individuals, the process may act to rehumanise the parties. It brings the individuality of the parties and the personal circumstances of those participating in the restorative process to the fore.[73] This form of accountability can be contrasted with the typical criminal justice process, in which offenders can be viewed as 'objects' rather than as people: characterised and understood in terms of specific traits—whether they are employed, their age

---

[68] Braithwaite and Mugford (1994).
[69] Ward and Langlands (2009).
[70] Matza (1964).
[71] Aertsen et al (2013).
[72] Van Ness (2014).
[73] London (2011).

and if they have any previous criminal convictions—which may be used to assess their 'dangerousness', or risk of reoffending.[74] Similarly, the victim is often invisible in the criminal justice process; the importance of the offence and the harm or damage that may have resulted from the criminal act is less prominent to proving the elements of the offence. The offender is thus made the main focus of attention and the conflict is dealt with in terms of how the offender is punished, as a subject deserving sanction within the broader aims of sentencing such as retribution, deterrence, incapacitation or rehabilitation.

iii. Agency, Accountability and Criminal Justice

Taken together, our empowering concepts of agency and accountability differentiate restorative justice from conventional criminal justice and provide clearer goals and expectations for its delivery within the criminal process. Not only do they serve to empower participants through the process and outcomes of restorative justice, but they may also extend a sense of 'ownership' over the underlying conflict(s). This ownership extends beyond the victim and offender to their supporters and others involved in the restorative process and even extends to the wider community. It allows for a means of resolving conflicts in ways that can involve and strengthen civil society, thereby potentially creating a sense of 'democratic space' that may act to revive politics and 'democratise democracy'.[75] Thus empowerment theory provides a platform to better understand how conflicts arising from crime are mediated and resolved through restorative justice in an inclusive framework, compared to the exclusionary and marginalising impacts of the traditional criminal justice approach.

The agency–accountability framework is thus essential for the effective delivery of restorative justice within criminal justice and can be used both to guide practice and to inform the evaluation of restorative programmes. Gaining agency and accountability through restorative justice can be seen through the manner in which it is implemented from the beginning to the end of the process. As we illustrate in subsequent chapters, these concepts feature prominently in successful restorative programmes which place considerable emphasis on preparing individuals for the process, so they are able to actively engage in the process, gain a strong sense of agency and are willing to hold others *to account* and *to be accountable* to them. Similarly, during the restorative encounter itself, restorative justice agency and accountability need to be facilitated through negotiation and dialogue in which participants are able to actively engage in a constructive discussion about the offence, its consequences and participate in collective decision making. Such active engagement means that participants make themselves accountable to each other as a collective group and provide each other with a sense of agency through dealing with the consequences of the offence in a constructive

---

[74] See further Dimock (2015).
[75] Morison (2001).

and forward-looking manner. Conversely, subsequent chapters also show that that agency and accountability are frequently undermined by the prevalence of structures, including legalism and institutionalisation, resulting in less successful applications of restorative justice.

III. Conclusions

This chapter has argued that empowerment theory provides a strong theoretical framework for the role of restorative justice and how it is used within the confines of criminal justice. Empowerment theory is a particularly useful construct because it is concerned with the impact of disempowerment on individuals, relationships and communities and enables us to better understand the processes by which people gain control over their lives and the ability to participate in decisions that affect them. Thus it allows us to critically reflect the disempowering impacts of crime and criminal justice on one hand, and the empowering goals of restorative justice on the other.

A fundamental value of empowerment theory is its ability to connect strongly with the structure and functions of modern criminal justice, while providing a useful analytical tool through which we can examine how the values and practices of restorative justice play out at the individual, interactional and behavioural levels. We have argued that the processes and outcomes of restorative justice can be reconceptualised as through the lens of an agency–accountability framework. Viewed through the lens of empowerment theory much of what is sought within restorative justice processes can be understood as a quest for agency, while much of what is sought through restorative outcomes can be seen as a quest for accountability. Both our concepts of agency and accountability are taken in their positive and empowering sense, in which they provide the capacity to make choices and the opportunities to accept and create commitments across and within the parties. Together these empowering concepts allow for an analysis which takes us beyond the limited scope of the processes and outcomes typology which has dominated much of the literature to date. The agency–accountability framework provides a more theoretically informed framework and rationale as to how and why restorative justice works and to provide guidance and direction for its delivery and goals within criminal justice.

In the following chapters, our attention turns to the role of victim and offenders in restorative justice (chapter four), before moving on to consider its praxis within the criminal justice context. Here, we focus on its use in diversionary applications and those at the periphery of criminal justice (chapter five), in mediation-based practices (chapter six) and though mainstreamed applications (chapter six). Our objective is not only to illustrate the diverse range of practices across an international context, but also to demonstrate that effective practice should be underpinned by our empowering values of agency and accountability.

4

Victims and Offenders: Agency and Accountability in Practice

In contrast to the orthodox criminal justice system, which sees the voices of victims and offenders usurped by those of lawyers and legal professionals, restorative justice seeks to enable victims and offenders to engage in a dialogical process in order to address the harm caused by the offence. It is worth underlining at the outset, however, that the labels of 'victim' and 'offender' are not unproblematic; their usage implies a false dichotomy whereby each stakeholder can be categorised as a discrete and self-contained entity. In reality, there is a body of research evidence which confirms that there is often an overlap between victimisation and offending behaviour, with victims and offenders commonly being drawn from similar social groups. Many offenders have previous experience of victimisation and some victims have been previously been labelled as offenders by the criminal justice system.[1] In some cases, victims and offenders may even have long-standing and complex relationships, with both parties engaging in harmful behaviours toward each other.[2] That said, the labels still provide a useful reference for determining the nature and extent of the harm and reparatory interests that subsequently arise. Moreover, as we argue below, by maximising agency and accountability within the process, restorative justice has the potential to untangle the knots that underlie the harm(s) at stake. As the discussion progresses, we will consider the roles and experiences of victims and offenders, enabling us to better understand how agency and accountability maps on to their experiences. This casts light on the normative roles of each stakeholder, as well as providing key insights for effective practice.

In this chapter, we will begin by examining the role of the victim in restorative processes and considering the diverse ways in which victims can participate in restorative programmes, and the obstacles which prevent their effective participation. We draw on the evaluative literature concerning the experiences of victims, demonstrating how these align with the underpinning values of agency and accountability at the heart of our analytical framework. In particular, we highlight that restorative justice is not necessarily appropriate for all victims; indeed,

---

[1] Jennings et al (2012); Schreck et al (2008).
[2] Cunneen and Goldson (2015).

there are risks inherent in the process that can potentially lead to secondary victimisation. We then turn to the experiences of offenders in restorative schemes. Again drawing from the research literature, their experiences are explored in terms of what they contribute to the restorative dynamic and what they might expect in terms of benefits, through the agency–accountability framework. In addition, we explore a number of rights-based questions, including issues relating to proportionality, consent and power imbalances, which may impact upon the pursuit of agency and accountability within restorative programmes.

I. Victims and Restorative Justice

As noted in chapter two, the state has historically taken ownership of conflicts, transforming what were 'private' disputes into a matter that is dealt with by the state and the offender. In the orthodox criminal justice system, criminal offences have been constructed as transgressions against the state, with restoration or reconciliation relegated beneath the state's interest in denouncing and punishing unacceptable behaviour. While the public have a legitimate interest in the administration of criminal justice, victims experience the first-hand effects of the crime in a very real and tangible way. Whilst some of the earlier restorative interventions have been justified primarily on the basis of diversion or crime prevention,[3] it is now commonly accepted that one of the core objectives of restorative justice is to deliver a better sense of justice to victims of crime. As Strang has contended, this requires meeting three core needs of victims: first, victims want a less formal process where their views count and more information about the processing and outcome of their cases; second, they want to participate in their cases and be treated with fairness and respect; and, third, victims want some form of restoration, possibly material in nature, though symbolic forms of restoration, such as an apology, may be of equal, if not greater, importance.[4]

In order for these needs to be effectively met, some form of dialogical encounter with the offender is usually required. The typical bipartisan structure of adversarial criminal processes is not conducive to such encounters, and provides no formal channel for interaction between victims and offenders. By contrast, restorative justice locates the victim at the centre of the system, both in terms of process and outcomes. As well as having their questions answered, victims are given an opportunity to participate within the process and explain the impact that the offence has had on them using their own words in the form of free narrative.[5] Rather than being placated through the abstract knowledge that 'justice has been

[3] Marshall and Merry (1990).
[4] Strang (2002).
[5] Pranis (2007).

done' by punishing the offender, victims usually experience a more personalised justice, formulated by the participants themselves and tailored to meeting their own particular needs.[6]

However, it is important to note that restorative processes have inherent limits: not all victims of crime will find out who committed the offence against them.[7] If perpetrators are not identified, or if they refuse to accept responsibility, there will be little value in putting in place a restorative process for the victim alone. Moreover, victims must also have a free choice as to whether or not they feel that participating in such a process would be worthwhile. Thus, for the restorative encounter to work, both parties must make a free choice to enter the process.[8] The underlying assumption—as in empowerment theory—is that participants make their choice as to whether they participate, with one of the key aims that it should provide them with opportunities to accept and create a productive restorative encounter. Moreover, care should be taken to ensure that both the process and the outcome take into account the specific needs of both the victim and offender. There is significant variation in the manner in which crime impacts upon victims. While some may value the opportunity to confront the offender, others will wish to put the offence behind them as quickly as possible, or may feel uncomfortable about the prospect of engaging with the person who caused them harm. For example, in relation to violent or sexual offences, a victim may not wish to have any further involvement with the offender at all. By the same measure, victims of trivial offences may feel that there is little point in engaging in the process and that their time and energy could be better spent elsewhere. Such scenarios create difficulties for facilitators, although as we outline later in this chapter, programmes have deployed means to encourage participation or sidestep problems of non-participation so that a degree of restorativeness can be preserved.[9]

A. Victim Participation

Research has consistently shown that the majority of victims are willing in principle to meet with the person who has offended against them, provided they are properly prepared and the arrangements to do so are in place.[10] Yet the success of some restorative programmes has been undermined by relatively low levels of victim participation. In surveying the evaluative literature, and taking differing types of offences into account, Dignan estimated that 50 per cent of victims across all programmes would be happy to meet with the offender.[11] However, it might

---

[6] Latimer et al (2005); Saulnier and Sivasubramaniam (2015a).
[7] Dignan (2005); Johnstone (2011).
[8] McCold (2000); Wemmers and Canuto (2002).
[9] See below, II(B).
[10] See eg Shapland et al (2007); Johnstone (2015).
[11] Dignan (2007).

be added that this rough figure varied considerably depending upon the nature of the offence, the form of interaction proposed and the personal circumstances of individual victims and offenders.

Participation rates seem particularly low for some types of restorative interventions. For example, in relation to young offender panels in England and Wales, Crawford and Newburn found that victims failed to attend for a number of reasons.[12] Almost half (43 per cent) had not been offered a realistic opportunity to attend a meeting: victims had either not been identified or had not been contacted in a timely fashion. Other victims opted not to attend. In 2000 similar low levels of participation were noted in relation to police-led restorative cautioning. Little had changed over a decade later, and having observed 39 young offender panels, Rosenblatt found that only one panel included a participating victim.[13] Likewise, research carried out in Thames Valley by Hoyle et al found that just 16 per cent of victims participated in a programme of police-led restorative cautioning.[14] Of those who did not attend, 52 per cent stated that they did not wish to do so; 30 per cent had wished to participate, but were unable to; and 15 per cent had not been invited. It was found that often community panel members would attempt (unsuccessfully) to invoke empathy in young offenders by explaining how they might have felt; but such attempts were often futile. In a similar scheme operating in Northern Ireland for young offenders, O'Mahony et al found that victims only participated in 20 per cent of cases.[15]

These data contrast with evaluations of family group conferencing, which have generally yielded much more encouraging results. High levels of participation were uncovered in Northern Ireland, where Campbell et al found that there was at least some form of victim participation in 69 per cent of conferences.[16] Similarly high participation rates were reported in New South Wales,[17] and in the Australian evaluations of RISE and the Wagga Wagga scheme, levels of victim participation were higher still, at over 80 per cent.[18]

In most of the above studies, the researchers sought to uncover the main reasons for victims choosing to participate or not in restorative encounters. Looking at the literature as a whole, the same kinds of factors were routinely cited. Typically, victims place particular value on the opportunity to explain the effect the crime has had on them, to put a face to the offender, and to seek answers to questions such as 'why me?'.[19] This recurrent question is particularly important to victims, as they hope that answers may help to make sense of what has happened and can help

---

[12] Crawford and Newburn (2003).
[13] Rosenblatt (2015a).
[14] Hoyle et al (2002).
[15] O'Mahony et al (2002).
[16] Of these, 47% were victim representatives, 40% were personal victims and 13% were representatives attending where there was no identifiable victim: Campbell et al (2006).
[17] Trimboli (2000).
[18] Braithwaite (1999).
[19] Campbell et al (2006); Hayes and Daly (2004); Shapland et al (2007); Strang et al (2006).

restore order to their lives.[20] The vast majority of studies also reveal that victims who have taken part are happy to recommend conferencing to another person in similar circumstances.[21]

Far from seeking an outlet to vent anger or pursue vengeance against the victim, the overwhelming finding from this body of research is that most victims have largely altruistic motives for participating in restorative practices.[22] A particularly common theme in the majority of the evaluations to date is that victims are genuinely willing to help the offender and hope that their input may assist offenders to understand the consequences of their actions and develop empathy for victims so that they will desist from reoffending in the future.[23] Such findings ring true when considered in the light of empowerment theory; through offering participants opportunities to positively engage in the process of the restorative encounter enables them to influence the proceedings and so to gain a sense of agency. The agency–accountability framework plays out in the dynamics of productive restorative encounters when the participants are able to move beyond feeling of anger and hostility, towards shared understanding of the circumstances underlying the offence, and eventual acceptance.

In the same way, the literature highlights a number of common reasons for the absence of victims in restorative encounters. This often occurs where the victim has not been identified, or has not been contacted in a timely fashion. Some victims may feel it is not worth their time and effort to become involved since the loss or harm is considered too small or too trivial, or they consider that the matter has already been resolved. Others may feel too much time has elapsed since the incident and some may be fearful of the offender or be too angry with the offender to participate. Obviously the chances of victims eventually receiving some form of reparation are considerably lessened where they have chosen not to participate. Equally, however, not all victims of crime need a restorative intervention, particularly where the offence is relatively minor and its impact on the victim has been minimal.

B. Overcoming Non-participation

Variable levels of victim participation continue to hinder the success of restorative justice programmes worldwide. While for maximum effectiveness, the preferable role for the victim would seem to be that of a direct participant, another option is for the mediator or facilitator to offer the victim an opportunity to communicate with the offender indirectly either through a letter, written statement, audio

---

[20] Achilles and Zehr (2001); Strang (2002).
[21] Campbell et al (2006); Fercello and Umbreit (1998); McCold and Wachtel (1998); McGarrell et al (2000).
[22] Doak and O'Mahony (2006).
[23] Campbell et al (2006); Shapland et al (2006b), (2007); Wemmers and Canuto (2002).

recording or some form of 'shuttle' mediation. In this way, the mediator or facilitator may attempt to 'feed in' a victim's perspective by informing the offender of the reaction and impact of the offence upon a victim for that particular type of offence.

Alternatively, it may be possible to substitute the actual victim with a 'surrogate' or 'proxy' victim who has previously experienced a similar type of offence. In earlier research into police-led restorative cautioning that we carried out in Northern Ireland, the practice of using surrogate victims was commonplace.[24] The idea evolved from an earlier retail theft initiative which used a panel of volunteer shopkeepers to impress upon young shoplifters the impact of their actions on local businesses and the livelihoods of shopkeepers and their staff. The panel was incorporated into the new restorative cautioning scheme, and panel members were used to represent the views of the victim if the actual shopkeeper was unable to participate. Since many of the cases that were dealt with by the scheme involved shoplifting, it appeared to work well for offenders. It addressed a problem whereby it was difficult to get shopkeepers to attend conferences, especially when the value of the goods was generally low and they had usually been recovered immediately when the young person was apprehended. In that sense, the surrogates brought a victim's perspective into the process and appeared to have had more of an impact on the young people than the facilitator simply reading a letter from a victim or recounting something that the victim had said about the impact of the offence.

Yet the use of surrogates also carries a number of distinct disadvantages over using the actual victim. For instance, the potential for the type of emotionality that Rossner has cited as a key predictor of a successful conference[25] is considerably diminished by the fact that offenders cannot hear the voice of—and do not have to explain themselves to—the real victim at the conference. Using a surrogate also detracts from the restorative goals of conferencing, which seek to facilitate a process of empowerment, dialogue, negotiation and agreement between *all* the parties. From the victim's perspective there are obvious disadvantages too, as victims do not get the opportunity to meet offenders face-to-face, to ask them to explain their actions and, importantly, to attempt to understand the reasons behind the offence. Nor are victims able to negotiate issues like compensation or restitution, and move towards reconciliation—all of which are key to maximising the emotionality of the conferencing process.

Furthermore, there may be a danger that those organising conferences may find it easier to use a panel of surrogates who are easily available, rather than embarking on the more difficult process of encouraging actual victims to become involved in the process. Although there was no evidence of this practice in our own fieldwork in Northern Ireland, this would be counterproductive to achieving the restorative goals of conferencing. As research has consistently confirmed, victim absence impacts on offenders' perceptions of their accountability for their actions, thereby

---

[24] O'Mahony and Doak (2004).
[25] See ch 2, III(B).

undermining the overall restorativeness of the process.[26] This also seems to correlate with the likelihood that the offender will comply with the terms of the agreement; Maxwell and Morris found that restoration was more likely to have been carried out where victims were present in the conference, in cases where victims suffered personal harm.[27] In order to amplify the roles of agency and accountability within the process, the direct involvement of victims is therefore crucial. Obviously, it is much more difficult to instil a sense of agency in circumstances where the victim is not present to participate in the decision-making process. The empowering effect of agency is an essential part of this enabling process whereby the participants play an active part in the dialogue and in decision making, giving them the capacity to make choices and influence decisions in that process. In terms of accountability, the presence and the active participation of the victim may enhance the prospects of 'turning points' being achieved in the encounter, through which a sense of accountability is impressed on the offender.[28] A recent study by Saulnier and Sivasubramaniam confirms how victims can positively enable offenders to engage in meaningful apologies, which are impactful for victims, offenders and their supporters.[29] In this way, victim involvement may help to diminish any self-blaming on the part of the victim and discourage victim blaming on the part of the offender.

The question of victim participation may be difficult to assess in cases which do not involve direct harm or loss to an individual. So-called 'victimless crimes' include financial offences against large companies or corporations, such as frauds and deceptions against financial institutions, utility providers or insurance companies. Regulatory offences, such as supplying alcohol or pharmaceuticals without holding an appropriate licence, and certain drug-related offences are often viewed as victimless in nature, as are criminal damage to public property such as public parks, schools and sites of historical or cultural importance, and a wide range of motoring offences.

However, none of these offences can truly be regarded as 'victimless', since in all cases either the state, the taxpayer, the broader community or a company will ultimately suffer some degree of harm and will bear the cost of putting things right. Any act that is contrary to the criminal law is usually considered harmful and undesirable to society at large. Thus the objective of the 'restorative' process in these types of cases is to (a) make offenders aware of the consequences of their actions and (b) to enable some form of restoration to be made to the relevant victim, be that the state, community or company. In order to achieve this, representatives from corporate bodies may participate in restorative programmes to stress the consequences of such crimes to the company and even the wider community. A representative from an insurance company could, for instance, attend a

---

[26] Hill (2002); Saulnier and Sivasubramaniam (2015b); Shapland et al (2007).
[27] Maxwell and Morris (1993).
[28] See Rosser (2013); ch 2, III(B).
[29] Saulnier and Sivasubramaniam (2015b).

conference to explain how insurance fraud results in higher premiums for all customers. A representative from a local school could attend to explain how dealing with vandalism has meant that the school has been unable to afford to purchase new equipment for the children. Even those who have suffered harm or addiction as a result of drug abuse could explain the impact of using or supplying a particular drug. Alternatively, therapists or clinicians could explain the physical and psychological effects of addiction as well as the impact it has on individuals and their families. Even the impacts of motoring-related offences, such as speeding, drink driving, or careless/dangerous driving, could be explained to the offender by a past victim, paramedic or police officer.

There is, however, some evidence to question the effectiveness of this course of action in terms of impressing a sense of accountability on the offender. Hoyle and Rosenblatt, who compared restorative police cautioning with the operation of young offender panels, found that the practice was often ineffective:

> In comments similar to police cautioning facilitators 15 years ago ... community panel members often said, 'this is how I would feel if it happened to me.' For young offenders these guesses or attempts at victim empathy did not ring true. Neither did they allow the offender to empathize with a victim they had not met nor heard directly from. For example ... community panel members typically used an empty chair in the room as a means of representing the victim throughout the panel meeting. A community panel member reported that once she was explaining the meaning of the chair to a young person—'this empty chair is to remind us of someone that isn't in this room but has also been affected by your behaviour'—the young person giggled dismissively: "Yeah ... right!"[30]

Far from instilling a sense of accountability on the young person, the process outlined here portrays a process that was perceived as inept and absurd by the offender. So, rather than helping offenders relate to the consequences of their actions, such processes might even further belittle or trivialise the impacts of crime on victims. Clearly, the empowering potential of restorative justice can be undercut by well-intentioned, if somewhat whimsical, attempts to reinforce the harmful consequences of offending on others.

Notwithstanding the question over whether restorative processes are appropriate in cases where victims cannot be identified, or are unwilling / unable to attend, we would argue that processes that attempt to include a victim's perspective are still preferable to those which fail to do. However, such attempts need to be thoroughly prepared and carefully configured, so that they are meaningful to the offender, relevant to their circumstances and reflect the gravity of the offence. Ideally this should involve some form of dialogical encounter with someone—preferably someone with training but who is outside the professional circle of stakeholders—who is able to relate a personal story about how similar types of crime has affected himself/herself or family members in the past. As noted in chapter two, this can have added benefits; those with local knowledge and experience can help the

---

[30] Hoyle and Rosenblatt (2016), 39.

offender develop social bonds and identify services and facilities that might aid the process of reintegration.[31] While such a process could be described as 'partially restorative', it cannot routinely be expected to deliver the type of encounter that is capable of delivering a fully empowering and restorative experience for the offender. It can nevertheless provide a tool to help educate the offender on the consequences of crime, including how criminal actions impact victims or the community, by enabling the offender to listen to the account of someone who has been subject to a similar experience in the past.

C. The Experiences of Victims

The agency–accountability framework helps us understand why participation is so important for restorative justice. The capacity to engage effectively in restorative justice and influence the nature of outcomes that focus on re-empowering the participants are essential elements of productive encounters.

In general, victims who meet with offenders are far more likely to be satisfied with how they were treated and also report being less fearful about re-victimisation.[32] Empirical research has consistently shown that both victims and offenders report high levels of satisfaction with restorative mechanisms involving victims. The vast majority of studies to date report high levels of satisfaction among participating victims irrespective of the seriousness of the offence or cultural or geographical variations. Satisfaction rates are higher where comparative research has evaluated the experiences of victims who went through a restorative process compared with those who went through a conventional criminal justice processes. In an international meta-analysis of seven evaluations, Poulson found that restorative justice outperformed court procedures on almost every variable—including judgments of fairness, accountability, increased respect, emotional wellbeing and reductions in fear—for both victims and offenders.[33] Indeed, it is commonplace for studies to report high overall levels of satisfaction among victims, typically between 70–90 per cent.[34] Similarly, Latimer et al's meta-analysis found higher levels of victim satisfaction when compared with control groups in all but one of the 13 programmes examined.[35] Sherman and Strang's meta-analysis of restorative versus non-restorative interventions also led the authors to conclude that the former carried significantly higher levels of satisfaction than the latter and Strang et al found substantial benefits in restorative interventions for victims as well as evidence of improved cost-effectiveness.[36]

---

[31] Rossner and Bruce (2016).
[32] Umbreit et al (1999).
[33] Poulson (2003).
[34] Campbell et al (2006); Latimer et al (2001); Shapland et al (2006a); Trimboli (2000).
[35] Latimer et al (2001).
[36] Sherman and Strang (2007); Strang et al (2013). See also Beven et al (2005); McCold and Wachtel (1998); Umbreit and Coates (1992).

With specific regard to victim-offender mediation, satisfaction rates tend to be lower in the UK schemes compared with their counterparts in North America.[37] One possible explanation suggested by Dignan and Lowey is that a much higher proportion of cases are dealt with by means of indirect or shuttle mediation in Britain, whilst mediation tends to be face-to-face in North America.[38] This implies that victims are less likely to secure symbolic reparation through indirect mediation than they are in cases where they meet their offender face to face. Importantly, indirect mediation is also less likely to be perceived by participants as empowering. However, in a recent overview of the research, Umbreit et al concluded that, taking the findings of all recent studies into account, nine out of ten participants would still recommend a victim-offender mediation programme over no mediation at all.[39]

Differences in degrees of satisfaction between victims of property crime and those of violence has been uncovered as part of the Australian RISE programme. Victims of violent offences appeared to be more satisfied with the process than victims of property offences, though both groups expressed a 'moderately high level of satisfaction regarding procedural justice'.[40] The discrepancy in satisfaction levels between violent and property offences may be partly due to the impact and nature of these different types of crime on victims. The psychological effects of some violent crimes appears to be especially amenable to restorative justice, as having a restorative meeting with the offender may help victims address issues like fear, anxiety and anger. These findings align with our emphasis on agency, whereby the restorative process enables victims to exercise voice within the process and to contribute directly to decision-making.[41]

It would be misleading to present restorative processes as perfect in terms of what they deliver to all victims. Most studies report a minority of victims feeling dissatisfied with the process. Some studies report that victims felt that the process was overly offender-centric;[42] they felt ill-prepared or their expectations were not met.[43] Some felt unable to express themselves fully.[44] Others have reported feeling pressurised into either taking part or accepting an apology[45] and some felt there had been inadequate monitoring and follow up.[46] Some victims can find it difficult to come to terms with the impact of crime and may be particularly vulnerable to overly enthusiastic attempts, by well-meaning organisers, to persuade them to

---

[37] cf. United Kingdom: Dignan (1990); Umbreit and Roberts (1996). North America: Umbreit and Coates (1992); Umbreit and Bradshaw (1999).
[38] Dignan and Lowey (2000) 37.
[39] Umbreit et al (2006).
[40] Sherman et al (1998), 151.
[41] Choi et al (2012).
[42] Pemberton et al (2007); Strang (2002); Zernova (2007).
[43] Campbell et al (2006); Maxwell et al (2004); Umbreit (1995).
[44] Coates and Gehm (1989); Morris et al (1993); Umbreit (1995).
[45] Bazemore and Schiff (2005); Choi et al (2010); Kingi et al (2008); McCold and Wachtel (1998); Morris and Maxwell (1998).
[46] Coates and Gehm (1989); Shapland et al (2007).

meet the offender, especially if they are not ready to do so. Although it is a widely accepted principle of good practice that restorative processes must be entered into voluntarily, some studies report that a small number of victims felt that they had been pressurised into participating in the process.[47] Wemmers and Canuto found that attempts to bring the victim and offender together, when the victim's emotions are dominated by fear and anger, may actually exacerbate their suffering.[48] They proposed providing victims with more relevant information regarding the purpose of restorative justice programmes, particularly where serious crime is concerned, thus allowing them to make a more informed decision to participate, if and when they feel ready.

The risks of coercion run counter to the ethos of empowerment theory, and push against the restorative goals of agency and accountability which seek to provide victims with choice and give them opportunities to participate in decisions that impact them, rather than imposing processes and outcomes. As Walgrave argues, the use of any form of coercion or pressure would ultimately mean that restorative justice will never constitute anything other than a peripheral approach responding to crime.[49] It is thus vital that the principle of voluntariness should be properly applied on each and every occasion, and victims should never be coerced to meet an offender against their wishes.

As part of the preparatory process, expectations of both victims and offenders must be carefully managed; Ashworth has warned of the possibility that the victim may be instrumentalised as an 'agent of offender rehabilitation' as opposed to having their discrete interests properly discerned and addressed.[50] As such, the victim should receive full and accurate information as regards the purpose of the process, its voluntary nature, how it will be conducted and organised, and the types of outcomes that can be expected.[51] The organiser should ensure that the victim is open to the concept of restorative justice and that the victim is aware that the meeting will have the potential to become emotionally charged. Similarly, steps should be taken to ensure that the reparatory expectations of the victim are realistic; few offenders, especially young offenders, have sufficient means to offer any substantial monetary compensation, and—as noted above—a promise of 'closure' or 'healing' is far from guaranteed. Even issues such as expectations of an apology or expression of remorse must be handled sensitively; raising expectations on this front could be viewed as a form of inducement—particularly in cases of domestic violence where some abused partners may long to be reunited with their abuser.[52] For their part, offenders should also be carefully screened to ensure that they are

---

[47] Bazemore and Schiff (2005); Choi et al (2010); Kingi et al (2008); McCold and Wachtel (1998); Morris and Maxwell (1998).
[48] Wemmers and Canuto (2002).
[49] Walgrave (2007).
[50] Ashworth (2000), 199.
[51] Johnstone (2011); McCold (2000).
[52] Stubbs (2007).

prepared to take responsibility for their actions without engaging in tactics of denial or victim blaming.[53]

Ensuring that victims are properly informed before they participate in restorative encounters is crucial to delivering the agency–accountability framework, which emphasises giving individuals the ability to make informed choices that help them become active and productive in decision making. To ensure that the expectations of the victims are met, some form of initial assessment should take place to ensure that offenders genuinely accept responsibility for their actions, and have not simply taken what they perceive to be an easy alternative to being dealt with by a court.[54] If an offender fails to appear at the meeting, does not genuinely accept responsibility for the offence, fails to express remorse or makes an attempt to physically or verbally intimidate the victim, the distress caused to the victim is likely to be considerably exacerbated. While such findings raise legitimate concern about the appropriateness of restorative disposals for such cases, many of these issues can be addressed through comprehensive preparation, rigorous facilitator training and regular monitoring and evaluation.[55] Care must be taken to ensure that service providers make information on what is likely to happen at the restorative encounter and the types of outcomes that the parties might realistically expect readily available. With thorough preparation and support, victims can be enabled to make an informed decision as to whether restorative justice is the right option in their particular circumstances.[56] Moreover, such preparation has a vital role to play in facilitating agency and accountability within the process.

i. Restoration and Apology

Findings from research examining how conferences are delivered reveal that satisfaction levels are mostly high in relation to agreed outcomes.[57] Interestingly, however, levels of satisfaction appear to correlate with the extent of the victim's participation.[58] It is therefore not surprising that programmes with low levels of participation result in little or no reparation being made directly to the victim, and thus have lower levels of victim satisfaction.[59]

Even if victims do not get any financial reparation from the restorative event, the empowering potential of accountability shows how a sincere admission of responsibility and remorse by the offender—often accompanied by an apology—is one of the most important parts of being acknowledged as a victim and helps the healing process by defusing feelings of anger or vengeance.[60] As noted in chapter two,

---

[53] Gal (2011), 150; Stubbs (2007).
[54] Hoyle et al (2002); O'Mahony and Doak (2004).
[55] Wood and Suzuki (2016); Zinsstag (2012).
[56] Kilty (2010).
[57] Beven et al (2005); Campbell et al (2006); Maxwell et al (2004); Shapland et al (2006a); Strang et al (2013); Trimboli (2000).
[58] Shapland et al (2007).
[59] Crawford and Newburn (2003).
[60] Bennett and Earwaker (1994); Dhami (2012); Umbreit (1994); Strang et al (2013).

apologies may act as a catalyst for emotional 'turning points' in the conference, and are often associated with defusing feelings of anger or vengeance.[61] However, it is relatively easy for an offender to utter an expression of remorse without actually meaning it. To be effective, an apology must convey to the victim the offender's sense of shame,[62] and to that end it is vital that any apology is perceived to be authentic by the participants.[63] Empirical data are somewhat mixed on this point, with some studies indicating a high level of sincerity perceived by victims,[64] whilst others suggest that victims can be suspicious of offenders' motives.[65] In Daly's evaluation of youth conferencing of South Australia, it was reported that while just under a third of victims perceived the apologies that offenders gave to be genuine, almost twice that proportion felt that the apologies were insincere.[66]

Apologies are deemed to be most effective when delivered in a face-to-face setting, as opposed to through indirect means, such as shuttle mediation, reading a letter, relaying a message to the offender or using 'surrogate' victims.[67] While these kinds of actions may be useful tools for providers to boost victim participation rates, they are also associated with a number of drawbacks. First, not providing a face-to-face meeting between the victim and offender can leave participants uncertain about the point of the process. Shapland et al found that participants were unsure whether something further was supposed to happen after indirect mediation or whether the case was then closed.[68] Overall, the researchers found evidence that direct mediation between the parties created more satisfaction than indirect mediation. Secondly, and perhaps more significantly, where channels for emotional communication are limited there is a risk that apologies may lose a degree of moral force. Victims will not be afforded with the opportunity to assess facial expressions, gestures and physical posture.[69] Research has illustrated a positive relationship between visible indicators of remorse and the acceptance of an apology by victims.[70] So, a failure to meet in person is likely to undermine the emotionality of the encounter; there is likely to be a much reduced sense of shared experience, and no real opportunity for a new co-narrative to be constructed. This lack of inter-connectedness between the victim and offender is likely to further exacerbate the problem of victims perceiving apologies as insincere.

The sincerity and impact of the apology will also be influenced by the nature of the underlying relationship between victim and offender and the nature of the harm in question. Such case-specific factors are likely to be pivotal in terms

[61] See ch 2, III(B).
[62] Lazare (2004).
[63] Morris and Maxwell (1998); Schneider (2000).
[64] Strang (2002).
[65] Campbell et al (2006); Hoyle et al (2002); Sherman et al (2005).
[66] Daly (2002), 70.
[67] Petrucci (2002); Scheff (1998); Shapland et al (2007).
[68] Shapland et al (2007).
[69] Retzinger and Scheff (1996).
[70] Ohbuchi and Sato (1994).

of how apologies are perceived. Rossner has indicated that encounters are prone to becoming stratified according to power and class differentials,[71] and others have cautioned how apologies may be used in 'gendered' ways, enabling stronger parties—such as perpetrators of domestic violence—to use insincere apologies as instruments to lever victims to return to their abusers.[72] Vulnerable parties may thus fall to cultural and social pressure to accept an apology,[73] since 'inequality and power do not disappear simply because of a change in the legal forum'.[74] In many cases, such parties will have been involved in a long-standing and complex relationship, wherein the perpetrator will have exercised an abusive and controlling power over the victim for a period of time resulting in multiple forms of psychological, sexual and/or physical violence.[75] The paramount need for victim safety is considered in greater detail below.[76]

While apologies—in whatever context—are clearly desirable, our conception of agency requires that offenders should not be prompted to apologise against their will, and by the same token victims should not be placed under an expectation to forgive. Forgiveness may (or may not) follow immediately, or in the weeks or months following the encounter.[77] Instead, as Braithwaite contends, expressions of apology, forgiveness and mercy should be viewed as 'gifts' which only carry meaning 'if they well up from a genuine desire in the person who forgives, apologises or grants mercy'.[78] Irrespective of whether forgiveness is offered or not,[79] apologies—and indeed the restorative process in general—empower victims and enable them to begin to recover from the negative impacts of crime, particularly when they are perceived as genuine. Notably, a number of studies have reported a reduction in anger following the restorative encounter,[80] and victims participating in restorative programmes have reported being less fearful of being revictimised by the offender when compared with court-based samples.[81] In their evaluation of the Thames Valley initiative, Hoyle et al reported that two-thirds of victims found

---

[71] Rossner (2008).
[72] Hooper and Busch (1996); Miller (2011); Stubbs (2007).
[73] Bennett and Earwaker (1994).
[74] Cunneen (2010), 161.
[75] Hopkins et al (2004).
[76] See I(D).
[77] Unlike apologies which can be recorded and observed by empirical testing, forgiveness is not so easily assessed. Often studies are not clear regarding what indicators are used to measure it, whilst others tend to shy away from measuring it altogether. Of the data we do have, Shapland et al (2006a) note that express statements of forgiveness were extremely rare, with many victims instead implying a degree of acceptance of the apology through symbolic gestures. Strang et al (1999) observed forgiveness to occur in 42% of cases involving juvenile personal property crime, 43% of cases of drink driving, and 50% of cases of youth violence dealt with by conferencing. In New Zealand, Maxwell et al (2004) report that just over half of the young people agreed with the statement that there was some sense of forgiveness in the family group conference and three-quarters reported that the others involved had made it possible for them to put things behind them. In Northern Ireland, Campbell et al (2006) found that 82% of victims expressed 'some level of forgiveness' in follow-up interviews.
[78] Braithwaite (2002a), 571, as cited by Stubbs (2007), 177.
[79] See further Dzur and Wertheimer (2002); Miller (2011); Retzinger and Scheff (1996).
[80] Daly (2001); Strang et al (2006); Doak and O'Mahony (2006).
[81] Umbreit (1994).

the restorative encounter had positively influenced their perceptions of offenders and the vast majority found it helpful in coming to terms with the offence.[82] While such findings lend support to claims that restorative justice may carry a range of psychological benefits for victims,[83] it is important to heed Angel's warning that issues of emotional and psychological wellbeing are often conflated in the literature with more general inquiries as to overall levels of satisfaction.[84]

Empirical evaluations to date have made limited examination into the mental health issues of participating victims. One exception is Daly's analysis of the South Australian juvenile conferencing data, in which she devised a distress measure categorising victims according to the effects of crime.[85] Over a quarter (28 per cent) suffered no distress; 12.5 per cent were rated as low distress; over one third (36 per cent) were considered to have moderate distress; with 23 per cent suffering high distress. It was a matter of some concern that this latter group comprised mostly female victims, victims of personal crime, victims of violence and victims who were well known to their offender. Theft and property offences were generally found to cause less distress. When interviewed one year after the offence, 71 per cent of the 'high distress' victims had not completely recovered from the effects of the offence. This compared with 63 per cent of the 'moderate distress' victims, 78 per cent of the 'low' distress victims and 95 per cent of the 'no distress' victims. More positive findings were recently reported by Angel et al,[86] who found that post-traumatic stress symptoms experienced by burglary and robbery victims were significantly lower among those who had participated in restorative justice vis-à-vis those who had experienced the conventional criminal process. Most victims experienced significantly reduced levels of stress both immediately following a restorative conference and six months later.

However, these data also suggest that restorative interventions do not necessarily assist victims of some of the more serious offences, even when accompanied by the passage of time. While this evidence suggests that therapeutic benefits are more keenly felt by victims of less serious and property-based offences, Daly's findings may have been influenced by the complex nature of interpersonal violence between intimates, influenced by their ongoing difficult relationships, rather than being the result of the restorative intervention or the type of violent crime. Indeed, there is emerging evidence that restorative interventions can be beneficial to victims who have experienced some very serious offences, particularly when they provide additional opportunities to meet some of their psychological needs.[87] However, there is a pressing need for larger-scale longitudinal research to ascertain the true potential of restorative justice to address the psychological needs of victims.

---

[82] Hoyle et al (2002).
[83] Doak (2011); Schopp (1998); Sherman and Strang (2007).
[84] Angel (2005).
[85] Daly (2004).
[86] Angel et al (2014).
[87] See eg McGlynn et al (2012); Miller (2011); Walker (2015).

Key emotional benefits of restorative interventions include a reduced fear of the offender; a feeling that the offender was 'held to account'; a reduction in feelings of anger; and a sense of closure through acquiring an understanding that the offender has accepted responsibility by apologising or undertaking some form of reparation. There is also some evidence to suggest that restorative justice may help to assuage levels of distress or trauma. It is generally accepted that many victims will find the experience especially positive where they are given opportunities to participate. Levels of satisfaction and the other benefits for victims, such as reductions in feelings of fear, underline the centrality of agency and accountability in the process of delivering successful restorative interventions. In this sense, individual findings relating to aspects of the processes and outcomes can be taken as indicators of its empowering potential.

D. Safety as a Prerequisite for Delivering Agency and Accountability

Although we have argued that many of the risks of restorative justice might be countered by enhancing practice—for example, through more rigorous preparation, training, monitoring and evaluation—careful consideration is also needed on the question of victim safety. As noted above, where the process allows for power imbalances to remain unchecked, the victim may be at risk from further violence or abusive behaviour.[88] The safety of all parties is a prerequisite to providing a secure setting in which agency and accountability can be exercised; and in cases where this cannot be achieved restorative disposals will not be appropriate. For example, fears have been expressed about the impact that power imbalances may play within the meeting—particularly where a victim is young or otherwise vulnerable.

One criticism of restorative justice theory is that, in conceptualising the offence as primarily a private conflict between victim and offender, it 'fails to engage with questions of structural disadvantage and with race, class and gendered patterns of crime'.[89] This has led some commentators to question the capacity of restorative justice to deal with conflicts involving domestic and sexual violence; here the intervention is often not used to address the consequences of a one-off incident. While perpetrators may well accept responsibility for their actions within the confines of a restorative meeting, it has been contended that this is insufficient to deal with such offenders.[90] It has been suggested, for example, that reforms aimed at empowering victims of sexual and domestic violence should instead focus on reform of the conventional legal system—for example, through the use of specialist courts—to ensure adequate protection of the victim and exposure of the

---

[88] Hoyle (2010), 78.
[89] Stubbs (2007), 171.
[90] Daly and Stubbs (2006).

offender.[91] Yet the ability of the criminal justice system to address the harms of sexual offences has led others to suggest that sexual offences should be removed from the criminal justice system entirely and dealt with through welfare service provision.[92]

The New Zealand Law Commission has been exploring the use of restorative approaches as potential alternative responses to sexual offending,[93] and has recommended their adoption in certain cases where the victim expresses a desire to follow this route. There are also plans to develop wrap-around support provisions for victims of sexual offending throughout their time in the justice system in order to promote a better recovery process based around Herman's model on the victim's response to trauma.[94] Although such developments may enable restorative justice practitioners and professionals to help some victims of sexual violence more effectively,[95] it must also be recognised that this is a highly complex task and many victims of sexual violence may not want to participate in a restorative paradigm in their pursuit for justice.[96]

While some authors have articulated concerns relating to the lack of public denunciation, it could also be argued that restorative justice increases the safety of vulnerable victims by 'opening up ... knowledge and awareness on the part of the community', and thereby involving the friends and families of offenders in addressing the cause of the harm that might otherwise be neglected by the criminal justice system.[97] In this sense, restorative justice seeks to hold the offender to account in ways that conventional court processes are unable to do and thus may also support future desistance.[98] Moreover, from a victim's perspective, restorative justice could offer such victims a degree of agency and accountability that service-provision or specialist criminal courts are unable to provide. Just as power imbalances pose a risk to the process, it can be countered that the nature of restorative mechanisms mean that they have the potential to address such imbalances through re-empowering the victim and holding the offender to account. In many cases, victims may be unwilling to testify in criminal proceedings, which could mean that prosecutions do not proceed. While a self-standing restorative conference positioned outside the formal system may be imperfect and controversial, it may offer an alternative to 'no further action'.[99]

A further advantage offered by conceptualising restorative justice through our agency–accountability framework is that this lens allows us to identify and highlight these kinds of risks and achieve a clearer understanding of what restorative

---

[91] Cossins (2008).
[92] Seidman and Vickers (2005).
[93] New Zealand Law Commission (2015).
[94] Herman (1997).
[95] Julich and Bowen (2015).
[96] Julich (2006).
[97] McAlinden (2005), 305.
[98] Hudson (2002). See further ch 7.
[99] Hoyle (2010), 80.

justice can achieve. An absolute bar on the use of restorative justice based on the nature of the offence alone would be an extremely arbitrary step; to do so could diminish the agency of individual victims to exercise their voice and confront the offender, and similarly limit their accountability to hold the offender to account for their actions. The strength of victims in this regard should not be underestimated,[100] and facilitators for sensitive cases need to be aware of the heightened risks involved in these types of cases and be equipped to provide the additional level of support needed before, during and after such conferences.[101]

II. Offenders and Restorative Justice

Although restorative justice is often characterised as victim-centred, offenders have a vital role to play and potentially they too have much to gain. The notion of crime as a violation of a relationship informs the restorative conception of how offenders should be dealt with. In contrast to the orthodox notion that offenders ought to receive their 'just deserts' for a particular act, advocates of restorative justice tend to view these actions in the wider context of fracturing relations between the victim, offender, and broader community. 'Just deserts' and other orthodox justifications for punishment should thus 'give way to the goal of reinstating them to a position of being … members of the community'.[102] In this way, the restorative process provides a mechanism by which offenders can appreciate how their actions have affected the victim and other people, such as their family and the broader community. In providing an apparatus for dialogue, victims and offenders are both able to participate in the process to determine how to best respond to the crime, and may reap benefits from an agreement that enables all parties to move on with their lives.

Restorative programmes also confer direct benefits on offenders in that they provide a means by which a line may be drawn under the offence and offenders can be accepted as full members of the community. The causes of offending behaviour will generally be probed and ways to prevent future reoffending will be considered in any restorative forum. The outcomes should not only entail some form of reparation to the victim, but may also seek to provide some form of support for the offender. This may involve, for example, family counselling, mentoring, victim awareness sessions, anger management and/or drugs/alcohol addiction programmes.

Just as restorative justice seeks to boost opportunities for participation of victims, it also provides a means to amplify the voice of the offender. As outlined in chapter two, offenders in the orthodox court process tend to communicate

---

[100] McGlynn et al (2012).
[101] McGlynn et al (2012).
[102] Johnstone (2013), 56.

solely through legal counsel, except when giving evidence.[103] Whilst they may play a more proactive part in sentencing proceedings, it remains the case that their role is largely confined to answering questions put to them by the judge or by counsel. By contrast, in restorative settings, offenders are offered a deliberative channel of communication in the sense that they will be asked to explain in their own words the factors that contributed to their offending behaviour, and how it might be prevented in the future. Like victims, they too should achieve an enhanced sense of agency through having the opportunity to ask questions and respond to them in their own words. Accountability is also reinforced through offenders being asked to explain their actions, being offered new insights into the human consequences of their actions,[104] and having the opportunity to rectify the harm they have caused.

A. The Experiences of Offenders

As with victims, there is strong evidence from research to suggest that offenders are usually more satisfied with their experience of the restorative process than with the conventional criminal process.[105] For example, Shapland et al found that offenders who went through the restorative process were considerably more satisfied with the process than those who underwent traditional criminal justice disposals.[106] It is also clear that restorative encounters provide offenders with the opportunity to apologise much more readily than court-based processes,[107] with the latter offering no formal channel for dialogue between the victim and the offender. In a revealing meta-study of seven restorative justice programs, Poulson found that whilst almost three-quarters (74 per cent) of offenders apologised in restorative justice settings, around the same proportion (71 per cent) of offenders who went through the court process did *not* apologise.[108]

Much of the literature, similar to the victim-focused research, emphasises the importance of offender participation in restorative processes and outcomes, so that they feel able to actively engage and be part of the positive dynamic of the restorative interaction. For the most part, findings have been broadly positive. This underlines the importance of providing an environment that offers offenders the capacity to make choices and to be actively involved in taking responsibility for their actions. As such, restorative processes should seek to maximise a sense of agency through the active participation and involvement of offenders in the decision-making process. Likewise, accountability is delivered when the offender assumes responsibility, apologises and offers reparation to deal with some of the

---

[103] Morris and Young (2000).
[104] Hudson (2003).
[105] Beven et al (2005); Latimer et al (2005); Nugent et al (2003).
[106] Shapland et al (2007).
[107] Sherman et al (2005); Strang (2002).
[108] Poulson (2003).

harm. Together, these empowering values underline the need to transform the negative consequences of crime and criminal justice from isolation, silence and powerlessness, into support, shared healing and re-engagement.

B. The Rights of the Offender

While the research evidence identifies some challenges to ensuring that agency and accountability remain central to restorative justice processes for offenders, the overall findings are largely positive in relation to their experiences. However, these positive findings alone are not sufficient to provide a normative justification for restorative justice. Some concerns have been raised, for instance in seeking to maximise the agency of victims and offenders and minimise the involvement of lawyers and legal procedures, the due process rights of the offender may be put at risk as a by-product of the restorative process.

Although the belief that fundamental human rights—including due process—should be respected in restorative practices is 'near universal' among proponents of restorative justice,[109] there is a concern that restorative justice may potentially 'trample rights because of impoverished articulation of procedural safeguards'.[110] While the less formal processes of restorative justice appear to sit uneasily with the legalism that underpins due process and fair trial rights,[111] certain provisions of international children's rights instruments advocate the informal resolution of cases.[112] Indeed, the European Court of Human Rights has recognised that while the prospect of appearing in court can create a willingness to compromise, options to forgo court processes do not breach the right to a fair trial under Article 6 provided that the pressure to participate in restorative justice is not compelling and that the provisions of Article 7 are respected (viz, the right of persons not to receive sanction for conduct not amounting to an offence nor to receive harsher sanction than that applicable at the time of the offence).[113] Yet, by the same token, it is not particularly difficult to imagine how such rights might be breached where restorative justice is not properly conducted. In particular, two concerns are commonly raised: first, that restorative processes may result in pressure to plead guilty, participate in the process or agree to the conference plan; and, second, that restorative justice outcomes may result in the imposition of disproportionate or inconsistent penalties.

---

[109] Braithwaite (1999), (2002b).
[110] Braithwaite (1999), 101.
[111] Muncie (2005).
[112] For instance, Art 40 of the UN Convention on the Rights of the Child provides for children in conflict with law to divert away from formal and judicial proceedings where possible, but in doing so the rights and safeguards of the child need to be respected.
[113] *Håkansson and Sturesson v Sweden* (1990) 13 EHRR 1.

As far as coercion is concerned, the UN Basic Principles on Use of Restorative Justice Programmes require that these 'should be used only with the free and voluntary consent of the parties'.[114] As such, the majority of restorative schemes require that the offender fully consents to taking part in the process.[115] The offender's decision should be informed, with a full awareness of all the options available. However, in practice and given that the alternative is often sentencing by a court whose sanctions may be perceived as potentially more punitive, a young person may feel there is little choice. Cunneen highlights the dangers of obtaining consent in circumstances where the offender has had no independent legal advice and faces a police investigation which may make use of 'coercive tactics designed to force an offender to admit an offence', where the offender may wish to obtain the benefit of a diversionary alternative to court and the avoidance of a criminal record.[116]

Research evidence indicates that such risks must be taken seriously. For example, in New South Wales, a small-scale qualitative study of young people's experiences of the justice system questioned whether informed consent was always exercised when they were referred to a conference. Two-thirds of participants said they were either not told, or were unsure whether they had been told, that they had a right to legal advice.[117] In England and Wales, solicitors have been excluded from acting in Youth Offender Panel meetings on the grounds that the presence of a solicitor may prevent the young person from becoming fully involved in the process. However, Crawford and Newburn note that this could potentially lead to challenges under Article 6 of the European Convention on Human Rights.[118] Moreover, given the complexity of the justice process and legal questions of establishing guilt, it is clear that conferencing is not an appropriate forum to deal with questions of unresolved criminal responsibility.[119] As such, where there is any doubt about the offender having committed the offence in question, the restorative process should not be used as an avenue for disposal of the case.

Within the conference itself, practitioners must ensure that offenders, and especially young people, have the opportunity to be heard in proceedings affecting them and to be allowed to express their views freely. Problems may arise in a conference scenario if the negotiation process of a plan proves to be undemocratic. Young people, especially, may feel that they have no leverage and are 'obligated' to agree to suggestions put forward, regardless of their willingness or suitability given the pressure that may be created by a room full of adults.[120] This heightens the risk that key decisions are being taken by the professional in the room (for example, the coordinator or police), rather than through dialogue and consent among

---

[114] The UN Basic Principles on Use of Restorative Justice Programmes, Principle 7.
[115] Some, such as Young Offender Panels in England and Wales, do not. See ch 5, IV.
[116] Cunneen (2010), 146.
[117] Turner (2002).
[118] Crawford and Newburn (2003).
[119] Daly (2006).
[120] Haines and O'Mahony (2006).

the stakeholders themselves.[121] While acknowledging the progressive principles of the system, and that research shows that restorative processes are generally preferred over court, there is clearly an ongoing need for continued checks on participatory rights, especially for children.[122] Indeed, as Hopkins suggests, one means of doing this is through the extension of access to legal representation especially at the pre-court stage.[123]

The risks of coercion can be partly offset through active monitoring by the court. As Roche contends, ongoing oversight with the possibility that a case might be re-routed to court can act both as an incentive to participate and an 'escape route' where there is too much pressure or domination directed towards the offender.[124] Judicial oversight may also act as a safeguard in relation to a second prominent concern noted in chapter two, namely that restorative justice endangers proportionate and consistent outcomes. Specifically, critics warn that proportionality may be compromised in restorative practices where the victim, whose reaction to the offence will inevitably differ from case to case, has an unpredictable input into what happens to the offender.[125] Maxwell and Morris reported some evidence of disproportionate outcomes in New Zealand; noting that on a number of occasions the end result appeared to 'outweigh the gravity of the offence'.[126] In addition, research has revealed that plans can be burdened with restrictive elements, which are not always necessary for public safety, or in accordance with the aims of the New Zealand legislation.[127] Similarly, in relation to Referral Orders in England and Wales, it was noted that substitution effects in terms of traditional court orders occurred at relatively lower levels, thus displacing disposals such as the conditional discharge and fine, suggesting a danger of up-tariffing and net-widening.[128]

Our own research in relation to police-led restorative cautioning in Northern Ireland revealed similar concerns.[129] In particular, it was apparent that the well-meaning enthusiasm among some police officers to utilise the scheme resulted in some interventions being made on an arbitrary basis and allocated with a focus on 'welfare' rather than 'desert' grounds.[130] Potentially, if a conference is viewed as more 'beneficial' to an offender, other low-tariff disposals such as cautions or informal warnings may be bypassed. In such circumstances this could lead to a more intensive intervention than the offender would otherwise have received;[131]

---

[121] Maxwell et al (2004).
[122] Lynch (2008).
[123] Hopkins (2015) notes how children have access to free specialised legal representatives or 'Youth Advocates' when appearing before the courts; however, such free representation is not available at the pre-court stages, before children are brought before the courts.
[124] Roche (2003), 86.
[125] Ashworth (1993), (2000); Von Hirsch et al (2003).
[126] Maxwell and Morris (1993), 96.
[127] Maxwell et al (2004).
[128] Newburn et al (2002).
[129] O'Mahony and Doak (2004).
[130] O'Mahony and Doak (2004).
[131] Roche (2003).

thereby the process itself could be viewed, not as an alternative *to* punishment, but an 'alternative punishment'.[132]

In order to counter disproportionate sentences, Ashworth has suggested that upper limits should be established and 'decided by reference to publicly debatable and democratically determined policies that show respect for the human rights of victims and defendants'.[133] Most proponents of restorative justice support the view that outcomes should never be in excess of punishments enforced by the courts for the same offence.[134] However research largely rejects the notion of a 'vengeful victim' and suggests that victims are no more punitive than non-victims.[135] Indeed, studies have reported that victims prioritise involvement in the process over involvement in deciding the outcome.[136] This is particularly important in a restorative context, where the victim may be less likely to demand a punitive outcome after meeting the offender face-to-face and learning more about the offender.[137] The importance of reaching proportionate outcomes aligns with the 'integrated restorative justice' model proposed by Cavadino and Dignan, whereby 'retributive maximum' and 'retributive minimum' standards should be applied to conference agreements as a whole through judicial oversight, in order to strike a balance between the private interests and those of the wider community.

For the most part, proponents of restorative justice have not adequately engaged with the challenges relating to rights-based issues. Using empowerment theory as a construct for understanding how restorative justice should be delivered, the core values of agency and accountability can help safeguard the rights of offenders. Take, for instance, the principle of voluntariness, which is widely accepted as being a core right for all participants. As noted above, voluntariness can be compromised in situations where offenders feel they have little viable choice. The agency–accountability framework reinforces these rights; it requires the free and open consent of participants to achieve their goals of facilitating and enabling an interaction process that leads to offenders being willing to make themselves accountable and take active responsibility for the consequences of their actions. These same empowering values help us recognise the difficulties associated with the adversarial and punitive nature of orthodox criminal justice practices. Thus, providing an agency–accountability framework for a rights-based approach to restorative justice can encourage offenders to positively engage, take responsibility, make amends and ultimately reintegrate back into society. Similarly, we have noted that power imbalances may pose a threat to the rights of both victims and offenders in restorative conferences. Yet, if we seek to maximise the

---

[132] Daly (2000).
[133] Ashworth (2001), 359.
[134] Braithwaite (2002b).
[135] Hough and Park (2002); Maruna and King (2004); Mayhew and Van Kesteren (2002).
[136] Doak and O'Mahony (2006); Strang (2002).
[137] Doak and O'Mahony (2006).

agency of participants, organisers must engage in rigorous and thoughtful preparation in advance of conferences, drawing on the knowledge of experts in high-risk cases involving vulnerable victims or offenders. Empowerment theory not only recognises such imbalances, it is framed around addressing them and providing a process in which all participants are actively enabled. Again, our agency–accountability framework can help sharpen the goals and practice of restorative justice by articulating underlying objectives which connect to their processes and outcomes. In this way, the values of agency and accountability foster the capacity for choice and engagement in decision making and ensure praxis aligns with the demands of a rights-based framework.

III. Conclusions

This chapter has drawn on a range of empirical studies to better understand the roles and experiences of victims and offenders within restorative justice and how these connect with our agency–accountability framework. Empowerment theory can support the development of a more fundamental understanding of restorative justice within criminal justice and so help shape practice to be better delivered, providing more positive impacts for victims and offenders. In particular, we have sought to demonstrate how agency and accountability can be used to identify and manage the difficulties and conflicts that obstruct effective restorative interventions.

Victims often value the opportunity to meet the offender, with their primary motivation often being to have their questions answered, rather than seeking vengeance or retribution. The overwhelming body of research suggests that most victims who participate in restorative justice programmes are satisfied with the experience, particularly where they feel they have achieved a sense of empowerment and have been able to positively contribute to the restorative dynamic. However, it is also clear that the impact of crime can vary considerably from one individual to another, and victims have a diverse range of needs that have to be addressed before, during and after a conference. Thus both processes and outcomes have to be appropriately tailored to take into consideration the individual needs and characteristics of victims and offenders. These findings directly connect with the thrust of empowerment theory, which emphasises the importance of identifying and understanding how individuals have been disadvantaged, which can help inform strategies that build their capacity to regain their sense of control and empowerment. In this way, the agency–accountability framework can help direct effective restorative practice, ensuring that that participation is fully voluntary, that victims are given proper information and that their expectations are managed appropriately.

For offenders, the chapter highlights their involvement in restorative processes, in terms of what they bring to it and what they get from it. It is widely recognised that many of the goals and values that underpin restorative justice apply to victims and offenders alike. These include the need to provide a process that is characterised by the respectful treatment of all parties; the need to be able to participate in the process and be empowered by it; the ability to provide a flexible and responsive process that meets the needs of all of the participants, yet which provides safety for all; and the need for consensus amongst the participants, so that agreements are genuine, likely to be achieved and are productive and useful to individuals.

As with victims, many of the evaluations of restorative interventions worldwide indicate that offenders are generally satisfied with their experiences of restorative processes. Particularly in relation to young offenders, restorative justice places considerable importance on the role of the young person's family in achieving overall satisfaction within the process. Yet the process of participation for offenders goes beyond simply having to speak: it needs to be an active process that involves them in dialogue, holding offenders to account and engaging them in discussions and decision making, so that there is clear ownership of the dispute by all the parties. Again, the agency–accountability framework provides a clearer rationale to *why* a sense of ownership to participants is of such importance, as they seek to re-empower and facilitate all participants to become active, productive and capable through the restorative encounter.

Careful attention must be paid to potential breaches of offenders' rights as a by-product of the restorative process; particularly where these relate to issues of consent and the right to a fair hearing. Similarly, proportionality needs to be ensured in restorative practices where the victim has an input into the process and power imbalances need to be considered, so offenders are able to properly engage in the process. However, we contend that focusing on the goals of agency and accountability can help guide effective practice by highlighting these types of problems, geared around the goals of empowerment and the risks of disempowerment. In this sense, it provides a valuable framework to understand the negative impacts of orthodox criminal justice, and the potential of restorative justice.

5

Restorative Practices at the Periphery of Criminal Justice

I. Introduction

Having explored the evolution of restorative justice theory and considered the roles and experiences of victim and offenders alongside our argument for reconceiving restorative justice through the lens of empowerment theory, the following three chapters reflect on the extent to which agency and accountability are realised in practice. The purpose here is not to catalogue the full range of programmes that operate globally; such a task would involve an exhaustive and encyclopaedic effort well beyond the remit of this book. Rather, we seek to give a flavour of the main ways in which restorative justice operates in criminal justice systems across the United Kingdom, Europe, North America and Australasia. As noted in chapter one, these jurisdictions have been selected because they offer the most widely documented and evaluated programmes with a defined relationship to existing criminal justice structures. Despite a number of differences—most notably, perhaps, the difference between common law and civil law procedural traditions—they broadly share similar social, economic and cultural characteristics.

In this chapter we identify a range of mechanisms which can be regarded as being on the 'periphery' of the criminal justice system; most of these we class as 'restorative practices' rather than true 'restorative justice' programmes. This is not intended to be in any way a derogatory categorisation. In many cases, they represent innovative and empowering forms of alternative justice which are an improvement on the status quo. However, as most currently stand they have not yet realised their full potential to deliver a vision of restorative justice which embeds agency and accountability at the heart of its delivery. The programmes discussed in this chapter adopt a range of techniques and practices which use the language of restorative justice. Where they fail to fully bear this out in practice, impediments include deficiencies of practice, a lack of a legislative basis, the fact they are or have been experimental in nature, and that they have been designed to deal with specified classes of offenders or specified types of offences.

We begin by looking at the rise of so-called 'bottom up' programmes, which have often been founded, developed and run by civil society organisations. Some of these evolved from pre-existing indigenous justice schemes, while others spawned from dissatisfaction with, or disengagement from, formal criminal justice systems. We then explore the rise of restorative policing initiatives, which spread rapidly following their introduction in Australia in the early 1990s. For the most part, these were diversionary in character, and we question the extent to which they might properly be labelled as 'restorative justice' programmes given the relatively low participation rates of victims and the limited extent to which they are capable of 'undoing' harm. Our attention then turns to the operation of panels as diversionary mechanisms for young offenders, focusing in particular on Young Offender Panels in England and Wales. Finally, we explore a number of schemes aimed at adult offenders which have been somewhat slower to develop than their juvenile counterparts. Here we draw on examples from England and Wales, New Zealand, Belgium and North America. For the most part, these operate at the post-conviction stage of the criminal process and many take place within the confines of prison. Throughout our analysis of these restorative programmes we consider how they reflect our agency–accountability framework in their practice.

II. Community-based Programmes

Since the concept of 'community' plays such a dominant role within restorative justice theory, it is perhaps unsurprising that civil society has played a prominent role in the development of many restorative programmes. Many 'bottom up' initiatives began entirely independently of the criminal justice system, sometimes owing to a communal sense that conventional criminal justice processes and institutions were incapable of satisfactorily resolving conflicts and offending within their particular communities. Many such schemes have, over time, forged more formalised relationships with criminal justice agencies or have been co-opted by the state as a tool to deal with offending within such settings.

Many community-based programmes, particularly those outside Europe, have roots in indigenous forms of justice. In recent years, the literature has expanded considerably to give new insights into practices which before now were not commonly understood in the West. There is a relatively large body of literature which provides insights into the use of sentencing circles among the Native Americans and First Nations people of what now constitutes Canada and the United State,[1] and aboriginal forms of restorative justice in Australia[2] and among the Maori of New Zealand.[3] Although there is little evaluative evidence, excellent accounts

---

[1] Yazzie (1998); Yazzie and Zion (1996).
[2] Blagg (1997); Cunneen (2007).
[3] Council and Durie-Hall (1999); Tauri (1999), (2009).

are provided in respect of recent (and some longstanding) initiatives in the People's Republic of China, India, the Pacific Islands and other parts of Asia,[4] Latin America[5] and among the Arab, Druze and Bedouin communities.[6]

Community-based restorative traditions which have drawn on indigenous traditions have perforated traditional boundaries between indigenous and non-tribal peoples in many of these settings. Indeed, there are now believed to be over 300 mediation programmes in North America, many of which have developed close working relationships with criminal justice institutions at local levels.[7] For the most part, research findings on these programmes have been fairly favourable. Victims and offenders have reported feeling content about being involved and have felt that the process was fairly conducted;[8] there have been reports of very high levels of agreement,[9] with most agreements carried out in full.[10] However, studies have varied considerably in terms of evidence of recidivism, with some studies reporting significant decreases in reoffending,[11] while others found either no difference or small increases.[12]

It is difficult to generalise in terms of evaluatory findings, since the various programmes differ considerably in terms of approach, scope and the degree of contact with the formal system. Some programmes are extremely large and well organised, and cover a wide range of offences committed across large geographic areas, whilst others are smaller and limited to resolving neighbourhood disputes that may be petty or non-criminal in nature.[13] Some schemes mediate only with juveniles, whilst others focus on adult offenders. However, as with many of the restorative practices that developed within Native America and First Nation communities, the majority of community-based mediation initiatives have now forged some formal links with conventional criminal justice authorities. Some even take referrals from police, prosecutors or the courts, with resources provided from a range of criminal justice agencies at local, state and federal levels.[14]

Sometimes, community-based programmes stand entirely apart from the formal criminal justice system; particularly in settings where there is a lack of confidence among the community in the capacity of the existing institutional arrangements to respond to crime and neighbourhood disputes. For example, a perceived lack of police legitimacy within both republican and loyalist areas of

---

[4] Boriboonthana and Sangbuangamlum (2013); Dinnen and Jowitt (2010); Latha and Thilagaraj (2013); Ping Wang et al (2007).
[5] Bolívar et al (2012); Ungar (2009).
[6] Jabbour (199).
[7] Richards (2011).
[8] Coates and Gehm (1985); Severson and Bankston (1995); Umbreit (1994), (1995).
[9] Umbreit (1994).
[10] Umbreit (1994).
[11] Bonta et al (1998); Evje and Cushman (2000); Umbreit (1994).
[12] Bonta et al (1983).
[13] Umbreit, (1994).
[14] Van Ness and Heetderks Strong (2014).

Northern Ireland was instrumental in the development of localised restorative justice programmes in the mid-1990s.[15] Community Restorative Justice Ireland and Northern Ireland Alternatives both evolved as 'bottom up' initiatives which made use of restorative techniques to deal with criminal and anti-social behaviour—often involving juveniles—as an alternative to the administration of 'punishment beatings' by paramilitary groups in republican and loyalist areas respectively. Many of the leaders of these organisations were themselves former political prisoners, who had declared themselves to be committed to resolving conflict through exclusively peaceful means and to adhering to widely accepted principles of best practice and human rights.[16]

Until recently, these schemes operated entirely independently of the formal criminal justice system in Northern Ireland due to the ongoing legacy of suspicion and mistrust, despite the paramilitary ceasefires of 1994 and the relative success of the subsequent peace process. The schemes were subject to a major evaluation by Mika in 2006, who reported a total of 498 case interventions between 1999 and 2005.[17] These included facilitated meetings and negotiations between victims, offenders and local community representatives, a range of therapeutic and reparative activities, and some referral and liaison with statutory organisations. Outcomes included apologies and agreements to desist from future offending, restoration of damaged property and agreements to participate in community, and therapeutic and/or personal development programmes. In an overwhelmingly positive report, Mika noted that these programmes were believed to be effective in preventing, or at least curtailing, paramilitary punishments. The vast majority of interventions resulted in agreements being completed, with case monitoring confirming that about three-quarters of case clients had experienced no further problems within their respective communities. In addition to an overall sense of fairness among victims and offenders, community leaders also noted that the projects had become essential community assets poised to respond to local needs. The main limitations of the projects were the lack of any working partnerships between the programmes and statutory service providers, continual political criticism, and inadequate levels of resourcing.

As outlined in chapter seven, under the Justice Act (Northern Ireland) 2002, restorative justice for juvenile offenders was 'mainstreamed' and integrated into the criminal justice system in Northern Ireland, including the roll out of statutory youth conferencing for young offenders between the ages of 10 and 17.[18] While both the statutory and community schemes adopted a similar approach to juvenile offenders with, presumably, the same restorative-based goals in mind, there was little active consultation or exchange between them.[19] This tension was

---

[15] See further Mika and McEvoy (2001); McEvoy and Eriksson (2006); Eriksson (2008).
[16] McEvoy and Mika (2002).
[17] Mika (2006).
[18] See ch 7, II.
[19] Campbell et al (2006).

clearly untenable in the longer term, particularly given its potential for double jeopardy for offenders, whereby some might have found themselves involved in both the formal conferencing scheme and a community scheme for the same offence. After several years of stalemate in which disputes over policing and criminal justice reform precluded political progress, the St Andrews Agreement of 2006 heralded a fresh era of devolved government, with the political parties (in particular, Sinn Féin) offering their support for the police and new criminal justice structures. In January 2007, the Northern Ireland Office published a Protocol for Community-Based Restorative Justice Schemes which marked the beginning of a process which eventually resulted in 10 'Community Justice Northern Ireland' and 4 'Northern Ireland Alternatives' schemes being accredited by the Criminal Justice Inspectorate.[20] Subsequently, limited government funding was made available, with both the community-based schemes and the formal agencies of the state committing themselves to mutual co-operation.

III. Restorative Policing

The police have been involved in the development of restorative conferencing schemes, which usually seek to bring the offender and victim together with their supporters to devise a plan to address the harm that has been caused (as opposed to restorative cautioning, see below). One of the first schemes to be developed on an experimental basis was that in Wagga Wagga, New South Wales. Beginning in 1994, the programme initially sought to bring offenders together with their family and friends to decide how to respond to offending but it was soon extended to include victims and their supporters.[21] The programme has been subject to an intensive evaluation, known as the Re-integrative Shaming Experiments (RISE) project, which randomly assigned cases to a police-led conference or a court hearing and sought to compare the effectiveness of each procedure. To be eligible for conferencing the offender must have admitted the offence and have been resident in the area covered by the project. In addition, the offender must have been informed that the case had been randomly selected to be diverted to conferencing and must have been given the choice to be dealt with by a court if preferred.[22]

In terms of its evaluation, the researchers arrived at the 'inescapable' conclusion that 'both victims and offenders can name many ways in which they prefer conferences to court'.[23] Perceptions of fairness amongst victims and offenders were higher and observations reported greater participation, emotional intensity, procedural

---

[20] The Northern Ireland Office has now agreed funding for the projects which should secure the future of the projects in the short-term: see 'Goggins to fund restorative justice plan, despite row', *Belfast Telegraph*, 30 July 2008.
[21] Moore and McDonald (1995).
[22] Strang (2002).
[23] Sherman et al (1998), 165.

justice, apologies, forgiveness, and time and effort given to justice in conferences than in court.[24] Furthermore, conferences were said to increase offenders' respect for the law and the police, and over 70 per cent of contractual obligations were fulfilled by offenders.[25] Victim analyses were carried out only on juvenile property crime and youth violence. High levels of victim participation were reported, with 82 per cent of property victims and 91 per cent of violence victims in attendance. By contrast, victims whose cases were assigned to court attended very infrequently, except where they had been called to give evidence. It was also found that conferencing enabled many victims to receive an apology, whereas apologies were never made in court. In terms of satisfaction, victims found conferencing fairer than court.[26] Victims who had participated reported being more pleased with their treatment than those dealt with in court.[27] Interestingly, there was some difference in degrees of satisfaction between victims of property crime and those of violence, but there was nevertheless 'moderately high level of satisfaction regarding procedural justice' amongst both.[28] This discrepancy in satisfaction levels may be explained by the nature of the crime. Some victims of violence were said to have suffered substantial harm, illustrated by the fact that 62 per cent of these victims required medical treatment. By and large, the research reflects positively on the RISE experiment and concludes that 'as long as there is at least no difference in both costs and recidivism, the advantages of increased respect for police and greater victim involvement suggest that police-led conferencing is a desirable addition to the criminal justice system'.[29]

A similar diversionary scheme of youth conferencing was introduced in South Australia under the Young Offenders Act 1993. Under the Act, the police may refer a juvenile offender (aged 10–17 years) to a conference, provided that the offence is 'minor' in nature. Although the legislation itself does not define which offences are considered 'minor', the South Australian Police Department have issued protocols offering guidance. In practice, these stipulate that cases suitable for a conference include those involving any offence for which the youth has already been formally cautioned, any offence where the police considers it desirable for the victim to participate and any offence resulting in a loss of property between AU$5,000 and $25,000.[30] The extent of police discretion, coupled with the fact that magistrates can also refer court matters to a conference, has meant that quite serious cases may also be dealt with through conferencing, including some sexual assaults and robberies.[31]

---

[24] Sherman et al (1998).
[25] Sherman and Strang (2007).
[26] Strang et al (2013), 41.
[27] Strang et al (2013).
[28] Sherman et al (1998), 151.
[29] Sherman et al (1998), 160.
[30] Strang (2001).
[31] The scheme is purely diversionary in nature, but for a brief period in the early 1990s, the Port Adelaide Youth Court interpreted the Act as providing for the use of conferencing as a sentencing option: Strang (2001).

Although the Wagga Wagga programme has since been superseded by a statutory youth conferencing programme,[32] the non-statutory basis of the original project has been replicated by police forces in other parts of Australia, New Zealand and the United States.[33] The use of police-based diversionary conferencing outside of Australasia developed in the mid-1990s, following a series of training sessions in Minnesota and Pennsylvania conducted by police officers from the Australian Capital Territory. In Bethlehem, Pennsylvania, conferencing began in November 1995, and by the end of 1997, police had conducted some 64 conferences involving 80 juvenile offenders.[34] The scheme was confined to misdemeanours, with strict controls on the types of offence which could be referred: only minor assaults were eligible, no sex offences, or crimes related to drink or drugs were eligible, and it only applied to first-time offenders arrested locally. When a case met the criteria, a liaison officer could approach the offender, who then had the choice whether to admit the offence and undergo a conference, or contest the case at court.

Research findings on the Bethlehem model were broadly similar to those of RISE project. Of those who had undergone a restorative conference, over 90 per cent of both victims and offenders expressed satisfaction, felt they were treated fairly, and would recommend conferencing to others. Victim satisfaction seemed particularly high, with 96 per cent of victims expressing satisfaction, compared with 79 per cent whose cases were assigned to court and 73 per cent among those victims who had declined to participate in a restorative conference and whose cases subsequently were heard at court. Victims also stated that they felt their opinion was taken into account (94 per cent) and almost all offenders (94 per cent) said that they had acquired a better understanding of how the offence had affected the victim.[35] The study also reported that the vast majority of police officers were able to conduct conferences in conformity with restorative justice and due process principles, providing they were given adequate training and supervision. The Bethlehem Project has been replicated by numerous other police departments across North America, with broadly positive evaluations in Indianapolis[36] and in Regina, Canada.[37]

Further evidence has shown the police to be capable of delivering high quality diversionary restorative conferences. The Indianapolis family group conferencing project, which examined how restorative conferencing worked with relatively young first-time offenders compared with those given a court-ordered diversion programme, found that restorative conferences produced high levels of participation among victims, offenders and supporters.[38] Here, the young offenders dealt

---

[32] See Crimes (Restorative Justice) Act 2004.
[33] McCold (1998).
[34] McCold and Wachtel (1998).
[35] McCold and Wachtel (1998).
[36] McGarrell et al (2000).
[37] Wemmers and Canuto (2002).
[38] McGarrell and Hipple (2007).

with through conferences were considerably more likely to report that they had been treated with respect, that their rights had been respected and that they felt that they had been given opportunities to express themselves, than those given the court-ordered disposals.[39] Youths who received the restorative conferences were found to have reduced rates of reoffending; they were more likely to recommend conferencing and said that they believed it had helped them to solve problems. The researchers argue that the face-to-face encounters with victims in the conferences provided the offenders with a greater sense of realisation of the harm they had caused. The conference agreements thus increased the accountability of the offenders for the harm they caused by their actions. More generally, they argue, the conferences provided a vehicle for building a community of care for both offenders and victims.[40]

Similarly, in the United Kingdom, a large police-led restorative conferencing scheme in Northumbria which diverted individuals away from prosecution was subject to a controlled evaluation by Shapland et al.[41] This research revealed that the main reasons that participants (victims and offenders) gave for taking part in the conferences was the opportunity to communicate their feelings and speak directly to each other. Victims and offenders said that they wanted to have their say in how the incident was resolved and fix the harm done, as well as understanding the individual circumstances surrounding the offence. Offenders wanted to be able to apologise and offer recompense to victims. However, for both offenders and victims the main priority was the opportunity to communicate and the possibility of helping to solve the problems that had been caused by the offence. A number of months after the conferences, the researchers also asked offenders and victims why they had participated. Here it was revealed that they gave similar answers: they had developed strong altruistic reasons for taking part, saying they valued the opportunity that it had provided to help the victim and offender. Indeed, half of the victims said they specifically wanted to help the offender. Such altruistic motives have also been reported in other research and highlight the fallacy that victims of crime are mostly vengeful and preoccupied with seeing the offender punished harshly.[42]

In the Northumbria research both offenders and victims agreed that the police-led conferencing had given them the opportunity to express their point of view and the conferencing process was rated as being fairer than going to court. Participants were found to be active in the conferencing process and in problem solving for the future. In many respects, these results demonstrate the potential of the programme to deliver aspects of the agency–accountability framework. In particular, it was noted that restorative conferencing offers considerable advantages

---

[39] See further ch 7, IV.
[40] McGarrell and Hipple (2007).
[41] Shapland et al (2011).
[42] Doak and O'Mahony (2006).

as 'enfranchising offenders, victims and their supporters to discuss potential solutions to offending-related problems is potentially very effective'.[43]

Similar to the findings of many other evaluations on restorative conferencing, the police-led conferences in Northumbria were found to produce high levels of satisfaction amongst participants. This satisfaction related to both the restorative justice process (such as how the individuals were treated during the conferencing) and the outcomes (such as the agreements). It was noteworthy that participants who had expressed a desire to communicate and help solve problems arising from crime were particularly likely to be satisfied with the police-led conferences. Thus many victims cited being empowered and given the opportunity to communicate and deal with the harms caused by the offence as being considerably more important than receiving compensation or redress, and the researchers noted how 'victims put much greater stress on the symbolic reparation of offenders taking control of their lives and deciding to change their life patterns away from offending', as opposed to seeing offenders punished or receiving monetary compensation.[44] Victims also reported that the conferencing process helped them feel more secure and gave them a sense of closure.

Offenders said the best things about the police-led conferences included the opportunity to 'clear the air' and 'work it out' with the victim. So, offenders, like victims, particularly valued the opportunities provided by conferencing to communicate and explain what had happened, as well to apologise and make amends. These conferences were delivered in ways that participants found empowering and elements of the agency–accountability framework were evident in their practice. Thus offenders felt that conferencing had helped them realise the harm they had caused and also to gain a sense of closure, allowing them to think about the future in a positive way. Importantly, the research by Shapland et al was also able to demonstrate significant cost savings by providing police-led diversionary restorative conferences. In a two-year follow up, examining the costs of providing the conferences against reductions in reoffending and the financial costs of crime, it was found that the police-led conferences were able to produce an overall cost saving from reduced crime and criminal justice costs.

Reflecting on experiences of police-led restorative conferences, many have managed to engage victims and offenders together in a dialogical process that produced productive encounters and high levels of satisfaction for participants. Importantly, the most successful restorative interventions adapted elements of the agency–accountability framework. This helped victims and offenders feel the process was fairer, in part because it empowered them to participate, allowed them to have their say. By doing so, they became active participants within the decision-making process to address the harm caused by their offending.

---

[43] Shapland et al (2011).
[44] Shapland et al (2011), 164.

A. Restorative Cautioning

In a similar way to the police-led diversionary conferencing model discussed above, restorative cautioning has also evolved as a means to integrate restorative principles into the traditional form of police caution. However, unlike conferencing, victims are rarely directly involved in the process. The restorative caution is different to the traditional police caution, which has been described as a 'degrading ceremony' in which the young person, most often a first-time and minor offender, is given a stern reprimand by a senior police officer.[45] The restorative caution, by contrast, is achieved by first attempting to get the young offenders to realise the harm caused to the victim by their actions, but also the harm caused to themselves and their families. The process draws heavily on Braithwaite's concept of reintegrative shaming, which focuses on the wrongfulness of the action or behaviour rather than the wrongfulness of the individual. It seeks to reintegrate young offenders, after they have admitted what they did was wrong, by focusing on how they can put the incident behind them (for example by repairing the harm caused through reparation and apology). It then allows them to move forward and hopefully reintegrate with their community and family. The process is usually facilitated by a trained police officer and often involves the use of a script or agenda that broadly mirrors a conferencing process. Victims can be encouraged to play a part in the process, particularly to reinforce upon the young offender the impact of the offence on the victim, but as Dignan notes, most restorative cautioning schemes have (at least initially) placed a greater emphasis on the offender and issues of crime control, than on their ability to meet the needs of victims.[46]

The practice of police-led restorative cautioning has its roots in Australia and began to penetrate policing practice in the United Kingdom during the late 1990s. Championed by the Chief Constable of Thames Valley, Charles Pollard, the programme was rolled out to train police officers and implement a variety of restorative-based processes, including a complaints system and a comprehensive monitoring/evaluation package.[47] The Thames Valley scheme, which has since been widely replicated throughout the United Kingdom,[48] confers on police officers a degree of discretion as to when to use such an approach as an alternative to a traditional caution or, indeed, prosecution through the courts. Most commonly, it tends to be used with individuals who have committed relatively minor offences, have not offended before, and are considered unlikely to do so again.

---

[45] Garfinkel (1956).
[46] Dignan (2005).
[47] Wilcox and Young (2007).
[48] Although Wachtel (2009) estimates that around 50% of police forces in England and Wales operate some form of restorative justice scheme, the resource-intensive nature of restorative cautioning meant that by 2007, only Thames Valley and West Mercia Police were providing restorative cautions: Paterson and Clamp (2012). In 2004, the Scottish Executive announced the introduction of police restorative warnings for young offenders in cases involving minor offences: McDiarmid (2005).

The Thames Valley scheme was subject to an intense evaluation from 1998–2001.[49] Researchers reported that offenders and their supporters were mostly satisfied and felt that they had been treated fairly. However, a minority of offenders felt they had not been adequately prepared for the process, or felt they had been pressured into it. Nonetheless, offenders generally believed that the restorative caution helped them to understand the effects of the offence and inculcated a sense of shame in them, which is a particularly important goal of the restorative cautioning intervention. Over half of the participants reported gaining a sense of closure and felt better because of the restorative session, and four-fifths saw holding the meeting as a good idea. Indeed, almost a third of offenders entered into a formal written reparation agreement at the restorative caution. Within a year, it was reported that the vast majority of these had been fulfilled.

Initially, the researchers examining the Thames Valley scheme also found that the implementation of the restorative cautioning model in individual cases was sometimes deficient, with facilitators occasionally excluding certain participants or asking inappropriate questions (eg relating to prior offending or attempts to gather criminal intelligence). More generally, it was found that some officers tended to dominate discussions and did not allow other participants to express themselves freely. However, it was noted that practice had improved considerably towards the end of the research period. Overall, this evaluation found that restorative cautioning represented a significant improvement over traditional cautioning, and was more effective in terms of reducing recidivism.[50] The research showed the police to be enthusiastic and sincerely committed to the restorative process. They had been generally well trained and it was clear from the interviews with the young people involved in the process and their parents that they placed a high degree of confidence and support in the scheme. There was also some evidence that it had other beneficial effects, especially in terms of helping the police improve their community relations.

On a less positive note, it was clear that the vast bulk of restorative cautions (86 per cent) took place without a victim present. Victims who opted not to attend cited various reasons; 52 per cent stated that they did not wish to do so; 30 per cent wished to participate, but were unable to; and 15 per cent were not invited. In these circumstances, community representatives or police officers attempted to invoke empathy in a young offender by explaining how a particular offence might impact upon a victim or a local community, but such attempts were often futile.[51] In reality, there was little opportunity for the process to maximise agency and accountability, which leads us to question as to whether the scheme could be properly described as 'fully' restorative.[52]

---

[49] Hoyle et al (2002).
[50] Hoyle et al (2002). See further ch 8.
[51] See also Hoyle and Rosenblatt (2016).
[52] Hoyle et al (2002).

During the same period, the Thames Valley model of police cautioning was replicated in Northern Ireland, in a slightly different guise.[53] Our own evaluation of the police restorative cautioning scheme in Northern Ireland identified differences in practice between the two pilot areas. In the area where a restorative scheme evolved from traditional cautioning practice, the interventions appeared to be used as an alternative to the traditional caution. Here, similar to the Thames Valley evaluation, the vast majority of restorative cases were dealt with by way of a restorative caution without the presence of the victim, and only a very small number were dealt with by a restorative conference including a victim. In the other pilot area, however, the scheme had been developed from a local 'retail theft initiative', and generally dealt with cases involving shoplifting. Here, most of the cases resulted in a 'restorative conference', based on the Wagga Wagga model, however these mostly used surrogate victims who were drawn from a volunteer panel of local retailers, and few cases were dealt with by way of a restorative caution (without any victim representation at all).[54]

As with the Thames Valley evaluation, the Northern Ireland research showed that the police were strongly committed to restorative ideals and had applied considerable effort in attempting to make it a success. Moreover, there was clear evidence that the practice of delivering the restorative cautions was a significant improvement in police practice and participants were generally pleased with the way their cases were dealt with. However, a number of pertinent concerns were identified by the researchers, including the lack of meaningful involvement of victims in many of the interventions.

The restorative cautioning sessions in Northern Ireland were also found to be resource intensive, taking a considerable amount of police time to organise and administer, often for minor offences. Furthermore, there was some evidence that they were unnecessarily drawing some petty first-time offenders into what was a demanding and intense process. This gave rise to concerns that the majority of conferences were not being used as a genuine alternative to prosecution. Instead, they appeared to be used mostly for less serious cases involving very young juveniles (12–14 years) that previously might not have resulted in any formal action. For instance, over 90 per cent of the restorative conference cases were for minor thefts, and 80 per cent involved goods with a value of under £15. Indeed, in over half of the cases, the goods were worth less than £5. The profile of those given restorative cautions and conferences was more similar to those given 'advice and warning' than those 'cautioned' under the pre-existing regime. The people dealt with under the scheme were generally at the younger end of juvenile offenders; they usually had no previous police contact or had only committed trivial offences.

---

[53] O'Mahony and Doak (2004).
[54] O'Mahony et al (2002).

The Northern Ireland findings highlight the danger that when informal alternatives are introduced into the criminal justice system they may serve to supplement rather than supplant existing procedures.[55] The question is thus raised, whether it is appropriate to use restorative processes, which may involve victims and which are obviously costly, time consuming and onerous, for mainly first-time offenders involved in petty offences (like shoplifting sweets). It could be argued that a better course of action might be to deal with such minor cases by way of informal and diversionary police action, preferably using a restorative framework. Certainly, it was apparent from the research that attempting to deliver a restorative conference with a victim present for trivial, first-time offenders was difficult to justify.[56]

Meanwhile in England and Wales, the regime governing the police cautioning of juveniles was overhauled with the introduction of 'final warnings' under the Crime and Disorder Act 1998. The Act followed the government White Paper *No More Excuses—A New Approach to Tackling Youth Crime in England and Wales*, published by the Home Office in 1997.[57] The White Paper underlined that one of the core aims of this new system was to toughen the stance on dealing with young offenders by limiting the number of times they could be cautioned by the police. The Act saw the introduction of the new 'final warning' scheme replace the old police caution. However, the guidance issued to the police emphasised that final warnings should now be carried out using a 'restorative framework'.[58] Thus police officers administering final warnings were advised to organise a restorative final warning for all young offenders who would formerly have been dealt with by way of a traditional caution. Those affected by the offence, including the offender, victim and any relevant supporter or family member, could be invited to attend the final warning, and police officers received training on how to facilitate a restorative-based structured discussion about the harm caused by the offence and how it might be repaired.

The use of a restorative framework to deliver final warnings became the norm for the police across England and Wales. However, the direct involvement of victims in the delivery of restorative final warnings has not improved over time and the practice of providing a fully fledged restorative process has become rare.[59] The lack of victim participation is obviously a major drawback in the ability of such schemes to provide a meaningful restorative justice process. In many respects what appears to be the norm in terms of the delivery of restorative final warnings can best be described as providing only a 'partially restorative' process.

The marginalisation of the victim in terms of their involvement in final warnings using a restorative framework arises from a number of factors. Importantly,

---

[55] Dignan and Lowey (2000); O'Mahony and Deazley (2000).
[56] O'Mahony and Doak (2004).
[57] Home Office (1997).
[58] Home Office (2002).
[59] Hoyle (2009).

the guidance from central government suggested the inclusion of victims as a 'desirable' element.[60] However the process of delivering final warnings was overshadowed by the pressures of police performance targets, in which the delivery of the warning became the most important element. As such, little recognition was given to whether final warnings were actually delivered with or without a victim. There was also no recognition given to the considerable efforts needed to properly involve victims in the process. As such, there was little incentive to directly involve victims in final warnings and combined with limited resources and increasing case-loads, victim participation became even more marginalised.

Given the resource intensity that is generally required in order to realise 'full' restorative justice, a new Youth Restorative Disposal was introduced on a pilot basis across eight police force areas in 2008. This intervention allows police officers to deal with juveniles involved in minor offences at the scene of the incident by way of a summary disposal, in a manner similar to a reprimand or final warning. It seeks to challenge inappropriate behaviour by using restorative justice principles and is intended to provide the police with another tool to handle young people who have committed low-level offences without undertaking the process of setting up a formal restorative caution. The disposal has been designed to offer police officers more discretion, with a quick and alternative means of dealing with low-level, anti-social and nuisance offending. It is designed to deliver a swift response and reduce the amount of time that police officers spend completing paperwork and attending court. By the same token, it aims to enable the victim to have a role in the process.

A recent evaluation of the Youth Restorative Disposal has shown it to be effective in delivering a swift response to minor offending by young people, mostly involving shoplifting, assault and criminal damage.[61] It was shown to be popular with police officers, not just because it was perceived to save time, but because they felt that it offered a proportionate response, which was perceived to have a positive impact on young offenders. In practice, the majority of Youth Restorative Disposals are given on the spot, by police officers (usually on the street), with the consent of the offender and victim. However, the research shows that the disposal normally entails not much more than a simple verbal apology to the victim at the scene of the incident and few cases have been referred to Youth Offending Teams or involved in any further intervention. As such, and despite being termed a 'restorative disposal', there is little to suggest that the Youth Restorative Disposal involves any significant restorative intervention or a process of meaningful interaction between the offender and victim. In many respects, the disposal simply provides the police with another mechanism to informally deal with minor offending, on the spot, by way of an immediate warning that includes an apology.

---

[60] Home Office (2002).
[61] Rix et al (2011).

Other developments have seen the introduction of the Youth Conditional Caution, started on a pilot basis in 2010, to extend the use of conditional cautions for young people aged 10–17.[62] The Government agreed during the passage of the Criminal Justice and Immigration Act 2008 that the Youth Conditional Caution would be introduced in stages, beginning with 16–17 year olds. The scheme aims to reduce the number of young people being taken to court for low-level offences and can be used where the offender has not previously been convicted of an offence, admits guilt and consents to the caution. The caution can have conditions attached to it that include restorative provisions supporting rehabilitation and effecting reparation. It can also include a fine and/or an attendance requirement. It can be offered to those aged 16 and 17 at the time of the offence (for the duration of the pilots) where there is sufficient evidence to charge for an offence and the young person has admitted guilt. The decision to administer a Youth Conditional Caution has the effect of suspending any criminal proceedings while the young person is given an opportunity to comply with the agreed conditions. They are used where the offender has either committed an offence which is not suitable to be dealt with by way of the reprimand or final warning, or where the offender has already been subject to the reprimand or final warning scheme. The offender can accept or refuse the conditional caution and if the latter option is selected the offender will be placed before the court. Where the conditions attached to the caution are complied with, the case will be discharged and no further prosecution and/or proceedings for the offence(s) will be commenced. However, where there is no reasonable excuse for non-compliance, the caution offer can be withdrawn and criminal proceedings commenced for the original offence(s).

As with many 'restorative' experiments, there has been some reluctance to utilise the principles at the more serious end of offending or with adult offenders. However, similar restorative principles were extended to adult offenders in England and Wales through the 'conditional cautioning' scheme introduced by the Criminal Justice Act 2003. Conditional cautioning enables the Crown Prosecution Service (CPS) to issue a caution to a first-time or minor offender as an alternative to prosecution. A number of conditions are attached to the caution, which must be aimed at either rehabilitating the offender and/or ensuring that the offender makes reparation to the victim or the wider community, and it is envisaged that restorative justice processes will form a part of, or will contribute towards, these conditions. Offenders who fail to comply with the conditions will usually be prosecuted for the original offence. Participation in a scheme may form part of an offender's caution in and of itself, or the conditions themselves may represent the outcome of such a process.[63] The CPS may only offer

---

[62] Section 48 of the Criminal Justice and Immigration Act 2008 amended the Crime and Disorder Act 1998 to provide that 10–17 year olds would also be eligible to receive conditional cautions.
[63] Home Office (2005).

such a caution if: (1) the officer has evidence that the person has committed an offence; (2) the relevant prosecutor decides that there is sufficient evidence to charge the person with the offence and grounds for giving a conditional caution; (3) the offender admits the offence to the authorised person; (4) an explanation of the effect of a caution and the warnings about the consequences of failure to observe the conditions has been given; and (5) the offender signs a document that sets out details of the offence, an admission, consent to the caution and consent to the attached conditions.[64]

This scheme pays only very limited service to the idea of restorative justice for two reasons. First, conditional cautions are not intended to replace traditional non-statutory police cautions (the 'simple' police caution remains on a non-statutory footing and within the discretion of the police), and are only used in a small minority of cases.[65] The conditional cautions were also introduced as an alternative option where the imposition of conditions are seen as being a more effective way of addressing the offender's behaviour or making reparation to the victim or the community.[66] Second, like many of the other measures outlined above, it can be said to be only partly restorative, in so far as victims are not usually actively involved in the process and, as Dignan observes, 'no attempt is made to "privilege" or "prioritise" restorative over rehabilitative interventions, even in cases involving direct victims'.[67]

The development and experience of police-led restorative cautioning practice provides an improvement to the traditional caution, which was little more than a harsh warning used to deal with mostly first-time offenders who committed minor offences. The restorative cautioning model has helped focus attention on the consequences of crime for offenders and is often a more positive way of dealing with mostly first-time offenders. However, the way that restorative cautioning initiatives have evolved has limited their potential to deliver our agency–accountability framework. Practice shows that more emphasis is placed on restorative cautions delivering speedy and cost-effective alternatives to prosecution, than on delivering what might be a meaningful and empowering restorative encounter. Too often there is little opportunity given for victims to participate in the process and, more importantly, there is limited potential for victims and offenders to properly engage in in an encounter in which they are empowered to shape or be impacted by its outcomes. So, while restorative cautioning practice may represent an improvement in the delivery of police cautions, it falls well short of being able to deliver an empowering restorative encounter through our agency–accountability framework.

---

[64] Criminal Justice Act 2003, s 23.
[65] Hoyle (2009).
[66] Doak (2008).
[67] Dignan (2006), 273.

IV. Youth Offender Panels

As restorative policing initiatives have expanded, policymakers have simultaneously sought to integrate restorative practices within the sentencing proceedings. This is particularly marked in the field of youth justice, where a form of reparation panel (known as Youth Offender Panels) were introduced in England and Wales under the Youth Justice and Criminal Evidence Act 1999. The panels, which comprise two community members who are volunteers from the local area and a professional from the local multi-agency youth offending team, aim to provide first-time offenders with 'opportunities to make restoration to the victim, take responsibility for the consequences of their offending and achieve reintegration into the law-abiding community'.[68]

When a young person is given a 'referral order' by the court, the panel itself decides how the offending should be dealt with and what form of action is necessary. If the victim wishes, they may attend the panel meeting and describe how the offence affected them. Parents are required to attend the panel meeting (if the young person is under the age of 16) and meetings are usually held in community venues. Government guidelines state that young people should not have legal representation at panel meetings, as this may hinder their full involvement in the process, but a solicitor may attend as a 'supporter'.[69]

It falls on the panel to draw up an agreed plan which can provide reparation to the victim or community and include interventions to address the young person's offending. This can include victim awareness, counselling, drug and alcohol interventions and forms of victim reparation. The length of the order should be based on the seriousness of the offence, but panels are free to determine the nature of intervention necessary to prevent further offending by the young person.[70] The young person must agree to the plan. However, if they refuse they will be referred back to the court for sentencing. Once a plan is agreed it is monitored by the Youth Offending Team and if the young person fails to comply with its terms they may be referred back to court for sentencing.

Referral orders were piloted in 11 areas across England and Wales between March 2000 and August 2001. An evaluation by Newburn et al found that, in the main: 'within a relatively short time youth offender panels have established themselves as constructive, deliberative and participatory forums in which to address young people's offending behaviour'.[71] The orders were rolled out across the rest of England and Wales in April 2002, and they currently form an important sentencing option for young offenders.

---

[68] Home Office (2002).
[69] Home Office (2002).
[70] Home Office (2002).
[71] Newburn et al (2002).

In an extensive evaluation, Newburn et al concluded from their research that the new orders were working well and that many young offenders played an active role in their panel meetings. They found that 84 per cent of the young people felt they were treated with respect and 86 per cent said they were treated fairly. The research found that 75 per cent of the young people agreed that their plan or contract was 'useful' and 78 per cent agreed that it should help them stay out of trouble.[72] Parents also appeared to be positive about the orders, and compared with the experience of the youth court, parents appeared to understand the referral order process better and felt it easier to participate. Generally, panel sessions were found to be 'constructive, deliberative and participatory forums'.[73]

Unlike most restorative-based interventions available in England and Wales, the referral order has been incorporated into the courts and criminal justice process as a key response to youth offenders who plead guilty the first time they are prosecuted. However, a number of concerns have been raised concerning the operation of referral orders. It has been argued that the system raises questions about informed consent if some young people and parents feel forced into agreeing plans. Concern has been raised that children as young as 10 years, without legal representation, may be drawn into what may be traumatic confrontations with adults, and that they may end up signing into contracts involving deprivations of their liberty.[74] Moreover, it has been argued that the discretion of magistrates has been severely curtailed in the legislation, whereby minor first-time offenders *have* to be referred to panels, effectively making this a mandatory sentence.[75] Research by Newburn et al (2002) confirms that 45 per cent of the magistrates interviewed felt that the lack of discretion in the legislation served to undermine their role. Crawford and Newburn also found that some panels had difficulty devising suitable plans because of a lack of local resources, yet panel members believed that adequate local facilities and resources were crucial to the success of panels.[76]

More fundamental problems with the referral order include the low levels of victim involvement in the process, with research revealing victims attending in only 13 per cent of cases where at least an initial panel meeting was held.[77] Victims failed to attend for a number of reasons. Almost half (43 per cent) had not been offered a realistic opportunity to attend a meeting: victims had either not been identifiable or had not been contacted in a timely fashion. Other victims had opted not to attend.

Disappointingly, over a decade later little had changed. Having observed 39 panels, Rosenblatt found that only one included a participating victim.[78]

---

[72] Newburn et al (2002).
[73] Newburn et al (2002), 62.
[74] Cullen (2004); Cunneen and Goldson (2015); Haines (1998).
[75] Ball (2000).
[76] Crawford and Newburn (2003).
[77] Crawford and Newburn (2003).
[78] Rosenblatt (2015a).

Such low levels of victim participation obviously limit any chance of realising the fundamental principles of our agency–accountability framework, let alone offering opportunities for 'encounter, reparation, reintegration and participation'.[79]

Moreover, research has yet to establish whether such orders are having any net-widening effects such as unnecessarily drawing minor offenders further into the criminal justice system; the extent to which such orders are truly proportionate to the offence committed; and their longer-term impact on recidivism, especially by comparison to other disposals.[80] The extent to which referral orders encapsulate the core features of restorative justice remains questionable; as such they might be more aptly described as a form of restorative *practice* as opposed to an exemplar of restorative *justice*. As we noted in chapter three, the challenge of maximising agency and accountability often hangs on active victim participation. This inevitably impacts on the restorative potential of outcomes. As Rosenblatt reminds us, on occasion providers failed to distinguish rehabilitative measures (ie those concerned with the reintegration of the offender) from reparatory measures.[81] In a number of the Youth Offending Panels agreements that she analysed there was a tendency to put in place 'menu' style or 'one size fits all' agreements. The depersonalised nature of such interventions clearly undermines the agency and accountability of both victims and offenders, in terms of empowering them to be active participants in a restorative process. This is even more likely to occur in cases where victims are not afforded a voice in the process. Certainly, in their current format referral orders have limited scope to provide a meaningful restorative encounter that is capable of realising our agency–accountability framework. This is especially relevant for victims, given their low levels of inclusion and the minimal opportunities available to properly participate, contribute or help shape such encounters.

V. Schemes for Adult Offenders

While restorative responses for youth crime have been growing in popularity for some time, there has been greater reticence to adopt such practices for adults. A number of reasons have been mooted for this, including the perception that young people may be more responsive to rehabilitation efforts[82] and may commit less serious crimes,[83] and also the fact that—owing to its propensity to be less politicised than adult justice—youth justice has traditionally tended to be

---

[79] Van Ness and Heetderks Strong (2014).
[80] Mullan and O'Mahony (2003).
[81] Rosenblatt (2015b).
[82] Bruce et al (2012).
[83] Bruce et al (2012).

more open to innovation and experimental interventions.[84] As we note in the final section of this chapter, many of the adult restorative-based programmes have tended to evolve in custodial settings, after conviction and sentencing. Certainly, the development of restorative justice for adult offenders by referral from the courts or other criminal justice agencies has been relatively slow and uneven, although more recent times have seen it become increasingly recognised as a feasible mainstream option. The next section provides an insight into New Zealand and England and Wales, both of which have taken steps to integrate restorative options into their adult criminal justice systems.

A. New Zealand

As noted above, New Zealand was the first jurisdiction to mainstream the use of restorative justice for juvenile offenders. Schemes for adult offenders were later embedded in the justice system. The first adult schemes with restorative elements emerged as community panel pilots, including Project Turnaround, Te Whānau Awhina and the Community Accountability Programme in 1995.[85] These were designed to divert first-time adult offenders from prosecution, and were the subject of a relatively positive evaluation.[86] In 2001, court-referred conferencing pilots were introduced in Auckland, Waitakere, Hamilton and Dunedin District Courts. The programmes were designed to be triggered after a guilty plea for certain serious offences,[87] with the conference agreement then being considered by the court in sentencing.

Research conducted in 2002 by Bowen and Boyack examining the pilot schemes notes that up to early 2003 there had been 750 referrals from judges or magistrates in the pilot courts; however, only 260 cases had been completed.[88] The researchers suggest the relatively low levels of completion were often due to the victim or offender being unwilling or unable to meet. Further research on the pilot schemes, published by the New Zealand Ministry of Justice in 2005,[89] found high levels of satisfaction amongst those who participated in the programmes. It was also found that many victims who participated said they felt better about the criminal justice system following the conference. Victims reported having a better understanding of why the offence occurred and its likelihood of reoccurring. They appreciated being given the opportunity of being able to say what they wanted and

---

[84] Muncie (2005); Souhami (2012).
[85] Maxwell and Hayes (2007).
[86] Morris and Maxwell (2003), 265–67.
[87] Eligible offences were property offences with a maximum of two years' imprisonment, or another offence for which the maximum penalty was between two and seven years. Some offences, such as family violence, were excluded: Bowen et al (2012).
[88] Bowen and Boyack (2003).
[89] Triggs (2005).

generally said the conference agreements were fair and they were satisfied with the conferencing process. The results showed that fewer offenders who went through conferencing were sent to prison, which resulted in a cost saving. An analysis of reoffending rates also showed that those sent to conferencing were less likely to reoffend than a matched sample of offenders dealt with solely in the criminal courts. Moreover, most of the judges said the reports from the conferences were useful to them in the sentencing process.

More recent research, published in 2011,[90] confirms that victims, in particular, continue to view the programmes in a largely positive light. In a survey of 154 victims, over three-quarters of respondents reported that they were satisfied with their overall experience of restorative justice, before, during and after the conference and 80 per cent said they would be likely to recommend restorative justice to others in a similar situation. Almost all respondents (94 per cent) reported that they had felt safe at the conference and had the chance to explain how the offence affected them.

Indeed, following the Court of Appeal case in *R v Clotworthy*,[91] the Sentencing Act 2002 introduced provisions which oblige sentencing judges to take into account restorative processes and outcomes that are agreed between the parties in determining the appropriate sentence for the offender.[92] Additionally, provided that restorative justice processes are available, there is an identifiable victim, the offender pleads guilty and no restorative process has previously taken place, the trial judges must adjourn sentencing and refer the case to a community-based restorative justice programme.[93] An assessment is then made as to the suitability of the case for restorative justice; the willingness of all parties to participate will be ascertained before the conference takes place. Similarly, the Victims' Rights Act 2002 provides that all victims have the right, in principle, to request a restorative justice conference at any time during criminal proceedings.[94] Following this raft of legislation, concern began to emerge about the ad hoc manner in which programmes were developing throughout the country, and the lack of uniform standards which were being applied. To this end, the Ministry of Justice published

---

[90] New Zealand Ministry of Justice (2011).

[91] (1998) 15 CRNZ 651. Here the Court acknowledged the importance of the restorative intervention and the views of the victim in how the matter was disposed of. It substituted a custodial sentence with a suspended sentence.

[92] Under Sentencing Act 2002, s 10 stipulates that the court must take into consideration any offer, agreement, response or measure to make amends, whether financial or by the performance of work or service, made by or on behalf of the offender to the victim; any agreement between the offender and victim; the response of the offender or his/her family; and any agreement between the offender and the victim as to how to remedy the wrong, loss or damage; any compensatory measure taken or proposed to be taken by the offender, including an apology. Courts also have the power to adjourn cases until any such agreements are fulfilled: s 10(4).

[93] Sentencing Act 2002, s 24A.

[94] Victims' Rights Act 2002, s 9 provides that where the victim makes such a request, a member of court staff, the police, or probation must, if satisfied that the necessary resources are available, refer the request to a suitable person who is available to arrange and facilitate a restorative justice meeting.

a document in 2004, *Principles of Best Practice*, which set out eight key principles which providers were expected to follow.[95]

Thus, while existing research on the adult restorative measures in New Zealand reveals their empowering potential, especially in providing victims with opportunities to have a say in the process and being able to explain how the offence impacted them, there are concerns over the direction and manner in which restorative interventions are currently evolving and expanding. There is obviously a need to ensure that new and existing adult schemes are delivered in a manner that maximises their restorative potential and allows for the agency–accountability framework to be realised for both victims and offenders. However, without significant financial investment and clear guidance, which enshrines these empowering values to the delivery of restorative justice, there is every danger that their rapid growth could undermine the quality of service needed for an effective restorative justice experience.

B. England and Wales

Although England and Wales had been among the first to experiment with restorative interventions aimed at adults during the 1980s,[96] the government chose to focus its efforts largely on youth justice during the 1990s and only recently has interest in its potential application for adult offenders begun to re-emerge. Under the Home Office's Crime Reduction Programme, announced in 2002, funding was established for three separate pilot projects to gauge how they worked with adults who had been charged with more serious offences. These programmes were quite distinct from each other in terms of being provided by different organisations, offering alternative types of interventions and working at different stages of the criminal justice system. The first was a London-based scheme focused on providing a variety of restorative interventions including mediation (direct and indirect) and conferencing for adult offenders who had committed a wide variety of offences. The second was a scheme that provided conferencing across a number of locations for adult offenders involved in burglary and street crime with the restorative intervention taking place after a guilty plea and prior to sentence. The third took cases for mediation across various stages of the criminal justice system, ranging from police final warnings to resettlement prior to release from prison.[97]

---

[95] New Zealand Ministry of Justice (2004).The principles are: (1) restorative justice processes are underpinned by voluntariness for both the victim and the offender; (2) full participation of the victim and offender should be encouraged; (3) effective participation requires that participants particularly the victim and the offender are well informed; (4) restorative justice processes must hold the offender accountable; (5) flexibility and responsiveness are inherent characteristics of restorative justice processes; (6) emotional and physical safety of participants is an overriding concern; (7) restorative justice providers and facilitators must ensure the delivery of an effective process; and (8) restorative justice processes should be only undertaken in appropriate cases.

[96] See generally Marshall and Merry (1990).

[97] See Shapland et al (2007).

The schemes were subject to an extensive evaluation by a team based at the University of Sheffield.[98] Overall, the research found that the schemes were generally successful in providing services that both victims and offenders found useful and productive. Victims and offenders who participated in conferencing or mediation were generally positive about the experience.[99] They were particularly happy with the opportunity to communicate with each other. In the final interviews with victims involved in conferencing, 90 per cent said the offender had apologised to them and in two-thirds of cases these apologies were perceived to be sincere. Satisfaction levels towards the conferences were ranked highly by both victims and offenders, as were the conference outcomes. Any dissatisfaction tended to be related to other aspects of the conference.

Aspects of our agency–accountability framework were evident in their delivery as the majority of victims and offenders felt that the restorative intervention had helped them deal with the aftermath of the offence. Similarly, victims stated that offenders usually came to recognise the harm they had caused and it had helped them achieve a sense of closure. The conferences also provided a forum in which offending-related problems were addressed and discussed. Most victims said participating in the scheme had lessened the negative effects of the offence and most offenders felt the intervention would lessen their likelihood of reoffending. Indeed, nearly three-quarters of participants mentioned that they would recommend the process to others for similar offences.[100]

The schemes which provided direct mediation prompted better reactions from the participants than those that provided indirect (not face-to-face) mediation. Thus the researchers suggest direct mediation may be a better way of providing a restorative environment in which the potential of restorative justice may be more likely to be achieved, especially in terms of facilitating communication and moving forward. Overall, the research was positive about the restorative interventions for adults and showed them to offer considerable advantages, particularly for the participants. Research focusing on their potential to reduce reoffending has also been positive, showing participants in such programmes to be less likely to have been reconvicted than those dealt with through the traditional route.[101]

Despite an initial reluctance to act in light of the positive findings of research, the 2010 Green Paper *Breaking the Cycle* signalled that the Coalition Government was taking seriously the prospect of introducing a statutory platform for restorative justice for adults. Yet, notwithstanding the positive rhetoric in its response to the consultation,[102] ultimately the Government shied away from proposing

---

[98] Shapland et al (2004), (2006a), (2007), (2008).
[99] Shapland et al (2007).
[100] Shapland et al (2007).
[101] Shapland et al (2008). See further ch 8.
[102] Ministry of Justice (2011).

legislation, until the Crime and Courts Act 2013 placed restorative justice on a modest statutory footing by enabling the criminal courts to defer sentencing pending the outcome of a restorative intervention.[103]

On the one hand, this legislation can be welcomed in the sense that courts have, for the first time, been directed towards statutory recognition of restorative justice for adult offenders. Moreover, the requirement for 'a face-to-face meeting ... [or] an alternative type of RJ activity'[104] allows for a wide range of interventions to be utilised, and these are not restricted to any particular offence. On the other hand, courts retain the discretion to decide if—and when—sentencing should be deferred and even where a restorative event is to be held. The legislation also provides no guidance as to what weight judges ought to place on the outcome in the sentencing exercise. In light of this, it remains to be seen how readily the judiciary will apply the powers under the Act. Moreover, in a climate of austerity, there is concern that the Government's enthusiastic rhetoric for restorative justice may not be matched by the financial commitment required to resource the intensive work necessary to deliver a properly functioning system capable of effectively delivering an empowering process utilising elements of our agency–accountability framework.[105]

VI. Prison-based Restorative Programmes

Another sphere of criminal justice that has seen growth in restorative types of programmes is within the prison system. Prison-based restorative programmes have expanded considerably in recent years across many jurisdictions, although often in a somewhat fragmented manner. For example, in England and Wales, many of the recent programmes have evolved through individual projects developed in specific prisons, but with no overarching strategy to guide them. English prisons have a long history of offering generic rehabilitation activities, including forms of education, community and environmental work, and victim awareness. Perhaps the most well known of these is the Sycamore Tree Project, an international programme (with a strong presence in the United Kingdom),[106] which involves volunteers delivering an 8–12 week course in which inmates learn about the effects of crime on victims, offenders and the community, and the need to take personal responsibility for one's actions. Usually, a victim of crime will attend one or more of the sessions to give a personal account of the impact of offending, and in the final session offenders are offered the opportunity to express remorse

---

[103] Crime and Courts Act 2013, sch 6, inserting s 1ZA into the Powers of Criminal Courts Act 2000.
[104] Ministry of Justice (2014a), 6.
[105] See Cavadino et al (2013), 128.
[106] http://www.prisonfellowship.org.uk/what-we-do/sycamore-tree/ (accessed 28 November 2016).

through letters, poems, music or arts or crafts. An extensive evaluation of the programme in England and Wales, undertaken by a team from Sheffield Hallam University in 2009, found significant positive attitudinal changes across the whole sample, with offenders of all types demonstrating an increased awareness of the impact of their actions as well as a reduced anticipation of reoffending.[107]

Notwithstanding, actual opportunities for victims and offenders to engage with each other have been somewhat thin on the ground, and whether formal arrangements can be arranged or not will depend on the capacity of individual institutions to deliver them. Although a number of examples of good practice can be identified,[108] the more general picture is a system that provides very limited victim-focused work, especially programmes that could be classified as restorative in nature. The lack of a planned approach in the prison service in England and Wales means that promising programmes often run for a very limited period, even if they have shown themselves to be successful. This approach has resulted in many worthwhile programmes failing because of a lack of medium or longer term support for their work. The difficulties of bringing promising programmes into the prison system is further hampered by persistent prison overcrowding and a lack of funding, which often means that prison control is prioritised over programmes which address rehabilitation or reintegration. Prisoners may be placed some distance from their community owing to overcrowding, making efforts to engage them with local services and their victims even more difficult to achieve.

Even programmes shown to be promising have had considerable difficulty in maintaining themselves. For example, despite the encouraging results from the Home Office pilots conducted by Shapland et al,[109] few have had the resources to continue to function, let alone expand. For young offender institutions the situation is similar and it has been recognised that despite research evidence generally supporting the use of restorative schemes in prisons and with examples of good practice, there is still little common understanding or policy guidance from the centre which supports the longer term establishment and retention of such programmes in a meaningful way, particularly in difficult economic circumstances.[110]

Turning elsewhere, we can look to the considerable array of prison-based restorative programmes running across the United States and Canada. Notable research has taken place into programmes operating in Alabama,[111] Minnesota[112] and Philadelphia.[113] For the most part, these schemes do not include direct

---

[107] Feasey et al (2005).
[108] For example, a project in young offenders' institutions involving direct and indirect mediation between offenders and their victims was awarded the Butler Trust prize in 2000 for good practice within the prison service. Similar schemes operate in HMYOI Brinsford and HMYOI Huntercombe.
[109] Shapland et al (2007).
[110] HMIC et al (2012).
[111] Swanson (2009).
[112] Pranis (2006).
[113] Roeger (2003).

mediation or conferencing approaches, but rather try to encourage empathy and remorse on the part of offenders.[114] To provide a snapshot of how such schemes operate, we consider briefly three of the most established schemes: the *Citizens, Victims, and Offenders Restoring Justice* (CVORJ) programme based at Washington State Reformatory, the *Resolve to Stop the Violence* programme based in San Francisco and the *Victim Offender Mediation/Dialogue Program* based in British Columbia.

The Washington-based CVORJ programme began operating in 1997 as a pilot, and was based around three restorative courses designed for victims, offenders and community members. The courses brought together victims, offenders and community members and engaged them in a process of dialogue. Victims were offered the opportunity to recount personal experiences about the aftermath of crime and offenders were provided with the opportunity to reflect on their actions and respond to any questions that the victims may have. Many of the offenders and victims had been involved in violent crime and the courses, facilitated by staff and experienced mediators, gave participants the opportunity to learn from their experiences in a series of restorative encounters.

Research evaluating the programme found that although most offenders had rarely recounted or discussed their crimes whilst in prison, they actually wanted to do so and as a result of their discussions they felt more able to take responsibility.[115] Both victims of crime and community members who worked with the prisoners felt it had been a positive experience and had increased their awareness of how to help victims and offenders. For victims, the results indicated the programme was useful in reducing their fear of victimisation and that they felt less ashamed about what had happened to them. Other victims reported that it made an important contribution to their healing. The majority of victims, offenders and community members considered the programme a success.[116]

A second notable scheme is the *Resolve to Stop the Violence* project which started in San Francisco in 1996. A collaboration between Community Works and the San Francisco Sheriff's Department, the programme brought together victim advocates, ex-offenders and community members to deliver an intensive programme for violent inmates. The programme contained three main elements: offender accountability, victim restoration and community involvement.[117] It also brought victims into prisons to tell the inmates of their experiences, and of how crime had affected their lives, as well as providing the opportunity for offenders to meet victims. The programme itself was an intensive experience for participants, in which offenders were involved in counselling and group work which explored their violent past and alternatives to violent conflict.

---

[114] Wood and Suzuki (2016).
[115] Helfgott et al (1999).
[116] Helfgott et al (1999); Lovell et al (2002).
[117] Gilligan and Lee (2005).

Victims played a part in the delivery of the programme by telling inmates of their experience of crime and its aftermath, giving them a first-hand appreciation of the impact of crime. It was delivered in a restorative context in which offenders were encouraged to reflect on the consequences of their actions. The programme also provided an opportunity for victims and their family members to meet the individual offender who had had harmed them. These meetings were carried out on a face-to-face basis or through other means such as a video link. Where appropriate, representatives from a variety of welfare, criminal justice agencies and support groups assisted victims and their families in preparing for the sessions and accompanied them if desired.[118] The meetings were mediated by trained facilitators and gave the participants the opportunity to talk through the crime and how it had impacted them, as well as providing opportunities for both sides to better understand the offence and its impact. The programme was evaluated positively by victim participants and was shown to have had a positive impact on the behaviour of inmates while they were serving their sentences.[119]

One of the most widely known restorative-based programmes in Canadian prisons was the Victim Offender Mediation/Dialogue Program which was established in Langley, British Columbia in 1991. This therapeutic programme was designed to facilitate and support restorative interactions between inmates and victims with a particular emphasis on serious crimes, including aggravated sexual assaults, murders and armed robberies. The scheme, which has now been replicated across other prisons in Western Canada, is facilitated by professional therapists who work in three-member teams with individual victims and offenders to help them to come to terms with the aftermath of the offence. Much of the work is one-to-one in nature, though interaction is facilitated through letters and video messages and, where meetings take place, these will usually be convened by two therapists who provide participants an opportunity to meet in a safe environment should they so wish.

An evaluation of the programme revealed a number of positive findings, including showing that inmates were better able to understand the impact of their offence on their victims and they were better able to develop empathy towards their victims.[120] For their part, victims also expressed high levels of satisfaction with the programme and indicated two primary motivators for participating: to know more of why the perpetrator committed the offence and to make the offender aware of the impacts of the crime. Moreover, the programme led to a stronger sense of community amongst inmates and staff within the institutions and there were fewer problems and disciplinary incidents within the unit using the restorative programme.[121] Unfortunately, the programme closed in 2005 following a change of the management in the prison service.

---

[118] Gilligan and Lee (2005).
[119] Gilligan and Lee (2005).
[120] See eg Roberts (1995), Umbreit (1995).
[121] Roberts (1995).

Similar in many ways to experiences in England and Wales, these examples of prison-based restorative programmes in North America show the potentially positive impacts of managed encounters between victims and offenders. It is evident that many such programmes can produce enhanced levels of victim awareness and offer inmates a chance to reflect on the consequences of their actions on others and themselves. Programmes that facilitate face-to-face interactions with victims appear to carry greater impact than methods of indirect mediation.

However, these prison-based restorative programmes are often limited in their capacity to deliver agency and accountability. As victims and offenders only occasionally meet in person, stakeholders are unable to engage in an emotionally-rich dialogue that is capable of addressing the individual—and often very complex—needs of victims and offenders. Moreover, since offenders in prison have already been sentenced through a punitive and exclusionary process, the true extent to which victims and offenders are empowered to assume a sense of ownership over the crime is questionable. Aside from the prison sentence itself, other issues relating to the reparatory interests of victims or the rehabilitation of offenders tend to fall beyond the reach of any restorative process. Thus, the capacity of prison-based schemes to facilitate agency and accountability is curtailed by lack of coherency and engagement in how many of the fundamental questions surrounding the offence and its aftermath are addressed. As a result, most prison-based restorative programmes are not 'full' forms of 'restorative justice' since they only encapsulate limited elements of our agency–accountability framework.

However, Belgium offers an innovative and well-developed prison-based restorative programme, which has evolved from a pilot study and action-research across six prisons carried out by the Universities of Leuven and Liege in 1998. Based on the positive results of the scheme, the Ministry of Justice assumed a central role in driving forward prison-based restorative justice on a national basis. The Federal Prison Plan of 2000 signalled that restorative justice should play a central role in national penal policy, with reintegration and reconciliation between the victim and offender among the key goals identified. All prisons were directed to employ a full-time 'restorative justice advisor' who, in addition to working on individual cases with victims and inmates, would also support the development of a restorative 'culture'.[122] Although the role was abolished in 2008, restorative justice continues to be integral to the Belgian system,[123] with programmes including victim awareness schemes, as well as direct and indirect mediation services.

Recent research exploring the motivations for prisoners participating in the scheme found that the majority of respondents felt genuinely remorseful for their past behaviour, and that this—along with their eagerness to offer explanations and answers the victims' questions—were the main reasons that offenders wished to participate.[124] The researchers also found that prisoners serving shorter

---

[122] Aertsen (2015); Stamatakis and Vandeviver (2012).
[123] Aertsen (2015).
[124] Stamatakis and Vandeviver (2012).

sentences (less than 10 years) were most likely to feel empathy for their victims and acknowledge the impact of their crime compared with those serving longer sentences.

Some prisons have also adopted restorative practices into their disciplinary regimes for both inmates and staff.[125] Importantly, parole and early release decisions are often influenced by evidence of the offender's efforts to address the harm he or she caused through their offending, particularly towards their victim. Similarly, the Corrections Act 2004 in New Zealand requires the parole board to take into account any restorative interventions that have been completed, when considering applications for release from prison. The result of the Belgian initiative has seen the use of restorative interventions and mediation becoming a central part of its prison regime. This has also led to the development of an independent restorative fund, to which prisoners can contribute through community service inside or outside prison. The proceeds of this work are put in a fund used to help compensate victims of crime.[126] Thus, the benefits of bringing restorative measures into the prison system can have broader positive impacts, beyond increasing inmates' awareness of victims and the consequences of their actions on others. However, a clearer focus on the empowering values of restorative justice can assist in guiding and informing future developments of restorative-based interventions in prisons, underlining the need for more meaningful interactions between victims and offenders, as well as a more joined-up approach to forging restorative outcomes that are better targeted towards the individual needs of both victims and offenders. There is also potential for the outcomes of prison-based restorative encounters to influence decisions that are taken in respect of licensing/parole or early release decisions.

VII. Conclusions

Clearly, there is a diverse and eclectic range of restorative interventions within diversionary, community and prison settings. Some of these schemes enable offenders and victims to come together and agree how to deal with a crime and its aftermath; the RISE police-led conferencing project is one such example. However, fully restorative practices like these are more the exception than the rule. Given that most of the programmes detailed here sit at the periphery of criminal justice, operating largely in a diversionary capacity (excluding the prison programmes), they are generally used for less serious types of offences. It is difficult to justify the significant investment of bringing offenders and victims together in the

---

[125] See generally Van Ness (2007).
[126] Eyckmans (2005).

demanding process of restorative justice when the offence is minor and the harm to the victim may be minimal. Thus it is unsurprising how much of the restorative practice on the ground can best be described as 'partially restorative', with only elements of restorative justice employed and limited opportunities for empowering interactions to deal with these mostly minor offences.

Methods used across police-led cautioning practices are usually only partially restorative; for example in England and Wales the vast bulk of restorative cautions took place without a victim present.[127] Police officers would usually try to provide some form of victim input into the process, highlighting how the victim was impacted, thereby attempting to make the offender more aware of the consequences of their actions. The process also sought to emphasise the wrongfulness of the offence, rather than the wrongfulness of the offender, thus underlining the importance of reintegrating the offender, once they had accepted the consequences of their actions. Similarly, in Northern Ireland, it was found that only a small number of offenders given restorative cautions had a victim present in the process and of those that did, many used surrogate victims, drawn from a volunteer panel or victim support organisations. Likewise, many of the community-based programmes used mediation and other partially restorative methods and Youth Offender Panels in England and Wales have rarely been able to directly involve victims in their restorative practices. Thus, in reality there is only a limited potential for fully restorative programmes which are capable of more fully delivering the agency and accountability for victims, offenders and other participants at the periphery of criminal justice.

There has been a significant growth in these partially restorative programmes, but difficulties can arise when diversionary and other types of programmes operating at the periphery of the criminal justice system adopt the restorative label, to promote what they do. For example, in our research on the pilot Northern Ireland police-led restorative cautioning schemes, we found evidence of net-widening, whereby some petty first-time young offenders ended up being formally cautioned, largely because there was a perception that the process was a 'good thing' to do. Prior to the introduction of the scheme, such cases were usually given informal warnings or the police would take no further action. This highlights the danger of 'attractive' diversionary alternatives supplementing rather than supplanting existing formal criminal procedures.

Diversionary practices at the periphery of criminal justice sometimes adopt the restorative label, yet really deliver little of what could be described as a restorative intervention. For instance, the Youth Restorative Disposal was established to use a restorative framework for dealing with minor youth offending. Yet, research has shown it to have limited restorative potential. There is certainly little prospect of empowering victims or offenders or achieving a meaningful sense of agency and accountability for them when the disposal results in little more than a verbal

---

[127] Wilcox and Young (2007).

apology given on the street without meaningful engagement between the parties and a lack of any follow up through Youth Offending Teams. Interventions like this highlight the priority given to reducing policing costs and increasing the speed at which offenders are processed, rather than providing any real attempt at providing restorative interventions which could empower victims or offenders.

A similar danger occurs when criminal justice practices explicitly use the restorative justice label, yet provide little opportunity for it to be practised. This not only misrepresents the practice, but also dilutes our understanding of what restorative justice seeks to achieve. An example of this is the Referral Order in England and Wales, which is described as primarily seeking to prevent reoffending by providing a 'restorative justice' approach within a community context.[128] While early research described them as constructive and participatory forums in which to address young people's offending,[129] very low levels of victim participation in the process have been uncovered, significantly limiting their potential to realise the fundamental principles of restorative justice.[130] Research also describes the depersonalised nature of such interventions and the use of standardised outcomes[131] which clearly undermine the potential for them to deliver the agency–accountability framework which restorative justice programmes should provide, for both victims and offenders.

However, it is also important to highlight that many partially restorative practices are still an improvement on previous practices. This can be seen in restorative cautioning, which has been enthusiastically taken up by many police forces. Research has shown this to be to be a significant improvement in practice over the old-style reprimand.[132] Equally, elements of restorative practice can provide some degree of empowerment when they help offenders to actively participate in the process and realise the consequences of their actions on others. Many prison-based restorative programmes have been successful in raising prisoners' awareness of the consequences of their actions, both on their victims and on themselves and their families. Indeed, such programmes can provide rarely available opportunities within prison for prisoners to discuss their crime and its consequences in a constructive manner. Partially restorative practices like these can tap into the values of agency and accountability, at least in a limited sense, by providing offenders with a forum in which they speak for themselves and participate in an active process, thereby imbuing elements of agency. Likewise, aspects of accountability can be delivered by the offender accepting responsibility for the consequences of their actions and by being willing to apologise (even indirectly) or provide some form of restitution.

---

[128] Ministry of Justice (2015), 8.
[129] Newburn et al (2002).
[130] Rosenblatt (2015b); Newburn et al (2002).
[131] Rosenblatt (2015b).
[132] Wilcox and Young (2007); O'Mahony and Doak (2004).

In many respects the evolution of the partially restorative practices which are being increasingly used across diversionary interventions are an appropriate response to the often minor types of offences that they are employed to deal with. We know that many of the offences that are dealt with at the diversionary stages of the criminal justice system (before prosecution or court) are usually a result of less serious crimes and offenders are often young and do not have offending histories. In these circumstances there is a danger that fully fledged restorative interventions like conferences may be used, even though these are onerous, time consuming and costly to organise, and may be disproportionate for such cases. Thus it may be better to deal with minor offences through the range of partially diversionary practices that are continuing to emerge. Likewise, some petty offending may be more appropriately dealt with informally, through a verbal warning (given restoratively) rather than through any formal programme or onerous procedures. The broader value of empowerment theory and our agency–accountability framework in this context is their potential to guide and inform the continued development and implementation of diversionary practices which employ at least a partially restorative focus. Such goals and values could help diversionary restorative practice to recalibrate its focus and objectives and may even help clarify its role and purpose within criminal justice into the future.

6

Mediation and Restorative Justice in Continental Europe

I. Introduction

While police-led restorative initiatives have expanded considerably in many common law jurisdictions, the development of mediation and restorative justice in continental Europe has tended to be led by the public prosecutor. In contrast to many common law jurisdictions, where the prosecutor's role is adversarial to the offender, the prosecutor in most civil law jurisdictions occupies a quasi-judicial role, with an overall duty to ensure that the criminal investigation is carried out impartially and the offender is dealt with fairly.[1] For example, in Germany and Austria the prosecutor is viewed not as an adversary of the defendant, but as a neutral advocate for the state. As such, they exercise close oversight over the criminal investigation, and are also seen as a largely objective source of information which the court will usually rely upon heavily for the purposes of sentencing.

Restorative interventions in continental Europe generally take the form of victim-offender mediation and are aimed primarily at juveniles.[2] Many of these programmes were developed during the 1980s, but have expanded dramatically since the turn of the century.[3] The continued growth of these programmes has been promoted by European and international standards, which have advocated mediation and other restorative practices.[4] While the growth of restorative justice is reflected in the expansion of such practices throughout Europe, it has proven to be particularly popular in Austria, Belgium, Finland, the Netherlands and Norway. The majority of the mediation projects available are used as forms of diversion away from criminal sanctioning and are usually restricted to less serious property and minor personal offences,[5] although, as we outline below, there is an increasing willingness to experiment at the 'deeper end' of the justice system. Most mediation-based programmes are not explicitly restorative. Although mediation

---

[1] Doak (2008).
[2] Dünkel et al (2015).
[3] Dünkel et al (2015); Pelikan and Trenczek (2006).
[4] See ch 1, II.
[5] Miers and Willemsens (2004).

is traditionally settlement-driven, recently, there has been an increasing emphasis on providing mediation programmes that have a stronger restorative focus, whereby they focus on the needs of the participants and are driven by dialogue and consent.[6]

Many descriptive accounts of the various European mediation-based programmes exist and there is considerable variation in what they do and how they operate.[7] However, there has been a general lack of research to evaluate such schemes, although more concrete data has emerged in recent years. In this chapter, we examine a range of mediation and restorative practices, drawing, in particular, from evaluations of the more developed programmes across the continent. It is not our intention to provide a comprehensive description of individual programmes; that task that has been admirably accomplished elsewhere.[8] Rather, we aim to give an insight of the range of practices that exist, the factors which have served to either propel or hinder their development, and the extent to which they might be capable of delivering a restorative and empowering experience whereby participants are able to achieve a strong sense of agency and accountability.

II. Background and Context

Moves towards alternative penal approaches in Europe were triggered in the late 1970s and early 1980s. As noted in chapter one, this period saw an increasing interest among both academics and policymakers in less retributive and more reparative forms of justice. For example, a report to the Norwegian Parliament in 1978 encouraged the Government to test a range of new ways of dealing with young offenders.[9] Mediation in Finland was first piloted in 1983 and rolled out nationwide during the 1990s.[10] Sweden followed a little later, with police-led schemes being introduced in 1987 before mediation schemes were placed on a statutory footing in 2002.[11]

Belgium is currently the only European jurisdiction which offers restorative justice for both juveniles and adults for all types of offences, and is particularly noteworthy insofar as it is the first civil law jurisdiction to have introduced conferencing as a mainstream option for juvenile offenders.[12] As in the Nordic countries,

---

[6] Strang et al (2013).
[7] Shapland (2012).
[8] See Dünkel et al (2015).
[9] Kemény (2005). It can be noted, however, that Norway lacks any distinct juvenile justice system; the age of criminal responsibility is 15 years and young people below this age are dealt with under the social welfare system. For those over the age of 15, the Municipal Mediation Service Act 1991 placed mediation on a statutory footing and specific powers to make referrals to mediation and to discontinue proceedings are provided to prosecutors under the Criminal Procedure Act 1998: Lundgaard (2015).
[10] Lappi-Seppälä (2015).
[11] Marklund (2015).
[12] Put et al (2012).

the welfare-orientated nature of the youth justice system in Belgium has proved conducive to the development of restorative justice.[13] Mediation—largely diversionary in nature—expanded significantly during the 1990s in Belgium,[14] with a number of programmes being developed by both the police and Public Prosecutor. The Flemish Parliament opted to roll out restorative justice initiatives across all judicial districts in 1999,[15] and in the following year a family group conferencing model, *Hergo*, was piloted across five judicial districts in Flanders to deal with more serious young offenders.[16] Under the Youth Justice Act 2006, mediation and conferencing are regarded as the primary disposals for youth crime,[17] and must be offered to the offender in every case where a victim has been identified.[18] In most instances, referral will occur at the prosecution stage of proceedings;[19] the case may only proceed to the Youth Court once the offer has been made or where the reasons for non-referral are specifically explained.[20] The Youth Court may then either make its own referral or proceed to deal with the case in the conventional manner. As far as adults are concerned, there are two models, both based on mediation. Penal mediation for minor offences is overseen by probation officers, where authority has been given by the public prosecutor; and 'mediation for redress' implemented by non-governmental organisations (NGOs) under the auspices of the Ministry of Justice, is available for all types of offences.[21]

Similarly in France, *médiation pénale* was developed in the early 1980s through various localised pilot projects, with express provision introduced into the criminal code in 1993.[22] Despite some initial scepticism among lawyers and magistrates, France was one of the first jurisdictions to enact statutory provision for mediation. In August 2014, a further amendment provided that mediation had to be made available at all stages of the criminal procedure, including sentencing.[23] Thus the prosecutor may refer a case to mediation at the pre-sentence stage of criminal proceedings. Usually, such cases are minor in nature, though more serious offences such as theft and criminal damage can be referred for mediation also.[24]

These developments were mirrored in Germany, where mediation (*Täter-Opfer-Ausgleich*) was piloted in a number of cities across the Federal Republic

---

[13] Aertsen (2015).
[14] Bolívar et al (2015).
[15] Aertsen (2015).
[16] Vanfraechem et al (2012).
[17] Put et al (2012), 88.
[18] Put et al (2012), 89.
[19] Put et al (2012).
[20] Aertsen (2015).
[21] Zinsstag et al (2011), 281.
[22] Article 41(6) of the *Code de Procédure Pénale* was amended, as a result of which a prosecutor may 'prior to his decision on further action and with the agreement of the parties, decide on mediation if it seems to him that such a step would ensure reparation of the damage caused to the victim, put an end to the difficulties arising from the breaking of the law and help in the rehabilitation of the individual': Lazerges (1998); cited by Miers et al (2001), 31.
[23] *Code de Procédure Pénale*, Art 10-1: Cario (2015).
[24] Tränkle (2007).

of Germany in the mid-1980s. During the 1990s, formal legal provision for mediation was gradually integrated into the German Criminal Procedure Code (StPO) and the Juvenile Criminal Code (JGG). As far as the latter is concerned, judges are empowered to refer any case to victim-offender mediation (s 10.1.7 JGG), and the public prosecutor can opt to halt procedure if the juvenile engages in a reconciliation process (s 45.2.2 JGG). For adult offenders, courts and prosecutors in Germany have considerably less discretion to make referrals, since the principle of legality dictates that the criminal law should be fully enforced (s 152 StPO). In 1999, victim-offender mediation assumed greater prominence under the law. Prosecutors and judges were placed under an obligation, at every stage of the process, to consider whether victim-offender mediation between the victim and offender might be feasible (s 155a StPO), and should, where appropriate, initiate or foster any reconciliation attempts by the parties. These programmes expanded rapidly and there are currently approximately 400 schemes in operation, dealing with an annual caseload of around 20–30,000 cases.[25] Around two-thirds of these involve juveniles.[26]

Another noteworthy scheme, from an international perspective is the HALT scheme of the Netherlands, which was established during the early 1980s as a police-led referral programme for first and second-time young offenders under the age of 16 involved in minor property offences. The scheme was one of the earliest crime prevention measures to be established in Europe with a clear restorative component and was enacted into legislation in 1995.[27] The programme is primarily offender-orientated; although victims are occasionally invited to participate in mediation, reparation is normally directed towards the wider community.[28]

III. Administration and Referral

As one might expect across a wide range of legal traditions, there is little homogeneity in terms of how mediation and restorative practices are administered. For the most part, state-based agencies centred on probation, social welfare or youth justice exercise an organisational role, either on a national or local level. In Norway, for example, responsibility for organising mediation passed from municipal authorities to the Ministry of Justice in 2004; the National Mediation Service now operates nationwide across 22 regional centres.[29] As in other Nordic countries, programmes are serviced by NGOs or trained volunteers and many

---

[25] Dünkel and Păroşanu (2015); Kilchling (2005).
[26] Dünkel and Păroşanu (2015); Pelikan and Trenczek (2006).
[27] Code of Criminal Procedure, Art 77(e).
[28] Blad (2006).
[29] Lundgaard (2015).

programmes operate outside the umbrella of the formal statutory scheme.[30] In Finland, mediation services are well established and are overseen by the Ministry of Social Affairs and Health, but financed and managed by local authorities. While practices vary considerably from one municipal district to another, the *Law on Mediation* (1015/2005), passed in 2006, has helped to ensure more consistency.[31] In other countries, such as Belgium, the Netherlands and the Czech Republic, programmes are largely dependent upon professionals, often with a background in social work, probation or law enforcement.[32] In Austria, mediation is organised and conducted by NEUSTART, a private organisation under the umbrella of the Ministry of Justice,[33] whilst in France the National Institute of Victim Assistance and Mediation (INAVEM) enters into local agreements with prosecutors' offices.[34] German programmes vary from state to state, with a range of public, private and voluntary sector provision.[35]

Across the continent as a whole, referrals tend to be diversionary in nature, and are made by the police or prosecutor (although they may also emanate from local government, the civil courts or the parties themselves),[36] with only a very small number of referrals ordered by courts as part of a community sentence or as a special condition of a suspended sentence.[37] Typically, prosecutors will make a determination whether the case is suitable for referral to mediation, yet usually this discretion will hinge upon the legislative scope of the provision in question. The efficacy of individual programmes is often contingent upon good working relationships between individual mediators or agencies and the more established criminal justice agencies.[38] For the most part, there are no concrete rules as to how types of offences should be disposed of; police or prosecutors are generally given discretion to determine whether or not a case is suitable for referral and it is rarely mandated. In some jurisdictions, such as Finland, referrals may also be made by judges and even the parties themselves.[39]

---

[30] The Red Cross, for example, has collaborated with schools, the police and other criminal justice agencies as part of its 'Street Mediation' project, which trains young people to act as mediators themselves in conflicts involving gangs and groups of young people. The Minhaj Mediation Service operates in a number of Norwegian cities and specialises in resolving conflicts involving young people from Muslim backgrounds: Lundgaard (2015).

[31] Whilst the new legislation did not radically alter the practices which had been developing throughout Finland over the past 20 years, it did amend the criminal code to provide that an agreement or settlement between the offender and the victim can now act as a possible ground for mitigation in sentencing, and could result in diversion from prosecution altogether when punishment is deemed unnecessary and the offender has reconciled with the victim, or has undertaken other reparative actions. This diversionary application is most widely applied to juvenile offenders: Lappi-Seppälä (2015).

[32] Dünkel et al (2015).

[33] Gombots and Pelikan (2015).

[34] *Code de Procédure Pénale*, Art 41(1) authorises the prosecutor to refer the offender 'to a medical, social or professional agency' as an alternative to mediation.

[35] Dünkel and Păroşanu (2015).

[36] Dünkel et al (2015).

[37] Kemény (2005); Lundgaard (2015).

[38] Hofinger et al (2002); Dünkel et al (2015).

[39] Pelikan and Trenczek (2006).

Generally, where legislation is in place, there are strict parameters on the types of offences and/or offenders which are deemed suitable for mediation or restorative interventions. These tend to fall at the lower end of the spectrum; in Norway, for instance (which arguably has the highest number of referrals per capita in Europe),[40] typical cases include theft, criminal damage, joyriding and less serious violent offences.[41] Providing that guilt has been established and the parties agree on the facts of the case and consent to the process, mediation may then be offered as an alternative at the sentencing stage.[42]

Similarly, in Austria, mediation may be ordered where there is no 'serious culpability' on the part of the suspect, provided that the facts and circumstances of the case have been adequately clarified, and that the maximum punishment prescribed by law for the offence does not exceed five years' imprisonment.[43] Here mediation is only possible where the offender has agreed (1) to accept responsibility for the offence; (2) to make some effort to try to repair the damage; and (3) to reflect on the reasons that led to the offence. The victim's consent is also necessary in cases involving adult offenders, unless this consent is withheld for reasons that are not relevant to the criminal proceedings.[44]

In France, the prosecutor may:

> prior to his decision on further action and with the agreement of the parties, decide on mediation if it seems to him that such a step would ensure reparation of the damage caused to the victim, put an end to the difficulties arising from the breaking of the law and help in the rehabilitation of the individual.[45]

In August 2014, an amendment to the *Code de Procédure Pénale*, provided that mediation must be made available at all stages of the criminal procedure, including sentencing, though only the prosecutor may refer a case to mediation at the pre-sentence stage of proceedings. Again, the types of cases referred tend to be minor in nature, though there appears to be a growing willingness to make referrals in cases of theft and criminal damage.[46]

As we noted above, Belgium is unique as the only continental jurisdiction to place conferencing on a statutory platform, with no upper limits as to the seriousness of the offence. Unlike mediation which tends to be used primarily for minor offences, *Hergo* is generally reserved for more serious offences where a victim has been identified. The offender must consent to the process and must

---

[40] See Miers and Willemsens (2004); Lundgaard (2015).
[41] Similar types of offences appear to be subject to referral in France, Germany and Austria: Gombots and Pelikan (2015); Kerner and Hartmann (2005); Tränkle (2007).
[42] Kemény (2005).
[43] Gombots and Pelikan (2015).
[44] Hofinger et al (2002).
[45] Code de *Procédure Pénale*, Art 46(3).
[46] Tränkle (2007). Since 2010, 'victim-inmate meetings' (*Rencontres Détenus-Victimes*) have been rolled out across a number of prisons, while 'victim-sentenced person meetings', which take place post-release in the community have been piloted across a number of regions since 2015: Cario (2015).

accept responsibility. Victims are offered the opportunity to participate, though their attendance is not compulsory and they may opt to participate indirectly (ie through writing a letter or through being represented by a friend or family member). Conferencing is also used in the Netherlands, albeit without a statutory framework. Here, referrals are accepted by private organisations from welfare agencies, the courts and affected communities.[47] Although originally geared towards problematic behaviour among juveniles, conferences now deal with a range of conflicts, including low-level crime, neighbourhood disputes and even domestic violence.[48]

The level of divergence in the organisation and referral systems which exist across (and sometimes within) various jurisdictions means that access to mediation and restorative programmes is highly variable. In some jurisdictions, such as Austria, Belgium and Finland, it seems that mediation is well embedded in the criminal justice system, whereas the availability of services in other jurisdictions, including France and Germany, varies considerably depending on the attitudes and working practices of criminal justice agencies.[49] However, it is clear that recent years have witnessed the emergence of more far-reaching restorative programmes, especially in Belgium and the Netherlands, allowing participants to become more empowered and delivering agency and accountability through their conferencing models.

IV. Process and Agreement

While the process of victim-offender mediation varies between each programme, it is usually governed by a central set of protocols overseen by a central agency. These tend to include commonly accepted best practice (eg voluntariness, consent, preparation and risk assessment). Generally, service providers outside the criminal justice system assess the suitability of the case, prepare parties for the meeting, facilitate it and oversee its implementation and monitoring. While some programmes, such as those in Norway, only provide for direct mediation, others (such as some in Germany and Austria) allow for shuttle mediation where one party declines to meet face-to-face.[50] There is evidence that direct mediation tends to result in a higher rate of offender-compliance with resulting agreements, than where it was indirect.[51] Most schemes allow parents or supporters of the parties

---

[47] Van Pagée et al (2012).
[48] Zinsstag et al (2011).
[49] Jullion (2000), cited by Miers et al (2001), 28.
[50] Kilchling (2005).
[51] Miers et al (2001).

to attend (indeed, this is a requirement in France).[52] Some programmes, such as those in Finland and Germany, also permit legal representation. Describing the French mediation system, Miers et al note how it comprises four distinct phases:

> Most associations structure their mediation practice into four phases. The preliminary phase comprises information exchange between prosecutor and association, analysis of the conflict, and initial meetings with the parties. The two central phases are the mediation itself and the completion of an agreement between them. The final phase comprises implementation, closure and evaluation. The association (or individual mediator) formally reports to the prosecutor on the process and the outcome.[53]

The Finnish process, as described by Iivari, is usually overseen by two mediators:

> The mediation process starts with preliminary contacts. The mediation office or one of its mediators contacts both parties separately, asking whether they are willing to take the matter into mediation. If all parties are agreed, the first mediation session will be held. For the majority of the cases this will suffice, but if needed, more sessions are arranged. During these sessions the mediator's principal role is to mediate; he/she does not try to lead the parties into one direction or another, but tries to mediate between them so that they both, understanding one another's viewpoint, can come to an agreement … If mediation is successful, a written contract is prepared. The contract includes the item (offence type), the content of the settlement (how the offender has consented to repair the damage), place and date of restitution as well as the consequences of a breach of contract.[54]

What is evident from the administration and operation of most established mediation programmes across continental Europe is the currently limited extent to which they have fully embraced restorative goals. Their focus, at least initially, has been on providing mediated settlements between parties, allowing for compensation or restitution. Yet there is real potential to provide a more empowering process that maximises the potential for empowering participants through the agency–accountability framework.

Indeed, some countries have begun to adopt a more mainstreamed restorative approach. For example, Belgium is currently practising restorative youth conferencing widely, having secured a statutory foothold under the auspices of the Youth Justice Act 2006. As noted above, conferencing also operates in the Netherlands, although here it remains largely on the periphery of the system and is unregulated by law. However, in both countries there is no restrictive threshold regarding offence severity.[55] Conferencing generally involves a much greater number of participants than mediation; parents of the young person must attend, while supporters, family members, police officers, social workers and teachers may attend.[56] Its format broadly mirrors that of the New Zealand model (explored

---

[52] Milburn (2002).
[53] Miers et al (2001), 29.
[54] Iivari (2000), 199.
[55] Dünkel et al (2015).
[56] Aertsen (2015).

in chapter seven) with the offender, the victim, their respective supporters and a police officer all present. Conferences are organised and co-ordinated by independent facilitators, with each participant being given an opportunity to speak and ask questions, and to contribute to the action plan.

The Dutch and Belgian approaches to conferencing differ from the New Zealand model in two key respects. First, they tend to consist of a larger circle comprising the families and friends of victims and offenders, along with community representatives and other professionals such as social workers. Van Pagée et al note that average attendance tends to be around 13 people.[57] A second distinctive feature of these conferences is that the co-ordinator and other professionals will usually leave the conference once the discussion around the offence has taken place, leaving the circle of participants with 'private time' in order to develop their own action plan.[58]

After an introduction, the facilitator invites the police officer to open with a factual account of events, with parties then having the opportunity to ask questions of each other. One distinctive feature is that parties are offered 'private time' at the end of the conference. This is designed to enable the offenders and their supporters to propose a plan to repair the harm which should consist of three main elements: reparation to the victim, reparation to the broader community and measures to prevent future reoffending.[59] In Flanders, offenders may draw on a special fund that is made available to juveniles who have no financial means to reimburse victims for the damage they have caused.[60] If agreement is reached, the conference plan is then signed by all parties before being forwarded to the Youth Court which may approve or reject it. If approved and successfully fulfilled, the case is closed; otherwise the court may opt to organise a second conference or follow an alternative route.[61] Clearly, the Dutch and Belgian approaches offer a much more restorative experience for participants. There is considerable scope within these programmes for engagement in dialogue and for agreed outcomes which foster agency and accountability.

In terms of outcomes, financial compensation has long been regarded as the norm in many of the larger European jurisdictions, including France and Germany. A small scale study carried out in Finland in 2003 suggested that many of the agreements were not very creative; reparation tended to be limited to solely monetary compensation, with other symbolic forms of reparation generally ignored.[62] While satisfaction levels have been found to be generally high, some offenders were seemingly reluctant to participate in the programme. However, as discourse around the notion of symbolic reparation has increased, it seems that many jurisdictions are adopting a more holistic stance as to what the mediation

[57] Van Pagée et al (2012).
[58] Van Drie et al (2015).
[59] Zinsstag et al (2011).
[60] Aertsen (2015).
[61] Zinsstag et al (2011).
[62] Elonheimo (2003).

agreement seeks to achieve.[63] In Austria, for instance, victim/offender mediation or *Außergerichtlicher Tatausgleich* has a long tradition in the country.[64] While literally translated as 'out-of-court offence compensation', the concept implies much more than a victim and offender simply negotiating a financial settlement. Instead, the process is designed to ensure that a comprehensive form of restitution is delivered which is 'socially constructive and more directly related to the victim: its goal—as an additional instrument of the penal system—is restoration of public peace after an offence'.[65] Mediation agreements thus aim to encapsulate three distinct components: compensation for any personal injury, loss or damage caused; reconciliation between victims and offenders; and, in exceptional cases, community service or payments to public welfare institutions (so-called 'symbolic restitution').[66] In Finland, recent data show that although 39 per cent of the agreements included financial compensation, other symbolic forms of reparation such as apology and the promise not to repeat the behaviour also featured prominently.[67] Apologies alongside some form of financial recompense were also observed relatively frequently in Bulgaria, Croatia, Latvia, Poland and Portugal.[68]

Although mediation is an out-of-court procedure, the final decision of whether to drop criminal charges or to pursue criminal proceedings in France remains in the hands of the prosecution authorities. Notwithstanding any agreement that may have been reached, it is still open to the prosecutor to continue the case if necessary to do so. In other jurisdictions such as Belgium, the courts have a role in ratifying the agreement and may impose additional measures as necessary to ensure that the harm is made good.[69] Likewise, in Finland, if the offence is relatively minor in nature (known in Finnish law as a 'complainant offence'), the agreement will usually bring the matter to a close and the prosecutor will generally drop the charges.[70] However, if the offence is more serious in nature, it can be treated as a 'non complainant offence', and the fact that the parties have been involved in a successful mediation will not necessarily bring the matter to a close. The principle of legality dictates that the case will still usually be heard by a court. Depending on the gravity of the offence and a range of other factors, the prosecutor may then use his or her discretion to drop the case; this is likely to follow if subsequent prosecution would seem 'either unreasonable or pointless' due to a reconciliation and if non-prosecution would not violate 'an important public or private interest'.[71] However, even where the case does proceed to court, the judge may opt to mitigate the sentence or even refrain from imposing a sentence altogether.[72]

---

[63] Dünkel et al (2015).
[64] Gombots and Pelikan (2015).
[65] Löschnig-Gspandl and Kilchling (1997), 59.
[66] Löschnig-Gspandl and Kilchling (1997).
[67] Lappi-Seppälä (2015).
[68] Dünkel et al (2015).
[69] Put et al (2012); Vanfraechem et al (2012).
[70] Iivari (2000).
[71] Lappi-Seppälä (2011).
[72] Iivari (2000).

V. Evaluation

As Miers and Willemsens note in their 2004 survey of restorative justice across Europe, the paucity of evaluative data makes comparisons problematic, and we caution against over-interpreting these data.[73] Although there has been a raft of studies published in the years since this survey, some jurisdictions (perhaps most notably France and Germany) have been subject to little evaluative research. Nevertheless, in recent years there has been an increase in research across Europe, with the European Union funding a number of major comparative projects.[74]

This research base provides valuable insights into the state of restorative justice across many European jurisdictions where information has previously been difficult to access. However, they rarely present primary data that is capable of supporting meaningful comparison. One exception is a recent study by Vanfraechem et al, which sought to collect and compare data on victims' experiences with mediation across Austria, Finland and the Netherlands.[75] The same questionnaire was used across all three jurisdictions with a total of 197 victims interviewed (67 based in Austria, 48 in Finland and 82 in the Netherlands). Satisfaction levels were broadly high in terms of the preparation, the experience of the mediation process itself and the outcome. However, respondents tended to be less optimistic in terms of the longer term cathartic effects of the intervention on either the offender or themselves.[76]

Some differences were noted between the jurisdictions; Austrian and Finnish victims appeared more satisfied with the amount of information they received prior to the process than those in the Netherlands.[77] Likewise, concerns emerged from Finnish data regarding the attitudes of mediators, who were sometimes observed in engaging in 'small talk' with the offender.[78] Differences also existed in terms of whether victims in each of the countries considered the harm to have been 'repaired'; this was considerably higher in Austria and in Finland than in the Netherlands. The researchers suggest this may be attributable in part to the participants equating 'repair' with the notion of financial compensation, which tends to be more common in the former jurisdictions than in the latter.[79] However, as Zinsstag notes in a comparative review of mediation and conferencing programmes, many share similar broad objectives and the conferencing model appears to be

---

[73] Miers and Willemsens (2004).
[74] See eg Dünkel et al (2015); Miers et al (2001); Miers and Willemsens (2004); Vanfraechem et al (2015); Zinsstag et al (2011).
[75] Vanfraechem et al (2015).
[76] Bolívar et al (2015), 141.
[77] The researchers suggest this may be attributable to 'differences between the countries in terms of processes of preparation (e.g. some Finnish and Austrian respondents mentioned no preparation or short preparation prior to the meeting), which may relate to their different relationships with the criminal justice system …': Bolívar et al (2015), 137.
[78] Bolívar et al (2015), 138.
[79] Bolívar et al (2015), 139.

permeating mediation practice in a growing number of jurisdictions.[80] Given the pace of growth of diversionary mediation and restorative programmes throughout Europe in recent years, it is hoped that these will be the first of many studies which enable more meaningful comparisons to be made across national borders.

Studies which are confined to a single jurisdiction are difficult to synthesise given differing methodologies and divergent legal procedures, as well as semantic questions over the meaning of key terms such as 'restoration', 'juvenile', 'community', 'reparation' and 'reconciliation'. However, it is possible to discuss some broadly generalisable findings. For instance, it appears that high levels of agreement between the parties have been recorded in Finland, Norway and the Netherlands.[81] Hofinger et al summarise a range of studies from Austria which suggest a very high degree of willingness among both victims and offenders to take part in victim-offender mediation, with around three-quarters of all cases resulting in a successful outcome.[82] In Germany, recent figures show that 80 per cent to 90 per cent of offenders and victims typically agree to participate in mediation, with an overall settlement figure of 89 per cent of cases mediated.[83]

Likewise, there are some indications of overall satisfaction levels within individual countries. Relatively high levels of victim and offender satisfaction have been reported in Austria, Norway and Romania.[84] In addition, there is evidence from Finland suggesting that the outcome-driven focus means that little attention was afforded to the wrongfulness of the crime itself and the emotions of both parties,[85] though a more recent evaluation showed high satisfaction rates, with the overwhelming majority of participants finding the mediation had been useful and fairly conducted.[86] Most Finnish victims also reported high levels of satisfaction and a sense of increased empowerment; they particularly appreciated the 'lightness' of the procedure and the opportunity to share their experiences directly with the offender. The research findings are not, however, universally positive. Some victims experienced a sense of betrayal when the case was subsequently prosecuted through the courts, in which case they felt that their input into the process had been usurped, while the lack of post-mediation support and aftercare was also criticised.[87] One of the few studies that has taken place in France (albeit on a very small scale) relating to mediation gives cause for concern; Tränkle reports that participants did not seem to know what was going on and what the procedure was

---

[80] Zinsstag (2012).
[81] Finland: Lappi-Seppälä (2015) reports an agreement rate of over 90%; Norway: Kemény (2005); Netherlands; Netherlands: Van Pagée et al (2012); Miers and Willemsens (2004).
[82] Hofinger et al (2002). More recent figures show that around two-thirds of all cases are usually successful, with over three-quarters of all cases being subsequently dropped by prosecutors: Gombots and Pelikan (2015).
[83] Dünkel and Pǎroşanu (2015).
[84] Austria: Kilchling and Löschnig-Gspandl (1998); Norway: Paus (2000); Kemény (2005); Romania: Pǎroşanu (2015).
[85] Elonheimo (2003).
[86] Iivari (2010).
[87] Honkatukia (2015b).

about, with the process often grinding to a halt after an initial meeting.[88] Many mediators were observed not to have been 'professionalized sufficiently', with overly formal and developed 'asymmetric relationships' with the other participants.

A broader concern that emerges through the evaluations is the considerable professional resistance—or at least scepticism—found in many jurisdictions. For example, Miers et al cite research published in 1997 which showed that of 450 judges and 667 public prosecutors throughout Germany, only 3 per cent and 11 per cent per cent respectively had made any mediation referrals in the previous year.[89] Indeed, Trenczek notes that only 5 per cent of criminal cases in Germany are dealt with by mediation, in spite of the fact that over 25 per cent of all charges are eligible.[90] Scepticism and/or limited understandings of mediation and restorative approaches have also been recorded in Poland and Bulgaria.[91] It seems that many lawyers and the gatekeepers of the criminal justice system see such practices as a burdensome and time-consuming process.[92] Resistance may be attributable to the fact that most public prosecutors and judges are unfamiliar with such procedures,[93] or that they see them as infringing on their own traditional role in administering the criminal process on behalf of the state.[94] Although positive attitudes towards mediation and restorative justice based interventions are widely held in Sweden and the Netherlands, it would seem that a perceived conflict between restorative and retributive values lead many professionals to conclude that mediation and restorative interventions should be used as a separate, complementary justice measure, as opposed to becoming an integral part of the criminal justice system.[95]

More positive results have been reported from Belgium. The initial *Hergo* pilot, based on the New Zealand model of youth conferencing, showed high levels of satisfaction among victims (75 per cent stated the process was fair and 77 per cent were satisfied with the outcome) and offenders.[96] A majority of agreements were successfully implemented, and there were some tentative indications that re-offending tended to be of a less serious nature.[97] Judges, prosecutors, police and social workers involved in the process were generally satisfied with the model.

The largely positive results from the evaluation prompted the mainstreaming of restorative justice throughout Belgium under the Youth Justice Act 2006. Yet, despite the national roll out provided for by the 2006 legislation, there is evidence that the system is still in its infancy, revealed by relatively few referrals, low

---

[88] Tränkle (2007).
[89] Miers (2001), 57.
[90] Pelikan and Trenczek (2006).
[91] Poland: Zalewski and Părosanu (2015), 134. Bulgaria: Chankova (2015).
[92] Trenczek (2001).
[93] Bannenberg (2000).
[94] Dünkel et al (2015), 1065.
[95] Sweden: Marklund (2015); Netherlands: Van Drie et al (2015). See further Dünkel et al (2015).
[96] Vanfraechem (2005).
[97] Zinsstag et al (2011).

levels of victim involvement, and a lack of direct face-to-face encounters.[98] While placing restorative justice on a statutory footing may have incentivised its use to some extent, it is clear that entrenched working cultures and attitudes need to be addressed. As Vanfraechem et al note:

> For many different reasons there seems to be reluctance to use this alternative justice mechanism. Although some juvenile judges are real champions of the cause, most of them are not yet convinced or find the application of conferencing too complicated.
>
> Moreover, in the interviews it became clear that there is a tendency to blame each other between the judiciary and the conferencing services for the failure of a proper implementation and running at a large scale of conferencing. Reference was also made to the time and labour consuming nature of conferencing and to the lack of funding and staff. For all these reasons, conferencing is reserved for more serious cases; including cases of sexual assault by juvenile offenders for whom the model has been applied successfully.[99]

Despite the national roll out of conferencing in Belgium, it seems that mediation remains a significantly more popular option than conferencing which is considerably more complex and time-consuming.[100] The decision to refer to mediation is complex, and contingent upon several elements, including the seriousness of the case; the prosecutor's personal perspectives; timing; the nature of the relationship between the mediation service and the prosecutor's office; and the role of criminologists attached to the prosecutor's office.[101] Put et al have also identified a widespread 'procedural misunderstanding', whereby some prosecutors send a case to the Youth Court whilst at the same time beginning mediation. Judges thus conclude that there would be little or no value of making an additional referral to conferencing.[102] Research also appears to indicate a dearth of knowledge of what conferencing entails among the judiciary and mediators themselves. Some judges seem to be unaware of the distinction between conferencing and mediation, and there also appears to be some confusion over the roles of the police and social services, as these are not prescribed in the legislation.[103] Such problems appear to be particularly acute in the Wallonia region, where referral rates to conferencing remain very low and are also marked by an unwillingness among victims to participate.[104] In part, these may be attributed to the fact that the initial *Hergo* pilots were only trialled in Flanders; here, it seems that judges, in particular, are more comfortable with the scheme than their Wallonian counterparts. Initiatives were introduced in 2011 to attempt to increase the referral rates in both jurisdictions,[105] though it remains to be seen whether these have been successful.

---

[98] Aertsen (2015).
[99] Zinsstag et al (2011), 282–285.
[100] Aertsen (2015).
[101] Couck and Tracqui (2009), cited by Put et al (2012).
[102] Put et al (2012), 92–93; Zinsstag et al (2011).
[103] Vanfraechem et al (2012).
[104] Vanfraechem et al (2012).
[105] Vanfraechem et al (2012).

Ultimately, the question as to 'what works' for each country has not yet been addressed through a systematic programme of evaluative research. Overall, it can be noted that the implementation of mediation and restorative justice based strategies are heterogeneous when one looks at the details. Thus, rather than attempting to superimpose a detailed one-size-fits-all strategy, it is vital that implementations of restorative justice take into account and are tailored to the context in which they are applied.[106] However, it is clear that more restorative types of interventions are taking place and that mediation practices are increasingly broadening their approach so that they incorporate a restorative focus. This is a positive development, increasing their potential to deliver a process for participants that is empowering and facilitates the agency–accountability framework.

VI. Developing Restorative Justice in Continental Europe

As with many criminal justice policy innovations, ideas that seem to attract instant and burgeoning interest are sometimes implemented in a haphazard and incoherent fashion on the ground. Certainly, international standards and governmental and non-governmental bodies such as the European Union and civil society organisations have played an important role in raising the overall profile of restorative justice across the continent. As such, there can be little doubt that the number of programmes and number of referrals has increased significantly and there has been a discernible drive in many jurisdictions to afford greater prominence to restorative initiatives. For instance, in Finland mediation expanded to cover over 10,000 referrals in 2013 compared with an average of 3,000 cases per annum during the 1990s.[107] Generally, these programmes constitute a welcome shift towards more reparative and reintegrative forms of justice and are a welcome improvement on conventional top-down practices. Yet, as often happens with new initiatives, initial enthusiasm seems to have waned. Even in jurisdictions such as Austria where mediation has been relatively widespread, something of a stagnation appears to have taken place; Gombots and Pelikan report a recent 'prevailing impression that there has been a loss of interest in this mode of reacting to crime'.[108]

In common with many other non-European jurisdictions, there is still a noticeable reluctance to make use of restorative justice for more serious offences. In the majority of jurisdictions, mediation and restorative approaches are used on a discretionary basis for low-level offences or non-criminal behaviour, mostly

---

[106] Dünkel et al (2015).
[107] cf Honkatukia (2015a); Miers et al (2001).
[108] Gombots and Pelikan (2015), 20.

committed by juveniles. Moreover, the focus within continental Europe has been on the development of mediation as opposed to restorative conferencing. Aside from Belgium, conferencing continues to lie on the periphery of almost all justice systems; it lacks statutory foothold and tends to be used in a localised, haphazard manner.[109] In practice, the line between conferencing and mediation is often blurred since many mediators will also adopt a script, while some mediation sessions involve the family and friends of the victim and offender.[110] However, as we argue in the next chapter, a conferencing model is inherently more likely to deliver on the core values of agency and accountability through enabling a wide range of the stakeholders to assume ownership of the offence and play an active role in repairing the harm.[111]

An obstacle to the success of restorative justice in Europe seems to be a cultural misfit between restorative justice concepts and the existent professional cultures of the legal profession and other criminal justice agencies. This means that, in practice, restorative mechanisms have carried a relatively minor impact on existing practices. As Cario notes in respect of France, 'measures such as mediation, family group conferencing etc. have had only a minor impact on juvenile law and practice'.[112] Similarly, while restorative principles seem to be widely supported in Finland, professionals appear unsure regarding its use, especially in respect of more serious offences, with lawyers, police officers and mediators commenting that the law is unclear.[113]

Germany provides another example of how the full potential of mediation is hindered by the reluctance of lawyers and judges to acknowledge the potential of the procedure. In particular, official communication of formal co-operation between mediators, prosecutors and the court seems to be poor, with little discussion of which cases might be suitable for referral. The manner in which the process of mediation itself is conducted is subject to very little regulation, thus standards and styles vary considerably.[114] Some federal states publish their own guidance and training standards, but these are by no means uniform throughout the country. Increasingly, however, there appears to be a move towards consensus on issues

---

[109] Dünkel et al (2015).
[110] Zinsstag et al (2011). One such example is the so-called 'Grand Meeting', which is a device used in Norway in cases where there are multiple victims or offenders involved. These are becoming more common place where 'it is unclear who is committing the crimes and who is "only hanging around"'. *Grand Meeting for Youth with a Youth Plan* has also been the basis behind a new programme aimed at 15–18 year olds who have a history of serious or repeat offending, or are deemed to be at high risk of re-offending. Following conviction, the offender is referred to a form of conferencing, known as *stormøte*, which involves a meeting with a wide circle of community representatives. The presence of the victim is not required. The aim of the conference is to agree a plan of action which aims to help the young person desist from future offending. Typical components of the plan may include school/work attendance, counselling, steps to address drug or alcohol addiction and other forms of interventions. Plans are put in place for a fixed period, and the young person will be returned to court for conventional sentencing in the event that it is breached: Lundgaard (2015).
[111] Shapland et al (2011), 132.
[112] Cario (2015).
[113] Iivari (2010).
[114] Pelikan and Trenczek (2006).

of good practice. In 2002, the National Mediation Association (*Bundesverband Mediation*) published a 1,500 page handbook designed to guide practice, and most schemes now conduct their work according to these standards.[115] However, Tränkle found a number of problems in the German mediation sessions she observed.[116] These included a lack of understanding among the participants of the purpose and value of mediation; an overly formal 'business-like' approach by some mediators; an over-emphasis on legality and a failure to provide victims and offenders with adequate information in advance of mediation.

The principle of legality, which features so heavily in many continental systems has arguably led to the 'excessive judiciarization of mediation'.[117] As we argue in chapter nine, a legalistic perspective tends to result in agreements and outcomes being construed in monetary terms, with insufficient attention being paid to the more fundamental task of tailoring symbolic forms of repair which are more suited to the individual circumstances to hand. The mediation process in Finland provides one such example, where despite a long established and widely used system, research has shown that what is currently provided is largely focused around achieving financial settlements, rather than exploring the impacts of the crime on the parties and forming resolutions that would be restorative in nature.[118] These kinds of mediation practice, which primarily concentrate on achieving material compensation, often fall short of providing a vehicle for empowering interactions in which the participants are likely to gain a sense of agency or accountability. While research has shown participants may be generally happy with outcome-driven processes which prioritise financial settlements, there is a lack of consideration of the wrongfulness of the crime or the emotional and moral needs of the participants—elements we argue are crucial to the successful delivery of an empowering and restorative process. Thus in their current format there is relatively little potential for these particular types of mediation to deliver a sense of agency to participants, allowing them to feel that they are able to actively participate and have some control over their 'case'. Nor is there much potential for the concept of accountability to be delivered, outside a financial settlement for compensation.

However, other jurisdictions are embracing a more holistic approach to their diversionary mediation programmes that go well beyond the financial and compensatory needs of participants. For example, the popular diversionary mediation programme established in Austria, noted above, has moved away from out-of-court mediation that simply sought to achieve compensation, to a scheme that is now orientated around reconciliation between the participants. The focus of the mediation process has expanded to become socially constructive, allowing for symbolic restitution and remorse, and emphasising the importance of the

---

[115] Kilchling (2005).
[116] Tränkle (2007).
[117] Rodrigues et al (2015), 140.
[118] Elonheimo (2003).

offender reflecting on the reasons that led to the offence and accepting responsibility. This mediation process has grown to allow for the victim and offender to gain some sense of agency through this process, enabling them to play an active and hopefully empowering part in the mediation and the decisions made in their interests. Equally, aspects of accountability are reflected in the Austrian process by a requirement that offenders take responsibility for the harm and consequences of their actions, thus holding them to account and allowing them to be accountable for their actions.

Similarly, the Norwegian diversionary mediation programmes have become more progressive and restorative in their orientation. They have long been focused on providing an alternative to the punitive outcomes of criminal justice and have sought to bring offenders and victims together to address and resolve the conflict and harms caused by crime. Many European programmes have thus evolved to take a more restorative focus and give offenders and victims opportunities to become empowered in a process dealing with the impact and consequences crime. Indeed, the relatively widespread use of mediation across continental Europe bodes well for these to further develop and evolve into more restorative focused interactions for participants.

There are promising signs that mediation-based programmes can orient themselves to provide a more restorative justice based encounter for participants. However, as noted above, programmes face cultural and attitudinal barriers, particularly from legal professionals within criminal justice. As Dünkel contends, mediation is likely to 'continue to play more or less the role of an additional educative/rehabilitative sanction within the traditional juvenile or adult criminal justice system, and—if left as is—will not be a step towards a fully-fledged restorative justice strategy'.[119] Thus, developing mediation programmes and incorporating restorative principles into practice is more likely to be overcome through mandating their use, with a clear restorative focus. Aside from Belgium, where every juvenile must be offered the possibility of either mediation or conferencing in cases where a victim is identified, the optional model of provision is the norm, making referrals dependent on the discretion and will of criminal justice personnel.

VII. Conclusions

Until relatively recently, restorative justice remained on the periphery of most European criminal justice systems, with practice largely centred on offender-orientated mediation and targeted primarily at juveniles involved in minor offences.[120] The policy dynamic began to change as international organisations

---

[119] Dünkel (2015), 78.
[120] Pemberton et al (2007). This remains largely true, though no limits on offence severity are currently in place in either Belgium or The Netherlands: Dünkel et al (2015).

such as the United Nations, Council of Europe and European Union exerted a downward pressure on national governments to develop restorative justice throughout the criminal process. Although mediation is now rooted in legislation in many jurisdictions, the scope of the legislation is frequently unclear and service coverage remains uneven. Clearly, mediation is more popular in some jurisdictions than others and continues to be more developed in cases involving juveniles than those involving adults. Even in countries such as Austria, Finland and Norway which have a long and established history of mediation, there is little evidence of efforts to 'mainstream' such interventions, for example by placing the prosecution or courts under a statutory obligation to refer particular types of offences or offenders to the procedure.

The majority of mediation projects are used as forms of diversion away from criminal sanctioning and courts are rarely involved either in making referrals or approving agreements. As such, usage tends to depend upon the individual attitudes of referral agencies which may vary, even within individual countries.[121] Germany constitutes one such example, where there are various well-established systems of mediation across its constituent states, yet resistance to using mediation is still prevalent amongst professionals within the criminal justice system.

While mediation remains the dominant model in continental Europe, restorative justice based conferencing appears to be now taking root and greater efforts are being made to increase the 'restorativeness' of mediation in many jurisdictions.[122] This is already evidenced in Belgium, where conferencing has been mainstreamed for juveniles since 2006 and in the Netherlands (although here it remains on the periphery of the justice system). Positive developments have also taken place in Norway, where efforts have been made to widen the circle of stakeholders by making greater use of the wider community in mediation process; here the Government has invested in and actively encouraged the use of conferencing. As we argue in chapter seven, a restorative conferencing model that is rooted in legislation and mandated for a wide range of offences offers the best opportunity to realise the goals of agency and accountability. However, the now well-established practices of mediation across Europe provide a strong foothold for the ongoing development of restorative justice based interventions.

---

[121] Zinsstag et al (2011).
[122] Zinsstag and Vanfraechem (2012).

7
Mainstreamed Restorative Justice: Youth Conferencing

I. Introduction

Many of the restorative interventions documented in the previous two chapters are led by the police or prosecution, rather than the courts. Although some may also be applied by the courts or other criminal justice agencies at later stages of the criminal process, the majority focus on diversionary efforts, aimed at keeping offenders outside the 'net' of the criminal justice system. Similarly, while much of the victim-offender mediation outlined in the previous chapter is grounded within legal frameworks, this has not generally been the case in common law jurisdictions where these schemes often lie on the periphery of the legal order and are operationalised on a largely ad hoc basis by various criminal justice agencies. The exception to this can be found in the arena of juvenile justice, where examples of restorative justice programmes have been 'mainstreamed' in a number of jurisdictions. By mainstreaming, we refer to the practice of giving restorative justice a statutory foothold within the criminal justice system. In other words, legislation is used to specify whether and how restorative justice mechanisms ought to be used to deal with a particular type of offence or offender once the offender enters the criminal justice system. In this context, it is worth noting that the conferencing model has been the preferred option among policymakers where attempts have been made to mainstream restorative justice.

As outlined in chapter one, the conferencing model for delivering restorative justice has its origins in New Zealand. The 1990s witnessed its expansion to Australia and beyond, and variations of the model have since been used many times across the world. Like restorative justice itself, conferencing lacks a universally accepted definition or international prototype and the boundary between conferencing and other forms of restorative justice may at times be blurred.[1] However, broadly speaking, conferencing involves a range of actors, including

---

[1] See further Vanfraechem and Zinstaag (2012), who provide the examples of a conference where only the victim and offender are present, or a mediation involving a wider circle of supporters or community representatives.

parties beyond the direct victim and offender, and is led by an independent facilitator. As such, from a theoretical perspective at least, conferencing is well positioned to undertake a holistic enquiry surrounding the circumstances of the offence and to tailor the most effective outcomes for the range of stakeholders involved. Consequently, mainstreamed restorative conferencing maximises the prospects for an empowering process, whereby agency and accountability can be realised within the criminal process.

In this chapter, we analyse two established and extensively evaluated restorative conferencing programmes which have been mainstreamed into the juvenile justice systems of New Zealand and Northern Ireland. Both of these schemes are particularly noteworthy as they are subject to an automatic statutory trigger, whereby the courts are required to make referrals to them. Although the past decade has seen a rapid proliferation of conferencing types of schemes across Europe, Australia and North America, the richness of data generated from New Zealand—and in particular our own experience of observing conferences in Northern Ireland—grants us a valuable insight into how these exemplars work in practice and the lessons that can be drawn from them. As appropriate, we also draw links with the very considerable body of literature that continues to flow from other contexts where conferencing has been researched and evaluated.

First though, looking beyond Northern Ireland and New Zealand, there are notable examples of restorative conferencing such as the Canberra RISE experiment outlined in chapter five, which offer insights into how it can work in relation to adult offenders. This is also the case in relation to Shapland et al's evaluation of restorative justice in England and Wales—two of the three schemes evaluated by Shapland et al in England made use of conferencing. Similarly, in New South Wales juvenile justice in the state is organised around a hierarchy of interventions based on the nature of the offence and any previous contact the young person may have had with the criminal justice system.[2] However, unlike New Zealand and Northern Ireland, conferencing is not mandatory, though the young person has an 'entitlement' to be dealt with by conference following an eligible offence. Thus it falls to a specialist youth officer to determine whether it would be more appropriate to deal with the young offender by commencing criminal proceedings or by giving a caution, largely based on what is in the best interests of justice.[3] Likewise, as noted in the previous chapter, Belgium introduced a pilot scheme (*Hergo*), based on the New Zealand model, to deal with serious young offenders from 2000. Following the relatively positive results of the pilot, the Belgian Youth Justice Act 2006 was introduced to provide a statutory basis for the programme on a national basis. The legislation provides the courts with 12 possible options for intervention, including both mediation and conferencing. These are now considered to be the primary disposals for youth crime.[4]

---

[2] Indeed, conferencing for juveniles and adults is now widely available throughout Australia: see Larsen (2014).
[3] Young Offenders Act 1997 NSW, s 37.
[4] Put et al (2012), 88.

While space does not permit an extensive description of these or the many other broader conferencing programmes that continue to evolve across the globe, our focus on New Zealand and Northern Ireland enables us to conduct a rigorous analysis of how these two well-established programmes operate in practice. It is notable that both schemes are focused solely on juveniles. We acknowledge that, on some levels, juvenile justice is fundamentally different from adult justice. It is widely accepted, for instance, that juveniles lack the same cognitive capacity of adults to control their impulses and understand the consequences of their behaviour.[5] Most youth offending is also seen as a 'transient phenomenon of adolescence', with the majority of more serious crime being committed by adults.[6] Many justice systems also acknowledge—on paper at least—the specific welfare and rehabilitative needs of juveniles over and above purely retributive or punitive rationales. Notwithstanding these important differences between the juvenile and adult systems, the restorative conferencing approach remains the underlying mechanism, and our focus on the conferencing arrangements in New Zealand and Northern Ireland enables valuable lessons to be gleaned in terms of how statutory-based restorative justice operates in practice and the potential that it can offer across the criminal justice system as a whole.

The chapter begins by briefly detailing the operation of restorative youth conferencing as practised in New Zealand and Northern Ireland, before discussing the more important findings of the evaluation data. Our analysis of this data leads us to conclude that mainstreamed approaches to conferencing are generally better calibrated than the diversionary approaches documented in the previous chapters towards embedding our agency-accountability framework within criminal justice.

II. The Process of Youth Conferencing

Youth conferencing was first introduced in New Zealand under the Children, Young Persons and Their Families Act 1989. The programme was designed to devolve decision-making, or at least the power to make recommendations as to how youth offenders should be dealt, back to those most directly impacted by the offence—namely the victim, offender and the offender's family.[7] The legislation provided that the Youth Court must refer all cases to a youth conference (except for certain very serious offences such as murder and manslaughter) and take into

---

[5] Souhami (2012), 222.
[6] Cavadino et al (2013), 256.
[7] The New Zealand model of restorative conferencing places particular emphasis on the role of family, emphasising the need for family time and for decisions to be made in a collective sense, see Mutter et al (2008).

consideration the recommendations of the conference when sentencing. In this respect, it provided the first statutory platform whereby conferencing became mainstreamed within a juvenile justice process.

The family group conference comprises the young person who has offended, members of their family and others in the family who they may wish to invite, the victim and others to support the victim, a police officer and a youth justice coordinator (employed by the Department of Social Welfare). Other possible attendees may include social workers, probation officers and lawyers. Conferences are usually held in facilities provided by the Department of Social Welfare, though they may be held at other venues with the consent of the participants.

The conference can only proceed if the young person admits to the offence, or if the offence has been proved in court. The conference is then expected to formulate recommendations for the court as to how the young person should be dealt with. These should be based on deliberations in the conference which consider the offence; its impact on the victim; the reasons for offending; the views of the offender's family; as well as prior offending and previous sentences. The meeting is intended to be a less formal gathering than a court appearance and is supposed to help the participants actively engage with each other and agree to recommendations to be passed to the court for sentencing.[8] The meeting is conducted in an informal manner, and is intended to offer stakeholders the freedom to express their views in a safe environment, without being dominated by criminal justice professionals.

The typical process will begin with an opening statement by the conference coordinator, followed by a summary of the facts by the police officer. Agreement of these facts is confirmed by the young person; if disputed, the case will be referred back to the court. The conference then usually hears from the victim who explains how the offence affected him or her before the young person explains the circumstances surrounding the offence and why he or she committed the offence. Everyone is encouraged to describe how the offence impacted them and the group usually splits up, with the offender and their family considering what plans and recommendations they wish to make to address the needs of victims and steps that might be taken to prevent further offending by the young person. Once the family are ready, the group reconvenes to discuss their proposals and to reach agreement on what measures might be most effective in the case at hand. Typically, conference plans can include an apology, community work, reparation, and involvement in programmes of treatment, for example to help the offender with problems with alcohol, substance abuse, family issues or anger management. Finally, the recommendations are recorded and then passed on to the Youth Court for consideration in sentencing. Provided they are accepted by the Youth Court, they become binding and are effectively the sentence of the court. With early evaluations

---

[8] See further Maxwell et al (2006).

yielding largely positive results,[9] the programme caught the attention of policy-makers and academics alike, and similar approaches were adopted in other youth justice systems.

Turning to the evolution of the conferencing system in Northern Ireland, it has many similarities to the New Zealand model. It emerged at the time of the peace process in Northern Ireland, when there was an opportunity for fundamental change to the entire criminal justice system following the Belfast Agreement of 1998.[10] In line with 'recommendations for arrangements most likely to inspire confidence of all parts of the community in the future',[11] the Criminal Justice Review Group made 294 recommendations for change, including that a new restorative justice approach should be adopted in all cases involving young persons aged 10–17.[12] In opting for a restorative youth conferencing model, the Group signalled that it wished to maximise participation within the criminal justice system as a means to boosting its legitimacy through a 'partnership between the criminal justice system, the community, and other external bodies'.[13]

Some of the New Zealand family group conferencing arrangements were transplanted under the Justice (Northern Ireland) Act 2002, but the Northern Ireland youth conferencing model placed a much stronger emphasis on the central role of the victim in the process. The legislation placed youth conferencing on a statutory platform and established an independent Youth Conferencing Service to organise and facilitate conferences.[14] Two forms of conference are provided for: those that are diversionary in nature (and are ordered by the Public Prosecution Service), and those that are intended to substitute traditional punitive sentences (and are ordered by the court). Both forms of conference take place with a view to providing a recommendation to the prosecutor or court as to how the young person should be dealt with for the offence.[15]

Diversionary conferences are convened following referral to the Youth Conferencing Service from the Public Prosecution Service. The prosecutor is expected to make a referral in those cases where they would otherwise have instituted court proceedings. Thus, conferencing is not intended as a prosecutorial disposal for first-time offenders or those committing petty offences.[16] Rather, diversionary

---

[9] See eg Maxwell and Morris (1993); Morris and Maxwell (1998); Morris et al (1993).
[10] O'Mahony and Campbell (2006).
[11] Criminal Justice Review Group (2000), 7.
[12] Criminal Justice Review Group (2000), 205.
[13] Criminal Justice Review Group (2000), 30.
[14] The restorative youth conference process was started in December 2003 in the form of a pilot scheme and initially was available for all 10–16 year olds living in the Greater Belfast area. In mid-2004, the scheme was expanded to cover young people living in more rural areas, including the Fermanagh and Tyrone regions. Section 63 of the Justice (Northern Ireland) Act 2002 provided for the extension of the youth justice system to cover 17-year-olds in the jurisdiction of the youth courts, which took effect from August 2005.
[15] O'Mahony (2015); O'Mahony and Campbell (2006).
[16] Such persons should be dealt with by the police, either by way of warning and advice or a formal caution.

conferences are intended for young people who may have offended in the past or where formal action is deemed necessary, but falls short of referral through the courts. As in New Zealand, for the conference to take place, two preconditions must be met: the young person must admit to the offence and he or she must consent to the process. If either of these conditions is not met, the young person will not be dealt with through this process and may be referred through the court for prosecution.

Similar provision for court-ordered conferences is made in the Northern Ireland legislation. Where the Public Prosecution Service has deemed the case unsuitable for diversion, the young person is prosecuted in the usual way, but must then be referred to conferencing by the court. As with diversionary conferences, referral will only occur where the young person admits to the offence and consents to the process. If there is a dispute of the facts, these will be heard by the court and following a finding of guilt the case may only then proceed to conferencing, which is mandatory for the vast bulk of cases; the only offences that fall outside the scheme are those which carry a penalty of life imprisonment, and offences which are triable under indictment only, and scheduled (terrorism) offences *may* be referred.[17] The Youth Conference Service must emphasise the centrality of the victim in the process and the conference plan is devised and negotiated with all the parties present. This plan takes the form of a negotiated contract, with implications if a young person does not follow through what is required them.[18] Agreement is a key factor in devising the contract, and the young person must consent to its terms. Ideally, the contract will ultimately have some form of restorative outcome, addressing the needs of the victim, the offender and wider community.

Overall, both the New Zealand and Northern Ireland approaches to restorative conferencing share many similarities in that they have a clear legislative base, they are mainstreamed within their respective youth criminal justice processes and referral to them through the courts is mandated. They share similar working practices and arrangements for the delivery of the conference, albeit with the Northern Ireland model having a stronger emphasis on the role of the victim while New Zealand has placed slightly more emphasis on the importance of the offender and their family in proceedings. Also, as previously noted, both have been subjected to substantial research and evaluation studies which allow us to reflect on their practices. In the following sections we seek to synthesise this research through the lens of our agency-accountability frame, assessing their capacity to deliver an empowering process for participants.

---

[17] Justice (Northern Ireland) Act 2002, s 59.
[18] Once a plan is accepted by the court it becomes a 'youth conference order' and any breach of the conditions of the order can be dealt with by the court, allowing for the order to be varied, new proceedings to be commenced or the young person to be resentenced. See generally O'Mahony (2015).

III. Participation in Youth Conferencing

The participation of victims, offenders and their supporters in restorative justice is vital to its effective delivery. Restorative interactions are dependent on participants taking part and being able to properly engage with the process, thus empowering them and facilitating the agency-accountability framework. The evaluations of youth conferencing in New Zealand and Northern Ireland have yielded promising results in terms of levels of participation with the process. Importantly, this research found that most participating victims wanted to meet with the person who committed the offence.[19] In New Zealand, for example, early research by Maxwell and Morris found that only 50 per cent of victims had participated in conferences. For the most part, however, this was attributable to the fact that the programme was still very much in its infancy and a number of logistical and organisational problems had to be addressed.[20] Participation rates improved as the family group conferencing process became more established.[21] Looking elsewhere, similar participation rates were uncovered in South Australia's Youth Conferencing Scheme,[22] though rates of participation were slightly lower (at 42 per cent) in the police-based family group conference scheme in Bethlehem, Pennsylvania.[23] However, Shapland et al's evaluation of three programmes in England adopting different methods had very high levels of victim participation, with up to 77 per cent victim participation in cases involving adult offenders and up to 89 per cent victim participation in cases involving young offenders.[24]

Relatively high levels of victim participation were also noted in Northern Ireland, where Campbell et al found that there was at least some form of victim participation in 69 per cent of conferences.[25] Similarly high participation rates have been reported in New South Wales[26] and, as we noted in chapter five, levels of victim participation in the RISE experiment were higher still, at over 80 per cent.[27] A revealing aspect of the research is the desire that many victims have to participate in their case, which—as noted previously—is effectively denied to them in traditional criminal justice proceedings.

The research also provides an understanding of the motivations of victims when deciding whether to accept or decline the invitation to participate in conferencing.

---

[19] Maxwell and Morris (1993).
[20] Maxwell and Morris (1993); Maxwell et al (2006).
[21] Maxwell et al (2004); Maxwell (2007).
[22] Daly (2001).
[23] McCold and Wachtel (1998).
[24] Shapland et al (2007).
[25] Of these, 47% were victim representatives, 40% personal victims and 13% were representatives attending where there was no identifiable victim: Campbell et al (2006).
[26] Trimboli (2000).
[27] Braithwaite (1999).

In Northern Ireland, of those willing to participate in youth conferencing, some 79 per cent said they were actually 'keen' to do so. Victims there expressed a number of reasons for participating in the conference process and these often related to a desire for information and a forum in which to state their views. Thus, 88 per cent of victims in Northern Ireland attended in order to hear what the young person had to say and 86 per cent wanted the young person to know how the crime had affected them. Almost all (91 per cent) said the decision to take part was their own and not a result of pressure to attend. Such findings show the importance of agency to victims; victims want to be given information and an active role in the process, as well as wanting to have a say in proceedings that impact them.

The reasons to attend conferences reveal other motivations, as over three-quarters (79 per cent) of victims in our research said they attended 'to help the young person' and many victims said they wanted to hear what the young person had to say and the young person's side of the story: 'I wanted to help the young person get straightened out.'[28] Only 55 per cent of victims said that the main reason they attended the conference was to hear the offender apologise. Therefore, while it was clear that many victims (86 per cent) wanted the offender to know how the crime affected them, the participation of victims in the process was clearly not driven by motivations of retribution or a desire to seek vengeance.

Although fears have been expressed in some quarters that restorative justice processes may skew the justice process by incorporating the punitive views of victims,[29] our own research found little evidence of this. Rather, it was apparent that victims' reasons for participating were based around seeking an understanding of why the offence had happened; they wanted to hear and understand the offender and to explain the impact of the offence to the offender. These themes again resonated with our agency-accountability framework. For their part, victims were offered a sense of agency through opportunities to become involved and be part of the process of dealing with their case. Through explaining the impact of the crime to the offender and having their questions answered, they were able to hold the offender to account. These findings tend to support broader victimological research which suggests that victims of crime are no more punitive than the general public.[30] They also show how victims seek accountability in a positive and empowering way, by wanting to hear what the young person has to say, rather than just focusing on punishment.

Evaluations of other programmes have also shed light on reasons why some victims opt not to participate in the conference process. On some occasions, low rates of victim attendance are attributable in part to practical matters such as inadequate notice and/or preparation, or that the time or venue of the conference

---

[28] Campbell et al (2006).
[29] Ashworth (1993), (2001).
[30] Hough and Park (2002); Mattinson and Mirrlees-Black (2000). See further Doak and O'Mahony (2006).

was unsuitable for them.[31] On other occasions, non-participating victims referred to personal reasons for the decision not to attend, such as not wishing to meet the young person face to face, or a belief that the offence was not serious enough to warrant attending the conference, or simply that they wanted to 'move on' after the offence.[32] However, many of the reasons why victims do not attend conferences can be addressed by good working practices, whereby victims are properly prepared, supported and given realistic expectations of what can be achieved.[33] Indeed, the reasons given by victims for attending conferences in Northern Ireland demonstrates the potential of this type of intervention to deliver a strong sense of agency. By giving victims opportunities to express themselves, have a say in the process, gain information on their cases and understand why they have been the target of criminal behaviour, they are empowered and able to achieve the elements of agency that we argue are vital to the successful delivery of restorative interventions.

Research has also provided insights into the motives of offenders for consenting to the process, and demonstrates how the conferencing process can hold them to account. In Northern Ireland, the majority of offenders said they wanted to attend their conference, giving reasons such as wanting to 'make good' for what they had done, or wanting to apologise to the victim.[34] The most common reasons for attending were to make up for what they had done, to seek the victim's forgiveness and to be given the opportunity to tell their side of the story. These reasons reinforce the centrality of accountability within restorative justice, whereby offenders are willing not only to be *held* to account, but also actively seek to hold *themselves* to account for their actions and assume responsibility. Even though some offenders who participated in conferences said they did so to avoid going through court, most felt it provided them with the opportunity to take responsibility for their actions, seek forgiveness and put the offence behind them. Indeed many offenders appreciated the opportunity to interact with the victim and wanted to 'restore' or repair the harm they had caused.[35]

A. Consent and Engagement

Notwithstanding this general sense of voluntariness, the Northern Ireland research gives rise to concerns about the potential role that coercion may have played in the decisions of young people to participate. Over a quarter (28 per cent) of the offenders said they initially did not want to take part in the conferencing

---

[31] Maxwell and Morris (1993); Maxwell et al (2004); Campbell et al (2006).
[32] See Campbell et al (2006) in respect of Northern Ireland; Maxwell et al (2004) in respect of New Zealand.
[33] Maxwell et al (2004).
[34] Campbell et al (2006).
[35] Campbell et al (2006).

process. It is very possible that in many cases this was due to a reluctance to engage in a challenging process which involved them coming face to face with their victim, rather than a lack of consent per se. Of greater concern however, is that around a quarter (24 per cent) of those who attended also said their decision to participate was made under some pressure, especially from their parents, or that they felt the court had 'made' them come. Similarly, about a quarter (25 per cent) said they felt they had to agree to the conference plan and also felt they had no real choice, as the court 'expected' a plan.

These findings highlight some of the difficulties of gaining consent and understanding, particularly amongst young offenders when they are faced with the demanding task of having to assume responsibility for what they have done. As noted in chapter four, questions have been raised concerning the place of children's rights within the conferencing process. The conferencing process can create power imbalances, whereby a young person in a room full of adults can feel disadvantaged.[36] They are also likely to experience difficulties because of the knowledge imbalance (in terms of what the process involves, what form reparation might assume and how it compares with court etc) which can create further barriers to active participation based on informed consent. Indeed, looking at the experience of New Zealand, Lynch notes that conferencing can be challenging and difficult, especially for younger children.[37] In particular, some children may not feel properly involved in the decision-making process and feel unable to participate fully. Furthermore, large case-loads and limited resources can negatively impact on practice, raising questions as to the extent to which adequate preparation is in place for children and their families. Similarly, the external pressure of the plan having to be ratified by the court may exert pressure on individuals to consent to things they may not be completely happy with. Indeed, we argue that these types of issues highlight the need to ensure that good restorative practice is driven by the clear goals of agency and accountability, whereby participants are empowered to participate effectively in the process and do not feel coerced—thus they are also willing to hold themselves to account for the consequences of their actions.

Turning to the engagement of participants in the conferencing process, much of the research shows that victims and offenders are able to actively and constructively engage in conferencing which is core to their potential to deliver an empowering experience. The Northern Ireland research shows victims reacting well to conferencing and being able to engage well with the other participants.[38] Overall, 98 per cent of victims were observed to be talkative in conferences and it was clear that the conference forum was largely successful in providing victims with the opportunity to express their feelings and gain a sense of agency, whereby they felt they had a legitimate part to play in the process. Though most victims

[36] See Daly (2003); Haines and O'Mahony (2006); Hoyle and Noguera (2008).
[37] Lynch (2008).
[38] Campbell et al (2006).

(71 per cent) displayed some degree of frustration toward the young offender at some point in the conference, the vast majority listened to and seemed to accept the young person's version of the offence either 'a lot' (69 per cent) or 'a bit' (25 per cent) and 74 per cent of victims even expressed a degree of empathy towards the offender. However, while a minority of victims were nervous at the beginning of the conference, this usually faded as the conference wore on and nearly all reported that they were more relaxed once the conference was underway. In addition, the overwhelming majority (93 per cent) of victims displayed no signs of hostility towards the offender at the conference.

The ability of victims to engage effectively in the process was strongly related to the intensive preparation they had been given prior to the conference. The Northern Ireland research revealed that a lot of work was put into preparing victims for conferencing and thus they were generally well prepared. Only 20 per cent of victims were observed to be visibly nervous at the beginning of the conference, by comparison to 71 per cent of the offenders. They were also able to engage and play an active part in the conferencing process; 83 per cent of victims were rated as 'very engaged' during the conference; and 92 per cent reported that they had said everything that they wanted to during the conference. These findings show how the conferencing process can be productively used to help participants to achieve a strong sense of agency whereby they are empowered to engage effectively and do so in a positive and constructive manner.

B. A 'Soft Option'?

Our analysis also indicates that, contrary to some perspectives, restorative justice should not be considered a 'soft option'.[39] Participation in restorative conferencing certainly entails more than simply having to speak. In order to embed a meaningful sense of accountability it needs to be an active process that involves dialogue, both holding individuals to account and engaging them so that there is clear ownership of the dispute by all the parties.[40] Such a vision clearly deviates from the orthodox criminal process; as we noted in chapter two, standard sentencing proceedings afford a largely passive role to both victims and offenders. For their part, young offenders often do not speak at sentencing proceedings other than to confirm their name, plea and understanding of the charges; they are normally represented and spoken for by legal counsel throughout their proceedings. Similarly, victims often find themselves feeling excluded and alienated, or simply they have been used for evidential purposes if the case is contested. While the conferencing model clearly holds considerable potential to facilitate agency and accountability, these values should not be assumed to be inherent to the process. Although programmes require that

---

[39] See further DUCKfoOT (2012).
[40] Wemmers and Canuto (2002).

offenders consent to take part in the process, in some instances they may fail to properly engage in it, and may show a lack of remorse or appear defiant. Some victims may be reluctant to engage with or be disinterested in the offender's account.

In one of the major early evaluations in New Zealand, Maxwell and Morris found that young people were generally able to play an active part in the conference process.[41] Nearly half of young people in this study felt involved in conferences, and said they also felt involved in reaching the decision and coming up with the recommendations. This evaluation found that decisions in the conferencing process were very much driven by the young person and his or her family, rather than being imposed by the coordinator. It was apparent that families of the young people were involved in the conferences, as family members were present in almost all conferences and extended members of the family were involved in about 40 per cent of conferences. The young people and their supporters were able to engage in a dialogue that considered the needs of the victim and offender and many viewed the participation of the victim as a particularly positive feature, since it gave them the opportunity to understand the victim's perspective and to apologise directly. Indeed, research that followed up offenders six years after their conference (through a factor analysis) found that those who did not go on to become persistent offenders had experienced 'successful' conferences. These successful conferences were identified as being: memorable; where the offender was not made to feel like a 'bad person'; where the offender felt involved in the decision making: where he or she agreed with the outcome and completed the task; where the offender felt sorry for what he or she had done; where the offender had met and apologised to the victim; and where the offender felt that he or she had repaired the damage caused.[42] These findings tie in very well with our goals of agency and accountability, whereby conferences are more likely to be deemed successful if they can deliver such empowering outcomes for participants through a productive restorative encounter.

As more recent research by Maxwell et al has uncovered,[43] the overall picture regarding involvement and engagement in conferences is far more positive than for young people who appear in the courts. Furthermore, there was little doubt that those participants who had experienced both court and conferencing preferred the conference. Their comments highlighted the participatory nature of the conference and the greater degree of support provided, by comparison with the stress that often accompanied a court appearance; although there has also been some evidence—particularly in the early study—that some conferences were not so well managed, with some families reporting they were not well prepared or provided with the information they needed to participate effectively.[44]

---

[41] Maxwell and Morris (1993).
[42] Maxwell and Morris (2001), 261.
[43] Maxwell et al (2006).
[44] Maxwell and Morris (1993); see also Lynch (2008).

Our research in Northern Ireland found young people displayed some discomfort and found the conference to be a challenging experience; the prospect of coming face to face with their victim was particularly difficult for them. For instance, 71 per cent of offenders displayed some degree of nervousness at the beginning of the conference and only 28 per cent appeared to be 'not at all' nervous. They were often observed at the beginning of the conference to be visibly nervous. This could be seen through their posture and body language, for example avoiding eye contact, looking at the floor, fidgeting and shaking. Despite their nervousness, the observations revealed that as conferences progressed, offenders were usually able to engage effectively, with nearly all (98 per cent) being able to talk about the offence in a full and frank manner. Most young offenders also appeared to listen to the victim when they expressed their feelings, maintained good eye contact and showed evidence of shame and/or remorse in their body language. These results demonstrated that young offenders were willing to be held to account and were listening carefully and responding to the feelings and emotions of victims, and in doing so they were further empowering themselves to take responsibility for what they had done. The research revealed that young offenders felt they had a better understanding of the consequences of what they had done following the conference. Interviews carried out with the young people after conferences revealed that most felt involved in the decision-making process and were satisfied with the outcome. The majority of young people reported that they had the opportunity to say what they wanted and almost all said that they understood the decisions that were made. Again, these results demonstrate how a sense of agency is integral to the successful delivery of restorative justice, whereby participants are given the opportunity to become actively involved in and part of the decisions and outcomes that impact them.

The Northern Ireland research also revealed that failure to engage on the part of the young person was generally a result of nervousness, embarrassment, lack of recall (as a result of passage of time or consumption of drugs and/or alcohol at the time of the offence), the lengthy nature of conferences, and, in a few cases, defiance. As noted in chapter four, some offenders have less developed verbal skills and struggle to engage effectively with the other participants. They may also feel reticent to speak in a group environment in light of the shame they experience. Offenders with histories of substance abuse and learning disabilities may also be impaired in their ability to empathise and understand alternative viewpoints.[45] This can pose something of a conundrum to facilitators and other professionals present, insofar as their archetypal roles as may become blurred. On the one hand, it is incumbent on facilitators to maintain an air of neutrality and non-dominance, yet by the same token, creative and supportive interventions may be required in order to safeguard the parties, encourage dialogue and ensure that the emotional dynamics of the conference are maximised. Research has shown that facilitators,

---

[45] Cunneen (2010).

and indeed the other professionals present, often hold substantial leverage when devising plans—and what they suggest is likely to be the outcome when parents and young are given little opportunity to consider the plan.[46]

These challenges were apparent in a number of the conferences we observed in Northern Ireland. Stress, the inability to recall details of the offence and the inability to verbalise their feelings resulted in some young people becoming frustrated and requiring breaks in their conference. Although the progressive staging of the conference would suggest that the apology might ordinarily follow from discussion about the impact of the offence, observations showed that participant input was often erratic. Again, this underpins the importance of our goals of agency and accountability in guiding the dynamics of the conference. The 'turning points' for victims and for offenders within conferences are often different and they need to be guided by an understanding of what the process seeks to achieve more broadly. For example, in one conference the victim was observed to pass their personal notes to the victim supporter who provided all input on the victim's behalf. Interestingly, this did not detract from the young person's appreciation of the impact of the offence and may have encouraged a heightened sensitivity toward the victim. In interview, the young person stated that the account and realisation of the impact of their behaviour, 'nearly made me cry', and that the best thing about the conferencing was 'apologising to [victim] and knowing that she knows I meant it'.[47] In one other instance where the conference operated via video link, the child victim refrained altogether from engaging in any discussion about the offence. It is difficult to ascertain whether or not this lack of engagement can be attributed to the physical distance or loss of immediacy between the victim and young person, but there is little doubt that the victim remained disinterested, resorting to monosyllabic answers throughout.

As Roche reminds us, accounts of restorative justice describing 'how people should respond are confused with the reality of how people do respond'.[48] Clearly, offender engagement is a key goal which should be 'actively encouraged by those arranging youth justice processes'.[49] To this end, it is vital that offenders feel comfortable expressing themselves within the conference environment; as a minimum starting point an admission of responsibility by the offender should be in place, as well as informed consent to participate in the process. If offenders feel coerced into attending, attend a restorative programme against their will, or dispute their guilt, there will be little prospect for a positive outcome.[50] Where this occurs, it is also likely to be an extremely unsatisfactory experience for the victim. On the other hand, we argue that the practice of conferencing could be substantially enriched if driven by a shared understanding based on our agency-accountability framework.

---

[46] Maxwell and Morris (1993), 85; Maxwell et al (2006).
[47] Campbell et al (2006), 96.
[48] Roche (2003), 33.
[49] Maxwell and Morris (1993), 128.
[50] Strang (2002).

The individual circumstances of each conference often require skilful or creative interventions on the part of the facilitator, or indeed other participants. Although in our Northern Ireland evaluation police officers often played a peripheral role, merely providing an outline of the facts of the offence, on some occasions they were observed to assume certain roles that might more commonly be attributed to those of a facilitator or supporter. In one conference, the police officer was observed to praise the young person, stating that they had provided a comprehensive version of events. When the coordinator requested further response the police officer stated, 'you basically got all the answers you needed from [young person's] opening statement …'.[51] The police officer then provided encouragement to the young person who was visibly upset, 'it's to your credit you are here kid'.[52] In another conference the police officer commended the young person's behaviour since commission of the offence, 'from a police point of view we have had no bother from you since. Would like it to stay that way—please keep at it'.[53]

The key competences of any facilitator are the abilities to use appropriate language and to present the proceedings in a way that permits all participants to understand. The Northern Ireland research found that a number of victims felt that this aspect of facilitation was extremely important, and facilitators were never observed to speak in an inappropriate manner. In the vast majority of conferences, facilitators were effective and displayed particular skill in their ability to be inclusive and to treat every participant in fair and respectful manner. However, it is equally clear that effective facilitation requires more than good interpersonal and negotiation skills. Having a clear understanding of what restorative justice is trying to achieve is equally important, and being able to communicate and manage the process in a way that facilitates agency and accountability is essential for an effective and successful conference.

IV. Satisfaction and Procedural Justice

The inclusion and active participation of the offender is clearly vital to the restorative process, but achieving this may depend upon the extent participants perceive the process to be fair and just, or procedurally just. As noted in chapter four, research has consistently reported positive results among participants, with levels of satisfaction and procedural justice being higher in restorative settings when compared with participants' experiences of the conventional court process. Offenders are said to be more likely to obey the law where procedural justice takes place[54] and, as such, this ought to be regarded as an important benchmark of

---

[51] Campbell et al (2006), 97.
[52] Campbell et al (2006), 97.
[53] Campbell et al (2006), 97.
[54] Tyler (1990); Tyler (2006).

restorative practice. Indeed, the RISE experiment found evidence that conferencing is more conducive to perceived procedural justice than court.[55]

In specific relation to conferencing, some of the earlier research from New Zealand gave cause for concern; Maxwell and Morris reported in 1993 that just a third of young people (34 per cent) felt involved in the process and only 9 per cent felt that they ultimately decided the outcome.[56] In addition, just half of all victims reported that they were satisfied; while over a quarter (27 per cent) felt worse.[57] The most frequent reasons cited were the young person did not come across as being genuinely remorseful, or that victims felt unable to express themselves fully. Some commented that their concerns were not properly addressed, or they had not been listened to. However, later research suggests that many of these issues had been subsequently addressed through improved practice, with only 5 per cent of those victims interviewed saying that they felt worse after the conference and 81 per cent of victims saying they felt better.[58]

More recent research by Maxwell et al[59] shows an improvement in the experience of victims and offenders when compared to the results from the earlier data.[60] The research found decisions in the conferencing process were more likely to be driven by the young person and his or her family, than imposed by the coordinator. In post-conference interviews, the majority of young people said they had the opportunity to say what they wanted and almost all said they understood the nature of the decisions that had been made. Although some offenders complained that they did not feel fully involved and felt too intimidated to express themselves, the overall picture regarding involvement and participation in conferences was significantly more positive than for young people who appear in the courts. Furthermore, there was little doubt that those participants who had experienced court and conferencing preferred the conference.[61]

Satisfaction rates also showed a marked improvement among victims. Around 60 per cent said they found the conference to be helpful, positive and rewarding. Aspects of the conference that they found particularly rewarding included being given the opportunity tell the young person what they had felt as a result of the crime and being able to contribute to the decision process on what should happen to the young person. Providing victims with a voice in conferences was obviously important for victims, as was being able to come face-to-face with the young person and his or her family, so they could better understand why the offence had occurred. Only 5 per cent of victim respondents stated that they felt worse following the conferencing.[62]

---

[55] Sherman et al (1998); Tyler et al (2007).
[56] Maxwell and Morris (1993).
[57] Maxwell and Morris (1993).
[58] Maxwell et al (2004).
[59] Maxwell et al (2004).
[60] Maxwell and Morris (1993), (evaluation carried out during 1990/91).
[61] Maxwell et al (2006).
[62] Maxwell et al (2004).

Maxwell et al's study indicated that those victims who attended conferences were able to express their views and were given a chance to explain how the offence had impacted on them.[63] When contrasted with the earlier study, these results arguably reflect an improvement of practice over time as conferencing has gradually become more embedded in the justice system. In particular, preparation, better training and follow-up meetings have helped to ensure that the needs of victims and offenders have been more effectively addressed and that they are have more realistic expectations of what can be achieved.

Our own evaluation of the Northern Ireland youth conferencing arrangements found that perceptions of fairness and satisfaction were extremely high.[64] Almost all victims (92 per cent) experienced the process as having been fair, and 98 per cent stated that their views were definitely or 'sort of' taken seriously. Almost three-quarters (71 per cent) of the young offenders were satisfied with the process,[65] and their generally positive perceptions of the procedural aspects of the conference process were echoed by victims. Indeed, the vast majority of victims (88 per cent) and offenders (86 per cent) would recommend the process to another young person in their situation and preferred it over court (81 per cent and 91 per cent respectively). Our observations confirmed that coordinators showed particular skills in progressing conferences towards agreement and ensuring all participants were included in the discussion.

Yet, as Van Camp and Wemmers observe, procedural justice is just one (albeit an important) factor in overall satisfaction levels. Their own interviews with victims of violent crime who had been engaged with some form of restorative intervention reveal that flexibility, the provision of care, the opportunity for dialogue and the capacity to address 'pro-social' motives were also deeply valued by the participants.[66] Similar findings were uncovered in relation to Northern Ireland conferencing; while notions of procedural justice were important, so too were the practicalities such as the location, timing and the lapse in time from the date of the offence to the actual conference.[67]

Satisfaction with the restorative process—particularly in cases involving young offenders—appears to be linked to the role of the young person's family. Research by Maxwell et al[68] shows an improvement in the experience of families when compared to the results from 1990–91.[69] At least 80 per cent of families interviewed felt satisfied with their preparation for the conference, and were overwhelmingly positive about their experience of the process. In relation to outcomes, 85 per cent

---

[63] Maxwell et al (2004).
[64] Campbell et al (2006).
[65] Of all the young people interviewed, only one reported feeling 'very unsatisfied' with the process: Campbell et al (2006), 100.
[66] Van Camp and Wemmers (2013).
[67] Campbell et al (2006), 102.
[68] Maxwell et al (2004).
[69] Maxwell and Morris (1993).

agreed with the decisions made at the conference. However, only half indicated that they were given ideas about how to respond to the offending. Comments from the families suggest that these feelings are often related to feeling responsible for the actions of the young person. Similarly, in the Northern Ireland research the majority of families welcomed the opportunity to attend the conference and believed it had a positive impact.[70] In considering the experience of conferencing in Nova Scotia, results from follow-up interviews with families show that the majority remain in agreement with outcomes, are happy with progress post-conference and feel better able to cope with the young person.[71] Thus, issues of procedural justice and satisfaction with the restorative justice process are clearly inherent to the agency-accountability framework. Participants revealed this through the value they placed in being involved in and participating in the decision-making process, being given a voice and this value also extended to other family members who were given the opportunity to share in the process.

V. Agreement: Restoration and Apology

The findings from research reveal that satisfaction levels are highest in relation to outcomes that are agreed amongst the participants.[72] This clearly underpins the importance of agency and accountability to the delivery of restorative justice. Participants are more likely to gain a sense of agency when they actively participate in dialogue that leads to agreement, particularly in the sense that they become involved and can gain a sense of ownership through being able to positively influence outcomes that are agreed. Similarly, accountability is strengthened when victims and offenders are willing to agree the outcome, in that they accept their commitments and demonstrate that they are willing to take on that commitment. In Northern Ireland, nearly all of the plans (91 per cent) were agreed by the participants and victims were, on the whole, happy with the content of the plans. Interestingly, most of the plans centred on elements that were designed to help the young person and victim, such as reparation to the victim or attendance at programmes to help the young person. Relatively few plans (27 per cent) had elements that could be classed as primarily punitive, such as curfews or restrictions on the young person's whereabouts; in most cases the outcomes focused on making restoration to the victim. The fact that 73 per cent of conference plans had no specific punishment element was a clear manifestation of their restorative nature. Crucially, this was also indicative of what victims sought to achieve through the

---

[70] Campbell et al (2006).
[71] Clairmont (2005).
[72] Beven et al (2005); Campbell et al (2006); Maxwell et al (2004); Shapland et al (2006a); Strang et al (2013); Trimboli, (2000).

process, since notions of retribution were not found to be high on the agenda for victims when it came to devising how the offence and offender should be dealt with.

The research also highlighted challenges and difficulties in providing restorative youth conferences, particularly for the relatively large number of cases dealt with by the Youth Justice Agency. For instance, a minority of victims (9 per cent) were unhappy with the outcome of their conference and these individuals appeared to have experienced difficulties in the direct aftermath of their victimisation. While there was no correlation between the seriousness of the offence and dissatisfaction with the outcome—so victims of more serious offences were generally not more dissatisfied than others—the finding highlights that restorative disposals are not universally welcomed by every victim. Equally, it should be noted that some victims of crime also express dissatisfaction with the outcome and their treatment in the traditional criminal justice process. The challenge for those providing restorative interventions is to recognise the diverse needs and expectations of victims and then assesses the likelihood of being able to meet those needs. Just as some offenders are not suitable for participation in conferencing, because they are unwilling to accept responsibility or express remorse, some victims are not suitable for participation, because they are unlikely to gain any benefit and perhaps because they may be particularly vulnerable at that time.

In relation to the view of victims, the early research in New Zealand found that about half of victims expressed satisfaction with the outcome of the conference and about a third were dissatisfied.[73] For many, the outcome of the conference was felt to be either too harsh or too lenient. Others were dissatisfied because the outcome did not appear to be followed through or they were not informed about the actual outcome. Again, the later study reports significant improvements in the levels of satisfaction amongst victims: 87 per cent said that they agreed with the outcome, 90 per cent said they had been treated with respect and almost three-quarters said that their needs had been met at the conference.[74] The research highlights that the findings on victims' experiences of conferences are particularly favourable when contrasted with the exclusion of victims in conventional youth justice or the juvenile courts. The vast majority of victims who had participated in a pilot scheme involving adult offenders in New Zealand also stated that their needs at been at least partly met.[75]

However, Bradley et al have questioned the extent to which the conferencing process in New Zealand actually delivers restorative outcomes for victims.[76] The researchers point to evidence that suggests some victims can end up feeling neither restored nor empowered if they enter into agreements as passive participants.

---

[73] Maxwell and Morris (1993).
[74] Maxwell et al (2004).
[75] Triggs (2005).
[76] Bradley et al (2006).

This may be particularly likely in conferences where agreements have been drawn up by facilitators, rather than through product of genuine dialogue and agreement between conference participants. While acknowledging and endorsing the positive contribution of the family group conferencing process, they warn of the need to enhance the potential for participants to be able to achieve positive reparative and restorative outcomes. Similarly New Zealand research by Morris and Maxwell found that 84 per cent of young people and 85 per cent of their parents said they were satisfied with the outcomes of the family group conferences.[77] Only a small number of young persons (9 per cent) and their parents (11 per cent) said they were dissatisfied with the outcome. For parents, an issue that appeared to cause dissatisfaction was the perception that the kind of help or treatment that they thought necessary was not offered. For offenders it was more often related to their perceptions of the outcome and whether they felt the penalty was too severe. Such findings clearly connect with our agency-accountability framework in terms of how agreements should be made in conferences. If the process is driven by a clear and shared understanding that seeks to empower participants, then the problems posed through victims and offenders adopting a more passive stance in the conference can be addressed. Similarly, the element of accountability highlights the importance of agreeing to outcomes that participants feel are fair and are achieved through dialogue which allows participants to take responsibility for their actions, rather than it being imposed by others.

However, a more sinister threat to the widely recognised progressive and non-punitive focus of the youth justice system in New Zealand is emerging from sustained political and media discourse which appears to connect with aspects of popular punitivism. The adult system in New Zealand and other similar jurisdictions have seen a continuing move towards more punitive rhetoric within political and media circles.[78] Lynch notes how the principles of diversion, decarceration, the acknowledgement of victims' interests and the importance of the input of the family have all contributed to the largely non-punitive system that has managed to divert up to 80 per cent of apprehensions without recourse to prosecution[79] and to low rates of custody. However, a change in government and new legislation introduced from 2010 have seen the introduction of new powers to allow the prosecution of even younger offenders, the extension of harsher sentences, parental orders and the introduction of military type training as disposals.[80] This apparently punitive agenda poses a direct threat to the fundamentals of the restorative family group conferencing process. While criminal justice practitioners and the judiciary seem to have largely stemmed this punitive turn in the short term, the future of New Zealand's progressive youth justice system appears to be under considerable strain.

---

[77] Maxwell and Morris (1993).
[78] Lynch (2012).
[79] New Zealand Ministry of Justice (2010), cited by Lynch (2012).
[80] Lynch (2012).

In Northern Ireland, young people and their families report high levels of satisfaction; for example, 84 per cent of young people and 85 per cent of their parents said they were satisfied with the outcomes of the family group conferences.[81] The overwhelming majority (92 per cent) of the young offenders felt the conference had helped them realise the harm that they had caused and 93 per cent felt that the conference plan was fair.[82] Only a small number of young persons (9 per cent) and their parents (11 per cent) said they were dissatisfied with the outcome. For parents, an issue that appeared to cause dissatisfaction was the perception that some kind of help or treatment they thought necessary was not offered. For offenders it was more often related to their perceptions of the outcome and whether the penalty was severe. Young people who received the most severe penalties were three times more likely to express dissatisfaction than those who received less severe penalties.

Other qualitative research on the youth conferencing process in Northern Ireland has noted how the longer-term impacts of youth conferencing process on young offenders in Northern Ireland has also found 'many of the post-conference outcomes were positive'[83] and a report produced by the Criminal Justice Inspectorate in 2008 has corroborated those findings.[84] However, the researchers also found that some young people can feel worse following their conference.[85] Maruna et al describe how some of the young people they interviewed following conferencing thought that they had gained little from the process. Some even felt the process was negative for them, especially if they had been expected to accept all the blame and responsibility for a crime, when they themselves felt they were not completely responsible for what had happened. Like the earlier evaluation by Campbell et al, it is clear that restorative youth conferencing in Northern Ireland does not always work well all of the time and in all of the cases. It is thus vital that the process is targeted in a manner that facilitates participants to become empowered and involved in how they are dealt with and that it allows them to actively accept personal responsibility, where appropriate, rather than simply being in a process that imposes responsibility upon them.

As we suggest in chapter four, apologies may act as a catalyst for emotional 'turning points' in the conference, insofar as they are associated with defusing feelings of anger or vengeance.[86] In Northern Ireland, almost all (97 per cent) of offenders accepted responsibility for their actions,[87] and in 87 per cent of cases the young person apologised or agreed to apologise (the majority of conferences without an apology involved a victim representative and not a personal victim). Nearly all victims who attended conferences (91 per cent) received at least an

---

[81] Maxwell and Morris (1993).
[82] Campbell et al (2006).
[83] Maruna et al (2007), 2.
[84] Criminal Justice Inspection Northern Ireland (2008).
[85] Maruna et al (2007).
[86] Doak (2011).
[87] Campbell et al (2006).

apology and 85 per cent said they were happy with it and felt it was genuine. On the whole, they appeared to be satisfied that the young person was sincere in what they said and were happy that they got the opportunity to meet them and understand more about the young person and why they had been victimised. In general, most victims were more interested in 'moving on' or putting the incident behind them and 'seeing something positive come out of it'.[88] Indeed, it is somewhat ironic that while the majority of young people felt that the conference offered a more manageable sentence, the apology (a feature predominantly absent from court proceedings) was identified as the most difficult aspect of the conference.

On the whole, a mutual feeling emerged among victims and young people that conferencing offered an environment that was more meaningful to them. Indeed, this overall positive outcome relates to the empowering sense of accountability revealed through the research in which offenders felt that conferencing helped them realise the harms they had caused and that it offered them opportunities both to take responsibility and address harms through agreeing to restorative outcomes. Similarly, a strong sense of agency was promoted in successful conferences when victims reported the importance of being able to meet with the offender, discuss the impacts of the offence, understand why they had been the target of criminal behaviour and agree to outcomes that helped address the harms that they had experienced. In this way victims were given a sense of agency which helped them feel less like victims and more like individuals who could constructively deal with the negative consequences of crime.

VI. Conclusions

The restorative justice schemes developed in Northern Ireland and New Zealand use conferencing models that adhere closely to what can be described as a 'mainstreamed' form of restorative justice. They are based on voluntary participation and consent. They seek to bring victims and offenders together to discuss the offence and actively involve the parties in deciding how the matter is to be dealt with. The schemes are entrenched in legislation and require the courts to refer cases for conferencing. They are used for more serious offences and repeat offenders. The conferencing process is integral to the sentencing process, rather than a diversionary measure. Both systems were brought about through major changes to their juvenile justice systems and they received significant financial investment and support when established. The schemes clearly show that restorative justice can be successfully implemented within youth justice and victims can play an integral part in that process. They also offer a structure in which the agency-accountability framework can be delivered in praxis.

---

[88] Doak and O'Mahony (2006).

By any measure, the youth conferencing arrangements in New Zealand and Northern Ireland have been successful in promoting levels of engagement and participation among both victims and offenders that were not previously in place under the former systems of youth justice. Most victims and offenders expressed a strong preference for the conference process as opposed to going to court and considered that the conference offered a more meaningful environment for them. In contrast to court, there is a right and an expectation for both parties to become involved in the decision-making process. In this sense, youth conferencing provides offenders and victims with a much more defined voice within the decision-making process. Indeed, the goals of agency and accountability were evident in successful restorative conferences, with agreements being negotiated in a non-coercive manner and with plans delivering restorative justice in an empowering and inclusive framework.

There is a growing body of evidence to show that schemes which fully embrace restorative principles and deliver the goals of agency and accountability are considerably more effective in producing higher levels of satisfaction and even reduced levels of reoffending.[89] Certainly, research confirms that victims are often willing to participate in restorative justice processes and they are generally positive about their experience of the process and outcomes. In Northern Ireland, for example, victims identified the best features of their experience which fall under three broad themes: the notion that the offender has been helped in some way; the belief that the young person will be less likely to offend in future; and, crucially, that they have been held to account for their actions. These features underline the centrality of the agency-accountability framework in that victims want to be involved and not excluded from how their case is dealt with, they want to see something positive emerge from their negative experience of crime and they want the offender to realise the harm they caused and to be less likely to do so again. Such symbolic forms of agency and accountability also occur through helping offenders to become positively accountable for their actions and to realise the nature and extent of the harm they have caused, as well as providing them with constructive opportunities to make amends to their victims by apologising, making reparation, or performing some form of community work or service. Indeed, offenders identified the most meaningful aspect of the conference as the opportunity to apologise to the victim, a feature that is central to our notion of accepting accountability, yet virtually absent from the court process. Interestingly, they also identified the apology as one of the most difficult parts of the process, underlining that actively accepting accountability is a more challenging process in contrast to having responsibility imposed by others.

This is not to suggest that the mainstreaming of restorative justice through youth conferencing works effectively all the time and in all cases. As we have noted, some cases are not suitable for conferencing, such as where the young person

---

[89] Sherman and Strang (2007).

is unwilling to actively participate, or where the evidence or facts are disputed. However, when used for suitable cases, and where the goals of agency and accountability are used to frame the process, the research evidence is largely positive and there is now a considerable international body of research demonstrating advantages of integrating restorative justice within criminal justice for offenders, victims and the broader community.[90]

Ultimately, realising the theoretical potential of conferencing to facilitate agency and accountability within the criminal justice system hinges upon the system's structural capacity to deliver it. As Maxwell notes, good outcomes depend on good practices.[91] Any attempt to introduce radical reform to criminal justice on a large scale will inevitably encounter structural, cultural and attitudinal obstacles. These are explored further in chapter nine. These challenges are likely to be even more acute as efforts are made to expand the use of conferencing beyond juvenile cases and into the realms of adult justice.[92]

It is important to recognise that 'doing' restorative justice well requires a considerable investment. A high quality and effective service built around the core values of agency and accountability requires adequate resourcing. Enthusiasm among facilitators to deliver best practice risks being undermined by increasing case-loads and diminishing resources.[93] Less time then becomes available to prepare participants, to deliver quality restorative conference, or to follow up and monitor the outcomes of conference plans. Indeed, as conferencing has become mainstreamed, so too has the pressure to standardise the facilitation and application of conferences and plans. This can threaten the individuality of tailor-made restoration packages with the capacity to address the very specific needs of both victims and offenders. If the key steps of thorough preparation, skilled facilitation and extensive follow up are undermined, the restorative nature of the conferencing process may become endangered, which is likely in turn to lead to increased dissatisfaction and poor outcomes for participants. Such concerns highlight the importance of aligning restorative justice interventions to our agency-accountability framework to ensure the quality and purpose of interventions are not lost in drives for efficiency and standardisation or, indeed, as part of a wider policy disbursement towards popular punitivism.

---

[90] See eg Miers (2001); Sherman and Strang (2007). For an alternative view, see Goldson (2011) who is critical of restorative youth conferencing—especially as a model for criminal justice reform as proposed by the Independent Commission on Youth Crime and Antisocial Behaviour (2010).
[91] Maxwell (2007), 65.
[92] Julich (2006).
[93] See further Barnes (2016).

8

Restorative Justice and Recidivism

I. Introduction

In this chapter we move on from the question of how restorative justice is used across criminal justice systems, and to take up the specific question of whether restorative justice reduces reoffending (or recidivism). There has been considerable debate on this question, and the proposition that restorative justice offers a cost-effective tool for reducing reoffending or recidivism clearly appeals to policymakers.[1] Evaluating the success or failure of restorative justice through headline reoffending figures may, prima facie, provide a simple and objective tool to determine whether or not restorative justice 'works'.[2] However, as we argue below, such claims are not derived from the theoretical underpinnings of restorative justice, as it is not primarily intended to deter future offending. The danger of making such claims, as Johnstone notes, is to imply that restorative justice is simply a new technique for crime prevention, which is clearly not the case.[3] Similarly, our agency-accountability framework is not primarily focused on the future behaviour of offenders. Rather, it seeks to clarify and guide the effective delivery of restorative justice within criminal justice, for the benefit of *all* participants.

As highlighted in chapter two, the objectives of restorative justice contrast with traditional justice systems which have largely been justified on the basis of punishing offenders and providing procedural safeguards to protect the innocent from conviction. Conventional criminal justice promotes these goals over the rights and interests of victims, where this focus has been justified by reference to both general and individual deterrence. We know from international evidence that traditional criminal justice sanctions are not effective at deterring crime. Indeed, the severe sanction of the loss of liberty through the imposition of a custodial sentence has been proven to be one of the most ineffective methods of reducing recidivism, with international research evidence consistently showing very high reoffending rates following imprisonment.[4]

---

[1] Braithwaite (2002a); Strang et al (2013).
[2] Bergseth and Bouffard (2007); Saulnier and Sivasubramaniam (20015a).
[3] Johnstone (2011).
[4] See eg Burnett and Maruna (2004); Cullen et al (2011); Lloyd et al (1994).

It is against this backdrop that the issue of reoffending and restorative justice is now considered. While there is broad agreement that reducing the probability of offenders reoffending ought to be a goal for criminal justice, current interventions are generally ineffective at achieving this. It is therefore important to view restorative justice interventions as primarily providing a better and more accountable form of justice, with any reductions in reoffending that are gained adding benefit—but the prospect of reducing recidivism should not be seen as the core rationale for restorative justice.

In this chapter we aim to untangle a range of questions that emanate from a range of research findings in relation to recidivism through the lenses of agency and accountability. Much of the research evidence is international in nature and covers a diverse range of restorative praxis; the evidence broadly reflects this heterogeneity. In the first section, evidence and claims regarding the early police-led restorative cautioning practices in the United Kingdom are critically examined. We then proceed to consider broader reoffending studies that have examined international reoffending rates across various types of restorative interventions. Next, the chapter explores meta-analyses, which pool the results of various studies to give us an overall indication of their effectiveness, in terms of reducing reoffending. Finally, more detailed studies are considered and we reflect on the kinds of factors that appear to most positively impact upon the effectiveness of restorative programmes in reducing recidivism and how such factors link to our core goals of agency and accountability.

A. Restorative Cautioning and Recidivism

Research conducted in England and Wales following the introduction of restorative police cautioning provides a useful illustration of some of the complexities that can arise in attempting to measure recidivism. This body of research highlights the dangers of making claims that restorative interventions have a dramatic impact in reducing recidivism and reveals how evidence to show changes in reoffending levels can easily be misinterpreted.

As noted in chapter five, the Thames Valley restorative cautioning programme differed significantly from the traditional police caution, which has been likened to a 'degradation ceremony'.[5] By contrast, the restorative caution focuses on the offence and its consequences, underlining the negative consequences of the act and its impact on the victim. Drawing from a restorative framework, it underlines the importance of shaming of the young person in a way that is reintegrative, through reinforcing that the young person can learn from their experience, make good for the harm they caused, and move forward in a positive way.

---

[5] Garfinkel (1956).

Introduction

The introduction of restorative cautioning was part of a wider set of reforms on cautioning and police practice that emerged in the 1990s. During this era there was an increasing emphasis on the use of diversionary practices, which were focused on keeping young people out of the court system, especially first-time offenders and those who had committed relatively minor offences.[6] The restorative caution was promoted not only as a better practice for administering cautions, but also as a more effective method, that could significantly reduce reoffending compared with traditional cautioning methods.[7]

The Thames Valley restorative cautioning programme was subjected to a study by the Home Office Police Research Group, which concluded that it was 'highly effective' in reducing reoffending, particularly for first-time offenders.[8] The research boldly asserted that the scheme resulted in a reoffending rate of just 3 per cent, compared with 35 per cent for first-time offenders dealt with using traditional caution methods. Further, the average time spent by officers dealing with cases in the restorative scheme was found to be about half that spent on offenders dealt with in the conventional way. These startling results acted as a catalyst for the rapid development of similar restorative cautioning schemes throughout the UK and Ireland.[9]

Further results on another restorative cautioning scheme based in Aylesbury, released to the media in 1997, suggested that it was highly successful in reducing reoffending from 30 per cent to just 4 per cent.[10] Such claims were headline-grabbing news and were even quoted in the House of Commons as evidence of the great success of the programme,[11] and further spurred on the drive to change traditional police cautioning practices. The Home Secretary, Jack Straw, was highly impressed with the new restorative techniques and both the subsequent Crime and Disorder Act 1998 and the Youth Justice and Criminal Evidence Act 1999 were heavily influenced by the apparent early success of restorative cautioning.

However, the research which had reported this overwhelming success of the schemes in reducing reoffending soon came under further scrutiny. One of the key caveats of the Thames Valley research, which was often missing when the research was quoted, was that those who chose to attend the conferences as a group were probably more motivated to stop offending than those who did not (and who were cautioned in the traditional manner).[12] As McCulloch explained in the research report, 'one cannot exclude the possibility that those who chose to attend the scheme are those who are least likely to re-offend anyway'.[13] Therefore, the

---

[6] Home Office (1994).
[7] Dignan (2001).
[8] McCulloch (1996).
[9] Wilcox and Young (2007).
[10] This figure was released by Thames Valley police to a number of media outlets in October 1997: see Wilcox and Young (2007), 144–45.
[11] *Hansard*, HC Deb, 11 May 1998, col 8.
[12] McCulloch (1996).
[13] McCulloch (1996), 1.

results as they were broadly reported failed to properly control for the motivation of the subject. This drew into question their internal validity, as motivation is a well-established factor for predicting success or failure in criminological interventions.[14] Moreover, it would appear that the research failed to properly control for the length of the follow up—so some individuals on the scheme were only followed up for a matter of months, yet these results were compared with the national five-year figures.[15] The results therefore exaggerated the effectiveness of the restorative scheme by comparison to traditional cautioning practice.

A second study of the Aylesbury programme, conducted by a consultancy firm, compared offenders in the scheme with offenders cautioned in another similar area (Nottinghamshire) which did not operate the scheme. The results were considerably more positive for those who attended the scheme than those cautioned in the traditional manner.[16] However, as in the first study, this work failed to control for the motivation of participants in the restorative caution group. Those in the restorative scheme had chosen to attend and thus were probably more motivated, while arguably those in the control group were not given a choice, meaning it contained both motivated and unmotivated individuals.

The schemes were subsequently exposed to much more rigorous research when they were being rolled out in other places. This research explored reoffending rates as well as aspects of best practice in terms of delivering restorative cautions.[17] Based on an analysis of official records and data from self-reported offending, the study suggested that about a quarter of the offenders had been helped to desist from crime, due at least in part to the restorative caution they had received. These findings, which were based on an in-depth analysis of a smaller number of individuals showed reductions in reoffending to be considerably more modest than the previous research claimed. The researchers also called for a large scale and detailed analysis of reoffending rates to be completed.[18]

The Home Office accepted the gauntlet and funded one of the largest and most complete studies of restorative cautioning in the United Kingdom at the time.[19] The cautioning practice in the Thames Valley police force area between 1998 and 2001 was evaluated by a team based at the University of Oxford. The sample included just under 20,000 cases where either traditional or restorative cautions were given. These were compared with cautions given over the same time period in Sussex and Warwickshire (which only used the traditional caution), and offenders were followed up over a two-year period from the date of the caution. 'Reoffending' included any conviction, caution, final warning or reprimand resulting from an offence within two years of the caution. The basic reoffending

---

[14] Clear and Cadora (2001).
[15] Goold and Young (1999).
[16] Goold and Young (1999).
[17] Hoyle et al (2002).
[18] Hoyle et al (2002).
[19] Wilcox et al (2004).

Introduction

rates showed that offenders in the Thames Valley area were less likely to be reconvicted (30 per cent) than those in Sussex (34 per cent) or Warwickshire (35 per cent). However, these differences were considerably more modest than the previous research had claimed (just 3–4 per cent were reported as reconvicted in the previous research). The research also showed that reoffending rates had decreased substantially from 1998 to 2001 and the differences between the forces decreased over this time period.[20] Most importantly, the research revealed that once other important variables were controlled for (including gender, age, previous cautions and number of offences) those exposed to the restorative cautioning were not any less likely to reoffend than those in the traditional scheme (nor were they more likely to reoffend).

This rigorous study demonstrated that the restorative cautioning projects did not have a major impact on reoffending rates and that claims of wide and substantial decreases in reoffending were incorrect. However, the research also illustrates that reoffending is only one measure of effectiveness, as the scheme was shown to be generally successful in delivering other important benefits to offenders and victims, including agreements for reparation, apologies and expressions of remorse. The schemes had proved successful in helping the large majority of offenders understand the effects of the offence and most participants were supportive of the police initiative.[21]

One of the key lessons from the experience of the early restorative cautioning research is the danger of making claims that it, or similar restorative measures at the periphery of the criminal justice process, can dramatically reduce reoffending rates. If such claims are exaggerated or unfounded, this can lead to over-selling and unrealistic expectations which may ultimately prove counterproductive to the future development of restorative schemes. In fact, the research revealed that the police-led restorative cautions only involved victims in about 16 per cent of the conferences, so often fell short of being able to achieve restorative environment for victims and offenders.[22] More generally, it is unrealistic to expect the impact of a single restorative session, often without the victim present, to have a dramatic effect on reoffending. An alternative approach to the evaluative research would have been to focus on the original aims of restorative schemes based around police cautioning, centring on whether it provided a process which was more open and accountable, and more balanced, which took into account victims' needs and concerns and which could be more useful to participants than traditional cautioning practice. Such research might have been better able to reflect the success of such schemes. While reductions in offending may 'add benefit' for restorative-based interventions such as these, they should not be regarded as the key yardstick of success.

---

[20] Wilcox et al (2004).
[21] Wilcox et al (2004).
[22] Hoyle et al (2002). See further ch 5, III.

B. Restorative Justice Programmes and Recidivism

A number of studies have reviewed research evidence examining the impact of restorative interventions on reoffending. For example, Umbreit, Voss and Coates completed a broad review of restorative-based programmes within criminal justice or with cases referred by criminal justice agencies.[23] The authors examined data relating to reoffending rates and evidence of success or otherwise, drawing on 85 studies from mostly North American research which included examples such as mediation, conferencing and sentencing circles. The review included studies with at least some type of control group; studies that simply reported overall reoffending rates with no comparison were excluded. While many of their findings found relatively high levels of satisfaction among participants,[24] it was also found that many restorative programmes had positive results in terms of reducing recidivism rates in comparison with traditional criminal justice interventions. Programmes that included victim-offender mediation and mediation that involved direct face-to-face contact between the victim and offender were shown to be more effective than programmes in which there was only indirect mediation between the parties. While noting that the goal of preventing reoffending may be used as a long-term measure of the effectiveness of restorative interventions, they caution against using it in isolation.[25] Rather, they advise that, in order to gauge the overall effectiveness of a programme, a broad range of measures should to be taken into account.

Indeed, research by Nugent et al which reviewed 14 different studies and involved over 9,000 cases, found those who participated in mediation had a statistically significant (25 per cent) lower rate of recidivism.[26] A broadly similar study conducted by the Canadian government showed that restorative programmes including mediation and group conferencing yielded greater reductions in recidivism compared with other non-restorative approaches, and offenders in restorative programme types (mediation and group conferencing) were significantly more successful during the follow-up periods.[27] Similarly, Latimer et al examined over 20 studies focusing on the impact of restorative justice programmes across a number of settings and found the majority produced positive and significant results in terms of reducing reoffending; these results were supported by a subsequent review of research by Bonta et al.[28]

Programmes involving group conferencing and sentencing circles research seemed to produce more mixed results.[29] For the most part, studies have been

---

[23] Unbreit et al (2006).
[24] See further ch 4.
[25] Umbreit et al (2006).
[26] Nugent et al (2003).
[27] Latimer et al (2001).
[28] Latimer et al (2005); Bonta et al (2006).
[29] Umbreit et al (2006).

generally positive and show that those who had gone through a conferencing process are less likely to reoffend. However, studies report differing results for different types of offenders. For instance, the RISE experiments from Australia showed a reduction in reoffending for violent crimes, but no statistically significant reduction for the other categories of offences studied (mostly property offences).[30] Similarly, research conducted by McCold and Wachtel of police-led conferencing found that conferences had a more positive impact on recidivism rates for participants whose offences were violent.[31]

Research from Northern Ireland has also examined reoffending rates of young people given a range of sentences, including those given through restorative youth conferences.[32] It demonstrates that reoffending rates vary considerably by the type of disposal. This can largely be explained by differences in the characteristics of offenders given each disposal. For example, those given community disposals were generally at a lower risk of reoffending than those given custodial sentences. However the research shows that those released from custody had the highest rates of reoffending (72 per cent). Those given restorative conferencing had a relatively low level of reoffending (38 per cent), which was better than those given by most of the other community-based disposals (47 per cent), such as probation, community service or attendance centre orders.[33]

Regarding longer-term outcomes, Bergseth and Bouffard found that young people referred for restorative justice and traditional juvenile court processing using multiple measures of offending or reconviction had significantly better outcomes for more serious offences. These results were also found to be consistent over a three-year follow-up period.[34] Moreover, their study was able to demonstrate significant reductions in reoffending in the restorative sample by comparison to those processed through the traditional court process, while controlling for key variables such as age, race, gender, seriousness of offence and the number of previous police and court contacts. Indeed, they note the effectiveness of restorative justice programming for more serious offenders 'would then suggest that it may be possible to expand the types of potential offenders to whom restorative approaches are applied'.[35] The authors followed up their study with a larger sample of treatment and control groups and the results also revealed strong evidence of the restorative

---

[30] Sherman et al (2000).
[31] McCold and Wachtel (1998).
[32] Lyness (2008).
[33] Lyness (2008). More recently, statistics published in 2011 show a similar trend. The one year reoffending rate of those juveniles (10–17 years of age) released from custody was 68%. For community-based disposals (excluding youth conferences) it was 54%. For court-ordered restorative youth conferences 45% reoffended, while only 29% of those given diversionary youth conferences reoffended within a year. These latest statistics are encouraging, in that reoffending rates for restorative youth conferences have been shown to be lower than for those given other types of community-based sentences and considerably lower than those given custodial sentences. See Lyness and Tate (2011).
[34] Bergseth and Bouffard (2007).
[35] Bergseth and Bouffard (2007), 449.

justice intervention having a positive impact in reducing reoffending, especially amongst more serious types of offenders.[36] Similarly, in New Zealand, Lynn examined the effectiveness of family group conferencing with matched cohorts of offenders referred to court and was able to demonstrate significant reductions in the 12-month reoffending rate for those who were in the restorative family group conferencing sample.[37]

i. Meta-analyses

Moving beyond specific reviews of restorative and court-based interventions and their impact on reoffending, another type of evidence emerges from studies that rely on the technique of meta-analysis. This method brings together the results of numerous studies and analyses them together, in an attempt to draw out common themes and conclusions from their collective weight. Such studies have the advantage of providing a more structured approach to reviewing diverse research findings and potentially provide a more robust set of conclusions relating to their impact on reoffending.

One of the first comprehensive meta-analysis studies looking at restorative interventions and their impact on reconviction was completed by Bonta and colleagues.[38] Their analysis was based on a wide review of differing programmes that had a restorative basis and included court imposed family group conferences and a range of community-based interventions. The analysis included studies with comparison samples and recidivism data. Some 39 studies were included and nearly half were situated within a court setting, covering a range of programmes based on restorative justice. The research revealed that many of the restorative programmes were targeted towards low-risk youth offenders and few included serious offenders, such as violent offenders. Similar to much of the general research on restorative programmes, victim and offender satisfaction levels were found to be high across the programmes evaluated. In relation to the impact of the restorative programmes on recidivism, it was found to produce a 7 per cent reduction over an average 17-month follow-up period.

Further analysis reveals that the impact of restorative programmes in the different studies was greater for those that had been evaluated after 1995. In general terms, it appears the older and more established programmes were less effective in reducing recidivism than the newer interventions. The researchers suggest this is related to the extent to which programmes over this period delivered restorative goals. Generally it was found that the newer programmes had clearer restorative objectives, goals and principles and appeared to provide a stronger restorative-based intervention. Furthermore, in all of the studies that included violent offenders, the effect of the restorative intervention was generally stronger,

---

[36] Bergseth and Bouffard (2013).
[37] Lynn (2011).
[38] Bonta et al (2006).

with a reduction in recidivism of about 15 per cent. However, the research also suggested that the restorative interventions were less effective with repeat offenders—who by definition have a much higher rate of recidivism.

Overall, the research by Bonta et al demonstrates that across a range of differing restorative interventions there was a modest but statistically significant reduction in reoffending. There were differences found between programmes, and there was a great degree of variation in the types of programmes evaluated, as well as variation in the types of offenders and offences. However, programmes which included more serious and violent offenders appeared to have a stronger effect and were able to produce statistically significant reductions in recidivism. These findings are generally supported by other similar research, such as the study by Luke and Lind, which concluded that restorative conferencing usually rendered modest but statistically significant reductions in the predicted risks of reoffending.[39] Only one study to date has found evidence that a restorative justice programme produced an increase in the probability of offending, though the programme was small and limited to one type of offence used for youth in Australia.[40]

Overall the meta-analysis of restorative interventions and reoffending produces similar findings to research which looked other types of interventions (not restorative) and their impact on offender rehabilitation.[41] This more general body of research shows that treatment programmes provided to offenders can have positive impacts in reducing reoffending.[42] Such findings are consistent with other reviews internationally and demonstrate that many offending programmes and interventions, including restorative interventions, have modest positive results in terms of reducing recidivism.[43] The broader research also shows, similar to the research based on restorative justice, that treatment interventions are commonly more effective for higher-risk offenders while programmes for low-risk individuals carry less impact.[44] These findings help us to understand why the police restorative cautions—which were directed towards low-risk first-time offenders—did not produce substantial reductions in reoffending, despite some of the claims that were made. Importantly, the research also shows that restorative interventions which include victims in a process of direct dialogue and those that use conferencing methods are more effective in producing lower levels of reoffending. Such results tend to support the proposition that restorative programmes which have the ability to deliver empowering goals of agency and accountability carry greater impact in terms of reducing reoffending.

---

[39] Luke and Lind (2002).
[40] Sherman et al (2000).
[41] Andrews and Bonta (2003).
[42] Andrews and Bonta (2003).
[43] McGuire (2001).
[44] Andrews and Bonta (2003).

ii. More Detailed Analyses of Recidivism

One of the more exhaustive studies of the international literature is provided by Sherman and Strang.[45] Their research adopted a different method for drawing the research evidence together compared to the meta-analysis studies noted above.[46] Sherman and Strang's research followed the methodology favoured by the UK National Institute of Clinical Excellence (NICE) to assess evidence on the effectiveness of medical treatments.[47] This involves looking in detail at every study in terms of what population the restorative intervention was provided for, and contrasting this with a comparison group for the outcomes provided. The method allows for a deeper analysis of the range of interventions and how they impact recidivism and seems better equipped to measure recidivism across a diverse range of programmes based in disparate community settings.

Most of the evidence used by Sherman and Strang is based on studies that used face-to-face conferences with offenders, victims and their supporters.[48] These types of programmes are more likely to fulfil the potential for restorative justice, in that the parties directly affected by the crime are present and can participate in the process and actively contribute to the restorative dynamic in such meetings. While other forms of restorative interventions, including those that use mediation or indirect communications between the parties, seek to achieve restorative outcomes, the way they are applied is less likely to result in the achievement of restorative outcomes for the parties.[49]

Similar to the meta-analysis studies, Sherman and Strang found that the vast majority of the restorative programmes they examined had a positive effect on reducing recidivism.[50] The success of the restorative programmes appeared to be most pronounced for violent crimes across the studies they analysed. Indeed, the largest effect of restorative interventions on recidivism was found for violent crime in the randomised experiments conducted in the Australian Canberra RISE project. In a two-year 'before' and 'after' comparison period, the frequency of arrests amongst white offenders under 30 years of age who were assigned to the restorative programme dropped significantly.[51] Furthermore, in six field tests the restorative justice intervention was found to reduce recidivism for adult or youth offenders referred for violent offences.

Sherman and Strang found similar results for a sample of young girls in England (Northumberland), who were less likely to be rearrested following a police-led

---

[45] Sherman and Strang (2007).
[46] See Bonta et al (2006).
[47] Sherman and Strang (2007).
[48] Sherman and Strang (2007).
[49] See Braithwaite and Mugford (1994); Claassen (1995).
[50] Sherman and Strang (2007).
[51] These effects were not found amongst the Aboriginal offenders, but the sample size for that group was also too small for effective comparisons, see Sherman et al (2006).

restorative intervention compared to those dealt with in the traditional manner.[52] Citing randomised experiments in the United States, they also claim that there is evidence for reductions in reoffending for violent offenders following restorative interventions; McGarrell et al reported that children between 7–14 years of age assigned to a restorative intervention for violent offences were less likely to be rearrested (28 per cent) than those in the control sample (34 per cent).[53] In relation to property crime, in comparison with violent offences, Sherman and Strang suggest the restorative interventions produced less pronounced effects in terms of reducing recidivism levels. Most of the studies they reviewed produced reductions in reoffending; however, some revealed little change by comparison with traditional interventions. One isolated study with Aboriginal youth offenders showed those who had undergone the restorative intervention were slightly more likely to reoffend—though this was an exception to the large body of evidence suggesting otherwise. Overall, five tests of restorative justice found reductions in reoffending for property offenders.

The findings from Sherman and Strang's research paint a broadly similar picture to other recent studies reviewing restorative programmes and their effectiveness in reducing recidivism. The conclusions show that restorative programmes can reduce crime, but the evidence is less clear as to the kinds of offences, or offenders for whom restorative justice is most effective. It is important to note that Sherman and Strang's research covers a wide range of restorative interventions, and forging a precise understanding of the specific circumstances in which it works is problematic. However, drawing on their data the authors predict that restorative programmes can produce 'substantial reductions in repeat offending for both violent and property crime'.[54] Furthermore, based on the evidence, they strongly support the development of restorative justice measures within criminal justice:

> Restorative justice offers a strategy for holding more offenders accountable, with many more victims helped, with more crimes prevented, and with the costs of government reduced. The evidence so far suggests that many elements of this strategy can work with some kinds of offenders and offences. That evidence is far more extensive, and positive, than the evidence base for most national roll-outs of new criminal justice policies in any government.[55]

More recently Strang et al produced a systemic review of studies examining the effects of face-to-face restorative justice conferencing.[56] This research examined randomised controlled trials where victims and offenders consented to meet prior to random assignment, as part of an 'intention to treat' analysis. A distinct advantage of this approach is that it selected studies that used very robust methodology

---

[52] Sherman et al (2006).
[53] McGarrell et al (2000).
[54] Sherman and Strang (2007), 8.
[55] Sherman and Strang (2007), 24.
[56] Strang et al (2013).

to conservatively estimate the impact of the restorative justice 'treatments' on reoffending. A total of 10 different experimental studies were examined, with strong methodological rigour and controls in place. These studies encompassed a range of applications, from diversion from prosecution, post-conviction prior to sentencing and post-sentencing applications in prison and probation samples. They also included violent and property crimes and covered youth and adult crime across differing samples.

Evaluating the studies, Strang et al found that while individually most were unable to produce statistically significant results, all but one showed less reoffending for the restorative justice conferencing samples than the control groups. However, when the average effect across all 10 studies was calculated the pattern of findings was statistically significant showing an overall modest benefit for the restorative justice conferencing programmes in terms of reducing reoffending. Similar to other studies, the impact of restorative conferencing appeared to produce more marked reductions in reoffending for violent offences than for property-related offences and there appeared to be slightly more positive results for the adult serious offenders than for juvenile offenders. Significantly, the research was also able to demonstrate cost advantages derived from estimating the costs of crimes that had been prevented through the restorative justice conferencing programmes. The restorative justice programmes appeared to offer substantial cost-effectiveness, especially for more serious and violent offenders who had longer criminal records, suggesting such programmes may be appropriately targeted towards such offenders, rather than younger and petty offenders.[57]

Not all reviews into reconviction have yielded such encouraging results. Some commentators have pointed to the methodological difficulties that beset many of the reconviction studies conducted to date.[58] In the real world, there are considerable obstacles to carrying out highly detailed and experimental studies that involve offenders, the courts and victims. Indeed, none of the research studies to date claim to be a perfect experiment producing totally reliable results that can be replicated exactly elsewhere. This is due to the difficulties in trying to conduct randomised controlled trials in the field, the problems in designing methods of controlling samples to allow for meaningful comparisons, and differences in the ways criminal justice is delivered across jurisdictions. There are also many different ways in which recidivism may be measured, ranging from arrests or court convictions, to the number and seriousness of subsequent convictions, all of which contribute to the complexities of making comparisons across studies.

It is therefore unsurprising that in a review of research on restorative justice interventions and reoffending from 2007 to 2012, Weatherburn and Macadam found

---

[57] Strang et al (2013), 48. The work of Shapland et al (2008) is particularly relevant in relation to cost and benefit-analysis, and underlines the importance of demonstrating the amount and types of crimes that can be avoided through restorative justice conferencing interventions, which can result in significant cost advantages.

[58] Bergseth and Bouffard (2007); Hayes (2007); Shapland et al (2008); Walgrave (2011).

'little reliable evidence that restorative justice reduces re-offending'.[59] They highlighted the many methodological problems encountered across studies conducted over this period; while 8 of 14 studies they examined were able to produce at least one statistically significant result in favour of restorative justice, six were unable to reach statistical significance. However, their overall conclusions may well have been overly pessimistic, given that they were able to find modest and statistically significant results and none of the studies they reported produced negative results. Indeed one of the studies they highlight produced 'significant results favouring the conferencing group … even after adjusting for each of the factors we earlier noted as critical controls. The effects, moreover, were quite substantial'.[60] Similarly, Livingstone et al reviewed studies examining restorative justice conferencing and its impact in reducing recidivism in young offenders (specifically aged 7–21).[61] Of the four randomised controlled trials they examined in their review, none were able to produce statistically significant differences in the rates of reoffending between those who were part of the restorative justice conferencing and those in the normal court proceedings. However, the authors acknowledged that restorative interventions may be effective for violent and more serious offending and that from the victims' perspective the restorative experience may well 'provide significant benefit over normal court proceedings'.[62]

These reviews of the research on restorative justice and reoffending placed high expectations on the quality of methodologies in order to include individual studies within their analysis. This resulted in many studies being excluded from their analysis, thus limiting the pool of evidence they could draw from. However, they do help temper the literature, highlighting the complexity of the relationship between restorative justice interventions and reoffending measures. Whilst most of the major reviews of the research have uncovered modest but favourable indications that restorative justice can help reduce reoffending, the evidence clearly demonstrates the need for further high-quality research on the issue.

iii. Factors Which Influence Recidivism

Despite the wide range of research that has looked at restorative justice programmes and reoffending, surprisingly little of this work sheds light on what specific elements of the process have the most significant impacts in reducing reoffending. In other words, much of the desistance-focused literature has been focused on just one output of restorative justice—measured as whether it results in reduced levels of reoffending. However, as noted above, reoffending is only one measure of success, which when taken in isolation reveals surprisingly little about the more fundamental questions of *why* restorative interventions may or may

---

[59] Weatherburn and Macadam (2013).
[60] Weatherburn and Macadam (2013), 9.
[61] Livingstone et al (2013).
[62] Livingstone et al (2013), 23.

not be successful. As such, reoffending provides a measure of success in terms of an important headline, but taken in isolation such data really tells us very little about the effectiveness of restorative justice as an intervention. This is one of the major disadvantages of using reoffending as the measure of success; the impacts of restorative justice go considerably beyond the offender and are evident across all of those involved in the process including the victim, peers, family members and even the broader community. It also touches upon wider issues of public trust and legitimacy of the criminal justice system.[63] Evaluating and understanding the effectiveness of restorative justice is therefore contingent upon gaining a fuller understanding of the complex sets of processes that revolve around the quality of the restorative encounter, how this is managed for the participants, as well as the agreed outcomes that flow from it, rather than through a simple measure that reoffending provides. Moreover, as with any criminal justice intervention, its ultimate effectiveness will also hinge on individual characteristics, demographics, personalities and life circumstances.[64]

For these reasons it is worth turning to a smaller body of research literature of detailed studies that have attempted to give more nuanced evaluations of the specific mechanics of *how* restorative justice may actually impact reoffending. In particular, these allow us to focus attention on the question as to why certain types of interventions and outcomes appear to be more effective than others. These studies are also important because they allow us to consider what role the empowering goals of agency and accountability play. An example of this kind of research is the work of Shapland et al who examined a range of different restorative programmes across England and Wales, mostly involving adult offenders, some of whom had been convicted of serious offences.[65] Three core restorative programmes were studied, including a programme that provided mediation and conferencing services for adult offenders. Most of these had been referred by the courts and these individuals were compared with a matched sample of offenders. The second group, which took referrals at different stages of the criminal justice process, also provided restorative services to adult offenders. This group used an experimental model where cases were randomly allocated to either a conference or a control group, after the victim's and offender's consent had been obtained. The third group offered direct and indirect mediation to adults and juveniles referred at different stages of the criminal justice process, ranging from police 'final warnings' to prison pre-release programmes. Referrals were taken from offenders, victims and the Probation Service and these cases were compared with matched samples of offenders who had not participated in mediation. This research study provides a detailed insight into three broadly different types of restorative programmes, run by different organisations and delivered to different types of offenders.

---

[63] Doak and O'Mahony (2011); Dzur and Wertheimer (2002); Tyler et al (2007).
[64] Saulnier and Sivasubramaniam (2015a).
[65] Shapland et al (2008).

Introduction

189

The research by Shapland et al measured reoffending by reviewing both whether individuals were reconvicted or not and the number of subsequent offences they committed. Their research shows those who participated in the restorative schemes were less likely to have been reconvicted over the subsequent two years[66] and they committed statistically fewer offences in the subsequent two years than offenders in the control groups. Since the research examined different schemes where the number of cases in some of the individual programmes was small, this impacted on their ability to provide statistically significant results for the smaller programmes. However, one programme which used an experimental model and had a larger sample showed a statistically significant reduction in the likelihood and seriousness of reoffending for those who took part and also showed fewer reconvictions in the subsequent two years than offenders in the control group. There was also no evidence that any of the programmes they evaluated resulted in an increase in convictions for participants.

Shapland et al's research is particularly useful because it gives a detailed account of the restorative practices used across the three broad schemes and provides an insight into the practice of restorative justice from the perspective of the offender and victim.[67] The research was able to examine the characteristics of offenders and victims, and whether this impacted on their likelihood of reconviction (though it was unable to identify statistically significant predictors). Thus they conclude from their evidence that no particular demographic group of offenders (such as age, sex, ethnic origin etc) appeared to benefit more substantially from restorative interventions than another. They also found that the victims' experiences in conferences did not affect the probability of offenders being reconvicted. So, it appeared that the views of victims and how they felt that conferences were delivered, or whether they accepted the apology of the offender, did not impact the offender's probability of reconviction.

Crucially, however, the research did shed light on the ways in which offenders experienced the conference process and this was related to subsequent levels of offending. Shapland et al reveal that offenders who reported that the conference had made them realise the harm they had caused and said that they had found the experience useful, as well as those who had wanted to meet the victim and were observed to be actively engaged in the conference, were all significantly and positively related to decreased subsequent offending.[68] As the authors note, 'conference experience itself and the communication with the victim had affected the likelihood of offenders' subsequent reconviction'.[69] Such findings support the broader theoretical work on effective practice, which emphasises the importance

---

[66] However, this result was not statistically significant.
[67] Shapland et al (2008).
[68] Shapland et al (2008), iv.
[69] Shapland et al (2008), iv.

of restorative elements, such as: bringing the parties together; working towards meeting needs; seeking to repair injuries caused and thus restoring relationships.[70]

These results provide evidence to support our contention that restorative justice ought to be framed around the empowering values of agency and accountability. This is evident in how participants were able to gain a sense of agency by being able to take ownership and involvement in the decisions impacting them. As Shapland et al's findings show, those offenders who were actively engaged in the restorative process (thereby exercising maximum agency) and were able to rate their experience as being useful were less likely to reoffend. Similarly, offenders who took part in conferences where levels of accountability were maximised—whereby offenders reported being willing to be held to account and exercised the choice to meet their victims—were less likely to reoffend. Furthermore, achieving accountability by taking steps to make amends for the harm caused, as well as deciding to make positive changes in their own lives were linked to reductions in reoffending. Thus aspects of both agency and accountability within the restorative process and its outcomes were positively related to decreased rates of reoffending.

The pertinence of our agency-accountability framework is also reflected in other studies that have looked in more detail at the experiences of participants in restorative justice programmes and how these may be related to reoffending. These studies broadly confirm the significance of the impact provided by the encounter between the victim and offender in a conference. For example, Maxwell and Morris interviewed offenders and found that those who perceived the process to be respectful and inclusive were less likely to reoffend.[71] These findings support the importance of agency within the restorative process and show how an inclusive and respectful process in which they are able to participate and actively engage with the other participants is more likely to assist in terms of reducing future reoffending. Indeed, in subsequent research that followed 108 young offenders for 6.5 years after their restorative conference found that previous life experiences and circumstances, such as poverty and unemployment, were important predictors of recidivism. However, what happened in the conference was particularly significant.[72] Especially relevant were indicators of agreement and compliance with conference outcomes, a sense of involvement in the process, a feeling of remorse, an apology and a lack of stigma and shame associated with the conference,[73] all of which resonate strongly with our concepts of agency and accountability and their importance to the successful delivery of restorative justice.

A larger and more recent follow-up study in New Zealand which analysed case files and data on offending for 1,003 young offenders and a large (520) sample of individuals who completed conferences reveals that reoffending was less likely when the conference was rated as inclusive, fair and forgiving.[74] It appeared that

[70] Claassen (1995).
[71] Maxwell and Morris (2001).
[72] Maxwell and Morris (2001).
[73] Maxwell and Morris (2002).
[74] Maxwell et al (2004).

allowing the young offenders to make amends for what they had done was important, as was avoiding stigmatising them as 'bad' individuals. Here too, the authors conclude that the quality of the restorative conference and the experience of the young person is an important determinant of subsequent reoffending. In other words, conferences that succeed in achieving empowering goals, especially for the offender, are also likely to reduce the probability of reoffending.

Further research in Australia has looked into how the impact of different variables may affect the probability of reconviction. Hayes and Daly analysed data from the South Australian Juvenile Justice project to examine how differing features of family conferencing relate to future offending.[75] They considered data from conferences that had been observed, along with data on previous offending, and found that sex, race and prior offending were factors in recidivism following a conference. More importantly, however, they showed that the young offenders who were remorseful and conference outcomes that were consensual amongst the participants were less likely to result in reoffending. Thus 'ritually successful' conferences are more likely to result in reductions in reoffending.[76] Earlier research in the Australian state of New South Wales, which compared reoffending by young people who participated in a conference with reoffending by young people who attended court, found that the conferencing produced a moderate reduction of up to 15–20 per cent in reoffending across different offence types.[77] In a further study, Hayes and Daly examined conferencing arrangements and offender characteristics and their relationship to subsequent offending in Queensland.[78] Again, this research supported the importance of offender characteristics, like previous convictions, age and sex, on recidivism after restorative interventions. However, it also highlighted how critical elements of the restorative process like remorse and consensual agreements impact reoffending, underlining the importance of agency and accountability to the delivery of effective restorative justice interventions.

These research studies highlight the importance of understanding what it is in the restorative encounter that helps it to deliver a process that is meaningful and worthwhile for participants. They show that when our agency-accountability framework is facilitated through successful restorative interactions, they can impact behaviour into the future by reducing reoffending. Thus the quality of the restorative encounter and its ability to empower participants are crucial to understanding why restorative justice works and how it can help reduce reoffending.

Connecting to this theme, Rossner's detailed research examining the microdynamics of restorative interactions underlines the importance of the situational variables and the micro-dynamics of interactions in restorative conferences (over the traditional individual characteristics like age, sex and ethnic origin).[79] Her emphasis on the quality and dynamics of the interactions in restorative justice

[75] Hayes and Daly (2003).
[76] Rossner (2013).
[77] Luke and Lind (2002).
[78] Hayes and Daly (2004).
[79] Rossner (2013). See further ch 2, III(B).

conferences provides a stark contrast to much of the evaluative research which simply measured reoffending. Indeed, Rossner highlighted how generalised comparisons between restorative justice interventions and traditional courtroom outcomes, as measured through offending, offer little in terms of furthering our understanding of the variations in restorative justice practice that may actually impact reoffending.

Rossner examined the extent to which restorative conferences which achieved positive dynamics in terms of solidarity, reintegration and positive emotional energy were associated with reductions in reoffending. While her analysis did not find positive emotional energy to be statistically related to offending, her concepts of solidarity and reintegration were both significantly associated with reductions in reoffending. In a multivariate analysis it was shown that individual level variables (age, sex and ethnicity) influenced arrest frequency, but conferences with high solidarity were most significantly related to less reoffending. Furthermore, where offenders had a previous offending history and experienced a reintegrative conference, reoffending decreased.

Rossner's findings reveal how important both situational factors and the dynamics of conferencing are to determining the success of restorative justice and to its deterrent impact. Moreover, her research allows for a more detailed account of the workings of restorative justice and can be used to better understand elements of the process that positively impact participants. She focused on the concepts of solidarity and reintegration, which were shown to be positively associated with reductions in offending, and which connect strongly with the agency-accountability framework. Agency is reflected through solidarity by the common emphasis on behaviours that unite people and aid group togetherness through inclusionary gestures, sustained eye contact and spontaneous physical contact. Such interactions help to empower participants and confer a sense of agency whereby they are enabled to play an active part in the process and take some ownership in the decision making. Similarly, restorative accountability is reflected in her concept of reintegration whereby participants are better able to engage with one another, fostering support and acceptance through the exchange of apologies and forgiveness. Accountability is thus fostered by individuals being able to take active responsibility for the consequences of their actions and they are empowered by gestures of acceptance and forgiveness. In this way, Rossner's work helps to show what is important in successful restorative justice encounters through the role of solidarity and reintegration and similarly reflects the empowering potential of our agency-accountability framework.

II. Conclusions

Research into restorative justice and recidivism spans a diverse range of research studies which have adopted a range of methodologies across highly divergent communities and legal jurisdictions. Studies have covered a wide range of restorative interventions, taking place at various stages in the criminal justice system and involving differing types of offenders and offences. Indeed, many had different ways of defining recidivism, ranging from re-arrests or cautions, through to convictions for offences committed after interventions. However, on balance, research indicates that restorative interventions have the ability to deliver lower levels of reoffending when compared with traditional court processing. They also appear to work better with people who have a higher probability of reoffending; for example, there is evidence that restorative interventions are more effective with offenders with previous convictions than with low-risk offenders without previous convictions.[80] These data are consistent with Wilcox et al's findings in England on restorative police cautioning by, which centred on first-time and low-risk offenders.[81] This research found little evidence of reductions of reoffending once relevant variables (age, sex and offending) were controlled.[82] But since the reconviction rate for those cautioned is already low, it would be difficult to reduce this already low rate further.[83] Moreover, as Ward and Langlands remind us,[84] restorative justice cannot operate in a vacuum. The restorative session has value in contributing towards future desistance, but ultimately it must work within an overarching rehabilitatory policy framework which promotes evidence-based interventions which operate in tandem with the restorative process.[85] Furthermore the broad international research, especially from North America and Australia, tends to support the hypothesis that restorative interventions are better able to reduce recidivism if they are targeted alongside other rehabilitation measures towards higher risk and more serious offenders.[86]

It is clear, however, that reoffending is just one measure of success in relation to restorative justice. There are many other positive impacts of restorative justice with research showing that offenders, victims and supporters take a wide range of positive experiences from the process and its outcomes. Research that has simply compared restorative interventions against traditional court outcomes in relation to offending actually tells us little, since it lacks sufficient detail concerning why restorative justice may or may not work, or what elements of the process are most beneficial to participants. Indeed, focusing on reoffending as the core indicator of success for restorative justice can even serve to undermine the other valuable impacts it has been shown to deliver, from facilitating the involvement of participants in a productive process dealing with the consequences of crime, to providing

---

[80] See Sherman and Strang (2007).
[81] Wilcox et al (2004).
[82] Wilcox et al (2004).
[83] Ministry of Justice (2016). The reoffending rate for juvenile offenders given a youth caution, reprimand or warning was 31%; by comparison the rate for juvenile offenders released from custody was 69.2%.
[84] Ward and Langlands (2009).
[85] Ward and Langlands (2009).
[86] See Sherman and Strang (2007); McGarrell et al (2000); Bonta et al (2006).

space for restoration and allowing for a process that is perceived to be procedurally fairer and more satisfying in terms of its outcomes.

Nevertheless, the weight of evidence demonstrates that most restorative justice interventions have a modest and positive impact in reducing reoffending. Whilst this still tells us little about how and why restorative interventions produce these positive impacts, evidence comparing restorative interventions with court-based outcomes show it to be more effective in certain circumstances. For example, restorative interventions are more likely to be effective when they involve face-to-face encounters as opposed to indirect contact between the offender and victim. Restorative interventions also appear to be more effective when they involve personal offences (like offences against the person as opposed to property offences) and more serious offences. They seem more effective when the intervention has clear restorative goals, such as in cases which where the outcomes were negotiated between the parties and where there are expressions of genuine remorse.

These findings lend strong support to the application of empowerment theory and our agency-accountability framework set out in this book as a mechanism for calibrating the quality and effectiveness of restorative justice interventions. The dynamics of restorative encounters that lead to empowerment are only likely to be able to present in situations where there is direct contact between the offender and victim. Similarly, the goals of agency and accountability are more likely to be achieved in situations where the parties are able to engage positively with each other, like face-to-face restorative conferencing. Likewise, evidence that restorative justice works best with offences of a personal and serious nature is also constant with the tenets of empowerment theory, since victims are more likely to be personally impacted by more serious offences and offences against the person than by property crimes (such as minor theft). Thus victims are more prone to benefit from a process that helps them to become re-empowered and to achieve a sense of agency and accountability. Similarly, a negotiated outcome that results in genuine remorse being expressed connects strongly with the goals of agency, by being able to participate in the decision-making process, and of accountability, by being willing to accept responsibility for the consequences, by expressing remorse.

The more detailed research that has been conducted examining the process of restorative justice and how it influences offending shows the importance of unpacking and understanding what really happens in restorative encounters and its influence on future behaviour. This research evidence also shows that restorative interventions that involve direct contact between the offender and victim are generally more successful than those that have indirect or no victim involvement. From a praxis perspective, this underlines the importance of restorative processes being centred around participants so they are able to meaningfully engage in dialogue and mutual understanding. Similarly, the detailed research demonstrates that restorative conferences are better able to impact reoffending if core elements of the restorative process are achieved which empower offenders to develop a sense of agency. The goal of agency can be seen in the findings that show conferences were more successful and resulted in less subsequent offending when the outcomes were consensual;[87] when they were rated as inclusive, fair and respectful;[88] when offenders actively participated and engaged in the conference and when they found the experience useful;[89] and when they were able to experience solidarity.[90] As such, agency is demonstrated by giving participants the opportunity to play an active role in the process and decision making that takes place in conferencing and in enabling a sense of collective ownership and capacity. Likewise, the goal of accountability is reflected in successful conferences where the outcomes were agreed and complied with; where offenders wanted to meet their victims[91] and the conferences helped them realise the harm they had caused; where they allowed offenders to make amends for what they had done and they were able to show remorse[92] and participate in what can be described as reintegrative conferences.[93] Thus, research supports the proposition that our agency-accountability framework is associated with reductions in reoffending when they are successfully facilitated within restorative justice conferences.

[87] Hayes and Daly (2003).
[88] Morris and Maxwell (1993).
[89] Shapland et al (2008).
[90] Rossner (2013).
[91] Shapland et al (2008).
[92] Hayes and Daly (2003).
[93] Rossner (2013).

9

Reimagining Restorative Justice: Towards Empowerment

I. Introduction

In this book we began by tracing the normative ideas underpinning restorative justice and the role of reparation within the criminal process. The growth of theoretical inquiry on restorative justice has not been satisfactorily charted against the diverse array of practice in the field, which has given rise to a diverse, sometimes disjointed, and occasionally conflicting body of literature, leading to Walgrave to describe the state of the field as a 'confused, seemingly incoherent assembly'.[1] There are a range of ongoing and unresolved debates on what restorative justice is attempting to achieve, the nature of its processes and outcomes, how it ought to complement the existing criminal justice system, and how effectively it operates in practice.

While it is recognised that the capacity of restorative justice to address harms within the criminal justice system is limited by what the state defines as a crime,[2] we argue that restorative justice can produce a more informed picture of the circumstances surrounding the offence and the needs of the parties than the orthodox criminal justice system. In creating a space for engaging multiple actors, restorative justice allows a multi-faceted understanding of the factors that led to the offending behaviour, including the impact of any previous conflicts between the parties. In enabling stakeholders to play an active role in tailoring the response to the crime, local community interests and civil society actors, restorative justice provides opportunities to provide outcomes that better meet the specific needs of the parties. This contrasts with the conventional criminal process, which often routinises cases which are similar in nature through a system which can feel like an assembly line to those drawn into it.[3] The lack of opportunity for meaningful interaction between victim and offender and limited means of communication to the courts often preclude proper consideration being afforded their views

---

[1] Walgrave (2011), 94.
[2] Cunneen and Goldson (2015); Pavlich (2005).
[3] Packer (1964), 4; Shapland et al (2011), 193.

and expectations by the judiciary. When correctly configured, restorative justice provides a more attuned means of gauging the needs of the parties to the conflict. Arguably, this enables it to deliver a more meaningful and responsive sense of 'justice' to each of the stakeholders involved. Indeed, as we have argued, this is best facilitated through our agency–accountability framework, giving clear direction and meaning to restorative interventions.

As far as victims are concerned, this may include emotionally intelligent measures (such as apologies and other symbolic reparatory gestures) as well as opportunities for pecuniary or proprietary redress. As regards offenders, non-stigmatic steps can also be taken to meet the particular challenges faced by an offender, ranging from education, counselling and support, to anger management and drug and alcohol treatment. The aim is to help to address any underlying issues relating to addiction, family life, education and work.

In chapter two we explored some of the most fundamental questions underpinning restorative justice discourse: *what* is being restored, *to whom*, *by whom* and *how*. In recent years, the percipience of philosophical and sociological insights into these questions have shed light on both the normative aims of restorative justice in terms of what its seeks to achieve and why, as well as the mechanics or micro-dynamics of the processes. In particular, recent observations underscore the need to maximise positive emotional energy (like anger, shame and empathy) in the conference in order to ensure its success.[4] This literature highlights the importance of the micro-dynamics of the interactions within the restorative encounters, and the role of emotions and rituals in such encounters, and underlines the centrality of interactions and emotional 'turning points' within the process. It is argued that such interactions are essential to the process of conferencing and can help participants overcome stigmatisation and defiance to produce solidarity and reintegration, which contributes to and helps underpin successful conference encounters.

II. Agency and Accountability as Keys to Empowerment

Against this backdrop, we set out to reimagine restorative justice within criminal justice and our vision of a criminal justice system which identifies *re-empowerment* as a fundamental normative goal. Fostering agency and accountability among participants are the underlying values which provide both the justification for that goal (ie *why* re-empowerment matters) as well as the key drivers that ought to inform *how* restorative justice can be best calibrated to deliver it in practice. In many respects, these twin values simultaneously flow from and respond to the negative and disempowering consequences that modern criminal justice processes

---

[4] Rossner (2013).

carry for many victims and offenders. Our argument is that the values and norms of restorative justice, as it operates within criminal justice, can be consolidated and clarified within our agency–accountability framework to allow for a clearer and more accurate explanation of how restorative justice works and the normative goals it ought to propel in practice. In other words, this framework lays down the normative goals and objectives for such interactions, and provides a sound theoretical foundation for restorative justice which is rooted in empowerment theory.

Research evidence suggests that victims and offenders are more likely to feel re-empowered through mechanisms that enable them to exercise agency and accountability. Agency is evidenced by the individual and collective autonomy of participants, being able to make free and informed choices and play an active role in decision-making. In turn, this can bolster levels of legitimacy and fairness in terms of both the process and its outcomes. Accountability, on the other hand, entails being *willing to hold* and *being held* to account. This is evidenced by participants rendering themselves accountable in a positive sense for the impact and consequences of crime on both themselves and others. As Maruna highlights, a distinction can be drawn between 'passive responsibility' where individuals are held responsible for their actions and punished, versus 'active responsibility' where individuals actively take responsibility for their actions and look to put things right.[5] Agency and accountability are thus conceived as forms of the latter, allowing participants to assume a sense of ownership over the conflict and the ways in which harms can be effectively addressed.

Participants have been shown to be most satisfied when they feel able to make choices and positively contribute to decision making in a collective enterprise. Both agency and accountability contribute to a sense of empowerment that gives participants the ability to move beyond feelings of anger and hostility, or shame and humiliation, towards a shared understanding of the circumstances underlying the offence and its impacts, and how it might be dealt with in a productive manner. Such interactions can bolster the prospects of significant turning points between victims and offenders, allowing for feelings of anger or vengeance to be defused and space to be created for a shared understanding that is beneficial to the parties. Not only does the instillation of agency and accountability guide victims and offenders towards the benefits of restorative justice, it may also lead to increased feelings of fairness and procedural justice. Moreover, the framework helps to secure both individual and collective rights by eliciting how power imbalances and negative dynamics of interactions can potentially undermine basic rights, such as consent and the right to a fair hearing. In this sense, agency and accountability can shape effective restorative interactions by articulating both the goals of empowerment and the risks of disempowerment, which play out through the potentially negative impacts of criminal justice processing and the opportunities that restorative justice presents.

---

[5] Maruna (2011b); see also Farrall et al (2011).

III. From Theory to Practice

By prioritising agency and accountability as the normative goals, we considered how they can help inform and guide the effective delivery of restorative praxis within criminal justice. In chapters five to seven, we analysed the nature and form of restorative justice interventions at various stages of the criminal process, along with its impacts on the experiences of victims and offenders. A number of trends are clearly identifiable. First, and most obviously, restorative justice has undergone considerable expansion over a relatively short period, particularly at the 'shallow' end of the criminal justice system. Indeed, restorative techniques are increasingly being adopted at the periphery of the criminal justice system and even at 'street' levels, with the rhetoric of restorative justice being used to promote practices involving the police brokering apologies or other forms of reparation.

However, practices at the margins of criminal justice carry substantial risks for both restorative justice as a practice and for participants, particularly if there is little prospect of a meaningful restorative interaction. Dangers include risks of widening the criminal justice net and of failing to provide better outcomes for those affected by crime. Far from maximising the prospects for agency and accountability to be realised, restorative justice as a 'quick fix' tends to eschew real opportunities for victims and offenders to enter into the type of emotionally driven deliberative encounter that has been shown to engineer positive effects and explain why restorative justice 'works'. In particular, 'off the shelf' reparatory packages, drawn up in haste without the considered involvement of the stakeholders, risk denying victims and offenders direct input into the task of making amends. In effect, this serves to undermine their agency. Likewise, if the reparatory measures themselves are not tailored to the specific needs of victims and offenders, with their input, it is highly questionable whether 'accountability' is achieved in any positive and meaningful way. Facing pressure from stretched resources and a creeping culture of performance-based targets,[6] criminal justice practitioners are often pressed for innovation, yet starved of the resources needed to deliver effectively. While some restorative-based interventions at the periphery of the criminal justice system and many mediation-based interventions represent an improvement on previous practice, they often have had to compromise the quality of what they can deliver. A disconcerting element of many of the practices at the margins of the criminal justice system is how the language of restorative justice is used to frame interventions which often cannot realistically grapple with the needs of victims, offenders and the wider community. As such, we question the extent to which this growing range of practices, which target diversion or aim to resolve low-level crime, can genuinely describe themselves as 'restorative' in nature.

By contrast, when restorative interventions are properly resourced, facilitated and target more serious harms at the deeper end of criminal justice, there

---

[6] Lister (2013).

are greater opportunities for the powerful effects of restorative justice to be manifested.[7] The less formal structures of restorative justice, the use of a neutral environment and its commitment to inclusivity should, in theory, create conditions which allow agency and accountability to be realised to a much greater extent than they can be within the setting of an adversarial courtroom. Participants should be thoroughly prepared and their informed consent gained, and facilitators should conduct their role in an encouraging, inclusionary and non-coercive manner, with appropriate monitoring and with sufficient provision of information. In these circumstances, victims, offenders and other participants can benefit from the positive and empowering goals of agency and accountability that restorative justice can deliver.

Not all cases are inherently suitable for restorative justice and it is not a panacea for all harmful behaviour. Some victims may not be ready or willing to participate and this should be respected. Similarly, some offenders will not be ready to hold themselves to account or constructively engage in a process of dialogue. Likewise, as with any criminal justice intervention, resources are finite and a balance must be struck between the need for high-quality fully restorative interventions and the types of offences that merit these interventions. Interventions must be targeted towards those cases and offences for which research shows they can offer the best prospects of success. Moreover, restorative justice lacks a fact-finding mechanism to deal with those cases where the offender disputes the facts, and some offenders will choose to have their punishment imposed by the court in the traditional manner.

While Daly asserts that 'the research and development phase of restorative justice has now passed',[8] we contend that, as practice has only recently begun to penetrate the deeper waters of the criminal justice system, there is still much to be learned. In that regard, there remains a key role for the ongoing development of theoretical understanding, through research, standard-setting, monitoring and evaluation. Certainly, we need more clarity on how and why restorative justice works and a greater degree of precision is needed in ascertaining which cases are most suitable for restorative disposals. There also is the need to consider how such restorative work is implemented in practice, for example whether it is offered as an option or is compulsory. Criminal justice professionals should consider whether there are particular types of offences and particular types of offenders (for example first-time offenders or repeat offenders) or particular types of victims which will merit these types of interventions. There are also complex questions to be unravelled concerning the utility of restorative justice in sexual violence and other cases where the offender is considered to be at high risk of reoffending.[9]

Nevertheless, much of the research evidence on restorative interventions and their impacts demonstrates them to be more effective when they involve personal

---

[7] Sherman et al 2000; Strang et al (2013).
[8] Daly (2016), 13.
[9] McAlinden (2008), 222.

offences (like offences against the person, as opposed to minor property offences) and more serious offence types. They also are more effective when the interventions have clear restorative goals, such as in cases which where the outcomes are negotiated between the parties and where there are expressions of genuine remorse. Agency and accountability are most readily facilitated in settings where there is an opportunity for direct dialogue between the offender and victim, rather than in 'shuttle mediation' or processes where surrogates or quasi-professionals attempt to integrate a 'victim perspective'. As such, direct dialogue is more likely to generate the degree of emotionality which can lead to 'turning points' in the conference that allow for the empowerment of participants.[10]

The use of the restorative conferencing model has certainly increased in recent years. In addition to New Zealand and Northern Ireland models which we examined in chapter seven, it is now placed on a statutory footing across much of Australia and in Belgium. Here, it is already being used at the deeper end of criminal justice, including cases involving serious violence. There are an increasing number of *ad hoc* programmes that also operate schemes for adult offenders at the court or post-conviction stages, but these are not yet mainstreamed in the sense that they are generally isolated in nature and tend to be subject to little or no statutory regulation.

By contrast, legislation permitting (though often not mandating) mediation is widely provided for in law across many continental European jurisdictions and there has been a growing trend for these to take on the restorative label.[11] As we explained in chapter six, many of these schemes have positive features; they are well embedded in the legal order and are generally not regarded with suspicion amongst the legal profession.[12] While they evoke aspects of restorative philosophy and practice, they evolved from very different political and legal traditions compared to contemporary restorative conferencing. In many European jurisdictions restorative approaches are widely perceived as diversionary tool bests suited for minor offences. As Dünkel et al note, just because the term 'reconciliation' has been used, this does not necessarily imply that a restorative process has taken place.[13] Agency and accountability do not feature strongly as values within most European schemes, and as such it is conceptually confusing to label them as true forms of restorative justice.[14] Nevertheless, it is encouraging that many programmes, including those in Austria, Belgium, Norway and the Netherlands are increasingly encompassing types of values that are inherent within our agency–accountability framework. The continuing growth of conferencing and trend towards mainstreaming means that we can afford to be optimistic about the future development of restorative justice across Europe.

---

[10] Rossner (2013).
[11] Dünkel et al (2015).
[12] Aertsen (2012), 241.
[13] Dünkel et al (2015), 216.
[14] Aertsen et al (2006), 284.

IV. Extending the Reach of Restorative Justice

There is now a range of data to suggest that restorative justice can and should work at the deeper end of criminal justice. After all, the personal impacts of serious crime, particularly involving violence to the person, are likely to be significantly greater than those of minor offences and property-based crime. If agency and accountability are to flourish as driving values within criminal justice the restorative justice conferencing processes need to be made more widely available. This should happen beyond diversionary types of schemes, and be used for the more serious types of crimes that come before the courts. The New Zealand and Northern Ireland conferencing models detailed in chapter seven show how restorative justice can be successfully implemented within criminal justice where victims and offenders play an integral part in the process. They offer a structure in which our agency–accountability framework can be facilitated in the practice of delivering an empowering form of restorative justice within criminal justice. The research from these models shows that victims and offenders often want to be involved in how their case is dealt with and they want to see something positive emerge from the negative impacts of crime. They gain through being positively involved in their case and influencing how it is dealt with. Being accountable creates constructive opportunities to make amends to victims. Indeed, offenders and victims identify the powerful impact of the restorative encounter and apology as important to their sense of empowerment and justice. Participants tell how conferencing offers an environment that is more meaningful than a court appearance, through being able to meet, discuss the impacts of the offence, understand why the crime occurred and agree outcomes to help address the harms. While victims and offenders should never feel that they are coerced into participation, by the same token they ought not be denied the opportunity simply because of the nature of the offence, or the personal attitude of criminal justice personnel, since this effectively hinders the agency of individuals to exercise their voices and influence the process and outcomes of interventions.

As our analysis of the literature on reoffending in the previous chapter shows, the priority afforded to agency and accountability can decrease the risks of re-offending. This is likely to occur where the process was rated as inclusive, fair and respectful;[15] where offenders actively participate and experience a sense of solidarity;[16] and where outcomes are consensual.[17] In short, restorative conferences are better able to impact reoffending if they are operationalised in a way that maximises agency and accountability. As such, agency is played out by giving participants the opportunity to play an active part in the process and decision making that takes place in conferencing and in enabling a sense of collective ownership

---

[15] Maxwell and Morris (1993).
[16] Rossner (2013).
[17] Hayes and Daly (2003).

and capacity. Likewise, the value of accountability is reflected in successful conferences where the outcomes are agreed and complied with; where offenders want to meet their victims[18] and the conference helps them to realise the harm they have caused; and where they allow offenders to make amends for what they have done, show remorse[19] and participate in what can be described as restorative justice.[20]

Obviously, restorative justice will not work for all offenders or all of the time, but the most reliable evidence shows there are prospects for modest reductions in reoffending for many types of cases, particularly for more serious and personal offences. The more detailed research on reoffending reveals the circumstances in which restorative interventions appear to be more successful. It reinforces the importance of agency and accountability as drivers behind its effectiveness, particularly for offenders. This work shows that the ways in which offenders experience conferencing is strongly related to subsequent levels of reoffending. The characteristics of offenders, such as age, sex and previous offending history, as well as their personal circumstances (like poverty, unemployment and life experiences) all have strong impacts on subsequent reoffending. However, conferences that achieve agency through actively involving and empowering participants have been positively associated with reductions in subsequent reoffending. Similarly, where accountability is facilitated and where offenders are willing to make *themselves* accountable through exhibiting the desire to put right the harm done,[21] and where they consequently express feelings of genuine remorse,[22] the evidence points to a clear association with a reduction in in reoffending. As Shapland et al highlight, restorative justice offers a more positive and forward-looking approach when attempting to address reoffending in comparison to the dominant state-centric paradigm which often serves to prevent participants from really thinking about the future consequences of offending, since its remit is focused on past actions and retrospective punishments.[23] Empowering offenders to take responsibility for their behaviour is a major part of getting them to think about the consequences of their offending, both on themselves and on others. Ultimately, restorative justice aids this process of empowerment, but restorative justice cannot succeed on its own and must work in tandem with other rehabilitation efforts.[24]

V. Challenges Ahead

We have argued for the mainstreaming of restorative justice within criminal justice to be built around the agency–accountability framework that we have developed

---

[18] Shapland et al (2008).
[19] Hayes and Daly (2003).
[20] Rossner (2013).
[21] Shapland et al (2008).
[22] Hayes and Daly (2004); Maxwell et al (2004); Rossner (2013).
[23] Shapland et al (2011).
[24] Ward et al (2014).

in this book. While we recognise that such an undertaking does not constitute a panacea for all of the ills of the existing criminal justice system, if delivered effectively it could offer a vast improvement on an adversarial system which is dominated by punitivism and undermines the rights of both victims and offenders. As Wood and Suzuki have neatly explained, 'over more than three decades, RJ practices have afforded victims (however imperfectly) more participation, more redress, and more agency than what existed prior—and offenders more opportunity to make amends in meaningful ways'.[25] As such, we argue that restorative justice has the potential to do a much *better* job of addressing the consequences of harmful behaviour than the traditional criminal justice system, and addresses the problem of exclusion experienced by participants in that system. Moreover, if the practice of restorative justice is grounded within our agency–accountability framework, it is much more likely to be able to deliver the promise of beneficial results for participants and contribute towards the broader transformation of criminal justice into a more legitimate, inclusive and emotionally intelligent enterprise.[26] Indeed, restorative justice holds the capacity to liberalise and humanise those areas it touches,[27] and holds a transformative potential for the criminal justice system as a whole.[28]

As change continues apace in modern criminal justice, the momentum behind restorative justice over the past two decades is likely to exert a strong influence on policy and practice agendas in forthcoming years. Although this may provide opportunities for the mainstreaming of restorative justice, there are also growing threats to its empowering potential. Indeed, the current trajectory of restorative justice's expansion is likely to bring it increasingly into conflict with the values and processes of the conventional criminal justice system.[29] Thus, we have identified three significant challenges ahead which ought to be addressed if agency and accountability are to be regarded as the normative hallmarks of restorative justice within the criminal process. We now consider, in turn, the threats posed by the tendency to prioritise quantity over quality; the operational barriers posed by legalism and institutionalisation; and, finally, cultural resistance to change.

A. Quantity over Quality?

The international growth of restorative justice has been tempered in part by popular punitivism, associated with the view that criminals are prioritised at the

---

[25] Wood and Suzuki (2016), 162.
[26] Participatory and deliberate democracy holds potential to address a sense of declining trust in liberal democracies (Roche, 2003). The procedural justice literature (see ch 4), and indeed our own research in Northern Ireland (see ch 7), provides some evidence that involvement with restorative justice processes can result in increased levels of public trust with criminal justice institutions (see further Doak and O'Mahony, 2011).
[27] Braithwaite and Parker (1999).
[28] Zehr (1990); Shapland et al (2011).
[29] Wood and Suzuki (2016).

expense of crime victims and the law-abiding public.[30] As Pratt notes, in many countries this penal populism is reflected in attempts to bolster state authority and thus there is the risk of restorative justice becoming engulfed by this drive, resulting in a reluctance to extend its use to the 'deep end' of criminal justice, and producing responses to crime and offenders that can lead to up-tariffing and net-widening.[31]

Since the current expansion of restorative initiatives shows little sign of decreasing, there is unlikely to be a fall in terms of the *quantity* of new restorative programmes. The real threat comes from the *quality* of practices which adopt the restorative label. In short, restorative justice risks becoming a victim of its own success. Programmes that are underdeveloped or poorly resourced are unlikely to deliver the empowering goals of agency and accountability and this can damage the restorative justice 'brand'. A useful illustration is provided by recent policy developments in England and Wales. On the one hand, the Government seemingly embraced restorative justice. In its 2010 Green Paper *Breaking the Cycle*, a clear commitment was made to develop the use of restorative justice at all stages of the criminal justice system for both young and adult offenders.[32] It outlined the need to increase the range of restorative justice approaches to support reparation and, in appropriate cases, making it a part of the sentencing process, whereby restorative justice is an element of a broader approach to support victims and witnesses. The Government recognised that restorative justice provides victims with opportunities to be heard and have a say in the resolution of offences and offenders can face the consequences of their actions; thus it can help offenders to rehabilitate and stop offending.[33]

On the other hand, the Government has also been clear that it views restorative justice as most appropriate for low-level offenders and suitable as an alternative to formal criminal justice action, or out of court and informal settlements.[34] Thus the promise to afford victims a more central role in the criminal justice system is effected through the more extensive use of victim impact statements and reparatory-based sentences, rather than any bold move to mainstream restorative justice across the criminal justice system. This is despite sustained calls to do so from various government agencies,[35] professional bodies,[36] and the voluntary sector.[37]

---

[30] See Pratt (2007), 12. More generally, see Garland (2001), Pratt et al (2013).
[31] O'Mahony and Doak (2004); Skelton and Frank (2004).
[32] Ministry of Justice (2010).
[33] Almost £30m has been pledged in funding over three years to 2018: Ministry of Justice (2014b).
[34] Ministry of Justice (2011).
[35] See eg Youth Justice Board (2006) which committed to placing 'restorative justice at the heart of the youth justice system' because of its potential to reduce offending, better support victims of crime and help build confidence in the criminal justice system.
[36] See eg Association of Chief Police Officers (2011).
[37] The Prison Reform Trust (Jacobson and Gibbs, 2009) specifically advocated for the adoption of a mainstreamed restorative justice programme, similar to that in Northern Ireland. The Independent Commission also made similar recommendations. It argued that restorative conferencing ought to be

The influence of popular punitivism and the political imperative of formulating a policy agenda seen as being 'tough on crime' has led to a reluctance to take the bold steps necessary to integrate restorative justice within criminal justice, particularly as a mainstreamed response to more serious types of offending.

The lack of commitment to deliver change at a more fundamental level is evidenced by the fact that restorative justice continues to operate at the periphery of criminal justice in England and Wales. Funding provision has been inadequate, by comparison to criminal justice spending, and it has been usually time limited, with financial support ending for most programmes within two to four years.[38] This has meant that some schemes began successfully yet were unable to sustain provision and services had to end when their funding ran out. Similarly, service providers such as Youth Offending Teams have seen significant cuts to their budgets which have resulted in them being unable to prioritise restorative and victim-focused work beyond their statutory obligations.[39] Indeed, the Government itself has recognised that local agencies lack the financial incentives and opportunities to develop or deliver effective alternative and restorative strategies.[40]

A recent Government action plan on restorative justice, detailing provision up to March 2018, still focuses attention on delivering restorative interventions at the shallow end and periphery of the criminal justice system.[41] Funding has been earmarked primarily to further develop policing initiatives, such as restorative cautioning and the Restorative Justice Disposal. A small amount has also been pledged towards developing the work of Youth Offending Teams, who deliver Referral Orders.[42] Yet, as detailed in chapter five, while police-led restorative cautioning practices may be an improvement over traditional cautioning methods, they have limited restorative potential. Research carried out over many years has repeatedly demonstrated police-led practices have low levels of victim participation, their reparative efforts are limited, apologies are sometimes 'extracted' from offenders, police officers may dominate the proceedings and they are usually used for trivial offences and first-time offenders.

Similarly, the newer police-led Restorative Justice Disposal, which has been shown to be popular with officers because it offers a quick and proportionate response to minor offending, also has limited restorative potential. It usually amounts to little more than an on-the-spot warning with an apology, with few

---

the centrepiece of responses to all but the most serious offences committed by young people in England and Wales. See also the Criminal Justice Alliance (2011), which proposes placing a 'duty' on all criminal justice agencies to offer restorative justice for victims of crime and offenders. See also Independent Commission on Youth Crime and Antisocial Behaviour (2011).

[38] O'Mahony (2012).
[39] See Sherman and Strang (2007).
[40] Ministry of Justice (2011).
[41] Ministry of Justice (2014b).
[42] Some £23m has been allocated to Police Crime Commissioners to build victim-initiated restorative capacity and £2.5m has been allocated to Youth Offending Teams over three years: Ministry of Justice (2014b).

offenders being referred on for further intervention and little by way of a meaningful restorative interaction between offenders and victims.[43] Likewise, early research on the Referral Order showed it to have low levels of victim involvement in the process[44] and over 15 years later Rosenblatt found little improvement, with victims rarely attending panel meetings.[45] Reparation activities have been found to be imposed on offenders, rather than being agreed between the parties, and there is a lack of evidence that such orders allow victims and offenders to engage in a meaningful dialogue or any real restorative interaction.[46] As Hoyle and Rosenblatt note, both restorative cautioning and youth offender panels suffer from poor victim involvement, they have limited community involvement and they are often driven by the professionals rather than led by the participants themselves.[47] Both types of schemes are firmly rooted as standard responses to low-level offending and reflect Hoyle's critique of restorative justice in England and Wales as being stuck in the 'shallow end' of criminal justice.[48] The danger of these kinds of interventions is they are unlikely to deliver the positive and empowering encounters we identify in this book and so they may end up being yet another discredited criminal justice intervention. Furthermore, they dilute and may even taint the restorative justice brand. While they might represent an improvement on existing criminal justice practice, in their current format they do not provide restorative justice.

As Strang et al observe, utilising restorative justice for minor offences at the expense of major offences constitutes a wasted opportunity; restorative justice is best suited to, and achieves the best return on investment, when it is used for offenders who have committed violent crime and offenders with previous convictions.[49] When offenders are able to exercise a direct voice in the process, meaningful interactions between participants are more likely to take place. The offence, its aftermath and the modalities of 'making amends' can be discussed in an enabling context where agency and accountability are maximised.[50] Yet both restorative cautioning and referral orders are unlikely to be able to deliver much by way of successful restorative justice processes or outcomes in their current configuration. The reoffending data also show that 'street' interventions and other approaches used with low-level offenders are unlikely to result in significant reductions in reoffending. Moreover, in the current financial environment, which prioritises funding for 'successful' programmes, it is unlikely that these limited practices will be able to deliver results that see real restorative justice provision being extended further into the deeper end of the criminal justice system.[51] Thus

---

[43] See Rix et al (2011).
[44] Newburn et al (2002).
[45] Rosenblatt (2015a).
[46] Rosenblatt (2015a).
[47] Hoyle and Rosenblatt (2016).
[48] Hoyle (2010).
[49] Strang et al (2013).
[50] See Sherman and Strang (2007).
[51] O'Mahony (2012).

it appears that the punitivism that has marginalised restorative practices into the shallow end of criminal justice in England and Wales may also limit its potential to deliver the success which fully fledged restorative justice programmes can achieve. Even countries where restorative justice is already mainstreamed for serious offences are not necessarily immune to these trends; Lynch detects a shift towards more punitive attitudes in New Zealand, where the recent introduction of a harsher penalties and measures for young offenders have emerged to threaten the progressive ethos of the conferencing system.[52] In this sense, the proliferation of 'restorative' interventions seem to be little more than repackaged criminal justice sanctions that fail to promote agency and accountability, or to meet the key needs of victims and offenders. In this context, the challenge for those advocating restorative justice is to look beyond the negative rhetoric associated with punitive politics and advocate the potentials that restorative justice can deliver when correctly targeted and properly provided.[53]

One of the core questions for the future is whether the continuing growth of restorative justice sees its essential values becoming clearer and more defined, with better practice and outcomes evolving in response to the research evidence, or whether we move towards even more diffuse forms of practice that result in further dilution of what we have identified as the overarching values of agency and accountability. We can already see evidence of the international proliferation of programmes and interventions which are labelled restorative, yet realistically have little or no potential to deliver core restorative justice goals.

B. Legalism and Institutionalisation

A second challenge comes in the form of legalism, which has many 'seductive qualities'.[54] If, as we argue, restorative justice ought to be mainstreamed as a criminal justice response, it must be accepted that it will need to operate within the confines of the justice system. Yet this produces an obvious tension; as we showed in chapters two and three, the values and process of restorative justice—as consolidated within our agency–accountability framework—are antithetical to the exclusionary and polarising character of the existing adversarial system. Legalism has clear limits; the complex nature of interpersonal conflicts is often too unwieldy to be neatly extrapolated by the legal process, with its underlying notions of guilt and innocence and the practical impact of burden of proof and other evidential rules. Writing in the context of transitional justice, McEvoy observed how legalism acts to 'thin out' the complexities of life and 'divorces' harms from their wider social, political and cultural contexts. In the same way, it might be said that the

---

[52] Lynch (2012).
[53] Note that the 'punitive turn' in policymaking does not always reflect public attitudes towards punishment: see eg Roberts et al (2011).
[54] McEvoy (2007), 417.

adversarial criminal justice process is fundamentally ill-equipped to disentangle the myriad of factors which underpin offending behaviour and the breakdown of interpersonal relationships. By contrast, restorative justice—when operationalised in an empowering manner—provides a mechanism whereby parties can deliberate directly with each other and take ownership of questions around how harm can be most effectively addressed.

Yet for all such shortcomings, some form of legal framework is required to establish how the restorative process operates within the broader mechanics of criminal justice. Criminal justice, by definition, involves the state determining certain harms to be so injurious as to warrant criminalisation; yet wider society also has legitimate interests in how the process is conducted and what outcomes are agreed.[55] The law, its institutions and its process exercise a key function in safeguarding the rights of participants, ensuring justice is meted out with uniformity and certainty and guarding against vigilantism or authoritarianism.[56] Legalism ensures compliance with international human rights obligations[57] and, as Braithwaite also acknowledges, it is not only the rights of the offender which are at stake: 'a battered woman with a lawyer standing beside her against a batterer and his lawyer is a more equal contest than one-on-one mediation between victim and offender'.[58] As Roche has argued, the state has a key role to play in minimising dominion and protecting rights.

The challenge is thus to consider whether, and if so how, restorative processes are capable of protecting legal rights to a similar (or perhaps better) extent than traditional adversarial court processes. Braithwaite considers that the presence of 'communities of care' may help to restore balance, but it is questionable whether supporters would be equipped to protect the legal rights of such parties (for example, where an agreement imposed overly onerous conditions on the offender). Some restorative programmes allow the presence of legal advisers; the Northern Ireland scheme is one such example. In practice, however, lawyers seem to attend infrequently and, even where they do attend, adopt a largely passive role.[59] This may be explained by the fact that the restorative encounter is supposed to be driven by participation of the parties, rather than their representatives; lawyers have a less defined role in this situation and may be uncertain as when, if ever, it is appropriate to exercise their voices.

Under our agency–accountability framework, we see no automatic barrier to the presence of a lawyer. Indeed, lawyers should be encouraged to attend and trained to intervene to ensure that the legal rights of their clients are protected. Indeed, a lawyer may aid vulnerable or less articulate participants to express their opinions. Rigorous preparation and diligent facilitation will ensure that the process remains

---

[55] Shapland et al (2011), 192.
[56] Dignan and Lowey, (2000); Shapland, (2003); Weisberg (2003).
[57] Particularly in cases involving juvenile offenders: see Lynch (2008).
[58] Braithwaite (2002a), 152.
[59] Campbell et al (2006).

firmly committed to the participation of the stakeholders. Similarly, the courts also should have an important role in the process. As in Northern Ireland, agreements should be subject to ratification by the courts to ensure that both the upper and lower limits of proportionality are preserved and that due process and fair trial rights are applied. Our argument for the involvement of lawyers and the courts in restorative conferences, particularly for serious offences, is rooted in the need for safeguarding the interests of participants and the need to work in tandem with the existing criminal justice apparatus. If agency and accountability are operationalised as guiding values behind its facilitation within criminal justice, there will be opportunities for more mainstreamed and 'fully' restorative programmes to flourish.

Yet the risks posed by legal formalism are real and if these are not kept in check there is a risk of restorative justice emerging as an *imitor paradox*.[60] Formal co-option of restorative justice poses a threat to its traditional 'oppositional focus and specificity', leading it to become 'colonised' by repressive and punitive practices that are deeply ingrained within the existing apparatus.[61] This is already evident within some of the programmes we have documented, such as restorative cautioning, which are not really alternative forms of justice but merely repacked elements of the pre-existing punitive and adversarial justice system. Even mainstreamed programmes are not immune. Lynch has observed how pressures to increase efficiency can become prioritised over the quality of its provision and the value it adds to victims and offenders, whereby the need to deliver numbers negatively impacts on the quality of the programme.[62] The risk, then, is that restorative justice service providers begin to mirror the role of a criminal justice provider, with interventions increasingly used where they are not needed, for example where there is no identifiable victim or where the harm caused has been trivial. This would obviously be counterproductive, since the proper facilitation of restorative justice is both demanding for participants and resource intensive.[63]

This, in turn, leads to a risk that the goals and values of restorative practices will be supplanted by 'system' goals and outcomes, such as case-processing targets, efficiency and growth.[64] Fears have already been expressed in New Zealand that youth conferencing has become increasingly state-sponsored and standardised in its application, thus becoming 'Eurocentric' and 'neo-colonial' in its approach;[65] Moyle and Tauri have noted that family group conferencing can be experienced by some Maori participants as a formulaic and standardised process devoid of culturally appropriate practice.[66] The authors call for the process to become more

---

[60] Pavlich (2005).
[61] Pratt (2007), 142.
[62] Lynch (2012).
[63] O'Mahony et al (2002); Hoyle et al (2002).
[64] Wood and Suzuki (2016), 155.
[65] Tauri (2009).
[66] Moyle and Tauri (2016).

culturally informed, which could in turn make it a more empowering experience for Maori participants.[67]

These are genuine dangers which cannot be ignored, particularly given that the underlying fabric of the criminal justice system is unlikely to unravel any time soon. Rather, in a climate of punitivism, the reach of the formal system is likely to extend further. The perceived need to 'get tough' on crime and reimpose the authority of the state may not only serve to hinder the development of new initiatives, but it also poses an ongoing threat to those restorative interventions that already exist since they are not immune to political interference or co-option by a larger political agenda. As such, proponents of restorative justice must consider the question as to how such risks might be minimised and how the restorative 'quality' of state-led processes can be protected. Just as McEvoy argues in respect of transitional justice processes,[68] there is a need to 'thicken' our understanding of the role of law in relation to 'ordinary' criminal justice in order to enable restorative processes to overstep the dangers of institutionalisation.

Critics of state-led schemes have often drawn on their failure to take account of grassroots customs, expertise and practical knowledge as well as forging links with 'bottom up' initiatives.[69] The task of safeguarding rights has long been associated with a state-centric, or 'top down' approach to justice.[70] As noted above, we advocate that the state ought to exercise certain functions in this regard, but this should not preclude the possibility that 'bottom up' programmes are also capable of protecting rights of their own accord.[71] In order to work effectively and enjoy some sense of legitimacy, some form of partnership between state-led programmes and grassroots/civil society is required. As Clamp has argued, effective partnerships between the state and the community sector are often difficult to engineer given that the state-based agencies are often hierarchical and are not naturally calibrated to working with those outside its formal parameters, and there is relatively little evidence to demonstrate how such a partnership might operate on a practical level with any level of success for a sustained period.[72] Yet, with proper resourcing and leadership, this too can be achieved. For example, the local community-based projects in Northern Ireland—which originated outside the formal system—developed a protocol to work with the state youth conferencing scheme following the St Andrews Agreement of 2007.[73]

An appropriate balance needs to be struck to give individual programmes the necessary social and political space to evolve and adapt in order to maximise their effectiveness within the communities that they serve.[74] By the same token, in order

---

[67] Moyle and Tauri (2016).
[68] McEvoy (2007).
[69] Boyes-Watson (1999); McEvoy and Eriksson (2006); McEvoy and Mika (2002).
[70] McEvoy (2007).
[71] See eg McEvoy and Eriksson (2006).
[72] Clamp (2014).
[73] See further Doak and O'Mahony (2011).
[74] Woolford and Ratner (2008).

to mainstream restorative justice as a cornerstone of the formal justice system, structures need to be put in place which are capable of maximising community participation within this system, and to ensure that protocols are observed which are capable of maintaining a stable, yet dynamic, relationship between schemes which operate at grassroots levels and those operated by the state.[75]

C. Cultural Resistance

A third barrier to mainstreaming our vision of restorative justice stems from the legalism and institutionalism noted above. The institutionalised and legalised structure of the criminal process has spawned a level of cultural resistance from some of the actors within the criminal justice system. This reflects Christie's analysis of 'conflicts as property'; there is a widespread underlying assumption that professionals assume that the justice system belongs to the state-led institutions and the staff of which it is comprised.[76] Even though there may be a genuine belief in restorative philosophies among criminal justice professionals, the pervasive nature of targets and ongoing drives for efficiency and cost-effectiveness often counteract this in practice. As Shapland et al note, 'though criminal justice was usually trying to be a friend of restorative, it was not a very flexible friend'.[77] Often, it is perceived as a product of a welfare-based model more suited to young offenders, rather than a concept that might be applied throughout the criminal justice system as a whole.[78] Cultural attitudes and existing working practices may thus constrain the capacity of restorative justice to operationalise our agency–accountability framework in practice. The gatekeepers of restorative justice (usually the police, prosecution service or the courts) have generally learnt their assigned roles from within legalistic, adversarial or punitive regimes, and it is perhaps unsurprising that there is empirical evidence that such deeply ingrained cultural attitudes and working practices may stifle restorative justice praxis.[79]

For example, in Germany, mediation is provided for in the criminal code and prosecutors and judges are under an obligation to consider it in cases where it might be appropriate to foster reconciliation between the parties. Although results from evaluations are positive in many respects, there continues to be considerable resistance by the legal profession and judges to refer cases to the mediation services, meaning that only about 5 per cent of criminal cases are dealt with by mediation despite the fact that over 25 per cent of charges are eligible.[80] It appears that much of the resistance of judges and prosecutors is linked to perceptions

---

[75] Northern Ireland provides an interesting example of how a working relationship was built over time between community-led programmes and the state-led youth conferencing system: see further Doak and O'Mahony (2011).
[76] McEvoy (2007), 423, citing Douglas (1986).
[77] Shapland et al (2011), 192.
[78] Mackay (2003).
[79] Campbell et al (2006); Shapland et al (2011).
[80] Bannenberg (2000).

that such processes are burdensome and time consuming and the desire to process cases quickly through the system means that they are not properly considered as alternatives.[81] Similarly, in New South Wales there is a well-established system of restorative interventions available across the criminal justice system and despite generally positive evaluations that have shown them as effective and well received by victims and offenders, the levels of referrals by criminal justice personnel remain stubbornly low. Indeed, estimates suggest that only about 2 per cent of cases dealt with by the police are referred to conferencing and there are also low levels of referrals from the courts.[82]

We found evidence of cultural resistance within our own evaluation of youth conferencing in Northern Ireland. Individual magistrates in the two pilot areas had vastly differing views as to whether conference plans should be ratified; while all conference plans were accepted by the youth courts in Fermanagh and Tyrone, over half of all referrals made by the Belfast youth court did not result in ratification. On occasion, some magistrates appeared to be dismissive of the scheme. Consent of offenders was not always sought and the nature of the process was not always explained to them.[83] Solicitors were often uncertain of their role; many did not attend conferences and some even advised their clients against taking part in the process. Many facilitators observed that there was a negative attitude within the legal profession towards both the philosophy and practice of youth conferencing. Those solicitors who attended conferences rarely participated, and many seemed unsure of the purpose or nature of the conferencing process.

Although these findings give some cause for concern, they may be explained by the fact that the imposition of any new policy initiative within an operational environment is likely to encounter some level of hostility and will take time to embed. It is well established in the organisational behaviour literature that the introduction of fundamental change will require individuals to question and develop their existing knowledge and skill-base; criminal justice professionals are no exception.[84] Even within the relatively short time-frame of our data collection, some facilitators reported that attitudes were beginning to change among legal professionals. Conversely, it is possible that such problems may actually intensify once a programme becomes established and initial enthusiasm begins to wane. As we noted above in respect of conferencing in New Zealand and Young Offender Panels in England and Wales, the risk thus heightens that the quality of interventions slip, with both processes and outcomes becoming routinised and formulaic. There may be a tendency of professionals and 'repeat players' to assume ownership of the process and seek to amplify their own voices over and above those of victims and offenders.[85]

---

[81] See Dünkel and Păroşanu (2015); Miers (2001); Trenczek (2001).
[82] Cunneen (2010).
[83] Campbell et al (2006).
[84] See eg Chan (1996); Trubek (1996).
[85] Hoyle et al (2002), Hoyle and Rosenblatt (2016); Lynch (2012).

There was, however, some evidence to suggest that the process might also make a modest contribution to breaking down barriers between lay participants and criminal justice professions. The mandatory presence of a police officer, coupled with the optional presence of a solicitor, enables lay and professional participants to have more constructive interactions with each other. Indeed, it has been argued that such encounters might even help break down some of the strongly held barriers towards the police and provide a space where individuals who feel alienated or antagonistic towards them may be able to interact in a more positive manner.[86]

VI. Effecting Change

In arguing for restorative justice to be for participants through the lens of the agency–accountability framework, this book has sought to move the debate beyond existing theoretical and operational issues, which have largely focused on the processes and outcomes of delivering restorative justice. Much of this work has helped clarify the deliverable aspect of restorative justice, through its focus on objectives like providing restitution, reparation and reconciliation, or on managing a process and outcomes that deliver practical elements such as collective decision making, remorse and apologies. However, this can lead us to overlook what we see as the more fundamental issues behind why these elements of practice are important and why they need to be rooted in theory. A practical example from our own research helps illustrate this point.[87] In a restorative youth conference we observed in Northern Ireland, a young woman who had stolen clothing from a local shop attended together with her mother, the shop owner, coordinator and a police officer. During the conference the young woman appeared upset and was crying through much of the process, so much so that there was little other input from her. But she repeatedly sobbed and said she was sorry, throughout. At the latter stages of the conference when it came to discussing what needed to be done for the conference plan, the shop owner appeared to feel sympathy for her and said he could see she was upset and sorry, so that was enough for him. But the coordinator reminded the conference the young woman had previous convictions and there would need to be consequences beyond saying sorry. The coordinator suggested that community work and a written apology would be appropriate. At this point the young woman suddenly stopped crying and forcibly said she was not going to do community work. She insisted her apology was enough and did not want to do anything further. Only when the shop owner and her mother agreed with the coordinator, did the young woman agree.

---

[86] Doak and O'Mahony (2011).
[87] Campbell et al (2006).

When assessing whether the conference was successful, it was the case that the offender showed remorse and apologised. After all she appeared to be upset, she was crying and repeatedly said she was sorry. In reality, however, the remorse and tears were used to avoid properly engaging with the other participants in the process and the apologies were little other than a deflection of her responsibility to face up to the consequences of her actions. Thus, by focusing on deliverable aspects of restorative justice, to ensure that remorse and apologies are being underpinned by agency and accountability, we can begin to better understand their purpose in relation to what restorative justice actually seeks to achieve. In this case the crying was used as a tool to avoid engaging with the other participants and the apologies were used as a to shield her from assuming her own accountability as she sought escape the difficult challenge of accepting responsibility for her actions and the need to make amends.

We propose that the fundamental goals of restorative justice should be reimagined through the lens of empowerment for participants, maximising the potential for agency and accountability, and this should be imbued at every state of the process. These values explain both the normative question as to *why* reparation ought to be prioritised within criminal justice and *how* this might be best effected in practice. Our hope is that the emphasis placed on these values will not only grant us a better insight as to the true reparative value of a particular practice, but will also improve insights into how the delivery of restorative justice can be improved.

Notwithstanding the burgeoning body of literature to emerge in recent years, there remains much work to be done in terms of innovating and refining the field. There is a significant pool of data from empirical evaluations, but it is important to also reflect on how those studies might give us a more accurate insight into the success of restorative justice, moving beyond the typical variables such as stakeholder satisfaction, the nature of specific outcomes, or reoffending rates. A deeper analysis looking beyond these individual measures is required in order to explore why restorative justice is successful or unsuccessful and how practice can be improved through better understanding the role of empowerment. By instilling agency and accountability as yardsticks of restorative justice interventions, empirical inquiries could be better tailored to see past the processes and outcomes and to focus on the extent to which our agency–accountability framework is realised in practice. Similarly, research needs to engage more proactively with practitioners, civil society actors and criminal justice professionals, as these sectors play an influential role in driving forward restorative justice innovation and praxis.[88] Developing research in this direction would enable richer and more meaningful analyses to take place.

Looking to the future, in making a case for mainstreaming restorative justice which uses our agency–accountability framework we recognise that much work

---

[88] See eg McEvoy and Mika (2002); McEvoy and Eriksson (2006); Lynch (2012); Wright (2002).

remains to be done in assessing how this would impact on the new roles that would inevitably emerge. This not only applies to the archetypal stakeholders in restorative justice (ie victims, offenders and the community), but also for police officers, lawyers, prosecutors, judges and probation; all of whom will have a vital, if changing, role to play as restorative justice continues to develop. This underlines the point that restorative processes are merely one part of a much larger and more complex criminal justice apparatus. Criminal investigation, court-based adjudication, meeting the needs of victims, and rehabilitating offenders are all aspects of the criminal process which might, in some measure, learn lessons from the role played by restorative justice in delivering a more humane and intelligent system of justice. Such a fresh commitment to restorative justice within criminal justice could enable a move beyond rhetoric, towards the evolution of a more empowering, more participatory and ultimately more legitimate criminal justice system.

REFERENCES

Abel, CF, and Marsh, FH (1984). *Punishment and Restitution: A Restitutionary Approach to Crime and the Criminal*. Westport, CT: Greenwood Publishing Group.

Achilles, M, and Zehr, H (2001). Restorative justice for crime victims: the promise, the challenge. In: G. Bazemore and M. Schiff (eds), *Restorative and Community Justice: Cultivating Common Ground for Victims, Communities and Offenders*. Cincinnati, Ohio: Anderson Publishing.

Aertsen, I (2012). Conferencing: concluding comments. In: E Zinsstag and I Vanfraechem (eds), *Conferencing and Restorative Justice. International Practices and Perspectives*. Oxford: Oxford University Press.

—— (2015). Belgium. In: F Dünkel, J Grzywa-Holten and P Horsfield (eds), *Restorative Justice and Mediation in Penal Matters—A stocktaking of legal issues, implementation strategies and outcomes in 36 European countries*. Mönchengladbach: Forum Verlag Godesberg.

—— Daems, T, and L Robert (2006), Epilogue. In: I Aertsen, T Daems and L Robert (eds), *Institutionalizing Restorative Justice*. Cullompton: Willan Publishing.

—— Parmentier, S, Vanfraechem, I, Walgrave, L, and Zinsstag, E (2013). An adventure is taking off. *Restorative Justice*, 1(1), 1–14.

Andrews, DA, and Bonta, J (2003). *The Psychology of Criminal Conduct* (3rd ed). Cincinnati, OH: Anderson.

Angel, C (2005). *Crime victims meet their offenders: Testing the impact of restorative justice conferences on victims' post-traumatic stress symptoms*. PhD thesis, Philadelphia, PA: University of Pennsylvania.

Angel, CM, Sherman, LW, Strang, H, Ariel, B, Bennett, S, Inkpen, N, Keane, A, and Richmond, TS (2014). Short-term effects of restorative justice conferences on post-traumatic stress symptoms among robbery and burglary victims: A randomized controlled trial. *Journal of Experimental Criminology*, 10(3), 291–307.

Arrigo, BA (2004). The ethics of therapeutic jurispudence: A critical and theoretical enquiry of law, psychology and crime. *Psychiatry, Psychology and Law*, 11(1), 23–43.

Arrigo, BA, and Williams, CR (2003). Victim vices, victim voices, and impact statements: On the place of emotion and the role of restorative justice in capital sentencing. *Crime and Delinquency*, 49(4), 603–26.

Ashworth, A (1993). Some doubts about restorative justice. *Criminal Law Forum* 4(2), 277–99.

—— (2000). Victims' rights, defendants' rights and criminal procedure. In: A Crawford and J Goodey (eds), *Integrating a Victim Perspective within Criminal Justice*. Aldershot, Ashgate.

—— (2001). Is restorative justice the way forward for criminal justice?. *Current Legal Problems*, 54, 347–76.

—— (2002). Responsibilities, rights and restorative justice. *British Journal of Criminology*, 42(3), 578–95.

Ashworth, A, and Player, E (2005). Criminal Justice Act 2003: The sentencing provisions. *Modern Law Review*, 68(5), 822–38.

Ashworth, A, and Von Hirsch, A (1993). Desert and the three Rs. *Current Issues in Criminal Justice*, 5(1), 9–12.

Association of Chief Police Officers (2011). *Restorative Justice Guidance and Minimum Standards*. London: ACPO.

Ball, C (2000). The Youth Justice and Criminal Evidence Act 1999 Part I: A significant move towards restorative justice, or a recipe for unintended consequences?. *Criminal Law Review*, 211–22.

Bannenberg, B (2000). Victim-offender mediation in Germany. In: The European Forum for Victim-Offender Mediation and Restorative Justice (ed), *Making Restorative Justice Work*. Leuven: University of Leuven Press.

Barnes, OM (2016) *Restorative Justice in the Criminal Justice System: the McDonaldization of diversionary youth conferencing*. PhD thesis. Belfast: University of Ulster.

Barnett, R (1977). Restitution: A new paradigm for criminal justice. *Ethics*, 87(4), 279–301.

Barton, C (2000). Empowerment and retribution in criminal justice. In: H Strang and J Braithwaite, (eds), *Restorative Justice: Philosophy to Practice*. Aldershot: Ashgate.

Bauman, Z (2001). *Community: Seeking Safety in an Insecure World*. Cambridge: Polity Press.

Bazemore, G (1998). Restorative justice and earned redemption communities, victims, and offender reintegration. *American Behavioral Scientist*, 41(6), 768–813.

Bazemore, G, and Dooley, M (2001). Restorative justice and the offender: The challenge of reintegration. In: G Bazemore and M Schiff (eds), *Restorative and Community Justice Cultivating Common Ground for Victims, Communities and Offenders*. Cincinnati, Ohio: Anderson Publishing.

Bazemore, G, and Schiff, M (2005). *Juvenile Justice Reform and Restorative Justice. Building Theory and Policy from Practice*. Cullompton: Willan Publishing.

Bazemore, G, and Umbreit, M (2001). A Comparison of Four Restorative Conferencing Models. *Juvenile Justice Bulletin*, 47(2), 1–20.

Bazemore, G, and Umbreit, MS (2004). Balanced and restorative justice: Prospects for juvenile justice in the 21st century. In: A Roberts (ed), *Juvenile Justice Sourcebook*. Oxford: Oxford University Press.

Bazemore, G, and Walgrave, L (1999). Restorative juvenile justice: In search of fundamentals and an outline for systemic reform. In: G Bazemore and L Walgrave (eds), *Restorative Juvenile Justice: Repairing the Harm of Youth Crime*. Monsey, New York: Criminal Justice Press.

Bazemore, G, Pranis, K, and Umbreit, MS (1997). *Balanced and Restorative Justice for Juveniles: A Framework for Juvenile Justice in the 21st Century*. Washington, DC: Office of Juvenile Justice and Delinquency Prevention.

Beck, U (1992). *Risk Society—Towards a New Modernity*. London: Sage.

Bell, E (2011). *Criminal Justice and Neoliberalism*. London: Palgrave Macmillan.

Bennett, C (2008). *The Apology Ritual*. Cambridge: Cambridge University Press.

Bennett, M, and Earwaker, D (1994). The effects of offender responsibility and severity of offense. *Journal of Social Psychology*, 134(4), 457–65.

Bergseth, KJ, and Bouffard, JA (2007). The long-term impact of restorative justice programming for juvenile offenders. *Journal of Criminal Justice*, 35(4), 433–51.

Bergseth, KJ, and Bouffard, JA (2013). Examining the effectiveness of a restorative justice program for various types of juvenile offenders. *International Journal of Offender Therapy and Comparative Criminology*, 57(9), 1054–75.

Beven, J, Hall, G, Froyland, I, Steels, B, and Goulding, D (2005). Restoration or renovation? Evaluating restorative justice outcomes. *Psychiatry, Psychology and Law*, 12(1), 194–206.

Bibas, S, and Bierschbach, RA (2004). Integrating Remorse and Apology into Criminal Procedure. *Yale Law Journal* 114, 85–148.

Blad, J (2006). Institutionalizing restorative justice? Transforming criminal justice? A critical view on the Netherlands. In: I Aertsen, T Daems, and L Robert (eds), *Institutionalizing Restorative Justice* Cullompton: Willan Publishing.

Blagg, H (1997). A just measure of shame? Aboriginal youth and conferencing in Australia. *British Journal of Criminology*, 37(4), 481–501.

—— (2001). Aboriginal Youth and Restorative Justice: Critical Notes from the Australian Frontier. In: A Morris and G Maxwell (eds), *Restorative Justice for Juveniles: Conferencing, Mediation and Circles*. London: Bloomsbury Publishing.

—— (2002). Restorative justice and aboriginal family violence: Opening a space for healing. In: H Strang (ed), *Restorative justice and Family Violence*. Cambridge: Cambridge University Press.

Bolitho, JJ (2012). Restorative justice: The ideals and realities of conferencing for young people. *Critical Criminology*, 20(1), 61–78.

Bolívar, D (2010). Conceptualizing victims' 'restoration' in restorative justice. *International Review of Victimology*, 17 (3), 237–65.

Bolívar, D, Brancher, L, Navarro, I, and Gutiérrez, M (2012). Conferencing in South America as an exercise of democracy? An exploration of the 'vertical' role of restorative justice. In: E Zinsstag and I Vanfraechem (eds), *Conferencing and Restorative Justice. International Practices and Perspectives*. Oxford: Oxford University Press.

Bolívar, D, Pelikan, C, and Lemonne, A (2015). Comparison of the main results: variations and similarities. In: I Vanfraechem, D Bolívar and I Aertsen (eds), *Victims and Restorative Justice*. London: Routledge.

Bonta, J, Boyle, J, Motiuk, L, and Sonnichsen, P (1983). Restitution in correctional half-way houses: Victim satisfaction, attitudes, and recidivism. *Canadian Journal of Corrections*, 20, 140–52.

Bonta, J, Jesseman, R, Rugge, T, and Cormier, R (2006). Restorative justice and recidivism: Promises made, promises kept. In: D Sullivan and L Tifft (eds), *Handbook of Restorative Justice: A Global Perspective*. Abingdon: Routledge.

Bonta, J, Roonery, J, and Wallace-Capretta, S (1998). *Restorative Justice: An Evaluation of the Restorative Resolutions Project*. Ottawa: Office of the Solicitor General.

Booth, T (2014). The restorative capacities of victim impact statements: analysis of the victim—judge communication dyad in the sentencing of homicide offenders. *Restorative Justice*, 2(3), 302–26.

Boriboonthana, Y, and Sangbuangamlum, S (2013). Effectiveness of the restorative justice process on crime victims and adult offenders in Thailand. *Asian Journal of Criminology*, 8(4), 277–86.

Bottoms, A (2003). Some sociological reflections on restorative justice. In: A von Hirsch, JV Roberts, AE Bottoms, K Roach, and M Schiff (eds), *Restorative Justice and Criminal Justice: Competing or reconcilable paradigms*. Oxford: Hart.

—— (1995). The Philosophy and Politics of Punishment and Sentencing. In: C Clarkson and R Morgan (eds), *The Politics of Sentencing Reform*. Oxford: Clarendon.

Bowen, H, and Boyack, J (2003). *Adult restorative justice in New Zealand/Aotearoa*. Paper presented at 4th International Conference on Conferencing, Sentencing Circles and Other Restorative Practices, Veldhoven, Netherlands, 28–30 August.

Bowen, H, Boyack, J, and Calder-Watson, J (2012). Recent developments within restorative justice in Aotearoa/New Zealand. In: J Bolitho, J Bruce and G Mason (eds), *Restorative Justice: adults and emerging practice*. Sydney: Federation Press.

Boyes-Watson, C (1999). In the belly of the beast? Exploring the dilemmas of state-sponsored restorative justice. *Contemporary Justice Review*, 2(3), 261–81.

Bradley, GV (2003). Retribution: The central aim of punishment. *Harvard Journal of Law and Public Policy*, 27, 19–31.

Bradley, T, Tauri, J, and Walters, R (2006). Demythologising youth justice in Aotearoa/New Zealand. In: B Goldson and J Muncie (eds), *Comparative Youth Justice*. London: Sage.

Braithwaite, J (1989). *Crime, Shame and Reintegration*. Cambridge: Cambridge University Press.

—— (1998). Restorative justice. In: M Tonry (ed), *The Handbook of Crime and Punishment*. Oxford: Oxford University Press.

—— (1999). Restorative justice: Assessing optimistic and pessimistic accounts. In: M Tonry (ed), *Crime and Justice: An Annual Review of the Research*, vol 25. Chicago: University of Chicago Press.

—— (2002a). *Restorative Justice and Responsive Regulation*. Oxford: Oxford University Press.

—— (2002b). Setting standards for restorative justice. *British Journal of Criminology*, 42(3), 563–77.

—— (2003). Principles of restorative justice. In: A von Hirsch, JV Roberts, AE Bottoms, K Roach, and M Schiff (eds), *Restorative justice and criminal justice: Competing or reconcilable paradigms?*. Oxford: Hart.

—— (2006). Responsive regulation and developing economies. *World Development*, 34(5), 884–98.

Braithwaite, J, and Daly, K, (1998) 'Masculinities, violence, and communitarian control' in SL Miller (ed), *Crime Control and Women: Feminist implications of criminal justice policy*. Newbury Park, CA: Sage.

Braithwaite, J, and Gohar, A (2014). Restorative justice, policing and insurgency: Learning from Pakistan. *Law and Society Review*, 48(3), 531–61.

Braithwaite, J, and Mugford, S (1994). Conditions of successful reintegration ceremonies: Dealing with juvenile offenders. *British Journal of Criminology*, 34(2), 139–71.

Braithwaite, J, and Parker, C (1999). Restorative justice is republican justice. In: G Bazemore and L Walgrave (eds), *Restorative Juvenile Justice: Repairing the Harm of Youth Crime*. Monsey, New York: Criminal Justice Press.

Braithwaite, J, and Roche, D (2001). Responsibility and restorative justice. In: G Bazemore and M Schiff (eds), *Restorative community justice: repairing harm and transforming communities*. Cincinnati, OH: Anderson.

Braithwaite and Strang (2001). Introduction. In: J Braithwaite and H Strang (eds), *Restorative Justice and Civil Society*. Cambridge: Cambridge University Press.

Brakel, SJ (2007). Searching for the therapy in therapeutic jurisprudence. *New England Journal on Criminal and Civil Confinement*, 33, 455–99.

Brennan, M, and Brennan, R (1989). *Strange Language: Child Victims under Cross-Examination*. Wagga Wagga: Riverina Murray Institute of Higher Education.

Brooks, T (2012). *Punishment*. London: Routledge.

Bruce, J, Mason, G, and Bolitho, J (2012). Restorative justice: From juveniles to adults. In: J Bolitho, J Bruce and G Mason (eds), *Restorative Justice: Adults and Emerging Practice*. Canberra: Institute of Criminology Press.

Burnett, R, and Maruna, S (2004). So 'prison works', does it? The criminal careers of 130 men released from prison under home secretary, Michael Howard. *Howard Journal of Criminal Justice*, 43(4), 390–404.

Button, M, Lewis, C, and Tapley, J (2014). Not a victimless crime: The impact of fraud on individual victims and their families. *Security Journal*, 27(1), 36–54.

Campbell, C, Devlin, R, O'Mahony, D, Doak, J, Jackson, J, Corrigan, T, and McEvoy, K (2006). *Evaluation of the Northern Ireland Youth Conference Service*, NIO Research and Statistics Series: Report No 12. Belfast: Northern Ireland Office.

Campbell, R (2006). Rape survivors' experiences with the legal and medical systems: Do rape victim advocates make a difference?. *Violence against Women*, 12(1), 30–45.

Campbell, T (1984). Compensation as Punishment. *University of New South Wales Law Journal*, 7(2), 338–62.

Cantor, G (1976). An end to crime and punishment. *The Shingle* (Philadelphia Bar Association), 39(4), 99–114.

Cario, R (2015). France. In: F Dünkel, J Grzywa-Holten, P Horsfield (eds), *Restorative Justice and Mediation in Penal Matters—A stocktaking of legal issues, implementation strategies and outcomes in 36 European countries*. Mönchengladbach: Forum Verlag Godesberg.

Cavadino, M, and Dignan, J (1997). Reparation, retribution and rights. *International Review of Victimology*, 4(4), 233–53.

Cavadino, M, Dignan, J and Mair, G (2013). *The Penal System: An Introduction*, 5th ed. London: Sage.

Cayley, D (1998). *The Expanding Prison: The Crisis in Crime and Punishment and the Search for Alternatives*. Toronto: House of Anansi Press.

Chan, J (1996). Changing police culture. *British Journal of Criminology*, 36(1), 109–34.

Chankova, D (2015). *Bulgaria*. In: F Dünkel, P Horsfield and A Păroşanu (eds) (2015). *European Research on Restorative Juvenile Justice: Volume I, Research and Selection of the Most Effective Juvenile Restorative Justice Practices in Europe: Snapshots from 28 EU Member States*. Brussels, International Juvenile Justice Observatory.

Choi, JJ (2008). *Opening the 'black box': A naturalistic case study of restorative justice*. PhD thesis. Lawrence, KS: University of Kansas.

Choi, JJ, Green, DL, and Kapp, SA (2010). Victimization, victims' needs, and empowerment in victim offender mediation. *International Review of Victimology*, 17(3), 267–90.

Choi, JJ, Bazemore, G, and Gilbert, MJ (2012). Review of research on victims' experiences in restorative justice: Implications for youth justice. *Children and Youth Services Review*, 34(1), 35–42.

Christie, N (1977). Conflicts as property. *British Journal of Criminology*, 17(1), 1–15.

Claassen, R (1995). *Restorative Justice Principles and Evaluation Continuums*. Clovis, California: Fresno Pacific College, National Centre for Peacemaking and Conflict Resolution.

Clamp, K (2014). *Restorative Justice in Transition*. London: Routledge.

Clamp, K, and Doak, J (2012). More than words: restorative justice concepts in transitional justice settings. *International Criminal Law Review*, 12(3), 339–60.

Clare, I, and Murphy, G (2001). Witnesses with learning disabilities. *British Journal of Learning Disabilities*, 29(3), 79–80.

Clairmont, D (2005). *The Nova Scotia restorative justice initiative: Final evaluation report*. Halifax, NS: Atlantic Institute of Criminology, Dalhousie University.

Clear, TR, and Cadora, E (2001). Risk and correctional practice. In: K Stenson and R Sullivan (eds), *Crime, Risk and Justice: The Politics of Crime Control in Liberal Democracies*. Cullompton, Willan.

Coates, RB, and Gehm, J (1985). *Victim Meets Offender: An Evaluation of Victim-Offender Reconciliation Programs*. Federal Way, Washington: Pact Institute of Justice.

Coates, RB, and Gehm, J (1989). An empirical assessment. In: M Wright and B Galaway (eds), *Mediation and Criminal Justice*. London: Sage Publications.

Collins, R (2004). *Interaction Ritual Chains*. Princeton, NJ: Princeton University Press.

Consedine, J (1995). *Restorative justice. Healing the Effects of Crime*. Lyttleton, New Zealand: Ploughshares.

Cordon, I, Goodman, G, and Anderson, S (2003). Children in court. In: PJ van Koppen and SD Penrod (eds), *Adversarial versus Inquisitorial Justice* (New York, Kluwer).

Cosemans, Z, and Parmentier, S (2014). Changing lenses to restorative justice: new directions for Europe and beyond. *Restorative Justice*, 2(2), 232–41.

Cossins, A (2008). Restorative justice and child sex offences: The theory and the practice. *British Journal of Criminology*, 48(3), 359–78.

Couck, J-V, and Tracqui, H (2009). *A partir de l'observation n.10: La réforme du champ d'action des sections jeunesse des Parquets sous l'angle de la déjudiciarisation*. Brussels: CIDE.

Council of Europe (2010). *Guidelines of the Committee of Ministers of the Council of Europe on Child Friendly Justice*. Adopted by the Committee of Ministers on 17 November 2010 at the 1098th meeting of the Ministers' Deputies. Strasbourg: Council of Europe.

Council, NZM, and Durie-Hall, D (1999). Restorative justice: A Maori perspective. In: H Bowen and J Consedine (eds), *Restorative Justice: Contemporary Themes and Practices*. Boston: Ploughshares.

Crawford, A, and Clear, T (2001). Community justice: Transforming communities through restorative justice? In: G Bazemore and M Schiff (eds) *Restorative Community Justice: Repairing harm and transforming communities*. Cincinnati, OH: Anderson Publications.

Crawford, A, and Newburn, T (2003). *Youth Offending and Restorative Justice*. London: Routledge.

Criminal Justice Alliance (2011). *Restorative Justice: Time for Action*. London: Criminal Justice Alliance.

Criminal Justice Inspection Northern Ireland (2008). *Inspection of the Youth Conferencing Service of Northern Ireland*. Belfast: Criminal Justice Inspectorate.

Criminal Justice Review Group (2000). *Review of the Criminal Justice System of Northern Ireland*. London: HMSO.

Croley, SP and Hanson, JD (1995). The nonpecuniary costs of accidents: pain-and-suffering damages in tort law. *Harvard Law Review*, 208, 1785–917.

Crow, G (2002). Community Studies: Fifty Years of Theorization. *Sociological Research Online*, 7(3), http://www.socresonline.org.uk/7/3/crow.html [accessed 3 May 2016].

Cullen, R (2004). The referral order: The main issues arising from its evaluation and the youth justice board's efforts to address them. *Childright*, 204, 8–9.

Cullen, FT, Jonson, CL, and Nagin, DS (2011). Prisons do not reduce recidivism: The high cost of ignoring science. *The Prison Journal*, 91(3), 48S–65S.

Cunneen, C (2007). Reviving restorative justice traditions. In: G Johnstone and D Van Ness (eds), *Handbook of Restorative Justice*. Cullompton, Willan.

—— (2010). The limitations of restorative justice. In: C Cunneen and C Hoyle, *Debating Restorative Justice*. Oxford, Hart.

Cunneen, C, and Goldson, B (2015). Restorative justice? A critical analysis. In: B Goldson and J Muncie (eds), *Youth, Crime and Justice*. London: Sage.

Daems, T (2008). Criminal law, victims, and the limits of therapeutic consequentialism. In: E Claes (ed), *Facing the Limits of the Law*. Springer: Amsterdam.

Daly, K (2000). Revisiting the relationship between retributive and restorative justice. In: H Strang and J Braithwaite (eds), *Restorative justice: Philosophy to practice*. Aldershot: Ashgate.

—— (2001). Conferencing in Australia and New Zealand: Variations, research findings and prospects. In: A Morris and G Maxwell (eds), *Restorative Justice for Juveniles: Conferencing, Mediation and Circles*. Oxford: Hart.

—— (2002). Restorative justice: The real story. *Punishment and Society*, 4(1), 55–79.

—— (2003). Mind the gap: Restorative justice in theory and practice. In: A von Hirsch, JV Roberts, AE Bottoms, K Roach and M Schiff (eds), *Restorative Justice and Criminal Justice: Competing or reconcilable paradigms*. Oxford: Hart.

—— (2004). Pile it on: More texts on RJ. *Theoretical Criminology*, 8(4), 499–507.

—— (2006). The Limits of Restorative Justice. In: D Sullivan and L Tifft (eds), *Handbook of Restorative Justice: A Global Perspective*. Abingdon: Routledge.

—— (2008). Girls, peer violence, and restorative justice. *Australia and New Zealand Journal of Criminology*, 41(1), 109–13.

—— (2016). What is restorative justice? Fresh answers to a vexed question. *Victims and Offenders*, 11(1), 9–29.

Daly, K, and Immarigeon, R (1998). The past, present, and future of restorative justice: Some critical reflections. *Contemporary Justice Review*, 1(1), 21–24.

Daly, K, and Stubbs, J (2006). Feminist engagement with restorative justice. *Theoretical Criminology*, 10(1), 9–28.

Davis, G (1992). *Making Amends: Mediation and Reparation in Criminal Justice*. Hove: Psychology Press.

Davis, G, Boucherat, J, and Watson, D (1988). Reparation in the service of diversion: the subordination of a good idea. *Howard Journal of Criminal Justice*, 27(2), 127–34.

Day, G (2006). *Community and Everyday Life*. London: Routledge.

Deem, DL (2000). Notes from the field: Observations in working with the forgotten victims of personal financial crimes. *Journal of Elder Abuse and Neglect*, 12(2), 33–48.

Deklerck, J (2008). Facing the limits of the law. In: E Claes, J Deklerck, W Devroe and B Keirsbilck (eds), *Restorative Justice, Freedom, and the Limits of the Law*. Bohn Stafleu van Loghum: Houten.

Dhami, MK (2012). Offer and acceptance of apology in victim-offender mediation. *Critical Criminology*, 20(1), 45–60.

Dignan, J (1990). *Repairing the Damage: An Evaluation of an Experimental Adult Reparation Scheme in Kettering, Northamptonshire*. Sheffield: Centre for Criminological and Legal Research.

—— (2001). Restorative justice and crime reduction: Are policy-makers barking up the wrong tree? In: E Fattah and S Parmentier (eds), *Victim Policies and Criminal Justice on the Road to Restorative Justice: A Collection of Essays in Honour of Tony Peters*. Leuven: Leuven University Press.

—— (2005). *Understanding Victims and Restorative Justice*. Maidenhead: Open University Press.

—— (2006). Juvenile justice, criminal courts and restorative justice. In: G Johnstone and D Van Ness (eds), *Handbook of Restorative Justice*. Cullompton: Willan.

—— (2007). The victim in restorative justice. In: S Walklate (ed), *Handbook of victims and victimology*. Cullompton: Willan.

Dignan, J, and Lowey, K (2000) *Restorative Justice Options for Northern Ireland: A Comparative Review*, Criminal Justice Review Research Report No 10. Belfast: HMSO.

Dimock, S (2015). Criminalizing dangerousness: How to preventively detain dangerous offenders. *Criminal Law and Philosophy*, 9(3), 537–60.

Dinnen, S, and Jowitt, A (eds) (2010). *A Kind of Mending: Restorative Justice in the Pacific Islands*. Canberra: ANU Press.

Doak, J (2008). *Victims' Rights, Human Rights and Criminal Justice: Reconceiving the Role of Third Parties*. Oxford: Hart Publishing.

—— (2011). Honing the stone: Refining restorative justice as a vehicle for emotional redress. *Contemporary Justice Review*, 14(4), 439–56.

—— (2015). Enriching trial justice for crime victims in common law systems: lessons from transitional environments. *International Review of Victimology*, 21(2), 139–60.

Doak, J, and McGourlay, C (2015) *Evidence in Context*, 4th ed. Routledge: London.

Doak, J, and O'Mahony, D (2006). The vengeful victim? Assessing the attitudes of victims participating in restorative youth conferencing. *International Review of Victimology*, 13(2), 157–77.

Doak, J, and O'Mahony, D (2011). In search of legitimacy: restorative youth conferencing in Northern Ireland. *Legal Studies*, 31(2), 305–25.

Doak, J, and Taylor, L (2013). Hearing the voices of victims and offenders: The role of emotions in criminal sentencing. *Northern Ireland Legal Quarterly*, 64(1), 25–46.

Dooley, M (1995). *Reparative Probation Program*. Waterbury, Vermont: Department of Corrections.

Doolin, K (2007). But what does it mean? Seeking definitional clarity in restorative justice. *Journal of Criminal Law*, 71(5), 427–40.

Douglas, M (1986). *How Institutions Think*. Syracuse, NY: Syracuse University Press.

DUCKfoOT (2012). *The General Public's Response to Restorative Justice, Community Resolution: Research Conducted on Behalf of Her Majesty's Inspector of Constabulary*. Somerset: DUCKfoOT Ltd.

Duff, RA (2003). Restoration and retribution. In: A von Hirsch, JV Roberts, AE Bottoms, K Roach and M Schiff (eds), *Restorative Justice and Criminal Justice: Competing or Reconcilable Paradigms*. Oxford: Hart.

Duff, RA, and Walgrave, L (2002). Restorative punishment and punitive restoration. In: L Walgrave (ed), *Restorative Justice and the Law*. Cullompton: Willan.

Duffee, D, Worden, A, and Maguire, E (2015). Directions for theory and theorising in criminal justice. In: D Duffee and E Maguire (eds), *Criminal Justice Theory: Explaining the Nature and Behavior of Criminal Justice*. London: Routledge.

Dünkel, F (2015). Germany. In: F Dünkel, P Horsfield and A Părosanu (eds) (2015). *European Research on Restorative Juvenile Justice: Volume I, Research and Selection of the Most Effective Juvenile Restorative Justice Practices in Europe: Snapshots from 28 EU Member States*. Brussels, International Juvenile Justice Observatory.

Dünkel, F, Grzywa-Holten, J, Horsfield, P (eds) (2015). *Restorative Justice and Mediation in Penal Matters—A stocktaking of legal issues, implementation strategies and outcomes in 36 European countries*. Mönchengladbach: Forum Verlag Godesberg.

Dünkel, F, and Părosanu, A (2015). Germany. In: F Dünkel, J Grzywa-Holten and P Horsfield (eds) (2015). *Restorative Justice and Mediation in Penal Matters—A stocktaking of legal issues, implementation strategies and outcomes in 36 European countries.* Mönchengladbach: Forum Verlag Godesberg.

Durkheim, E (1966) [1897]. *Suicide: A Study in Sociology.* New York: Free Press.

Dyck, D (2004). Are we-practitioner, advocates–practicing what we preach? In: E McLaughlin and G Hughes (eds), *Restorative Justice: Critical issues.* Maidenhead: Open University Press.

Dzur, AW, and Olson, SM (2004). The value of community participation in restorative justice. *Journal of Social Philosophy,* 35(1), 91–107.

Dzur, AW, and Wertheimer, A (2002). Forgiveness and public deliberation: The practice of restorative justice. *Criminal Justice Ethics,* 21(1), 3–20.

Easton, S, and Piper, C (2012). *Sentencing and Punishment: The Quest for Justice.* Oxford: Oxford University Press.

Eglash, A (1958). Creative restitution: A broader meaning for an old term. *Journal of Criminal Law and Criminology,* 48(6), 619–22.

—— (1977). Beyond restitution: Creative restitution. In: J Hudson and B Galloway (eds), *Restitution in Criminal Justice.* Toronto: Lexington.

Elechi, OO (1999). Victims under restorative justice systems: The Afikpo (Ehugbo) Nigeria model. *International Review of Victimology,* 6(4), 359–75.

Elonheimo, H (2003). *Restorative Justice Theory and the Finnish Mediation Practices.* Paper presented at the Third Annual Conference of the European Society of Criminology, Helsinki, 27–30 August.

Enright, RD, and Fitzgibbons, RP (2000). *Helping Clients Forgive: An Empirical Guide for Resolving Anger and Restoring Hope.* Washington DC: American Psychological Association.

Epstein, RA (1975). Intentional harms. *The Journal of Legal Studies,* 4(2), 391–442.

Eriksson, A (2008). Challenging cultures of violence through community restorative justice in Northern Ireland. *Sociology of Crime, Law and Deviance,* 11(2), 231–60.

Evje, A, and Cushman, RC (2000). *A summary of the evaluations of six California victim offender reconciliation programs.* Sacramento, CA: Judicial Council of California.

Eyckmans, D (2005). New Belgian Law on Mediation. *Newsletter of the European Forum for Restorative Justice,* 6(2/3), 9.

Farrall, S, Hough, M, and Maruna, S (2011). Introduction: Life after punishment: Identifying new strands in the research agenda. In: S Farrall, M Hough and S Maruna (eds), *Escape Routes: Contemporary Perspectives on Life after Punishment.* London: Routledge.

Faulkner, D (2001). *Crime, State and Citizen.* Winchester: Waterside Press.

Fattah, E (1998). Some reflections on the paradigm of restorative justice and its viability for juvenile justice. In: L Walgrave (ed), *Restorative Justice for Juveniles: Potentialities, Risks and Problems for Research.* Leuven: Leuven University Press.

Feasey, S, Williams, P, and Clarke, R (2005). *An Evaluation of the Prison Fellowship Sycamore Tree Project.* Sheffield: Centre for Community Justice, Sheffield Hallam University.

Feinberg, J (1984). *Harm to Others.* Oxford: Oxford University Press.

Fercello, C, and Umbreit, M (1998). *Client Evaluation of Family Group Conferencing in 12 Sites in 1st Judicial District of Minnesota.* Minneapolis, MN: Center for Restorative Justice and Mediation, University of Minnesota.

Finkelhor, D, and Browne, A (1985). The traumatic impact of child sexual abuse: A conceptualization. *American Journal of Orthopsychiatry,* 55(4), 530–41.

Foley, T (2014). *Developing Restorative Justice Jurisprudence: Rethinking Responses to Criminal Wrongdoing*. Abingdon: Routledge.

Fox, L (2007). *Conceptualising Home: Theories, Laws and Policies*. Oxford: Hart Publishing.

Frazer, E (1999). *The Problems of Communitarian Politics: Unity and Conflict*. Oxford: Oxford University Press.

Gal, T (2011). *Child Victims and Restorative Justice: A Needs-Rights Model*. Oxford: Oxford University Press.

Garfinkel, H (1956). Conditions of successful degradation ceremonies. *American Journal of Sociology*, 61(5), 420–42.

Garland, D (1996). The limits of the sovereign state: Strategies of crime control in contemporary society. *British Journal of Criminology*, 36(4), 445–71.

—— (2001). *The Culture of Control*. Oxford: Oxford University Press.

—— (2013). Penality and the penal state. *Criminology*, 51(3), 475–517.

Garvey, S (2003). Restorative justice, punishment and atonement. *Utah Law Review*, 1, 303–17.

Gavrielides, T (2007). Restorative justice theory and practice: Addressing the discrepancy. Helsinki: HEUNI.

—— (2008). Restorative justice—the perplexing concept: Conceptual fault-lines and power battles within the restorative justice movement. *Criminology and Criminal Justice*, 8(2), 165–83.

—— (2013). Restorative pain: a new vision of punishment. In: T Gavrieledes (ed), *Reconstructing Restorative Justice Philosophy*. Farnham: Ashgate.

Giddens, A (1982). *Profiles and Critiques in Social Theory*. London: Macmillan.

—— (1984). *The Constitution of Society: Outline of the Theory of Structuration*. Cambridge: Polity Press.

Gilligan, J, and Lee, B (2005). The Resolve to Stop the Violence Project: reducing violence in the community through a jail-based initiative. *Journal of Public Health*, 27(2), 143–48.

Glaser, D, and Frosh, S (1988). *Child Sexual Abuse*. London: Macmillan.

Goldson, B (2011). 'Time for a fresh start', but is this it? A critical assessment of the report of the independent commission on youth crime and antisocial behaviour. *Youth Justice*, 11(1), 3–27.

Goldstein, A (1982). Defining the role of the victim in criminal prosecution. *Mississippi Law Journal*, 52, 515–42.

Gombots, R, and Pelikan, C (2015). Austria. In: F Dünkel, J Grzywa-Holten, P Horsfield (eds), *Restorative Justice and Mediation in Penal Matters—A stocktaking of legal issues, implementation strategies and outcomes in 36 European countries*. Mönchengladbach: Forum Verlag Godesberg.

Goodman, GS, and Bottoms, BL (1993). *Child victims, child witnesses: Understanding and improving testimony*. London: Guilford Press.

Goold, BJ, and Young, RP (1999). Restorative police cautioning in Aylesbury—from degrading to reintegrative shaming ceremonies?. *Criminal Law Review*, 126–38.

Gray, P (2009). The political economy of risk and the new governance of youth crime. *Punishment and Society*, 11(4), 443–58.

Green, S (2014). *Crime, Community and Morality*. London: Routledge.

Greene, D (2013). Repeat performance: Is restorative justice another good reform gone bad? *Contemporary Justice Review*, 16(3), 359–90.

Griffiths, CT (1996). Sanctioning and healing: restorative justice in Canadian Aboriginal communities. *International Journal of Comparative and Applied Criminal Justice*, 20(2), 195–208.

Griffiths, CT, and Hamilton, R (1996). Spiritual renewal, community revitalization and healing. Experience in traditional aboriginal justice in Canada. *International Journal of Comparative and Applied Criminal Justice*, 20(2), 289–311.

Groenhuijsen, M (2004). Victims' rights and restorative justice: Piecemeal reform of the criminal justice system or a change of paradigm?. In: H Kaptein and M Malsch (eds), *Crime, Victims, and Justice. Essays on Principles and Practice*. Ashgate: Aldershot.

Haines, K (1998). Some principled objections to a restorative justice approach to working with juvenile offenders. In: L Walgrave (ed), *Restorative justice for juveniles: Potentialities, risks and problems for research*. Ithaca, NY: Cornell University Press.

Haines, K, and O'Mahony, D (2006). Restorative approaches, young people and youth justice. In: B Goldson and J Munice (eds), *Youth crime and justice*. London: Sage.

Hall, M (2012). *Victims and Policy-Making: A Comparative Perspective*. London: Routledge.

Hamlyn, B, Phelps, A, Turtle, J, and Sattar, G (2004). *Are special measures working?: Evidence from surveys of vulnerable and intimidated witnesses* (HORS No 283). London: Home Office.

Hanson, RF, Sawyer, GK, Begle, AM, and Hubel, GS (2010). The impact of crime victimization on quality of life. *Journal of Traumatic Stress*, 23(2), 189–97.

Harber, K, and Pennebaker, J (1992). Overcoming traumatic memories. In: S Christianson (ed), *The Handbook of Emotion and Memory: Research and Theory*. London: Lawrence Erlbaum Associates.

Harber, K, and Wenberg, C (2005). Emotional disclosure and closeness toward offenders, *Personality and Social Psychology Bulletin*, 31(6), 734–46.

Harland, A (1978). Theoretical and programmatic concerns in restitution: An integration. In: B Galaway and J Hudson (eds), *Offender Restitution in Theory and Action*. Boston, MA: Lexington.

Hays, S (1994). Structure and agency and the sticky problem of culture. *Sociological Theory*, 12(1), 57–72.

Hayes, H (2007). Reoffending and restorative justice. In: G Johnstone and D Van Ness (eds), *Handbook of Restorative Justice*. Cullompton, Willan.

Hayes, H, and Daly, K (2003). Youth justice conferencing and reoffending. *Justice Quarterly*, 20(4), 725–64.

Hayes, H, and Daly, K (2004). Conferencing and re-offending in Queensland. *Australian and New Zealand Journal of Criminology*, 37(2), 167–91.

Hegel, GWF (1821) (rep 1991). *Elements of the Philosophy of Right*. Cambridge: Cambridge University Press.

Helfgott, JB, Lovell, M, Lawrence, C, and Parsonage, W (1999). Development of the citizens, victims, and offenders restoring justice program at the Washington state reformatory. *Criminal Justice Policy Review*, 10(3), 363–99.

Herman, JL (1997). *Trauma and Recovery*. New York: Basic Books.

Herman, S (2004) Is Restorative Justice Possible Without a Parallel System for Victims?. In: H Zehr and B Toews (eds), *Critical Issues in Restorative Justice*. Cullompton: Willan.

HMIC (Her Majesty's Inspectorate of Constabulary), HMI Probation, HMI CPS and HMI Prisons (2012). *Facing Up To Offending: Use of Restorative Justice in the Criminal Justice System*. London: Criminal Justice Joint Inspectorate.

Hinks, N, and Smith, R (1985). Diversion in practice: Northants Juvenile Liaison Bureaux. *Probation Journal*, 32(2), 48–50.

Hill, RF (2002). Restorative justice and the absent victim: new data from the Thames Valley. *International Review of Victimology*, 9(3), 273–88.

Hoffman, M (2002). Therapeutic jurisprudence, neo-rehabilitationism, and judicial collectivism: The least dangerous branch becomes most dangerous. *Fordham Urban Law Journal*, 29, 2063–88.

Hofinger, V, Pelikan, C, and Birgit Z (2002). *Victim-Offender Mediation with Juveniles in Austria*. Paper presented at Victim-offender Mediation: Organization and Practice in Juvenile Justice Systems, Bologna, 19–20 September.

Home Office (1994). *The cautioning of offenders*, Circular 18/1994. London: Home Office

—— (1997). *No More Excuses: A New Approach to Tackling Youth Crime in England and Wales*. London, HMSO.

—— (2002). *The Introduction of Referral Orders into the Youth Justice System*, Home Office Research Study 242. London: Home Office.

—— (2005). *Cautioning of Adult Offenders*, Circular 30/2005. London: Home Office.

Honkatukia, P (2015a). Victim-offender encounters in Finland. In: D Bolívar, I Aertsen and I Vanfraechem (eds), *An empirical study of the needs, experiences and position of victims within restorative justice practices*. Leuven: European Forum for Restorative Justice.

—— (2015b). Restorative justice and partner violence: victims' view of Finnish practice. In: I Vanfraechem, D Bolívar and I Aertsen (eds), *Victims and Restorative Justice*. London: Routledge.

Hooper, S, and Busch, R (1996). Domestic violence and restorative justice initiatives: The risks of a new panacea. *Waikato Law Review*, 4, 101–30.

Hopkins, CQ, Koss, MP, and Bachar, KJ (2004). Applying restorative justice to ongoing intimate violence: Problems and possibilities. *Saint Louis University Public Law Review*, 23, 289–312.

Hopkins, Z (2015). *Diverted from Counsel: Filling the Rights Gap in New Zealand's Youth Justice Model*. Wellington: Fulbright New Zealand.

Hough, M, and Park, A (2002). How malleable are attitudes to crime and punishment? Findings from a British deliberative poll. In: J Roberts and M Hough (eds), *Changing Attitudes to Punishment*. Cullompton: Willan.

Hoyle, C (2009). Restorative justice policing in Thames Valley. *Journal of Police Studies*, 11(2), 189–213.

—— (2010). Debating restorative justice. In: C Cunneen and C Hoyle, *Debating Restorative Justice*. Oxford: Hart.

—— (2012). Victims, victimisation and restorative justice. In: M Maguire, R Morgan and R Reiner (eds), *The Oxford Handbook of Criminology*. Oxford: Oxford University Press.

Hoyle, C, and Noguera, S (2008). Supporting young offenders through restorative justice: Parents as (in) appropriate adults. *British Journal of Community Justice*, 6(3), 67–85.

Hoyle, C, and Rosenblatt, FF (2016). Looking back to the future: Threats to the success of restorative justice in the United Kingdom. *Victims and Offenders*, 11(1), 30–49.

Hoyle, C, Young, R, and Hill, R (2002). *Proceed with caution: An evaluation of the Thames Valley Police initiative in restorative cautioning*. York: Joseph Rowntree Foundation.

Hudson, B (2002). Restorative justice and gendered violence: diversion or effective justice?. *British Journal of Criminology*, 42(3), 616–34.

—— (2003). *Justice in the Risk Society: Challenging and Re-affirming 'Justice' in Late Modernity*. London: Sage.

Hudson, J, and Galaway, B (1996). Introduction. In: B Galaway and J Hudson (eds), *Restorative justice: International Perspectives*. Monsey, NY: Criminal Justice Press.

Huntington, SP (1996). The West: unique, not universal. *Foreign Affairs*, 75(1), 28–46.

Iivari, J (2000). Victim–Offender mediation in Finland. In: The European Forum for Victim-Offender Mediation and Restorative Justice (ed), *Victim-Offender Mediation in Europe: Making Restorative Justice Work*. Leuven, Belgium: Leuven University Press.

—— Providing Mediation as a Nationwide Service: Empirical research on restorative justice in Finland. In: I Vanfraechem, I Aertsen and J Willemsens, J (eds), *Restorative Justice Realities: Empirical Research in a European Context*. The Hague: Eleven International Publishing.

Independent Commission on Youth Crime and Antisocial Behaviour (2011). *Time for a Fresh Start*. London: Independent Commission on Youth Crime and Antisocial Behaviour.

Irani, GE, and Funk, NC (1998). Rituals of reconciliation: Arab-Islamic perspectives. *Arab Studies Quarterly*, 20(4), 53–73.

Independent Commission on Youth Crime and Antisocial Behaviour (2011). *Time for a Fresh Start*. London: Independent Commission on Youth Crime.

Jabbour, EJ (1996). *Sulha: Palestinian Traditional Peacemaking Process*. Montreal: House of Hope Publications.

Jacobson, J, and Gibbs, P (2009). *Making Amends; Restorative Justice in Northern Ireland*. London: Prison Reform Trust.

Jacobson, J, Hunter, G, and Kirby, A (2015). *Structured Mayhem: Personal Experiences of the Crown Court*. London: Criminal Justice Alliance.

James, A, and Raine, JW (1998). *The New Politics of Criminal Justice*. London: Longman.

Janoff-Bulman, R (1985). The aftermath of victimization: Rebuilding shattered assumptions. In: C Figley (ed), *Trauma and Its Wake: The Study and Treatment of Post-Traumatic Stress Disorder*. New York: Brunner/Mazel.

Jenkins, M (2006). Gullah Island dispute resolution: An example of Afrocentric restorative justice. *Journal of Black Studies*, 37(2), 299–319.

Jennings, WG, Piquero, AR, and Reingle, JM (2012). On the overlap between victimization and offending: A review of the literature. *Aggression and Violent Behavior*, 17(1), 16–26.

Johnstone, G (2007). Critical perspectives of restorative justice. In: G Johnstone and D Van Ness (eds), *Handbook of Restorative Justice*. Cullompton, Willan.

—— (2011). *Restorative Justice*, 2nd ed. London: Routledge.

—— (2013). The teachings of restorative justice. In: T Gavrielides and V Artinopoulou (eds), *Reconstructing Restorative Justice Philosophy*. Farnham: Ashgate.

—— (2015). Twenty-five years of Changing lenses—a symposium. *Restorative Justice*, 3(3), 419–24.

Johnstone, G, and Van Ness, D (2005). *The Meaning of Restorative Justice*. Paper presented at the British Society of Criminology Conference, Leeds, 12–14 July.

——, and Van Ness, D (2007). The meaning of restorative justice. In: G Johnstone and D Van Ness (eds), *Handbook of Restorative Justice*. Cullompton, Willan.

Jones, L, Hughes, M, and Unterstaller, U (2001). Post-traumatic stress disorder (PTSD) in victims of domestic violence: A review of the research. *Trauma, Violence, and Abuse*, 2(2), 99–119.

Julich, S, (2006). Views of justice among survivors of historical child sexual violence. *Theoretical Criminology*, 10(1), 125–38.

Julich, S and Bowen, H (2015). Restorative justice in Aotearoa, New Zealand: Improving our response to sexual violence. *Revisa de Asistenta Sociala*, 4, 93–104.

Jullion, D (2000). Victim-offender mediation in France. In: The European Forum for Victim-Offender Mediation and Restorative Justice (ed), *Victim-Offender Mediation in Europe: Making Restorative Justice Work*. Leuven, Belgium: Leuven University Press.

Karp, DR, and Drakulich, KM (2004). Minor crime in a quaint setting: Practices, outcomes, and limits of Vermont reparative probation boards. *Criminology and Public Policy*, 3(4), 655–86.

Kaufman, W (2008). The rise and fall of the mixed theory of punishment. *International Journal of Applied Philosophy*, 22(1), 37–57.

Kellas, J, and Manusov, V (2003). What's in a story? The relationship between narrative completeness and tellers' adjustment to relationship dissolution. *Journal of Social and Personal Relationships*, 20(2), 285–307.

Kemény, S (2005). Victim-offender mediation with juvenile offenders in Norway. In: A Mestitz and S Ghetti (eds), *Victim-Offender Mediation with Youth Offenders in Europe. An overview and comparison of 15 countries*.

Kerner, H-J, and Hartmann, A (2005). *Täter-Opfer-Ausgleich in der Entwicklung: Auswertung der bundesweiten Täter-Opfer-Ausgleichs-Statistik für den Zehnjahreszeitraum 1993 bis 2002*. Godesberg: Forum Vlg Godesberg.

Kilchling, M (2005). Victim-offender mediation with juvenile offenders in Germany. In: A Mestitz and S Ghetti (eds), *Victim-Offender Mediation with Youth Offenders in Europe. An overview and comparison of 15 countries*. Dordrecht: Springer.

Kilchling, M, and Löschnig-Gspandl, M (1998). Legal and practical perspectives on victim/offender mediation in Austria and Germany. *International Review of Victimology*, 7(3), 305–32.

Kilcommins, S, and Donnelly, M (2014). Victims of crime with disabilities in Ireland: Hidden casualties in the 'vision of victim as everyman'. *International Review of Victimology*, 20(3), 302–25.

Kilpatrick, DG, and Acierno, R (2003). Mental health needs of crime victims: Epidemiology and outcomes. *Journal of Traumatic Stress*, 16(2), 119–32.

Kilty, J (2010). Gendering violence, remorse, and the role of restorative justice: Deconstructing public perceptions of Kelly Ellard and Warren Glowatski. *Contemporary Justice Review*, 13(2), 155–72.

King, M, Freiberg, A, Batagol, B, and Hyamns, R (2014). *Non Adversarial Justice*, 2nd ed. Leichhardt, New South Wales: Federation Press.

Kingi, V, Paulin, J, and Porima, L (2008). Review of the delivery of restorative justice in family violence cases by providers funded by the Ministry of Justice. Wellington: New Zealand Ministry of Justice.

Klein, JF (1978). Revitalizing restitution: Flogging a horse that may have been killed for just cause. *Criminal Law Quarterly*, 20, 383–408.

Kohen, A (2009). The personal and the political: forgiveness and reconciliation in restorative justice. *Critical Review of International Social and Political Philosophy*, 12(3), 399–423.

Lappi-Seppälä, T (2011). Finland. In: F Dünkel, J Grzywa, P Horsfield and I Pruin (eds), *Juvenile Justice Systems in Europe—Current Situation and Reform Developments*. 2nd ed. Mönchengladbach: Forum Verlag Godesberg.

—— (2015). Finland. In: F Dünkel, J Grzywa-Holten, P Horsfield (eds), *Restorative Justice and Mediation in Penal Matters—A stocktaking of legal issues, implementation strategies and outcomes in 36 European countries*. Mönchengladbach: Forum Verlag Godesberg.

Larsen, JJ (2014). *Restorative justice in the Australian criminal justice system*, Research and Public Policy Report No 127. Sydney: Australian Institute of Criminology.

Latha, S, and Thilagaraj, R (2013). Restorative justice in India. *Asian Journal of Criminology*, 8(4), 309–19.
Latimer, J, Dowden, C, and Muise, D (2001). *The Effectiveness of Restorative Justice Practices: A Meta-analysis*. Ottawa, Department of Justice Canada.
——, (2005). The effectiveness of restorative justice practices: A meta-analysis. *The Prison Journal*, 85(2), 127–44.
Lazare, A (2004). *On Apology*. Oxford: Oxford University Press.
Lazerges, C (1998). A study of types of processes in criminal mediation in France. In: E Fattah and T Peters (eds), *Support for Crime Victims in a Comparative Perspective*. Leuven: Leuven University Press.
Lees, S (1996). *Carnal Knowledge: Rape on Trial*. London: Hamish Hamilton.
Liebmann, M (2007). *Restorative Justice: How it works*. London: Jessica Kingsley.
Lind, EA, and Tyler, TR (1988). *The Social Psychology of Procedural Justice*. New York: Springer.
Lind, EA, Tyler, TR, and Huo, YJ (1997). Procedural context and culture: Variation in the antecedents of procedural justice judgments. *Journal of Personality and Social Psychology*, 73(4), 767–80.
Lister, S (2013). The new politics of the police: Police and crime commissioners and the 'operational independence' of the police. *Policing*, 7(3), 239–47.
Livingstone, N, Macdonald, G, and Carr, N (2013). Restorative justice conferencing for reducing recidivism in young offenders (aged 7 to 21). *Cochrane Database of Systematic Reviews*, 2, 1–89.
Llewellyn, J, and Howse, R (1998). *Restorative Justice: A Conceptual Framework*. Ottawa: Law Commission of Canada.
Lloyd, C, Mair, G, and Hough, JM (1994). *Explaining reconviction rates: A critical analysis*. London: HMSO.
Lo, TW (2011). Resistance to the mainlandization of criminal justice practices: A barrier to the development of restorative justice in Hong Kong. *International Journal of Offender Therapy and Comparative Criminology*, 56, 627–45.
London, R (2011). *Crime, punishment, and restorative justice: from the margins to the mainstream*. Boulder, CO: First Forum Press.
Loschnig-Gspandl, M, and Kilchling, M (1997). Victim/offender mediation and victim compensation in Austria and Germany-stocktaking and perspectives for future research. *European Journal of Crime, Criminal Law and Criminal Justice*, 5, 58–78.
Lovell, M, Helfgott, J, and Lawrence, C (2002). Narrative accounts from the citizens, victims, and offenders restoring justice program. *Contemporary Justice Review*, 5(3), 261–72.
Luban, D (1995). Settlements and the erosion of the public realm. *Georgetown Law Journal*, 83, 2619–62.
Luke, G, and Lind, B (2002). Reducing juvenile crime: Conferencing versus court. *BOCSAR NSW Crime and Justice Bulletins*, 20.
Lundgaard, JM (2015). Norway. In: F Dünkel, J Grzywa-Holten and P Horsfield (eds), *Restorative Justice and Mediation in Penal Matters—A stocktaking of legal issues, implementation strategies and outcomes in 36 European countries*. Mönchengladbach: Forum Verlag Godesberg.
Lyness, D (2008). *Northern Ireland Youth Re-offending: Results from the 2005 Cohort*, Research and Statistics Bulletin 7/2008. Belfast: Northern Ireland Office.
Lyness, D, and Tate, S (2011). *Northern Ireland Youth Re-offending: Results from the 2007 Cohort*, Statistical Bulletin 2/2011. Belfast: Youth Justice Agency.

Lynn, R (2011). *Reoffending analysis for restorative justice cases 2008–2011*. Wellington: NZ Ministry of Justice.

Lynch, N (2008). Youth justice in New Zealand: A children's rights perspective. *Youth Justice*, 8(3), 215–28.

—— (2012). Playing catch-up? Recent reform of New Zealand's youth justice system. *Criminology and Criminal Justice*, 12(5), 567–91.

Mackay, RE (2003). Restorative justice and the children's hearings—A proposal. *European Journal of Crime, Criminal Law and Criminal Justice*, 11(1), 1–17.

Maguire, EMW (1982). *Burglary in a Dwelling: The Offence, the Offender and the Victim*. London: Heinneman Educational Books.

Mackenzie, D (2008). *An Engine, not a Camera: How financial models shape markets*. Cambridge, MA: MIT Press.

Marklund, L (2015). Sweden. In: F Dünkel, J Grzywa-Holten and P Horsfield (eds), *Restorative Justice and Mediation in Penal Matters—A stocktaking of legal issues, implementation strategies and outcomes in 36 European countries*. Mönchengladbach: Forum Verlag Godesberg.

Marshall, TF (1996). The Evolution of Restorative Justice in Britain. *European Journal on Criminal Policy and Research*, 4(4), 21–43.

Marshall, T (1999). *Restorative Justice: An Overview*. London: Home Office.

Marshall, T, and Merry, S (1990). *Crime and Accountability*. London, HMSO.

Maruna, S (2011a). Lessons for justice reinvestment from restorative justice and the justice model experience. *Criminology and Public Policy*, 10(3), 661–69.

—— Reentry as a rite of passage. *Punishment and Society*, 13(1), 3–28.

Maruna, S, and King, A (2004). Public Opinion and Community Penalties. In: A Bottoms, S Rex and G Robinson (eds), *Alternatives to Prison: Options for an Insecure Society*. Cullompton: Willan.

Maruna, S, Wright, S, Brown, J, van Merle, F, Devlin, R, and Liddle, M (2007). *Youth Justice Conferencing as Shame Management: Results of a Long-Term Follow-up Study*. Cambridge: ARCS (UK) Ltd.

Mattinson, J, and Mirrlees-Black, C (2000). *Attitudes to Crime and Criminal Justice: Findings from the 1998 British crime Survey*. London: Home Office.

Matza, D (1964). *Delinquency and Drift*. New Brunswick, NJ: Transaction Publishers.

Mawby, R (2013). *Burglary*. Abingdon: Routledge.

Mawby, R, and Walklate, S (1994). *Critical Victimology: International Perspectives*. London: Sage.

Maxwell, G (2007). The youth justice system in New Zealand: Restorative justice delivered through the family group conference. In: G Maxwell and J Liu (eds), *Restorative Justice and Practices in New Zealand: Towards a Restorative Society*. Wellington: Institute of Policy Studies.

Maxwell, G, Kingi, V, Robertson, J, Morris, A, and Cunningham, C (2004). *Achieving effective outcomes: Youth justice in New Zealand*. Wellington: Ministry of Social Development.

Maxwell, G, and Hayes, H (2007). Pacific. In: G Johnstone and D Van Ness (eds), *Handbook of Restorative Justice*. Cullompton, Willan.

Maxwell, G, and Morris, A (1993). *Families, Victims and Culture: Youth Justice in New Zealand*. Wellington: Victoria University of Wellington.

—— (2001). Putting restorative justice into practice for adult offenders. *Howard Journal of Criminal Justice*, 40(1), 55–69.

—— (2002). Restorative justice and reconviction. *Contemporary Justice Review*, 5(2), 133–46.
Maxwell, G, Morris, A, and Hayes, H (2006). Conferencing and restorative justice. In: D Sullivan and L Tifft (eds), *Handbook of Restorative Justice: A Global Perspective*. Abington: Routledge.
Mayhew, P, and Van Kesteren, J (2002). Cross-national attitudes to punishment. In: JV Roberts and M Hough (eds), *Changing Attitudes to Punishment, Public opinion, Crime and Justice*. Cullompton: Willan Publishing.
McAlinden, AM (2005). The use of 'shame' with sexual offenders. *British Journal of Criminology*, 45(3), 373–94.
—— (2008). *The Shaming of Sexual Offenders: Risk, Retribution and Reintegration*. Oxford: Hart.
—— (2011). Transforming justice: challenges for restorative justice in an era of punishment-based corrections. *Contemporary Justice Review*, 14(4), 383–406.
—— (2016). Risk, Regulation and the Reintegration of Sexual Offenders. In: C Trotter, G McIvor and F McNeill (eds), *Beyond the Risk Paradigm. Volume III: Developing Practices in Criminal Justice*. London: Routledge.
McCold, P (1996). Restorative Justice and the Role of Community. In: B Galaway and J Hudson (eds), *Restorative Justice: International Perspectives*. Monsey, NY: Criminal Justice Press.
—— (1998). Restorative justice—variations on a theme. In: L Walgrave (ed), *Restorative Justice for Juveniles: Potentialities, Risks and Problems*. Leuven: Leuven University Press.
—— (2000). Toward a holistic vision of restorative juvenile justice: A reply to the maximalist model. *Contemporary Justice Review*, 3(4), 357–414.
—— (2001). Primary restorative justice practices. In: A Morris and G Maxwell (eds), *Restorative Justice for Juveniles: Conferencing, Mediation and Circles*. London: Bloomsbury Publishing.
—— (2006). The recent history of restorative justice: Mediation, circles, and conferencing. In: D Sullivan and L Tifft (eds), *Handbook of Restorative Justice: A Global Perspective*. Abingdon: Routledge.
McCold, P, and Wachtel, B (1997). *Community is Not a Place: A New Look at Community Justice Initiatives*. Paper presented to the International Conference on Justice Without Violence: Views from Peacemaking Criminology and Restorative Justice. Albany, New York, 5–7 June.
McCold, P, and Wachtel, T (1998). *Restorative Policing Experiment: The Bethlehem Pennsylvania Police Family Group Conferencing Project*. Washington DC: U.S. Department of Justice.
—— (2002). Restorative justice theory validation. In: E Weitekamp and HJ Kerner (eds), *Restorative Justice: Theoretical Foundations*. Cullompton: Willan.
—— (2003). *In Pursuit of Paradigm: A Theory of Restorative Justice*. Paper presented at the XIII World Congress of Criminology, Rio de Janeiro, 10–15 August 2003.
McCulloch, H (1996). *Shop Theft: Improving the Police Response*, Crime Detection and Prevention Series Paper 76. London: Home Office.
McDermott, D (2002). Debts to society. *Journal of Political Philosophy*, 10(4), 439–64.
McDiarmid, C (2005). Welfare, offending and the Scottish children's hearings system. *Journal of Social Welfare and Family Law*, 27(1), 31–42.

McEvoy, K (2007). Beyond legalism: Towards a thicker understanding of transitional justice. *Journal of Law and Society*, 34(4), 411–40.

McEvoy, K, and Eriksson, A (2006). Restorative justice in transition: Ownership, leadership and 'bottom-up' human rights. In: D Sullivan and L Tifft (eds), *Handbook of Restorative Justice: A Global Perspective*. Abingdon: Routledge.

McEvoy, K, and McConnachie, K (2013). Victims and transitional justice voice, agency and blame. *Social and Legal Studies*, 22(4), 489–513.

McEvoy, K, and Mika, H (2002). Restorative justice and the critique of informalism in Northern Ireland. *British Journal of Criminology*, 42(3), 534–62.

McGarrell, EF, and Hipple, NK (2007). Family group conferencing and re-offending among first-time juvenile offenders: The Indianapolis experiment. *Justice Quarterly*, 24(2), 221–46.

McGarrell, E, Olivares, K, Crawford, K, and Kroovand, N (2000). *Returning Justice to the Community: The Indianapolis Juvenile Restorative Justice Experiment*. Indianapolis, IN: Hudson Institute.

McGlynn, C, Westmarland, N, and Godden, N (2012). 'I just wanted him to hear me': sexual violence and the possibilities of restorative justice. *Journal of Law and Society*, 39(2), 213–40.

McGuire, J (2001). What works in correctional intervention? Evidence and practical implications. In: DFG Bernfield and A Leschied (eds), *Offender rehabilitation in practice: Implementing and evaluating effective programs*. New York, NY: John Wiley & Sons.

McLaughlin, E, Muncie, J, and Hughes, G (2001). The Permanent Revolution: New Labour, new public management and the modernization of criminal justice. *Criminology and Criminal Justice*, 1(3), 301–18.

Meares, TL (2000). Norms, legitimacy and law enforcement. *Oregon Law Review*, 79, 391–415.

Menkel-Meadow, C (2007). Restorative justice: What is it and does it work? *Annual Review of Law and Social Sciences*, 3, 161–87.

Messmer, H, and Otto, H-U (1992). Restorative Justice: Steps on the way toward a good idea. In: H Messmer and H-U Otto (eds), *Restorative Justice on Trial*. The Hague: Kluwer Academic.

Miers, DR (2001). *An International Review of Restorative Justice*. London: Home Office.

Miers, D (2014). Offender and state compensation for victims of crime: Two decades of development and change. *International Review of Victimology*, 20(1), 145–68.

Miers, D, Maguire, M, Goldie, S, Sharpe, K, Hale, C, Netten, A, Uglow, S, Doolin, K, Hallam, A, Newburn, T, and Enterkin, J (2001). *An Exploratory Evaluationg of Restorative Justice Schemes*, Home Office Occasional Paper. London: Home Office

Miers, D, and Willemsens, J (2004). *Mapping Restorative Justice: Developments in 25 European Countries*. Leuven: European Forum for Restorative Justice.

Mika, H (2006). *Community based restorative justice in Northern Ireland: An evaluation*. Belfast: Institute of Criminology and Criminal Justice, Queen's University Belfast.

Mika, H, and McEvoy, K (2001). Restorative justice in conflict: Paramilitarism, community and the construction of legitimacy in Northern Ireland. *Contemporary Justice Review*, 3(3), 291–319.

—— (2002). Republican hegemony or community ownership? Community restorative justice in Northern Ireland. In: D Feenan (ed), *Case Studies in Informal Justice*. London: Ashgate.

Milburn, P. (2002). *La Médiation: Expériences et compétences*. Paris: La Découverte Coll.

Milburn, P (2005). Mediation and Reparation for Young Offenders in France. In: A Mestiz and S Ghetti (eds), *Victim-Offender Mediation with Youth Offenders in Europe. An overview and comparison of 15 countries*. Dordrecht: Springer.

Miller, S (2011). *After the Crime: The Power of Restorative Justice Dialogues between Victims and Violent Offenders*. New York: New York University Press.

Ministry of Justice (2010). *Breaking the Cycle: Effective Punishment, Rehabilitation and Sentencing of Offenders*. London, HMSO.

—— (2011). *Breaking the Cycle: Government Response*, Cmnd 8070. London: HMSO.

—— (2014a). *Pre-sentence Restorative Justice*. London, HMSO.

—— (2014b). *Restorative Justice Action Plan for the Criminal Justice System for the period to March 2018*. London: Ministry of Justice.

—— (2016). *Proven Reoffending Statistics Quarterly, January to December 2014* (England and Wales). London: HMSO.

Minow, M. (1998). *Between vengeance and forgiveness: Facing history after genocide and mass violence*. Boston, MA: Beacon Press.

Moore, D (1993). Shame, Forgiveness, and Juvenile Justice. *Criminal Justice Ethics*, 12, 3–25.

Moore, DB, and McDonald, JM (1995). Achieving the Good Community: A local police initiative and its wider ramifications. In: KM Hazelhurst, *Perceptions of Justice Issues in Indigenous and Community Empowerment*. Brookfield, Ashgate.

Morison, J (2001). Democracy, Governance and Governmentality: Civic Public Space and Constitutional Renewal in Northern Ireland. *Oxford Journal of Legal Studies*, 21(2), 287–310.

Morris, A (2002). Critiquing the critics: A brief response to critics of restorative justice. *British Journal of Criminology*, 42(3), 596–615.

Morris, A, and Maxwell, G (1998). Restorative justice in New Zealand: Family group conferences as a case study. *Western Criminology Review*, 1(1).

—— (eds) (2001). *Restorative justice for juveniles: Conferencing, mediation and circles*. London: Bloomsbury.

—— (2003) Restorative Justice in New Zealand. In: A von Hirsch, J Roberts, AE Bottoms, K Roach and M Schiff (eds), *Restorative Justice and Criminal Justice: Competing or Reconcilable Paradigms*. Oxford: Hart.

Morris, A, Maxwell, GM, and Robertson, JP (1993). Giving victims a voice: A New Zealand experiment. *Howard Journal of Criminal Justice*, 32(4), 304–21.

Morris, A, and Young, W (2000). Reforming criminal justice: The potential of restorative justice. In: H Strang and J Braithwaite (eds), *Restorative Justice: Philosophy to Practice*. Aldershot: Ashgate.

Morris, H (1968). Persons and punishment. *Monist*, 52, 475–501.

Moyle, P, and Tauri, JM (2016). Māori, family group conferencing and the mystifications of restorative justice. *Victims and Offenders*, 11(1), 87–106.

Mullan, S, and O'Mahony, D (2003). *A Review of Recent Youth Justice Reforms in England and Wales*. Belfast: Northern Ireland Office.

Muncie, J (2005). The globalization of crime control—the case of youth and juvenile justice Neo-liberalism, policy convergence and international conventions. *Theoretical Criminology*, 9(1), 35–64.

Mutter, R, Shemmings, D, Dugmore, P, and Hyare, M (2008). Family group conferences in youth justice. *Health and Social Care in the Community*, 16(3), 262–70.

Nash, CL, and West, DJ (1985). Sexual molestation of young girls: A retrospective survey in sexual victimization. In: DJ West (ed), *Sexual Victimization*. Brookfield, Vermont: Gower Publishing.

New Zealand Law Commission (2015). *The Justice Response to Victims of Sexual Violence: Criminal Trials and Alternative Processes*, Report R136. Wellington: New Zealand Law Commission.

New Zealand Ministry of Justice (2004). *Restorative justice in New Zealand: Best Practice*. Wellington: Ministry of Justice.

—— (2010). *Child and Youth Offending Statistics in New Zealand: 1992 to 2008*. Wellington: Ministry of Justice.

Newburn, T, and Crawford, A (2002). Recent Developments in Restorative Justice for Young People in England and Wales: Community Participation and Restoration. *British Journal of Criminology*, 45(2), 476–95.

Newburn, T, Crawford, A, Earle, R, Goldie, S, Hale, C, Hallam, A, Masters, G, Netten, A, Saunders, R, Sharpe, K, and Uglow, S (2002). *The Introduction of Referral Orders into the Youth Justice System: Final Report*. London: Home Office.

Nugent, WR, Williams, M, and Umbreit, MS (2003). Participation in Victim-Offender Mediation and the prevalence and severity of subsequent delinquent behavior: A meta-analysis. *Utah Law Review*, 137–66.

O'Mahony, D (2012). Restorative justice and youth justice in England and Wales: One step forward, two steps back. *Nottingham Law Journal*, 21(2), 86–106.

—— (2015). Northern Ireland. In: F Dünkel, J Grzywa-Holten and P Horsfield (eds), *Restorative Justice and Mediation in Penal Matters—A stocktaking of legal issues, implementation strategies and outcomes in 36 European countries*. Mönchengladbach: Forum Verlag Godesberg.

O'Mahony, D, and Campbell, C (2006). Mainstreaming Restorative Justice for Young Offenders through youth conferencing. In: J Junger-Tas and S Decker (eds), *International Handbook of Youth Justice*. Amsterdam: Springer.

O'Mahony, D, Chapman, T, and Doak, J (2002). *Restorative Cautioning: A Study of Police Based Restorative Cautioning Pilots in Northern Ireland*. Belfast: Northern Ireland Office.

O'Mahony, D, and Deazley, R (2000). *Juvenile Crime and Justice*, Criminal Justice Review Group Research Report 17. London: HMSO.

O'Mahony, D, and Doak, J (2004). Restorative justice—is more better?: The experience of police-led restorative cautioning pilots in Northern Ireland. *Howard Journal of Criminal Justice*, 43(5), 484–505.

—— (2006). The enigma of 'community' and the exigency of engagement: restorative youth conferencing in Northern Ireland. *British Journal of Community Justice*, 4(3), 9–24.

O'Mahony, D, McEvoy, K, Geary, R, and Morison, J (2000). *Crime, Community and Locale: The Northern Ireland Communities Crime Survey*. Aldershot: Ashgate.

O'Malley, P (2009). *The Currency of Justice: Fines and Damages in Consumer Societies*. Abingdon: Routledge.

Ohbuchi, K, Kameda, M, and Agarie, N (1989). Apology as aggression control: Its role in mediating appraisal of and response to harm. *Journal of Personality and Social Psychology*, 56, 219–27.

Ohbuchi, K, and Sato, K (1994). Children's reactions to mitigating accounts: Apologies, excuses, and intentionality of harm. *The Journal of Social Psychology*, 134(1), 5–17.

Orbuch, T, Harvey, J, Davis, S, and Merbach, N (1994). Account-making and confiding as acts of meaning in response to sexual assault. *Journal of Family Violence*, 9, 249–64.
Packer, HH (1964). Two Models of the Criminal Process. *University of Pennsylvania Law Review*, 113, 1–68.
Padfield, N (2012). Alternative futures for the magistracy. In: D Faulkner (ed), *The Magistracy at the Crossroads*. London: Waterside Press.
—— (2013). Exploring the success of sentencing guidelines. In: A Ashworth and J Roberts (eds), *Sentencing Guidelines: Exploring the English Model*. Oxford: Oxford University Press.
Păroşanu, M (2015). Romania. In: F Dünkel, J Grzywa-Holten and P Horsfield (eds), *Restorative Justice and Mediation in Penal Matters—A stocktaking of legal issues, implementation strategies and outcomes in 36 European countries*. Mönchengladbach: Forum Verlag Godesberg.
Paterson, C, and Clamp, K (2012). Exploring recent developments in restorative policing in England and Wales. *Criminology and Criminal Justice*, 12(5), 593–611.
Paus, K (2000). Victim-offender mediation in Norway. In: European Forum for Victim-Offender Mediation and Restorative Justice (ed), *Making Restorative Justice Work*. Leuven, University of Leuven Press.
Pavlich, G (2001). The force of community. In: H Strang and J Braithwaite (eds), *Restorative Justice and Civil Society*. Cambridge: Cambridge University Press.
—— (2005). *The Governing Paradoxes of Restorative Justice*. London: Glasshouse Press.
Peachey, D (1989). The Kitchener Experiment. In: M Wright and B Galaway (eds), *Mediation and Criminal Justice*. London: Sage Publications.
Pelikan, C, and Trenczek, T (2006). Victim offender mediation and restorative justice: The European landscape. In: D Sullivan and L Tifft (eds), *Handbook of Restorative Justice: A Global Perspective*. Abingdon: Routledge.
Petrucci, CJ (2002). Apology in the criminal justice setting: Evidence for including apology as an additional component in the legal system. *Behavioral Sciences and the Law*, 20(4), 337–62.
Pemberton, A, Winkel, FW, and Groenhuijsen, M (2007). Taking victims seriously in restorative justice. *International Perspectives in Victimology*, 3(1), 4–14.
Ping Wang (2007). Restorative Justice in Asia. In: G Johnstone and D Van Ness (eds), *Handbook of Restorative Justice*. Cullompton, Willan.
Poulson, B (2003). A third voice: A review of empirical research on the psychological outcomes of restorative justice. *Utah Law Review*, 1, 167–203.
Pranis, K (2006). Healing and accountability in the criminal justice system: applying restorative justice processes in the workplace. *Cardozo Journal of Conflict Resolution*, 8, 659–76.
—— (2007). Restorative values. In: G Johnstone and D Van Ness (eds), *Handbook of Restorative Justice*. Cullompton, Willan.
Pratt, J (2007). *Penal Populism*. London: Routledge.
Pratt, J, Brown, D, Brown, M, Hallsworth, S, and Morrison, W (eds) (2013). *The New Punitiveness*. London: Routledge.
Put, J, Vanfraechem, I, and Walgrave, L (2012). Restorative dimensions in Belgian youth Justice. *Youth Justice*, 12(2), 83–100.
Putnam, RD (2000). *Bowling Alone: The Collapse and Revival of American Community*. London: Simon and Schuster.
Radin, MJ (1993). Compensation and commensurability. *Duke Law Journal*, 43(1), 56–86.

Radzik, L (2009). *Making Amends: Atonement in morality, law, and politics*. Oxford: Oxford University Press.
Rahami, M (2007). Islamic restorative traditions and their reflections in the post-revolutionary criminal justice system of Iran. *European Journal of Crime, Criminal Law and Criminal Justice*, 15(2), 227–248.
Rappaport, J (1987). Terms of empowerment/exemplars of prevention: Toward a theory for community psychology. *American Journal of Community Psychology*, 15(2), 121–48.
Retzinger, SM, and Scheff, TJ (1996). Strategy for community conferences: Emotions and social bonds. In: B Galaway and J Hudson (eds), *Restorative Justice: International Perspectives*. Monsey, NY: Criminal Justice Press.
Richards, K (2009). Taking victims seriously—the role of victims' rights movements in the emergence of restorative justice. *Current Issues in Criminal Justice*, 21(2), 302–20.
—— (2011). Restorative justice and "empowerment": Producing and governing active subjects through "empowering" practices. *Critical Criminology*, 19(2), 91–105.
Rix, A, Skidmore, K, Self, R, Holt, T, and Raybould, S (2011). *Youth Restorative Disposal Process Evaluation*. London: Youth Justice Board.
Roberts, LD, Spiranovic, C, and Indermaur, D (2011). A country not divided: A comparison of public punitiveness and confidence in sentencing across Australia. *Australian and New Zealand Journal of Criminology*, 44(3), 370–86.
Roberts, T (1995). *Evaluation of the Victim Offender Mediation Program in Langley, B.C.* Victoria, BC: Focus Consultants.
Roche, D (2001). The evolving definition of restorative justice. *Contemporary Justice Review*, 4(3), 341–53.
—— (2003). *Accountability in Restorative Justice*. Oxford: Oxford University Press.
Rodrigues, AM, Cruz Santos, C, and Păroşanu, A (2015). Portugal. In: F Dünkel, P Horsfield and A Păroşanu (eds), (2015). *European Research on Restorative Juvenile Justice: Volume I, Research and Selection of the Most Effective Juvenile Restorative Justice Practices in Europe: Snapshots from 28 EU Member States*. Brussels, International Juvenile Justice Observatory.
Roeger, D (2003). Resolving conflicts in prison. *Relational Justice Bulletin*, 19, 4–5.
Rose, N (2000). Government and Control. *British Journal of Criminology*, 40(2), 321–39.
Rosenblatt, FF (2015a). *The Role of Community in Restorative Justice*. London: Routledge.
—— (2015b). Restorative justice and the blurring between reparation and rehabilitation. In: T Gavrielides (ed), *Offenders No More: An Interdisciplinary Restorative Justice Dialogue*. New York: Nova Publishers.
Rossner, M (2013). *Just Emotions: Rituals of Restorative Justice*. Oxford: Oxford University Press.
Rossner, M, and Bruce, J (2016). Community participation in restorative justice: Rituals, reintegration, and quasi-professionalization. *Victims and Offenders*, 1–19.
Ruback, RB, and Thompson, MP (2001). *Social and psychological consequences of violent victimization*. London: Sage.
Saulnier, A, and Sivasubramaniam, D (2015a). Restorative justice: Underlying mechanisms and future directions. *New Criminal Law Review*, 18(4), 510–36.
—— (2015b). Effects of victim presence and coercion in restorative justice: An experimental paradigm. *Law and Human Behavior*, 39(4), 378–87.
Sawin, JL, and Zehr, H (2007). The ideas of engagement and empowerment. In: G Johnstone and D Van Ness (eds), *Handbook of Restorative Justice*. Cullompton, Willan.
Scheff, T (1998). Community conferences: shame and anger in therapeutic jurisprudence. *Revista Juridica Universidad de Puerto Rico*, 67, 97–119.

Schiff, M (1997). Gauging the severity of criminal sanctions: Developing the Criminal Punishment Severity Scale (CPSS). *Criminal Justice Review*, 22(2), 175–206.

Schluter, M (1994). What is relational justice? In: J Burnside and N Baker (eds), *Relational Justice: Repairing the Breach*. London: Waterside Press.

Schneider, CD (2000). What it means to be sorry: The power of apology in mediation. *Mediation Quarterly*,17(3), 265–80.

Schopp, RF (1998). Integrating restorative justice and therapeutic jurisprudence. *Revista Juridica Universidad de Puerto Rico*, 67, 665–69.

Schreck, CJ, Stewart, EA, and Osgood, DW (2008). A reappraisal of the overlap of violent victims and offenders. *Criminology*, 46(4), 871–906.

Seidman, I, and Vickers, SH (2005). The second wave: An agenda for the next thirty years of rape law reform. *Suffolk University Law Review*, 38, 467–91.

Severson, MM, and Bankston, TV (1995). Social work and the pursuit of justice through mediation. *Social Work*, 40(5), 683–91.

Shapland, J (2003). Restorative justice and criminal justice: Just responses to crime?. In: A von Hirsch, J Roberts, AE Bottoms, K Roach and M Schiff (eds), *Restorative Justice and Criminal Justice: Competing or Reconcilable Paradigms*. Oxford, Hart.

—— (2012). Comparing conferencing and mediation: Some evaluation results internationally. In: E Zinsstag and I Vanfraechem (eds), *Conferencing and Restorative Justice: International Practices and Perspectives*. Oxford: University Press.

Shapland, J, and Hall, M (2007). What do we know about the effects of crime on victims?. *International Review of Victimology*,14(2), 175–217.

Shapland, J, Atkinson, A, Colledge, E, Dignan, J, Howes, M, Johnstone, J, Pennant, R, Robinson, G, and Sorsby, A (2004). *Implementing Restorative Justice Schemes (Crime Reduction Programme): A Report on the First Year*, Home Office Online Report 32/04. London: Home Office.

Shapland, J, Atkinson, A, Atkinson, H, Chapman, B, Colledge, E, Dignan, J, Howes, M, Johnstone, J, Robinson, G, and Sorsby, A (2006a). *Restorative Justice in Practice: The Second Report from the Evaluation of Three Schemes.* Sheffield: Centre for Criminological Research, University of Sheffield.

——, (2006b). Situating restorative justice within criminal justice. *Theoretical Criminology*, 10(4), 505–32.

——, (2007). *Restorative Justice: The Views of Victims and Offenders: The Third Report from the Evaluation of Three Schemes.* Sheffield: Centre for Criminological Research, University of Sheffield.

Shapland, J, Atkinson, A, Atkinson, H, Dignan, J, Edwards, L, Hibbert, J, Howes, M, Johnstone, J, Robinson, G, and Sorsby, A (2008). *Does Restorative Justice Affect Reconviction? The Fourth Report from the Evaluation of Three Schemes.* London, Ministry of Justice.

Shapland, J, Robinson, G, and Sorsby, A (2011). *Restorative Justice in Practice: Evaluating What Works for Offenders and Victims*. London: Routledge.

Shapland, J, Wilmore, J, and Duff, P (1985). *Victims in the Criminal Justice System*. Aldershot: Gower.

Sharpe, S (2007). The idea of reparation. In: G Johnstone and D Van Ness (eds), *Handbook of Restorative Justice.* Cullompton: Willan.

Sherman, L (2003). Reason for emotion: reinventing justice with theories, innovations, and research—The American Society of Criminology 2002 Presidential Address. *Criminology*, 41(1), 1–38.

Sherman, L, and Strang, H (2007). *Restorative Justice: The Evidence.* London: The Smith Institute.

Sherman, LW, and Strang, H (2012). Restorative justice as evidence-based sentencing. In: J Petersilia and KR Reitz (eds), *The Oxford Handbook of Sentencing and Corrections.* Oxford: Oxford University Press.

Sherman, L, Strang, H, Angel, C, Woods, D, Barnes, G, Bennett, S, and Inkpen, N (2005). Effects of face-to-face restorative justice on victims of crime in four randomized controlled trials. *Journal of Experimental Criminology,* 1(3), 367–96.

Sherman, L, Strang, H, Barnes, J, Braithwaite, J, Inkpen, N, and Teh, M (1998). *Experiments in Restorative Policing: a progress report on the Canberra Reintegrative Shaming Experiments.* Canberra: Australian Institute of Criminology.

Sherman, L, Strang, H, Barnes, G, and Woods, D (2006) *Preliminary Analysis of the Northumberland Restorative Justice Experiments.* Philadelphia: Jerry Lee Centre of Criminology, University of Pennsylvania.

Sherman, LW, Strang, H, Mayo-Wilson, E, Woods, DJ, and Ariel, B (2015). Are restorative justice conferences effective in reducing repeat offending? Findings from a Campbell systematic review. *Journal of Quantitative Criminology,* 31(1), 1–24.

Sherman, LW, Strang, H, and Woods, DJ (2000). *Recidivism patterns in the Canberra reintegrative shaming experiments (RISE).* Canberra: Australian National University.

Simon, J (2001). Entitlement to cruelty: neo-liberalism and the punitive mentality in the United States. In: K Stenson and RR Sullivan (eds), *Crime Risk and Justice.* Cullompton: Willan.

Skelton, A (2007). Africa. In: G Johnstone and D Van Ness (eds), *Handbook of Restorative Justice.* Cullompton: Willan.

Skelton, A, and Frank, C (2004). How does restorative justice address human rights and due process issues?. In: H Zehr and B Toews (eds), *Critical Issues in Restorative Justice.* Monsey, NY: Criminal Justice Press.

Skogan, WG (1987). The impact of victimization on fear. *Crime and Delinquency,* 33(1), 135–54.

Slobogin, C (1995). Therapeutic Jurisprudence: Five Dilemmas to Ponder. *Psychology, Public Policy and Law,* 1, 193–219.

Smith, N (2008). *I Was Wrong: The Meanings of Apologies.* Cambridge University Press.

Souhami, A (2012). *Transforming Youth Justice.* London: Routledge.

Spalek, B (2005). *Crime Victims: Theory, Policy and Practice.* London: Palgrave Macmillan.

Spencer, JR, and Lamb, ME (eds) (2012). *Children and Cross-Examination: Time to Change the Rules?.* Oxford: Hart.

Stamatakis, N, and Vandeviver, C (2012). Restorative justice in Belgian prisons: the results of an empirical research. *Crime, Law and Social Change,* 59(1), 79–111.

Stanko, EA, and Hobdell, K (1993). Assault on men: Masculinity and male victimization. *British Journal of Criminology,* 33(3), 400–15.

Strang, H (2001). *Restorative Justice Programs in Australia, Report to the Criminology Research Council.* Canberra: Australian Institute of Criminology.

—— (2002). *Repair or Revenge: Victims and Restoraive Justice.* Oxford: Clarendon Press.

Strang, H, and Braithwaite, J (2001) Introduction. In: H Strang and J Braithwaite (eds), *Restorative Justice and Civil Society.* Cambridge: Cambridge University Press.

Strang, H, Barnes, GC, Braithwaite, J and Sherman, L (1999). *Experiments in Restorative Policing: A Progress Report on the Canberra Reintegrative Shaming Experiments (RISE).* Canberra: Australian National University.

Strang, H, Sherman, L, Angel, CM, Woods, DJ, Bennett, S, Newbury-Birch, D, and Inkpen, N (2006). Victim evaluations of face-to-face restorative justice conferences: A quasi-experimental analysis. *Journal of Social Sciences*, 62(2), 281–306.

Strang, H, Sherman, LW, Mayo-Wilson, E, Woods, D, and Ariel, B (2013). *Restorative Justice Conferencing (RJC) Using Face-to-Face Meetings of Offenders and Victims: Effects on Offender Recidivism and Victim Satisfaction. A Systematic Review*. Oslo: Campbell Collaboration.

Stubbs, J (2007). Beyond apology? Domestic violence and critical questions for restorative justice. *Criminology and Criminal Justice*, 7, 169–87.

Sullivan, D, and Tifft, L (2001). *Restorative Justice: Healing the Foundations of Our Everyday Lives*. Monsey, NY: Criminal Justice Press.

Swanson, C (2009). *Restorative Justice in a Prison Community: Or Everything I Didn't Learn in Kindergarten I Learned in Prison*. Boston, MA: Lexington.

Sylvester, DJ (2003). Myth in restorative justice history. *Utah Law Review*, 1, 471–522.

Tauri, J (1999). Explaining recent innovations in New Zealand's criminal justice system: empowering Maori or biculturalising the state?. *Australian and New Zealand Journal of Criminology*, 32(2), 153–67.

—— (2009). An Indigenous Perspective on the Standardisation of Restorative Justice in New Zealand and Canada. *Indigenous Policy Journal* 10(3). Available: https://ipjournal.wordpress.com/2009/12/16/an-indigenous-perspective-on-the-standardisation-of-restorative-justice-in-new-zealand-and-canada/ [accessed 1 June 2016].

Tavuchis, N (1991). *Mea Culpa: A Sociology of Apology and Reconciliation*. Stanford, CA: Stanford University Press.

Theidon, K (2006). Justice in transition: The micropolitics of reconciliation in postwar Peru. *Journal of Conflict Resolution*, 50(3), 433–57.

Thibaut, JW, and Walker, L (1978). *Procedural Justice: A Psychological Analysis*. Hillsdale, NJ: L Erlbaum Associates.

Thompson, W, and Hickey, J (2005). *Society in Focus*. Boston, MA: Pearson.

Tonry, M (2005). Obsolescence and immanence in penal theory and policy. *Columbia Law Review*, 105(4), 1233–275.

Tränkle, S (2007). In the shadow of penal law: Victim offender mediation in Germany and France. *Punishment and Society*, 9(4), 395–415.

Trenczek, T (2001). Victim-offender mediation in Germany: ADR under the shadow of the criminal law?. *Bond Law Review*, 16(5), 364–80.

Triggs, S (2005). A summary of New Zealand court-referred restorative justice pilot: Evaluation. *Just Published* 39. Retrieved: http://www.justice.govt.nz/publications/global-publications/n/new-zealand-court-referred-restorative-justice-pilot-evaluation-may-2005/documents/nz-court-referred-restorative-justice-pilot.pdf [accessed 17 May 2016].

Trimboli, L (2000). *An Evaluation of the NSW Youth Justice Conferencing Scheme*. Sydney: NSW Bureau of Crime Statistics and Research.

Trubek, LG (1996). Embedded practices: Lawyers, clients, and social change. *Harvard Civil Rights–Civil Liberties Law Review*, 31, 415–41.

Turner, S (2002). *Young People's Experiences with the Young Offenders Act*. Sydney, NSW: Law and Justice Foundation of New South Wales.

Tyler, T (1990). *Why People Obey the Law*. Princeton, MA: Princeton University Press.

Tyler, TR (2006). Restorative justice and procedural justice: Dealing with rule breaking. *Journal of Social Issues*, 62(2), 307–32.

Tyler, TR, Sherman, L, Strang, H, Barnes, GC, and Woods, D (2007). Reintegrative shaming, procedural justice, and recidivism: The engagement of offenders' psychological mechanisms in the Canberra RISE drinking-and-driving experiment. *Law and Society Review*, 41(3), 553–85.

Umbreit, M (1994). *Victim Meets Offender: The Impact of Restorative Justice in Mediation*. Monsey, NY: Criminal Justice Press.

—— (1995). *Mediation of Criminal Conflict: An Assessment of Programs in Four Canadian Provinces*. St Paul, MN: Center for Restorative Justice and Mediation, University of Minnesota.

—— (2001). *The Handbook of Victim Offender Mediation. An Essential Guide to Practice and Research*. San Fransisco: Jossey-Bass.

Umbreit, M, and Bradshaw, W (1999). Factors that contribute to victim satisfaction with mediated offender dialogue in Winnipeg: An emerging area of social work practice. *Journal of Law and Social Work*, 9(1), 35–51.

Umbreit, M, and Coates, R (1992). *Victim Offender Mediation: An Analysis of Programs in Four States of the US*. Minneapolis, MN: Minnesota Citizens Council on Crime and Justice.

Umbreit, M, and Roberts, A (1996). *Mediation of Criminal Conflict in England: An Assessment of Services in Coventry and Leeds*. St Paul, MN: Centre for Restorative Justice and Mediation.

Umbreit, M, Bradshaw, W, and Coates, R (1999). Victims of severe violence meet the offender: Restorative justice through dialogue. *International Review of Victimology*, 6(4), 321–43.

Umbreit, MS, Coates, RB, and Vos, B (2002). The impact of restorative justice conferencing: A multi-national perspective. *British Journal of Community Justice*, 1(2), 21–48.

Umbreit, M, Coates, R, and Vos, B (2004). Victim-offender mediation: Three decades of practice and research. *Conflict Resolution Quarterly*, 22(1–2), 279–303.

Umbreit, M, Vos, B, Coates, R, and Armour, MP (2006). Victims of severe violence in mediated dialogue with offender: The impact of the first multi-site study in the US. *International Review of Victimology*, 13(1), 27–48.

Ua-amnoey, J, and Kittayarak, K (2004). Restorative justice: a paradigm shift in the Thai criminal justice system. *Corrections Today*, 66(1), 86–91.

Ungar, M (2009). Policing youth in Latin America. In: G Jones (ed), *Youth Violence in Latin America: Gangs and Juvenile Justice in Perspective*. London: Palgrave Macmillan.

United Nations (2006). *Handbook on Restorative Justice Programmes*. Vienna: United Nations Office on Drugs and Crime.

Van Camp, T, and Wemmers, JA (2013). Victim satisfaction with restorative justice: More than simply procedural justice. *International Review of Victimology*, 19(2), 117–43.

Van Drie, D, van Groningen, S, and Weijers, I (2015). Netherlands. In: F Dünkel, J Grzywa-Holten and P Horsfield (eds), *Restorative Justice and Mediation in Penal Matters— A stocktaking of legal issues, implementation strategies and outcomes in 36 European countries*. Mönchengladbach: Forum Verlag Godesberg.

Van Kesteren, J, Mayhew, P, and Nieuwbeerta, P (2001). *Criminal Victimisation in Seventeen Industrialised Countries: Key Findings from the 2000 International Crime Victims Survey*. The Hague: WODC.

Van Ness, D (1993). A reply to Andrew Ashworth. *Criminal Law Forum*, 4(2), 301–06.

—— (1996). Restorative justice and international human rights. In: B Galaway and J Hudson (eds), *Restorative Justice: International Perspectives*. Monsey, NY: Criminal Justice Press.

—— (1997). Perspectives on Achieving Satisfying Justice: Values and Principles of Restorative Justice. *The ICCA Journal on Community Corrections*, 7(1), 7–12.

—— (2004). *Contemplating a restorative justice system*. Paper presented at Building a Global Alliance for Restorative Practices and Family Empowerment, Richmond, BC, Canada, 5–7 August.

Van Ness, DW (2007). Prisons and restorative justice. In: G Johnstone and D Van Ness (eds), *Handbook of Restorative Justice*. Cullompton: Willan.

Van Ness, D (2014). Accountability. In: JJ Llewellyn and D Philpott (eds), *Restorative Justice, Reconciliation, and Peacebuilding*. Oxford: Oxford University Press.

Van Ness, D, and Heetderks Strong, K (2014). *Restoring Justice: An Introduction to Restorative Justice*, 5th ed. New Providence, NJ: Mathew Bender and Co.

Van Ness, D, and Nolan, P (1998). Legislating for restorative justice. *Regent University Law Review*, 10(1), 53–110.

Van Pagee, R, Van Lieshout, J, and Wolthuis, A (2012). Most things look better when arranged in a circle: Family Group Conferencing empowers societal developments in The Netherlands. In: E Zinsstag and I Vanfraechem (eds), *Conferencing and Restorative Justice. International Practices and Perspectives*. Oxford: University Press.

Van Stokkom, B (2015). Just emotions: rituals of restorative justice, *Restorative Justice*, 3(2), 303–06.

Vanfraechem, I (2005). Evaluating Conferencing For Serious Juvenile Offenders. In: E Elliott and R Gordon (eds), *New Directions in Restorative Justice: Issues, Practice, Evaluation*. Cullompton: Willan.

Vanfraechem, I, and Zinstaag, E (2012). Conferencing: Setting the scene. In: E Zinsstag and I Vanfraechem (eds), *Conferencing and Restorative Justice. International Practices and Perspectives*. Oxford: University Press.

Vanfraechem, I, Lauwaert, K, and Decocq, M (2012). Conferencing at the Crossroads between Rehabilitation and Restorative Justice. In: E Zinsstag and I Vanfraechem (eds), *Conferencing and Restorative Justice. International Practices and Perspectives*. Oxford: University Press.

Vanfraechem, I, Bolívar, D, and Aersten, I (eds) (2015). *Victims and Restorative Justice*. London: Routledge.

Vetten, L, Jewkes, R, Sigsworth, R, Christofides, N, Loots, L, and Dunseith, O (2014). Worth their while? Pursuing a rape complaint through the criminal justice system. *South African Crime Quarterly*, 32(1), 19–25.

Voice UK, Respond, and Mencap UK (2001). *Behind Closed Doors: Preventing Sexual Abuse against Adults with a Learning Disability*. London: Mencap.

Von Hirsch, A, and Jareborg, N (1991). Gauging criminal harm: A living-standard analysis. *Oxford Journal of Legal Studies*, 11(1), 1–38.

Von Hirsch, A, Ashworth, A, and Shearing, C (2003). Specifying aims and limits for restorative justice: A 'making amends' model. In: A von Hirsch, JV Roberts, AE Bottoms, K Roach and M Schiff (eds), *Restorative Justice and Criminal Justice: Competing or Reconcilable Paradigms*. Oxford: Hart.

Von Holderstein Holtermann, J (2009). Outlining the shadow of the axe—on restorative justice and the use of trial and punishment. *Criminal Law and Philosophy*, 3(2), 187–207.

Wachtel, J (2009). Restorative Community Policing in the UK: Dorset, Cheshire and Norfolk Constables Point the Way, *Restorative Practices EForum*. Retrieved: http://www.iirp.edu/eforum-archive/4415-restorative-community-policing-in-the-uk-dorset-cheshire-and-norfolk-constables-point-the-way [accessed 27 March 2017].

Walgrave, L (2002). Restoration and community, law and state—paradoxes, contradictions, convergences. In: L Walgrave (ed), *Restorative Justice and the Law*. Cullompton: Willan Publishing.

—— (2003). Imposing restoration instead of inflicting pain: reflections on the judicial reaction to crime. In: A von Hirsch, JV Roberts, AE Bottoms, K Roach and M Schiff (eds), *Restorative Justice and Criminal Justice: Competing or reconcilable paradigms*. Oxford: Hart.

—— (2007). Integrating criminal justice and restorative justice. In: G Johnstone and D Van Ness (eds), *Handbook of Restorative Justice*. Cullompton: Willan.

—— (2008). *Restorative Justice, Self Interest and Responsible Citizenship*. Cullompton: Willan Publishing.

—— (2011). Investigating the potentials of restorative justice practice. *Washington University Journal of Law and Policy*, 36, 91–139.

—— (2012). The Need for Clarity about Restorative Justice Conferences. In: E Zinsstag and I Vanfraechem (eds), Conferencing and Restorative Justice. Oxford: Oxford University Press.

Walgrave, L, and Bazemore, G (1999). Reflections on the future of restorative justice for juveniles. In: L Walgrave and G Bazemore (eds), *Restorative Juvenile Justice: Repairing the Harm of Youth Crime*. Monsey, NY USA: Criminal Justice Press.

Walker, L (2015). Re-entry circles for the innocent: The psychological benefits of restorative justice and taking responsibility in response to injustice. In: T Gavrieledes (ed), *The Psychology of Restorative Justice: Managing the Power Within*. London: Routledge.

Walker, MU (2006). *Moral Repair: Reconstructing Moral Relations after Wrongdoing*. Cambridge: Cambridge University Press.

Ward, T, Fox, KJ, and Garber, M (2014). Restorative justice, offender rehabilitation and desistance. *Restorative Justice*, 2(1), 24–42.

Ward, T, and Langlands, R (2009). Repairing the rupture: Restorative justice and the rehabilitation of offenders. *Aggression and Violent Behavior*, 14(3), 205–14.

Weatherburn, D, and Macadam, M (2013). A review of restorative justice responses to offending. *Evidence Base* 1. Carlton, Victoria: The Australia and New Zealand School of Government. Retrieved: http://apo.org.au/node/40204 [accessed 27 March 2017].

Weinrib, EJ (2012). *The Idea of Private Law*. Oxford: Oxford University Press.

Weisberg, R (2003). The Practice of Restorative Justice: Restorative Justice and the Danger of Community. *Utah Law Review*, 1, 343–74.

Wemmers, J (1996). *Victims in the Criminal Justice System*. Amsterdam: Kugler.

—— (2009). Where do they belong? Giving victims a place in the criminal justice process. *Criminal Law Forum*, 20(4), 395–416.

Wemmers, J, and Canuto, M (2002). *Victims' Experiences with Expectations and Perceptions of Restorative Justice: A Critical Review of the Literature*. Montreal: Department of Justice Canada.

Wemmers, J, and Cyr, K (2005). Can mediation be therapeutic for crime victims? An evaluation of victims' experiences in mediation with young offenders. *Canadian Journal of Criminology and Criminal Justice*, 47, 527–544.

Wexler, D (1998). Therapeutic jurisprudence forum: practicing therapeutic jurisprudence: Psycholegal soft spots and strategies. *Revista Juridica Universidad de Puerto Rico*, 67, 317–42.

Wheeldon, J (2009). Finding common ground: Restorative justice and its theoretical construction(s). *Contemporary Justice Review*, 12(1), 91–100.

Wielsch, D (2013). Relational justice. *Law* and *Contemporary Problems*, 76(2), 191–211.
Wilcox, A, and Hoyle, C (2004). *National Evaluation of the Youth Justice Board's Restorative Justice Projects*. London: Youth Justice Board.
Wilcox, A and Young, R (2007). How green was Thames Valley? Policing the image of restorative justice cautions. *Policing and Society*, 17(2), 141–63.
Wilcox, A, Young, R, and Hoyle, C (2004). *Two-year resanctioning study: A comparison of restorative and traditional cautions*. London: Home Office.
Winfree Jr, LT (2002). Peacemaking and community harmony: Lessons (and admonitions) from the Navajo peacemaking courts. In: E Weitekamp and HJ Kerner (eds), *Restorative Justice: Theoretical Foundations*. Cullompton: Willan.
Wood, WR, and Suzuki, M (2016). Four challenges in the future of restorative justice. *Victims and Offenders*, 11(1), 149–72.
Wood, M, Lepanjuuri, K, and Paskell, C (2015). *Victim and Witness Satisfaction Survey*. London: Crown Prosecution Service.
Woolford, A, and Ratner, RS (2008). *Informal Reckonings: Conflict Resolution in Mediation, Restorative Justice, and Reparations*. London: Routledge.
Wright, M (1991). *Justice for Victims and Offenders.* London: Sage.
—— (1996). Can mediation be an alternative to criminal justice?. In: B Galaway and J Hudson (eds), *Restorative Justice: International Perspectives*. Monsey, NY: Criminal Justice Press.
—— (2002). The court as last resort: Victim-sensitive, community-based responses to crime. *British Journal of Criminology*, 42(3), 654–67.
Yazzie, R (1998). Navajo peacemaking: Implications for adjudication-based systems of justice. *Contemporary Justice Review*, 1, 123–31.
Yazzie, R, and Zion, JW (1996). Navajo restorative justice: The law of equality and justice. In: B Galaway and J Hudson (eds), *Restorative justice: International Perspectives*. Monsey, NY: Criminal Justice Press.
Youth Justice Board (2006). *Developing Restorative Justice: An Action Plan*. London: Youth Justice Board.
Zalewski, W, and Păroşanu, A (2015). Poland. In: F Dünkel, P Horsfield and A Păroşanu (eds) (2015). *European Research on Restorative Juvenile Justice: Volume I, Research and Selection of the Most Effective Juvenile Restorative Justice Practices in Europe: Snapshots from 28 EU Member States*. Brussels, International Juvenile Justice Observatory.
Zedner, L (1994). Reparation and retribution: Are they reconcilable? *Modern Law Review*, 57(2), 228–50.
Zehr, H (1990). *Changing Lenses: A New Focus for Crime and Justice*. Waterloo, ON: Herald Press.
—— (2001). *Transcending: Reflections of Crime Victims: Portraits and Interviews*. Intercourse, PA: Good Books.
—— (2002). *The Little Book of Restorative Justice*. Intercouse, PA: Good Books.
—— (2005). Evaluation and restorative justice principles. In: E Elliott and R Gordon (eds), *New Directions in Restorative Justice: Issues, practice, evaluation*. Cullompton: Willan.
Zehr, H, and Mika, H (1998). Fundamental Concepts of Restorative Justice. *Contemporary Justice Review*, 1(1), 47–55.
Zernova, M (2007). Aspirations of restorative justice proponents and experiences of participants in family group conferences. *British Journal of Criminology*, 47(3), 491–509.
Zimmerman, MA (1995). Psychological empowerment: Issues and illustrations. *American Journal of Community Psychology*, 23(5), 581–99.

Zinsstag, E (2012). Conferencing: A developing practice of restorative justice. In: E Zinsstag and I Vanfraechem (eds), *Conferencing and Restorative Justice. International Practices and Perspectives*. Oxford: University Press.

Zinsstag, E, and Vanfraechem, I (eds) (2012). *Conferencing and Restorative Justice. International Practices and Perspectives*. Oxford: University Press.

Zinsstag, E, Teunkens, M, and Pali, B (2011). *Conferencing: A Way Forward for Restorative Justice in Europe*. Leuven: European Forum of Restorative Justice.

INDEX

NB–page locators in **bold** indicate information found in figures

accountability, *see* agency-accountability framework
adult offenders, schemes for, 4, 118–19, 201
  Belgium:
    conferencing, 133
    mediation for redress, 134
    penal mediation, 134
  continental Europe:
    Belgium, 133–34
    victim-offender mediation, 21
  England and Wales:
    changes in government policy, 122–23
    conditional cautioning scheme, 5, 114–15
    government policy reform, 205
    Home Office Crime Reduction Programme, 121
    mediation schemes, 121–22
    satisfaction rates, 122
  New Zealand:
    Community Accountability Programme, 119
    community panels, 119–21
    empowering nature, 121
    Project Turnaround, 119
    satisfaction rates, 119–21
  recidivism, 184–88
  victim participation, 157, 169
  youth justice compared, 152–53
adversarial system of justice, 20, 56, 97, 204
  criticisms of, 13–14, 43, 208–10
  inquisitorial system compared, 132–33
  state-led nature, 39
  victim participation and role, 41, 63, 76–77
  victimisation of the victim, 63
agency, *see* agency-accountability framework
agency-accountability framework, 129–31, 215–16
  accountability, 20
    restorative agency and accountability, 71–73
    safety of victims, 90–92
    'victimless' crimes, 81–82
    youth conferencing, 173–74
  adult offender, schemes for, 122–23

agency, 20
  restorative agency and accountability, 70–71
  safety of victims, 90–92
  youth conferencing, 173–74
civil law jurisdictions, 201
continental Europe:
  mediation schemes, 146, 140
development, 19–20
empowerment theory, 68–69, 197–98
European schemes, 201
mainstreaming restorative justice and, 199–204
offenders, 92–93, 98–99
  offender experiences, 93–94
  rights of offenders, 94–95
police-led conferencing, 107, 108
prioritisation as normative goals, 199
prison-based restorative schemes, 127
recidivism and, 190, 194–95, 202–03
  Australia, 191
  New Zealand, 190–91
restorative agency and accountability, 69–70, 74
  accountability, 71–73
  agency, 70–71
  agency, accountability and criminal justice, 73–74
restorative cautioning, 115
victims, 76–77, 98
  non-participation, 79–83
  sincere apology, 86–90
  victim experiences, 83–90
  victim participation, 77–79
  victim safety, 90–92
youth conferencing, 158–59, 172–74
youth offender panels, 118
see also agency and accountability; empowerment theory
agency and accountability:
  goals and values, 18, 19, 20–22, 97–99, 131, 174, 190
  coercion, 85
  conferencing, 80–81, 147, 161–62, 201

criminal justice and reform of criminal
    procedure, 15, 24–26, 202, 203–04,
    205–08
empowerment theory, 59, 65–69, **68, 69**,
    73–74, 128, 197–98
Europe, 201
experiences of offenders, 93–94
individual values and process values
    distinguished, 28–29
mediation programmes, 4–5, 139
prison-based programmes, 128, 130–31
reducing recidivism, 202–03
reparation, 44, 215
surplanting by 'system goals' and processing
    targets, 39, 210–11
translation into practice, 46–47, 57–58, 202,
    203–04, 205–08
see also agency-accountability framework;
    criminal justice; empowerment theory
apology, *see* sincere apology
Australia, 3:
    adult offenders, 13, 21–22
    community-based programmes:
        impact of indigenous practices, 101
    impact of indigenous practices, 17–18, 101
    informed consent, 95
    recidivism, 181, 183, 191, 193
    referrals from criminal justice system, 213
    restorative cautioning, 5
    restorative conferencing, 151–52
    restorative policing, 5, 104–05
        police-led conferencing, 21
        police-led restorative cautioning, 109
        youth conferencing, 87, 89, 105–06, 152,
            157
    RISE project:
        reduced recidivism, 181, 184
        satisfaction rates, 84
        victim participation, 78, 157
    victim impact statements, 41–42
    victim participation:
        RISE project, 78, 157
        Wagga Wagga programme, 78
        youth conferencing, 157
    Wagga Wagga programme, 104, 106
        victim participation, 78
    young offenders, 13, 17
    youth conferencing, 87, 89, 152
        participation, 157
Austria:
    agency-accountability framework, 201
    developing restorative justice, 146, 150
    mediation schemes, 132, 141
        administration, 136
        criminal justice system and, 138
        diversionary mediation programmes,
            148–49
        evaluation, 142–43

financial compensation, 140
referrals, 137
shuttle mediation, 138

Belgium, 21–22
    agency-accountability framework, 201
    mediation schemes, 133–34
        administration, 136
        evaluation, 144–45
        conferencing, 140
        mainstreaming of practice, 139
        referrals, 137–38
    prison-based restorative programmes,
        127–28
    restorative conferencing, 140, 152–53, 201
benefits of restorative justice:
    offenders, 92, 179, 198
    victims, 25, 43–44, 63, 83, 89–90, 179, 198
best practice, 6–7, 10–12, 67, **68**, 103, 138, 174,
    178
    see also standards
bottom up schemes, 3, 39–40, 101–04, 211
    see also community-based programmes
Bulgaria:
    mediation schemes:
        apologies, 141

Canada:
    First Nations tribes, 8
        sentencing circles, 101
    prison-based restorative programmes, 124–25,
        126
    victim impact statements, 41–42
    victim-offender mediation, 4–5
    see also North America
civil law jurisdictions:
    common law compared, 132
    see also mediation; *individual countries*
coercion, 28
    agency and accountability and, 173, 200
    consent and, **67**, 200
    empowerment theory and, 85
    rights of offender to protection from, 95–96
    rights of victim to protection from, 84–85
    *UN Basic Principles on Use of Restorative
        Justice Programmes*, 95
    youth conferencing programmes, 159–60,
        164, 173
common and civil law jurisdictions compared,
    132
common goals of restorative justice, 68
    encounter, **68**, 68–69
    participation, **68**
    reparation, **68**
    reintegration, **68**
common law jurisdictions:
    civil law compared, 132
    see also individual countries

Index

communities:
 community participation, 37–39
  benefits, 34–35
  criticisms, 35–36
 exclusion of those without community, 37
community reparation panels:
 adult offenders, schemes for, 119–21
 aims, 6
 origins, 6–7
 victim participation, 78
 referral orders, 7
 Youth Offender Panels, 7
Community Restorative Justice Ireland, 103, 104
community-based programmes:
 adult offenders, schemes for, 119–21
 First Nations and indigenous communities, 101–02
 levels of satisfaction, 102
 Northern Ireland, 103–04
  Community Restorative Justice Ireland, 103, 104
  government funding, 104
  Northern Ireland Alternatives, 103, 104
 positive outcomes, 101–02
 schemes entirely apart from criminal justice system, 102–03
  Community Restorative Justice Ireland, 103
  Northern Ireland Alternatives, 103
 see also communities; community reparation panels
compensation orders, 47–48, 55
conceptual challenges, 23–24
 criminal justice, 24–27
 restorative justice theory, 27–30
  outcomes, 47–53
  processes, 41–47
  victim and offender, 30–41
conditional cautioning:
 adult schemes, 5, 114–15
 Youth Conditional Caution:
  aims of the scheme, 114
  benefits of participation, 114
  conditions applicable, 114–15
  partly restorative nature, 115
 see also restorative cautioning
consent, 31, **67**
 breaches of offenders' rights, 99, 213
 continental European mediation programmes, 137–38
 informed consent, 11, 95–96, 117, 164, 200
 participation and, 27, 97
 UN Basic Principles on Use of Restorative Justice Programmes, 95
 young offenders, 117
  Youth Conditional Cautions, 114–15
  youth conferencing, 156, 159–62, 164, 172
  Youth Restorative Disposals, 113
continental Europe, *see individual countries*

Council of Europe:
 EU Framework Decision on the Standing of Victims in Criminal Proceedings, 11
 pressure on member states to develop restorative justice programmes, 149–50
 Recommendation (99)19 Concerning Mediation in Penal Matters, 11–12
criminal justice:
 agency, accountability and, 73–74
 criticisms of traditional paradigm, 25, 57–58
 development of restorative justice, 2–3, 23
  mainstreaming restorative justice within criminal justice system, 53–57
 historical background, 24
  concept of victim compensation, 24
  concept of victimisation, 24–25
 retribution, 3
 restitution, 2
 restorative agency and accountability, 69–70
  agency, accountability and criminal justice, 73–74
Croatia:
 mediation schemes:
  apologies, 141
cultural resistance to restorative justice, 212
 Australia:
  referral levels, 213
  concerns, 213–14
 Germany:
  mediation, 212–13
 Northern Ireland:
  youth conferencing, 213
Czech Republic:
 mediation schemes:
  administration, 136

damages, *see* reparation
direct contact between victim and offender, 79, 194
disempowerment through crime, 20, 59, 65, 74, 197–98
 agency and, 70–71
 breaches of offenders' rights, 99
 loss of personal autonomy, 60–62
 physical violence, 61
 property-related crimes, 61–62
 secondary victimisation, 62–63
diversionary practices, 21
 increasing emphasis, 177
 mediation, 132, 134, 136, 143, 148–49, 150
 restorative policing, 104–05, 112, 128–29, 131
  police-led diversionary conferencing, 105–08
 youth conferencing, 153, 155–56
 Youth Offender Panels, 116–18
 see also restorative policing
due process, 10, 15
 agency and, 70

opportunity to be heard, 95–96
police-led restorative cautioning, 96–97
proportionality of justice, 96–98, 210
protection from coercion, 95–96
protection of human rights, 26, 57, 106
rights of offenders, 94

emotions and ritual, 45, 46–47
　identity and, 45
　self-conscious emotions, 45
empowerment theory, 20, 60–61, 74, 196–97
　adult offenders, schemes for, 121
　agency and accountability, 59, 68–69, **69**, 197–98
　behavioural elements, 64
　empowering practices:
　　restorative practices compared, **67**
　interactional elements, 64
　interpersonal elements, 64
　offenders, 64
　restorative themes:
　　empowering values, 65
　　empowering processes, 65–66
　　empowering outcomes, 66
　socially excluded and marginalised populations, 64–65
　victims, 63–64
　values and principles, 66–67
　　overlap with restorative justice values and principles, 66, **67**
　see also agency-accountability framework; disempowerment through crime; restorative agency and accountability
encounter-based nature of restorative justice, 28
engagement of participants:
　youth conferencing, 160–61
England and Wales, 3
　adult offenders, schemes for, 21–22, 118–19, 188
　　changes in government policy, 122–23, 205
　　Home Office Crime Reduction Programme, 121
　　mediation schemes, 121–22
　　satisfaction rates, 122
　community reparation panels, 6–7
　compensation orders, 47
　final warning scheme, 112–15
　lack of government commitment, 206–08
　prison-based programmes, 123–24
　referral orders, 96, 130
　restorative cautioning
　　Thames Valley programme, 176–79
　restorative conferencing, 152
　restorative policing, 5–6, 129
　satisfaction rates, 63
　victim participation, 42–43
　young offender panels, 78, 95, 101, 116–18, 213

Youth Restorative Disposal system, 6
see also United Kingdom
European Convention on Human Rights, 95
European Court of Human Rights, 94
European Union:
　funding for research, 142
　international standards, 146
　pressure on member states to develop restorative justice programmes, 149–50

family group conferencing, 21, 106–07
　Belgium, 134
　development, 7–8
　evaluations, 78
　format, 154
　France, 147
　New Zealand, 3–4, 155
　origins, 7
　resistance of indigenous populations of New Zealand, 210–11
　satisfaction levels, 170–71, 182
　success of, 7–8
　victim participation, 78, 157
　youth conferencing, 154
final warning scheme:
　implementation, 112
　　impact of performance targets, 113
　　creation of Youth Restorative Disposal, 113
　introduction in England and Wales, 112
　marginalisation of the victim, 112–13
　Youth Restorative Disposal, 113
Finland:
　developing restorative justice, 146–47
　mediation schemes, 133, 148, 150
　　administration, 136
　　evaluation, 142–43
　　financial compensation, 140–41
　　legal representation, 139
　　referrals, 136, 146
First Nations tribes, 8, 102
　sentencing circles, 101
France:
　family group conferencing, 147
　mediation schemes, 134, 147
　　administration, 136
　　evaluation, 142–43
　　financial compensation, 140
　　legal representation, 139
　　referrals, 137
fully restorative programmes, 9, 20
fundamental values and principles, 28
funding:
　community-based programmes:
　　Ireland, 104
　EU funding, 142
　Home Office Crime Reduction Programme:
　　evaluation of adult-schemes, 121

inadequacy of funding in England and Wales, 124, 206, 207—08
lack of:
    impact on prison-based programmes, 124
    restorative cautioning, 206
    Restorative Justice Disposal, 201

Germany:
    cultural resistance to mediation, 212–13
    developing restorative justice, 147–48
    mediation schemes, 134–35, 150
        administration, 136
        cultural resistance to mediation, 212–13
        evaluation, 142–44
        financial compensation, 140
        legal representation, 139, 147–48
        shuttle mediation, 138

human rights, 12, 26, 35, 50, 103, 209
    offenders, 94–95
    victims, 97

inclusionary nature, 28, 112–13, 118, 165, 192, 200
indirect contact between victim and offender, 79–80, 194
institutionalisation:
    balance with community needs, 211–12
    dangers of Europeanisation of indigenous traditions, 210
    New Zealand, 210–11
'integrated restorative justice model', 55, 97
interventions, 21
    adult schemes, 118–19, 201
        Belgium, 133–34
        England and Wales, 114–15, 121–23
        New Zealand, 119–21
    family group conferencing, 21
    police-led conferencing, 21
    prison-based schemes, 123–28
    restorative policing, 21
    youth schemes:
        Youth Conditional Caution, 114–15
        youth conferencing, 153–74
        youth offender panels, 7, 116–18
        Youth Restorative Disposal system, 6, 113, 129–30

Latvia:
    mediation schemes:
        apologies, 141
legalism:
    operational barriers and, 208–10
    risks posed by legal formalism, 210
    see also institutionalisation

mediation schemes, 9, 132–33, 149–50
    administration, 135–36
    adult offenders, 121–22
    civil law jurisdictions:
        Austria, 136, 137, 139, 142, 143
        background and context, 133–35
        Belgium, 133–34, 136, 137–38, 139, 144–45
        Bulgaria, 144
        Czech Republic, 136
        Finland, 133, 136, 139, 142, 143
        France, 134, 137, 139, 142, 143
        Germany, 134–35, 136, 139, 142, 144
        Netherlands, 135, 136, 139, 142, 143, 144
        Norway, 133, 135, 137, 143
        Poland, 144
        Romania, 143
        Sweden, 133, 144
    diversionary mediation programmes, 148–49
    evaluation, 142–43
        professional resistance/scepticism, 144–46
        satisfaction rates, 143–44
    process:
        apologies, 141
        conferencing, 139–40
        direct and indirect mediation, 138–39
        financial compensation, 140–41
        legal representation, 139
        mainstreaming of restorative approaches, 139–40
        outcomes, 140–41
        shuttle mediation, 138–39
        variety across Europe, 138
    referrals, 136–37
        offender's consent and, 137–38
    shuttle mediation, 138–39
    see also individual countries
moral debt, 32
    to whom owed, 33, 34, 38, 50–51
mostly restorative programmes, 9

Netherlands:
    agency-accountability framework, 201
    mediation schemes, 135, 150
        administration, 136
        evaluation, 142–44
        conferencing, 139
        referrals, 138
New Zealand, 3
    adult offenders, schemes for, 118–19
        Community Accountability Programme, 119
        community panels, 119–21
        empowering nature of, 121
        Project Turnaround, 119
        satisfaction rates, 119–21
    community-based programmes:
        impact of indigenous practices, 101
        family group conferencing, 7–8
            resistance of indigenous populations, 210–11

impact of indigenous practices, 17–18, 101
police-led conferencing, 21
prison-based restorative programmes, 128
recidivism, 190–91
restoration cautioning, 5
restorative conferencing, 151–52
serious and sexual offences, 91
victim impact statements, 41–42
youth conferencing, 13, 153–55
  agreement and outcomes, 169–70, 171
  engagement of participants, 160–61, 173
  evaluation of conferencing, 162
  format, 154
  Northern Ireland compared, 156
  process, 154–55
North America:
  First Nations tribes, 8, 18
  mediation practice, 84, 102
  origins of restorative justice, 2–3
  police-led conferencing, 106
  police-led conferencing, 21
  prison-based restorative programmes, 124–27
  recidivism, 180, 193
  restorative policing, 5
  satisfaction rates, 84
  victim-offender mediation, 4–5
Northern Ireland:
  community-based programmes, 103–04
    Community Restorative Justice Ireland, 103, 104
    government funding, 104
    Northern Ireland Alternatives, 103, 104
  restorative conferencing, 152
  restorative policing, 5
    application, 111
    impact, 111–12
  youth conferencing:
    agreement and outcomes, 168–69
    apologies, 171–72
    coercion of young offenders, 159–60
    court-ordered conferences, 156
    diversionary conferences, 155–56
    engagement of participants, 160–61, 173
    evaluation of conferencing, 163
    evolution of youth conferencing, 155
    family group conferencing, 155
    New Zealand compared, 156
    process, 155–56
Northern Ireland Alternatives, 103, 104
Norway:
  agency-accountability framework, 201
  mediation schemes, 133
    administration, 135–36
    diversionary mediation programmes, 149
    evaluation, 142–43
    referrals, 137
    direct mediation, 138

obligation to restore and repair, 30–31
offenders:
  benefits of restorative justice programmes, 92, 98–99
  restorative justice and traditional justice compared, 20, 92–93
  rights of the offender, 99
    due process, 94–98
    opportunity to be heard, 95–96
    police-led restorative cautioning, 96–97
    proportionality of justice, 96–98
    protection from coercion, 95–96
  satisfaction rates, 93–94
outcome-based restorative justice, 27–28

partially restorative programmes, 9, 20, 83, 112, 129–31
participation in restorative justice programmes:
  agency-accountability framework, 77–79
    non-participation, 79–83
  coercion, 84–85
  common goals of restorative justice, **68**
  community participation, 37–39
    benefits, 34–35
    criticisms, 35–36
  community reparation panels, 78
  conditional cautioning:
    benefits of participation, 114
    Youth Conditional Caution, 114
  consent and, 27, 97
  England and Wales, 42–43
  evaluation of, 77–79
  family group conferencing, 78, 157
  overcoming non-participation, 79–83
  police-led conferencing, 78
  referral orders, 207
  RISE project, 78, 157
  surrogate victims, 80–81
  United Kingdom:
    conditional cautioning, 114
    youth offender panels, 78, 117–18
  victim participation:
    adult offenders, schemes for, 157, 169
    adversarial system of justice, 41, 63, 76–77
    community reparation panels, 78
    conditional cautioning, 114
    England and Wales, 42–43
    family group conferencing, 78, 157
    RISE project, 78, 157
    Wagga Wagga programme, 78
    youth conferencing, 157
    youth offender panels, 78, 117–18
Wagga Wagga programme, 78
Youth Conditional Caution, 114
youth conferencing, 157
  consent and engagement, 159–61
  evaluation of programmes, 158–59

motivations of offenders for consenting to
   participate, 159
motivations of victims for participation,
   157–58
youth offender panels, 78, 117–18
youth offender panels, 78, 117–18
youth conferencing programmes
   consent and engagement, 159–61
   evaluation of programmes, 158–59
   levels of participation, 157
   motivations of offenders for consenting to
      participate, 159
   motivations of victims for participation,
      157–58
   soft option, whether should be considered
      as, 161–65
personal injury:
   compensation orders, 47
   mediation agreements, 141
Poland:
   mediation schemes:
      apologies, 141
      scepticism about, 144
police-led cautioning, *see* restorative cautioning
police-led conferencing, 21
   recidivism, 181
   reintegrative shaming, 5–6, 24, 44–45
   restorative cautioning distinguished, 109
   RISE project, 104–05, 128
      participation rates, 78
   satisfaction rates, 108
popular punitivism, 40, 170, 174, 204–05, 206
Portugal:
   mediation schemes:
      apologies, 141
prison-based restorative programmes, 123–24
   Belgium, 127–28
   difficulties in the UK:
      distance of prisoners from community, 124
      lack of funding, 124
      overcrowding, 124
   limits to effectiveness, 127
   New Zealand, 128
   North America, 124–26
procedural fairness, 14, 28, 43–44, 57–58, 76, 83
   empowerment and, 64, 65, **67**, 68
   legitimacy and, 198
   perceptions, 43–44, 104, 167
   proportionality and, 27
process-based restorative justice, 27
process values, 28
processes and outcomes, 16, 20, 24, 29–30,
   41–46, 55–56, **68**, 74
   empowerment and, 90, 93, 98
proportionality, 15, 26, 48, 210
   agency, 70
   fairness and, 27

'integrated restorative justice model', 55
rights of offenders, 96–98, 99
public policy, 15, 204–06
   continental Europe, 146, 150
   focus on youth justice programmes, 121–23, 133
   lack of commitment, 206
   support for restorative justice, 4, 10
   Youth Conditional Cautions, 114
   youth offender panels, 116
public tariff:
   degree of reparation, 55

quantification of harms, 23–24, 48–49, 55
quantity of new restorative programmes:
   current UK policy, 205
   quality of practices and, 205–06

recidivism, 16, 22, 175–76, 192–95
   agency-accountability framework and, 190
      Australia, 191
      New Zealand, 190–91
   influences, 187–92
   meta-analysis studies, 182–83
   other studies, 184–87
   restorative cautioning and, 176–79
   restorative justice programmes:
      group conferencing, 180–81
      mediation, 180
      sentencing circles, 180–81
      youth conferencing, 181–82
referral orders, 7, 96, 116
   recidivism and, 130
   victim participation, 207
   youth offender panels, 116–18, 206–07
reform, 214–16
reintegrative shaming, 5–6, 24, 44–45
   see also Reintegrative Shaming Experiments
      (RISE) project
Reintegrative Shaming Experiments (RISE)
   project:
   Canberra programme, 152, 184
   participation rates, 78
   Wagga Wagga programme 78, 104, 106, 111
   see also reintegrative shaming
relational approach to justice, 31–32
reoffending, *see* recidivism
reparation, 47, 51–53, 207
   adversarial system of justice, 49–50
   calculation of damages, 48–49, 55
   compensation, 47–48
   forms:
      apologies, 50–51
   law of obligations, 48
   proportionality and, 48
   restorative justice, 50
restorative agency and accountability, 69–70
   accountability, 71–73

agency, 70–71
agency, accountability and criminal justice, 73–74
safety of victims, 90–92
see also agency-accountability framework
restorative cautioning, 6, 129
  Australia, 109
  conditional cautioning:
    aims of the scheme, 114
    benefits of participation, 114
    conditions applicable, 114–15
    partly restorative nature, 115
    Youth Conditional Caution, 114–15
  origins, 109
  police-led diversionary conferencing distinguished, 109
  process, 109
  reintegrative shaming and, 109
  rights of offenders, 96–97
  traditional police cautioning distinguished, 109
  UK:
    conditional cautioning, 114–15
    final warning scheme and, 112–13
    Northern Ireland, 111–12
    Thames Valley scheme, 109–10
    Youth Restorative Disposal, 113
restorative conferencing:
  Australia, 151–52
  Belgium, 152–53
  mainstreaming within criminal justice system, 151–53, 172, 201
  New Zealand, 151–52, 201
  Northern Ireland, 152, 201
  origins, 151
  youth conferencing:
    development of, 152–53
  see also youth conferencing
restorative justice, 19
  bottom up schemes, 3, 39–40, 101–04, 211
  concept, 1–2
  degree of restorativeness, 9
  delivery methods, 1
  development of practice, 1–2
  empowerment theory, 20, 197–98
  historical background:
    Mennonite movement, 2
    North America, 2–3
    origins, 2
    rise of restorative justice, 3–4
  First Nations and indigenous peoples, 8–9
  quick fix, as, 199
  restorative practice distinguished, 9
  transformative potential, 13–15, 199–200
  types of intervention:
    community reparation panels, 6–7
    family group conferencing, 7–8
    other forms, 8–9

restorative policing, 5–6
victim-offender mediation, 4–5
variety of practice, 9
youth justice schemes, 3
Restorative Justice Disposal, 206
restorative policing:
  advantages, 105
  Australia, 104–05
  evaluation of impact, 104–05
  North America, 106
  origins, 5, 104–05
  reintegrative shaming, 5–6
  restorative cautioning and traditional cautioning distinguished, 6
  UK:
    Northumbria, 107–08
    satisfaction levels, 108
    success, 108
  Youth Restorative Disposal system, 6
  see also restorative cautioning
restorative practice, 100–01, 128–31
  restorative justice distinguished, 9
  see also community-based programmes; prison-based restorative programmes; restorative policing; schemes for adult offenders; youth offender panels;
retributive justice, 1–4, 20, 39, 47, 169
  criticisms of, 13–14
  integrated restorative justice and, 97
  mediation and, 144
  public interest and, 54–56
rights of offenders:
  due process, 94
  opportunity to be heard, 95–96
  police-led restorative cautioning, 96–97
  proportionality of justice, 96–98
  protection from coercion, 95–96
RISE, *see* reintegrative shaming; Reintegrative Shaming Experiments (RISE) project

satisfaction levels, 15–16
  adult offenders, schemes for, 119–21, 122
  community-based programmes, 102
  England and Wales, 63
  family group conferencing, 170–71, 182
  mediation schemes, 143–44
  offender satisfaction levels, 93–94
  police-led conferencing, 108
  restorative policing, 108
  processes and outcomes, 16
  victim satisfaction levels:
    reintegrative shaming and, 84
    restorative justice and court procedures compared, 83
    victim-offender mediation, 84
    victims of property crime, 84
    violent crime, 84

youth conferencing, 165–68
youth offender panels, 117
secondary victimisation, 62–63, 76
sentencing circles, 8, 101–02, 180–81
serious and/or sexual offences, 4, 13, 22, 52, 131, 181–82, 193–94, 200–02, 208
   adult offenders, 114, 118–19, 121, 186, 188–89
   continental Europe mediation, 134, 137, 146–47
   experiences of victims, 83, 85, 89
   family group conferencing, 7
   lawyer involvement, 210
   prison-based programmes, 126, 128
   quantification of harm, 49
   youth conferencing, 152–53, 169
   youth offender panels, 116
shuttle mediation, 5, 79–80, 84, 87, 138–39, 201
sincere apology, 45, 50–51, 86–87
   agency and forced apologies, 88–89
   effectiveness, 87
   sincerity and impact, 87–88
standards:
   Council of Europe
      EU Framework Decision on the Standing of Victims in Criminal Proceedings, 11
      Recommendation (99)19 Concerning Mediation in Penal Matters, 11–12
      legislative provision and frameworks, 12–13
   Ministry of Justice (NZ)
      Principles of Best Practice, 120–21
   United Nations
      11th Congress on the Prevention of Crime and Treatment of Offenders, 10
      Basic Principles on the Use of Restorative Justice Programmes in Criminal Matters, 10
      Handbook of Restorative Justice Programmes, 11
      Vienna Declaration on Crime and Justice, 10
state intervention, 39–41
surrogate victims, 34, 80
   agency and accountability and, 201
   apologies, 87
   disadvantages, 80–81
   restorative cautioning, 111, 129
   Thames Valley model of police cautioning, 111
   victim participation, 80–81
Sweden:
   mediation schemes, 133
      evaluation, 144

Thames Valley restorative cautioning scheme, 37
   evaluation, 110
   impact on recidivism, 110, 176–79
   implementation, 109–10
   victim participation, 78, 88–89

United Kingdom:
   conditional cautioning:
      aims of the scheme, 114
      benefits of participation, 114
      conditions applicable, 114–15
      partly restorative nature, 115
      Youth Conditional Caution, 114–15
   police-led conferencing, 21
   prison-based restorative programmes, 123–24
   restorative cautioning:
      conditional cautioning, 114–15
      final warning scheme and, 112–13
      Northern Ireland, 111–12
      Thames Valley scheme, 109–10
      Youth Restorative Disposal, 113
   youth offender panels:
      community reparation, 7
      incorporation into the justice system, 117
      introduction, 116
      process, 116
      referral orders, 116
      satisfaction rates, 117
      victim participation, 78, 117–18
   see also England and Wales
United Nations
   11th Congress on the Prevention of Crime and Treatment of Offenders, 10
   Basic Principles on the Use of Restorative Justice Programmes in Criminal Matters, 10
   Handbook of Restorative Justice Programmes, 11
   pressure on states to develop restorative justice programmes, 149–50
   Vienna Declaration on Crime and Justice, 10

victim impact statements, 205–06
   disadvantages, 42
      restorative justice compared, 42–43
   types, 41–42
victim-offender mediation:
   aims, 4–5
   format, 5
   origins, 4
   relationship focus, 4–5
   see also mediation schemes
victimisation, 24–25
   adversarial system of justice:
      victimisation of the victim, 63
   disempowerment through crime, 62–63
   secondary victimisation, 62–63
'victimless' crimes, 33
   'accountability, 82
   assessment of harm, 81–82
victims, 75–76
   absent or untraceable victims, 33–34
   compensation, 24
   desire to support offenders, 79
   participation in restorative justice programmes, 77–79, 98

community panels, 78
family group conferencing, 78
overcoming non-participation, 79–83
police-led restorative cautioning, 78
reintegrative shaming projects, 78
satisfaction levels, 83–86
youth offender panels, 78
restorative justice, 76–77
sincere apologies, 86–90
traditional justice compared, 20
victim participation, 77–79
surrogate victims, 34, 80–81, 87, 111, 129, 201
victim visibility, rise of, 24–25
victimisation, 24–25

Youth Conditional Caution:
aims of the scheme, 114
benefits of participation, 114
conditions applicable, 114–15
partly restorative nature, 115
youth conferencing:
agency and accountability, 173–74
agreement and positive outcomes, 168–71
apologies, 171–72
challenges faced by you offenders, 163–65
family group conferences, 154
New Zealand, 153–55
agreement and outcomes, 169–70, 171
engagement of participants, 160–61, 173
evaluation of conferencing, 162
format, 154
Northern Ireland compared, 156
process, 154–55
Northern Ireland:
agreement and outcomes, 168–69

apologies, 171–72
coercion of young offenders, 159–60
court-ordered conferences, 156
diversionary conferences, 155–56
engagement of participants, 160–61, 173
evaluation of conferencing, 163
evolution of youth conferencing, 155
family group conferencing, 155
New Zealand compared, 156
process, 155–56
origins, 153
participation:
consent and engagement, 159–61
evaluation of programmes, 158–59
levels of participation, 157
motivations of offenders for consenting to participate, 159
motivations of victims for participation, 157–58
procedural fairness, perceived, 165–68
satisfaction levels, 165–68
soft option, whether should be considered as, 161–65
youth justice:
early restorative practice, 3
New Zealand, 21–22
youth offender panels:
community reparation, 7
incorporation into the justice system, 117
introduction, 116
process, 116
referral orders, 116
satisfaction rates, 117
victim participation, 78, 117–18
Youth Restorative Disposal system, 6, 113, 129–30